The Cambridge Companion to Ravel

This Companion provides a comprehensive introduction to the life, music and compositional aesthetic of the French composer Maurice Ravel (1875–1937). Leading international scholars offer a powerful reassessment of this most private and elusive musician, examining his work in detail within its cultural context. Supported by many music examples, the volume explores the full range of Ravel's work – piano repertory, chamber works, orchestral music, ballets, songs and operas – and makes illuminating comparisons with the music of Couperin, Gounod, Chabrier and Debussy. The chapters present the latest research focusing on topics such as Ravel's exoticism and Spanishness and conclude by analysing the performance and reception of his music, including previously untranslated reviews. Marking the 125th anniversary of Ravel's birth, the Companion as a whole aims to secure a solid foundation for Ravel studies in the twenty-first century and will appeal to all enthusiasts and students of his music.

The editor, Deborah Mawer, is Lecturer in Music at Lancaster University, where she specialises in French music (c. 1890–1939). She is author of *Darius Milhaud* (1997) and 'Darius Milhaud, *La Création du monde*' (1996), an analytical listening guide. She also writes on music analysis and education.

Cambridge Companions to Music

Composers

The Cambridge Companion to Bach
Edited by John Butt

The Cambridge Companion to Bartók
Edited by Amanda Bayley

The Cambridge Companion to Beethoven
Edited by Glenn Stanley

The Cambridge Companion to Berg
Edited by Anthony Pople

The Cambridge Companion to Berlioz
Edited by Peter Bloom

The Cambridge Companion to Brahms
Edited by Michael Musgrave

The Cambridge Companion to Benjamin Britten
Edited by Mervyn Cooke

The Cambridge Companion to Chopin
Edited by Jim Samson

The Cambridge Companion to Handel
Edited by Donald Burrows

The Cambridge Companion to Ravel
Edited by Deborah Mawer

The Cambridge Companion to Schubert
Edited by Christopher Gibbs

The Cambridge Companion to

RAVEL

EDITED BY
Deborah Mawer

CAMBRIDGE
UNIVERSITY PRESS

CAMBRIDGE UNIVERSITY PRESS
Cambridge, New York, Melbourne, Madrid, Cape Town, Singapore, São Paulo

Cambridge University Press
The Edinburgh Building, Cambridge CB2 2RU, UK

Published in the United States of America by Cambridge University Press, New York

www.cambridge.org
Information on this title: www.cambridge.org/9780521640268

First published 2000

A catalogue record for this publication is available from the British Library

Library of Congress Cataloguing in Publication data

The Cambridge companion to Ravel / edited by Deborah Mawer.
    p.   cm. – (Cambridge companions to music)
Includes bibliographical references (p.) and index.
ISBN 0 521 64026 1 (hardback) – ISBN 0 521 64856 4 (paperback)
1. Ravel, Maurice, 1875–1937 – Criticism and interpretation. I. Mawer, Deborah, 1961–
II. Series.
ML410.R23 C36 2000
780′.92–dc21 99–047568 CIP

ISBN-13 978-0-521-64026-8 hardback
ISBN-10 0-521-64026-1 hardback

ISBN-13 978-0-521-64856-1 paperback
ISBN-10 0-521-64856-4 paperback

Transferred to digital printing 2006

Contents

List of contributors [viii]
Acknowledgements [x]
Chronology of Ravel's life and career [xi]
Note on the text [xv]

Introduction *Deborah Mawer* [1]

Part I · Culture and aesthetic

1 History and homage *Barbara L. Kelly* [7]

2 Evocations of exoticism *Robert Orledge* [27]

3 Musical objects and machines *Deborah Mawer* [47]

Part II · Musical explorations

4 Ravel and the piano *Roy Howat* [71]

5 Harmony in the chamber music *Mark DeVoto* [97]

6 Ravel and the orchestra *Michael Russ* [118]

7 Ballet and the apotheosis of the dance *Deborah Mawer* [140]

8 Vocal music and the lures of exoticism and irony *Peter Kaminsky* [162]

9 Ravel's operatic spectacles: *L'Heure* and *L'Enfant* *Richard Langham Smith* [188]

Part III · Performance and reception

10 Performing Ravel: style and practice in the early recordings
Ronald Woodley [213]

11 Ravel and the twentieth century *Roger Nichols* [240]

Appendix: Early reception of Ravel's music (1899–1939)
Roger Nichols and Deborah Mawer [251]
Notes [267]
Select bibliography [283]
Index of names and works [287]

Contributors

Mark DeVoto, composer and writer, has been Professor of Music at Tufts University since 1981. He is the editor and co-author, with his late teacher Walter Piston, of the much acclaimed book *Harmony* (Gollancz, 1978; 5/1987); he has published extensively on Berg (and Bartók), including his recent edition of the *Altenberg Lieder*, Op. 4 (1997) for the Alban Berg *Sämtliche Werke*.

Roy Howat is a concert pianist known especially for his expertise in French music: among his teachers were two close associates of Ravel, Vlado Perlemuter and Jacques Février. His publications include *Debussy in Proportion* (Cambridge University Press, 1983), contributions to books on Schubert, Chopin, Debussy and Bartók, Urtext editions of music by Fauré and Chabrier, and several volumes of the *Œuvres complètes de Claude Debussy* (Editions Durand), of which he is one of the founding editors.

Peter Kaminsky is Associate Professor of Music Theory at the University of Connecticut at Storrs. He has published work on Schumann's piano cycles, Paul Simon, Mozart opera and score study in *Music Theory Spectrum, College Music Symposium, Theory and Practice, The Instrumentalist* and *Clavier*; current interests include endings in Brahms's music and the role of genre in the solo music of Sting.

Barbara L. Kelly is Lecturer in Music at Keele University and author of the new Ravel article for the forthcoming second edition of *The New Grove Dictionary of Music and Musicians*. She researches on late nineteenth- and early twentieth-century French music, including Darius Milhaud, and on issues of French national identity from 1870 to 1939.

Richard Langham Smith is Reader in Music at the University of Exeter and has been admitted to the rank of 'Chevalier de l'ordre des arts et des lettres' for his contribution to French music. Author and editor of several books on Debussy, including *Debussy Studies* (Cambridge Univeristy Press, 1998), he has also reconstructed Debussy's unpublished opera, *Rodrigue et Chimène*, which opened the new Opéra in Lyon in 1993.

Deborah Mawer is Lecturer in Music at Lancaster University and Vice-President of the Society for Music Analysis. Her research focuses on the analysis of early twentieth-century French music (1890–1939), including *Darius Milhaud: Modality and Structure in Music of the 1920s* (Scolar Press, 1997) and an analytical listening guide, 'Darius Milhaud, *La Création du monde*' (Teaching and Learning Technology Programme, 1996); she also writes on issues in music education.

Roger Nichols read music at the University of Oxford and subsequently lectured at various other universities before becoming a freelance writer and broadcaster in 1981. He has published widely on French music of the last 200 years, including *Ravel* (Dent, 1977) for the Master Musicians series, *Ravel Remembered* (Faber, 1987), *Debussy Remembered* (Faber, 1991) and *A Life of Debussy* (Cambridge University Press, 1998).

Robert Orledge is Professor of Music at the University of Liverpool. His research field is French music between 1850 and 1939 and his main publications are *Gabriel Fauré* (Eulenburg, 1979; 2/1983), *Debussy and the Theatre* (Cambridge University Press, 1982; 2/1985), *Charles Koechlin: His Life and Works* (Harwood, 1989; 2/1995), *Satie the Composer* (Cambridge University Press 1990; 2/1992) and *Satie Remembered* (Faber, 1995).

Michael Russ is Senior Lecturer in Music at the University of Ulster. He has published work on Webern, Bartók and Musorgsky, including a monograph on Musorgsky's *Pictures at an Exhibition* (Cambridge University Press, 1992).

Ronald Woodley is Senior Lecturer in Music at Lancaster University where he is active both as a musicologist (medieval and twentieth-century periods) and as a performer on clarinet. His publications range from *John Tucke: A Case Study in Early Tudor Music Theory* (Clarendon Press, 1993) to an essay on irony in Prokofiev in *The Practice of Performance*, ed. John Rink (Cambridge University Press, 1995); he is currently completing a book on the music of Steve Reich.

Acknowledgements

All contributors appreciatively acknowledge the pioneering work of Arbie Orenstein – documentary, editorial and biographical – that has facilitated the writing of *The Cambridge Companion to Ravel*. I am also grateful to Roger Nichols for his perceptive comments on the book chapters at draft stage and to Roy Howat, who has been generous both with his time and specialist knowledge. Thanks are due to Penny Souster at Cambridge University Press for her support and of course to the individual contributors to this volume. In particular, special thanks go to my partner, Ronald Woodley, who also took on the sizeable task of producing all the music examples with his characteristic meticulousness and finesse.

Additionally, I should like to acknowledge the generous financial assistance given to me as editor to assist the research stage of this book at the Bibliothèque Nationale de France, both by the British Academy/Humanities Research Board and by Lancaster University.

Chronology of Ravel's life and career

This chronology is compiled from various sources, but special acknowledgement should be made of Roger Nichols's work in cementing part of the biographical foundation in his *Ravel* (London: Dent, 1977). For any one year, entries within *contemporary events* are ordered as follows: history; science/literature/arts; musicians/music.

YEAR	RAVEL'S LIFE	CONTEMPORARY EVENTS
1875	Maurice Ravel born at Ciboure, near Saint-Jean-de-Luz (7 March); in summer family moves to Paris	Third Republic founded in France; new Paris Opéra opened; Bizet dies; *Carmen* premiered
1876		Mallarmé, *L'Après-midi d'un faune*; Falla born
1877		Edison invents phonograph
1878	Edouard Ravel (brother) born	Exposition Universelle (Paris)
1879		Sir George Grove, *A Dictionary of Music and Musicians* (London, 1879–89)
1880		
1881		telephone transmission of Paris Opéra performance; Musorgsky dies; Bartók born
1882	piano lessons with Henry Ghys	Stravinsky born
1883		Wagner dies; Webern born
1884		
1885		Berg and Varèse born
1886	harmony lessons with Charles René	Statue of Liberty, New York; Liszt dies
1887		
1888	meets Ricardo Viñes	Borodin dies
1889	attends Exposition; enters junior piano class at Paris Conservatoire	Exposition Universelle (Paris); Eiffel Tower completed; Cocteau born
1890		Nijinsky born; Franck dies
1891	first prize for piano; joins de Bériot's piano class and Pessard's harmony class	Rimbaud dies; Prokofiev born
1892		Milhaud and Honegger born
1893	plays Chabrier's music to the composer (with Viñes); composes *Sérénade grotesque* and *Ballade de la Reine morte d'aimer*	Gounod and Tchaikovsky die

1894		Chabrier dies; Debussy, *Prélude à l'après-midi d'un faune*
1895	leaves Conservatoire	Röntgen discovers X-rays
1896		Bruckner dies
1897	early Sonata for Violin and Piano and *Sites auriculaires* completed	Concerts Lamoureux (Paris); Brahms dies
1898	returns to Conservatoire for Fauré's composition class; private lessons with Gedalge	Spanish–American War (Treaty of Paris); Mallarmé dies; Gershwin born
1899	composes *Pavane pour une Infante défunte*; *Shéhérazade* (overture) first performed	Boer War begins; Chausson dies; Poulenc born
1900	enters Prix de Rome (first time); leaves Fauré's class	Paris Métro opened; Freud, *The Interpretation of Dreams*
1901	third prize in Prix de Rome; composes *Jeux d'eau*	Verdi dies
1902	failure in Prix de Rome; starts String Quartet	Debussy, *Pelléas et Mélisande* completed (begun in 1893)
1903	failure in Prix de Rome; starts *Sonatine*	Wright brothers' first flight; Wolf dies
1904	Quartet first performed; meets Godebski family	Balanchine born; Dvořák dies
1905	'l'affaire Ravel' (removed after preliminary round of Prix de Rome); signed up by Durand	Russian Revolution; Einstein, *Special Theory of Relativity*; Tippett and Jolivet born; Debussy, *La Mer*
1906	*Miroirs* and *Sonatine* first performed; starts *La Cloche engloutie* and *Histoires naturelles*	Shostakovich born; Schoenberg, Chamber Symphony No. 1
1907	*Histoires naturelles* and *Introduction et allegro* first performed; finishes *L'Heure espagnole* (vocal score); teaches Vaughan Williams	Picasso, *Les Demoiselles d'Avignon*; Grieg dies
1908	*Rapsodie espagnole* first performed; composes *Gaspard de la nuit*; starts *Ma Mère l'Oye*; father dies	Rimsky-Korsakov dies; Messiaen born
1909	*Gaspard* first performed; first concert abroad (London); orchestration of *L'Heure espagnole*; starts *Daphnis et Chloé*	inaugural season of Ballets Russes (1909–29); Albéniz dies
1910	*Ma Mère l'Oye* first performed at opening concert of Société Musicale Indépendante (SMI); finishes first version of *Daphnis* (piano score)	Balakirev dies; Stravinsky, *L'Oiseau de feu*; Debussy, *Préludes* (Bk. I)

1911	*Valses nobles et sentimentales* first performed (anonymously); *L'Heure espagnole* premiered at the Opéra-Comique on 19 May	Mahler dies; Stravinsky, *Petrushka*
1912	ballet productions from orchestrations of *Ma Mère l'Oye* and *Valses nobles* (as *Adélaïde*); *Daphnis* premiered by Ballets Russes on 8 June, Théâtre du Châtelet; leaves Paris for break	Massenet dies; Cage born; Schoenberg, *Pierrot lunaire*
1913	orchestrates Musorgsky, *Khovanshchina* (with Stravinsky) for Dyagilev's performance in June	Britten born; Stravinsky, *Le Sacre* premiered to uproar in Paris
1914	*Trois poèmes de Stéphane Mallarmé* first performed; orchestration of Schumann and Chopin for Nijinsky; London production of *Daphnis*; starts *Le Tombeau de Couperin*	outbreak of World War I
1915	Piano Trio first performed; produces edition of Mendelssohn; enlists as truck driver	French–American radio link from Eiffel Tower; Einstein, *General Theory of Relativity*
1916	illness: returns to Paris	Battle of the Somme; Granados dies
1917	mother dies; finishes *Le Tombeau de Couperin* (piano)	Bolshevik Revolution; Satie, *Parade*
1918	composes *Frontispice*; orchestrates 'Alborada' (*Miroirs*) and some Chabrier	Debussy dies; Stravinsky, *L'Histoire du soldat*
1919	holiday at Mégève; *Le Tombeau* first performed and four movements orchestrated	Paris Peace Conference (1919–20), including Treaty of Versailles
1920	holiday at Lapras; completes *La Valse* (piano score); declines Légion d'honneur; starts *L'Enfant et les sortilèges*; concert in Vienna; ballet production of *Le Tombeau*; concert performance of *La Valse*	formal inauguration of League of Nations; Ballets Suédois (1920–5); Stravinsky, *Pulcinella*
1921	moves to 'Le Belvédère'	Saint-Saëns dies
1922	Sonata for Violin and Cello first performed; orchestrates some Debussy; concerts abroad (England, Holland, Italy)	BBC set up; Joyce, *Ulysses*; Eliot, *The Waste Land*; Stravinsky, *Mavra*
1923	further concerts abroad (as above and in Belgium); starts Sonata for Violin and Piano and *Ronsard à son âme*	regular Eiffel Tower broadcasts; BBC music broadcasts; Stravinsky, *Les Noces*

1924	*Tzigane* first performed; concerts in Spain	Fauré and Puccini die
1925	*L'Enfant et les sortilèges* premiered on 21 March in Monte Carlo; starts *Chansons madécasses*	Satie dies; Boulez and Berio born
1926	concerts abroad (Belgium, Scandinavia, Germany, Britain); *L'Enfant* performed on 1 February at the Opéra-Comique; *Chansons madécasses* first performed; concerts in Switzerland	
1927	Sonata for Violin and Piano first performed; first signs of neurological upset; begins North American tour	Lindbergh Atlantic flight; Stravinsky, *Oedipus Rex*
1928	arrival in New York; back in France by late April; award of Hon. D.Mus. (Oxford); *Boléro* premiered at the Opéra; concerts in Spain	Janáček dies; Barraqué and Stockhausen born
1929	concerts abroad (England, Switzerland, Austria); starts the piano concertos; *La Valse* first staged at the Opéra	Wall Street crash, New York; Dyagilev dies
1930	'Quai Maurice Ravel' opened at Ciboure; finishes Concerto for the Left Hand	Stravinsky, *Symphony of Psalms*; Milhaud, *Christophe Colomb* premiered
1931	finishes Concerto in G; complete rest urged by doctor	d'Indy dies
1932	piano concertos first performed (Vienna and Paris); starts *Don Quichotte à Dulcinée*; taxi accident (October); concert in Switzerland	
1933	finishes composition of *Don Quichotte*; more obvious symptoms of degenerative brain disease	Hitler becomes Chancellor of Germany; Duparc dies
1934	treatment at Swiss clinic; orchestration and first performance of *Don Quichotte*	Elgar, Delius and Holst die; Birtwistle and Maxwell Davies born
1935	tour of Spain and North Africa with Léon Leyritz; second Spanish trip	Berg and Dukas die
1936	further decline in health	Spanish Civil War; BBC television broadcasts; Respighi and Glazunov die
1937	brain operation attempted; ten days later Ravel dies (28 December)	Paris Exposition; Gershwin and Roussel die; Shostakovich, Fifth Symphony

Note on the text

In order to avoid unnecessary repetition, references to frequently cited Ravel texts are given in short-title form in the supporting endnotes (and Appendix); the full reference can be found in the Select bibliography. Where no author is given for a short title, the item is usually an unsigned interview with Ravel (or his 'An autobiographical sketch', as dictated to Roland-Manuel). Unless otherwise indicated, endnote references relate to the most recent edition of any text detailed in the Select bibliography. More occasional references to Ravel (and non-Ravel) literature are given in full at their first citation in the notes for any one particular chapter.

Across the book, there are so many references to Arbie Orenstein's celebrated source book of Ravel readings that it makes sense to abbreviate this as follows:

RR   Arbie Orenstein (ed. and trans.), *A Ravel Reader* (New York: Columbia University Press, 1990).

References to articles or interviews reprinted in *RR* are given in their English translation; however, since *RR* is presently out of print, the original source is also included in the full reference (unless stated otherwise, page numbers are for *RR* only and include Orenstein's editorial notes). Titles given in French refer to the original source (or, if appropriate, to its reprint in Orenstein's French edition: *Maurice Ravel: Lettres, écrits, entretiens* (Paris: Flammarion, 1989)); translated quotations in the text have usually been supplied by the author of the chapter.

Musical references employ a mixture of bar numbers and rehearsal figures depending on the available editions of the work concerned. Rehearsal figures are still the main means of referencing orchestral or staged works, and so the following shorthand has been used in the main text: Fig. 1^{-1} refers to the bar preceding Figure 1; Fig. 1 denotes the relevant bar-line (analogous to the start of a movement or scene); Fig. 1^{+1} refers to the first full bar of Figure 1. This shorthand is used just to identify a particular starting point; to avoid any confusion, extent is indicated more fully, as in Fig. 1, bars 1–2.

In musical discussion the sign '/', as in G/F♯ or major/minor, indicates a simultaneity whereas the sign '–', as in G–F♯ or I–V, indicates a progression. Separation of pitches by commas indicates a neutral, basic listing, such as for the components of a scalic collection or chordal formation. Modes are referred to in the same way as major or minor scales (e.g. C major), hence C aeolian or E phrygian.

Introduction

DEBORAH MAWER

The many masks of Ravel

Our image of Maurice Ravel is still partly obscured by mystery and intangibility, and by some lingering misunderstandings. This situation arises as a result of various factors: Ravel's own actions, his elusive blend of French, Basque and Spanish traits and the quirks of reception across the years (for instance, the emphasis on his undoubted skills of orchestration has to some extent down-played the actual substance of much of his orchestral music). Even in his lifetime, an interviewer for *De Telegraaf* exclaimed, literally and figuratively: 'It is not easy to find the hiding place of Maurice Ravel.'[1]

How then might we think about Ravel? He himself sometimes adopted the metaphor of masks, so popular in contemporary dramatic and balletic productions. Castigating the self-conscious academicism of Georges Witkowski, a pupil of d'Indy, he declared: 'How far this repulsive intellectual logic is from sensibility! Nevertheless, behind this dour mask, one discerns a profound, vibrant musician at every moment.'[2] Among Ravel's early biographers, Vladimir Jankélévitch, especially, developed this image of masks in relation to the composer's compositional aesthetic: 'Ravel is friend to *trompe-l'œil*, deceptions, merry-go-round horses and booby-traps; Ravel is masked.'[3]

So what is the nature of the masks, or distorting mirrors, behind which we might seek Ravel? (In posing this question, we're aware of the impossibility of the quest: in peeling off one mask there is invariably another beneath; furthermore, the masks are so bound up with Ravel's identity that, at one level, they are part of him. No mask: no Ravel.) These devices for detachment and distancing take various forms and can embody contradictions. Fastidious neoclassical craftsmanship, abstracted, objectified and sometimes depersonalised, has a place in Ravel's compositional aesthetic; yet this is contrasted by the sheer sensuousness of *Daphnis et Chloé* and the wild abandon of *La Valse*. The reinterpretation of cultural 'otherness' – including Spanish exoticisms and jazz – offers another mask, while imagined otherness powerfully drives the psychological childhood fantasy of *L'Enfant et les sortilèges*. Additionally, some of Ravel's music shows a pronounced fluidity of genre, appearing in two or more guises.

[1]

Why the need for masks? In part, no doubt, because of his love of artefacts, musical objects and vehicles, but also because the Ravel who would be laid bare is such a private man – one who, both artistically and physically, exhibited unusual sensitivity and vulnerability,[4] yet still had to endure a succession of traumas.

Aim and summary of chapters

Marking the 125th anniversary of Ravel's birth (within a tradition of anniversary tributes from 1925, 1938, 1975, 1977 and 1987), this *Companion* seeks to celebrate Ravel's achievement by viewing his music and compositional aesthetic in its cultural context. It also aims to offer something of a reassessment at the start of the new millennium. Part of its *raison d'être* – which would also sustain several future volumes – is that Ravel's music has not yet received enough detailed study; Philip Russom's pronouncement of the mid-1980s is still largely true today: 'Music theorists have left Ravel's music untouched, with the exception of a few pages by Felix Salzer.'[5] An important supporting activity involves the production of new critical editions (currently restricted by copyright), and there are as yet no plans for a collected edition to balance that in progress for Debussy. We do, though, have access to *Ravel's Piano Music – A New Edition*, undertaken by Roger Nichols for Peters Edition, and to selected works at competitive rates courtesy of Dover Publications.[6]

In order to broaden the base for Ravel studies beyond France, it was important (beyond a core of eminent Ravel scholars) to bring in 'new blood' from other related areas. Thus scholars with reputations established by reference to Debussy, Satie, Milhaud and Koechlin have here offered fresh perspectives on Ravel's music, coloured by their distinctive backgrounds. Each chapter pursues a differentiated aspect of Ravel's aesthetic, musical style or reception, but it would be false and undesirable to claim that these compartments are airtight. In fact, one of the interesting things is how different trajectories have certain meeting-points. The most important cross-references (connecting discussions of a work or concept) are flagged up in the main text or endnotes as follows: author's surname, 'relevant subheading': chapter.

Part I aims to secure the background, concentrating on the essentials of Ravel's aesthetic and including aspects of biography. Barbara Kelly contextualises the composer's position within the French (and Austro-German) historical tradition, embracing matters musical, literary and more broadly cultural. Robert Orledge then highlights Ravel's interest in a wide-ranging eclecticism: an engagement with cultural 'otherness', manifested through

Spanish, Russian, Hebrew and Far Eastern inflections of exoticism, together with something of the blues and early jazz. Chapter 3 probes the idea of the 'Swiss clockmaker'; it examines Ravel's fascination with objectivity, especially in respect of machines, and explores the opportunities that this offered for aesthetic detachment and distancing. The complementary 'themes' of Part I enable an overview of Ravel's compositional identity and another way of grouping works beyond the genre-based divisions of Part II. This approach acknowledges that Ravel's music works do exhibit flexibility with regard to instrumentation and genre: to put it another way, particular musical objects may be viewed from varying stances.

Part II offers broad coverage of Ravel's music. While endorsing rhythmic, harmonic, motivic and voice-leading analytical enquiries, we endeavour to maintain accessibility for the general reader. Several chapters illuminate Ravel by comparison with Debussy. Works which cross generic boundaries are detailed in the single most appropriate place: as examples, *Valses nobles et sentimentales* and *Le Tombeau de Couperin* are regarded primarily as piano pieces, whereas *La Valse* is regarded primarily as a ballet.

Roy Howat brings his expertise to the seminal domain of Ravel's piano music, highlighting *Gaspard de la nuit* and *Le Tombeau* (in which he relates features of phrase structure to Malayan *pantun* poetry), while Mark DeVoto directs his interest in twentieth-century harmony to Ravel's chamber music (especially the Piano Trio and post-war sonatas), with its rethinking of traditional formulae such as the sonata and tonality itself. While not overlooking Ravel's consummate skills as the orchestrator of Musorgsky's *Pictures at an Exhibition*, Michael Russ probes the modality and thematic workings of Ravel's orchestral music from the early *Shéhérazade* through to the piano concertos.

The multi-dimensional art-form of ballet is seen in the Parisian context of the Ballets Russes and Stravinsky, focusing on the unifying concept of dance, conveyed so exquisitely in *Daphnis*. Beyond the War, *La Valse* represents the ultimate reinterpretation of an inherited classical legacy, while *Boléro* is an essay in the construction and destruction of a musical object, walking a tightrope between oppressive control and ecstatic release. In the genre of song, Peter Kaminsky demonstrates Ravel's insatiable appetite for exoticisms and explores both irony and 'literalism' in his text setting; the main points of arrival are *Trois poèmes de Stéphane Mallarmé* and *Chansons madécasses*. With reference to spectacle and text, Richard Langham Smith completes the musical explorations by considering *L'Heure espagnole* within a tradition of fanciful evocations of Spain and *L'Enfant et les sortilèges* within extended Freudian psychology.

Part III considers matters of performance and reception. Ronald Woodley brings his interest in performance issues to bear on selected early recordings of Ravel's music (mainly from the inter-war period, and including the composer's own piano rolls), and their relationship to more recent performing attitudes, as one dimension of reception. To balance this coverage, in the Appendix, Roger Nichols considers the press reception of Ravel's music within his own lifetime, focusing on Ravel's relations with critics and the composer's own views on criticism; this discussion is followed by a listing of selected first performance details and press clippings.

In the final Chapter 11, which continues the historical trajectory of Chapter 1 through to the present day, Nichols assesses Ravel's contribution and position more broadly. Typically, our perceptions are affected by Ravel's being regarded in association with, or as secondary to, Debussy (whose position is in turn perpetuated by the continuing wealth of Debussy literature). Beyond this, the well-practised response is that, essentially, the nature of Ravel's aesthetic – his highly polished art – seems just not to have been conducive to a 'Ravel School' (appropriately enough, Ravel disapproved of schools, believing them to have a stagnating effect). Nichols challenges this stance by surveying the views of composers writing today, although he still finds ambivalence and complexity in establishing Ravel's relationship with the undisputed twentieth-century 'greats': 'Ravel, it turns out, is a far more baffling, problematic and "deep" composer than he has so far been given credit for.'

So, while it is hoped that this book will go some way towards securing a solid foundation for Ravel studies in the twenty-first century, the mysteries are real and detailed musical enquiries must continue.

PART I

Culture and aesthetic

1 History and homage

BARBARA L. KELLY

One should not expect a composer's works to be entirely personal creations, offering no analogy whatever with the achievements of his predecessors. RAVEL[1]

An artist should be international in his judgments and esthetic appreciations and incorrigibly national when it comes to the province of creative art. RAVEL[2]

Ravel and authority: the Conservatoire and the Prix de Rome

Ravel informed Cipa Godebski in Spring 1914: 'I am transcribing a Forlane by Couperin. I will see about getting it danced at the Vatican by Mistinguett and Colette Willy in drag.'[3] This excerpt reveals Ravel's decidedly ambivalent attitude towards the establishment which was so marked during his early career and which he directs here towards the Church and hostile critics. Klingsor noted that the young Ravel was 'given to mocking but [was] secretly set in his purposes', while Cortot recalled 'a deliberately sarcastic, argumentative and aloof young man, who used to read Mallarmé and visit Erik Satie'.[4] Both these descriptions touch on crucial aspects of Ravel's character: a conflict between 'individual consciousness' and conformity. Ravel's sense of direction was already well developed from his days at the Conservatoire. He had willingly succumbed to the influence of Poe and Mallarmé, and his musical tastes included Chabrier and the anti-establishment figure, Satie. Much to the frustration of some of his teachers, Ravel was only teachable on his own terms. Reports from Bériot, his piano teacher, indicate an untameable temperament which is 'not always with full control' and 'needs to be held in check', and even the sympathetic Fauré damns with faint praise, stating that he was, in time, 'less exclusively attracted than before by pursuit of the excessive'.[5]

In 'Contemporary music' (1928), Ravel spoke of the two essential components of a composer's make-up: individual consciousness and national consciousness, the former amounting to the composer's individuality and the latter to his link with a national tradition. Noting American composers' reluctance to use blues and jazz to create a national style, he described 'those musicians whose greatest fear is to find themselves confronted by mysterious urges to break academic rules rather than belie individual consciousness. Thereupon these musicians, good bourgeois as they are, compose their music according to the classical rules of the European epoch.'[6] Despite his criticism, Ravel had faced a similar dilemma when entering for the Prix de Rome. In 1926, he admitted his failure as an impostor: 'I wrote the most terrible thing and was only awarded a third prize. The last time I entered a competition I was rejected because I had submitted a parody-cantata entitled "Sardanapalus' Favorite Slave" [*Myrrha*], at a time when I had already composed my Quartet and *Shéhérazade*. But that's the way I have always been.'[7] Nichols, in a similar tone, describes *Myrrha* as 'a brilliantly worked exercise in pastiche', and *Alyssa* and *Alcyone* as 'inherently false'.[8] (*Myrrha* (1901), *Alcyone* (1902) and *Alyssa* (1903) were Ravel's early unpublished cantatas entered for the Prix de Rome competition, each composed for three solo voices and orchestra.) Certainly, after *Alyssa* and *Alcyone*, Ravel would never again write anything so Wagnerian, or so suggestive of the nineteenth-century operatic tradition that he would later wish to supplant.

Ravel took his Prix de Rome attempts seriously, hoping, possibly expecting, to win. In his letter to Kiriac of 21 March 1900, he recalled his effort: 'I had patiently elaborated a scene from *Callirhoé*, and was strongly counting on its effect: the music was rather dull, prudently passionate, and its degree of boldness was accessible to those gentlemen of the Institute . . . All of this ended up in a miserable failure.' Moreover, the following year he boasted to Lucien Garban about his partial success, citing the approval of Massenet, Leroux, Vidal and even Lenepveu and declaring his intention to try again.[9] Yet Ravel was not able to maintain this conformity; Nichols interprets his uncharacteristically scrappy writing for the 1902 entry as a sign of reluctance, while the fugue submission in 1905 (with its deliberate parallel fifths and a seventh chord ending) suggests an irrepressible impulse to subvert. Distinguishing between these submissions and his real work, he was hurt that Dubois, in 1900, had directed his criticisms at *Shéhérazade* rather than at his cantata. Romain Rolland's response to Ravel's final elimination in 1905 pinpointed the problem when he argued that he could 'not comprehend why one should persist in keeping a school in Rome if it is to close its doors to those rare artists who have some originality – to a man like Ravel, who has established himself at the concerts of the Société Nationale through works far more important than those required for an examination'.[10] Despite experiencing momentary despair as a result of the protracted affair, Ravel did at least establish his reputation as a force to be reckoned with.

Rolland's view that Ravel was 'already one of the most highly regarded of the young masters in our school', was not, however, so universally accepted. The Société Nationale (SN) was dominated by the Schola Cantorum, which was distinctly hostile towards him. After the stormy receptions of *Sites auriculaires* and *Shéhérazade* at the SN, Ravel must have been aware that his *Histoires naturelles* was bound to cause a stir on account of its radical treatment of art song. Although the subject-matter and aspects of the piano accompaniment can be compared to Chabrier's animal songs, his naturalistic treatment of language was shocking even to the supportive Fauré.

Ravel's decision to break from the SN and to set up the Société Musicale Indépendante (SMI) was motivated by a desire for independence from the restricting and outmoded authority of the Schola. The new Society's aim to 'make known, through performance, French or foreign modern music, published or unpublished, without exceptions of genre or style' reveals a fundamental belief in freedom, a tolerance of difference and a firm rejection of dogma, which were central to Ravel's thinking.[11] His role in setting up the SMI indicates his growing stature, in that now he did not simply have to respond to events; his actions could make a difference.

Although d'Indy and Fauré could still refer to Ravel, Koechlin, Grovlez and Casadesus as 'the youth' in 1910, this perception quickly changed with World War I, the death of Debussy and the emergence of the post-war generation. If his refusal to accept the Légion d'honneur and election to the Institut de France was motivated by his earlier official neglect, Ravel, now regarded as the most important French composer, became a tool of the French establishment. In the mid-to-late 1920s and early 1930s, Ravel acquired a role as an ambassador in the eyes of the French authorities. The USA tour in 1928, particularly, presented an opportunity for the authorities to market him as a sign of French achievement. His European trip in 1932 with Marguerite Long and his new Concerto in G is fascinating on account of the political wrangling behind the scenes; high-level diplomacy was required to appease Georges Kugel on behalf of the Vienna Philharmonic and Furtwängler in Berlin when it emerged that Ravel was too unwell to play the concerto himself, but would be able to conduct. The Berlin Philharmonic reaction was particularly intransigent and it seemed that Hindemith would be invited in his place as a snub: a situation which René Dommange felt was an insult to France, demanding retaliation.[12] The matter was resolved when Ravel visited and conducted in Berlin on 20 March 1932. Represented by his agent and the director of the Association Française d'Expansion et d'Echanges Artistiques, Ravel was spared many of the details and, motivated largely by his love for travel, he accepted his ambassador's role.

Technique, imitation and influence

In many respects Ravel remained thoroughly attached to tradition; he stressed the importance of Gedalge for developing his own technique, and it is notable how much he valued technique, form, orchestration in others. Beethoven, Berlioz, Wagner, Brahms, Saint-Saëns, d'Indy and even Debussy were found by Ravel to be wanting in some of these areas. Ravel regularly consulted the treatises of Widor, Berlioz and Rimsky-Korsakov and the scores of many composers, including Strauss and Saint-Saëns.

At the heart of his teaching methods, Ravel emphasised mastery of technique through the imitation of models; originality would emerge from 'unwitting infidelity to the model'.[13] He could not comprehend the notion of fascist music, written to order, speculating 'Maybe they are writing Rossini-like music, but they shouldn't do that, because nobody needs bad Rossini. Good Rossini was created by the master himself, so we don't need any more of that either.'[14] Repetition or schools of composers were anathema because they were stagnant. In 1931, he spoke of 'this eternal desire to renew myself',[15] a quality which he admired in both Satie and Stravinsky.

In his writings and discussions with friends, Ravel adopted a detached manner of citing the model behind his works. He was particularly frank in relation to the Concerto in G and, in an interview for the *Excelsior* (1931), talked about the work as follows: 'As a model, I took two musicians who, in my opinion, best illustrated this type of composition: Mozart and Saint-Saëns.'[16] This attitude towards acquiring a style for a particular purpose indicates a rare distance from his own completed work. Basil Deane argues that Ravel's use of models, dance-forms and texts indicates a desire for detachment from direct experience; but, whereas Deane perceives this as a deficiency, Frank Kermode regards 'a writer's sense of the remoteness, the otherness' of his subject as essential to artistic creation.[17] Ravel viewed the model as the external trapping, shielding the inner emotion of the work; detachment from the subject did not equate with insensitivity, a charge frequently directed at his own work.

An essential difference between Ravel and Stravinsky lies in the value that they attached to models. While Stravinsky regarded them as suitable resources on which he could draw in order to forge something new, Ravel studied models principally in order to learn from them. Although achieving a similar fusion of old and new, Ravel's attitude indicates an awareness of his dependence on a history of composition (with a more spontaneous use of the past than that of Stravinsky).

Ravel and his immediate predecessors

Ravel accepted influence as inevitable and necessary. Alexandre Tansman recalled Ravel's comment that 'A composer who shows no influences should change his profession'.[18] In 'Take jazz seriously!', Ravel cited his indebtedness to Fauré, Chabrier, Gounod, Debussy and Satie, highlighting his keen awareness of the influence his immediate predecessors and older contemporaries had on him; his gratitude and occasional 'anxiety' towards the past took a number of forms, including frank acknowledgement in 'An autobiographical sketch' of stylistic influence in certain works.[19] It also manifested itself in acts of homage, pastiches, reductions, transcriptions, orchestrations and editions, in which Ravel engaged with the work or the style of a chosen composer. The degree to which Ravel's homages resulted in misreadings or 'unwitting infidelity' needs to be examined in each case.

Ravel's acknowledgement of Fauré's support is evident from the dedication of the String Quartet and of *Jeux d'eau*. Similarly, his *Berceuse sur le nom de Gabriel Fauré*, destined for the special musical supplement of *La Revue musicale* (October 1922), was written as a tribute to his *maître* and a token of appreciation for Fauré's continued support and his crucial role in attempting to bridge the chasm between the SN and the SMI. Fauré, for his part, described the homage as 'the most beautiful jewel in my crown', expressing his extreme satisfaction with the 'solid position which you [Ravel] occupy and which you have acquired so brilliantly and so rapidly. It is a source of joy and pride for your old professor.'[20] Although Fauré disapproved privately of some of Ravel's innovations, he continued to appreciate his student's importance. While Ravel never acknowledged Fauré's musical influence on any particular work, he rated highly his musicianship and his ability to admit that his opinion might be wrong. Ravel upheld Fauré's songs as his most significant achievement, pinpointing 'his nostalgic and tender lyricism, modest and without superfluous outbursts', which achieve 'a poignant and strong emotion'.[21] This lyricism and emotional restraint that he so admired in *Le Secret* are fundamental to Ravel's own writing, and it seems that Fauré succeeded in taming the more violent inclinations noted in Ravel's student reports.

After resisting Fauré's appreciation of Saint-Saëns as a student, Ravel grew to admire him from about 1910. Calvocoressi recalls his surprise at this new interest, which he detected musically in the Trio; the dedication of the Trio to Gedalge, however, suggests a more direct homage to his counterpoint teacher to whom he owed 'the most valuable elements of ... [his] technique'.[22] While the contrapuntal writing of the 'Passacaille' suggests Gedalge's teaching, the emphasis on technique and classical structure reflects the elements that he admired most in Saint-Saëns. Ravel's reduction and analysis of Saint-Saëns's *La Jeunesse d'Hercule* as a Conservatoire student is noteworthy for its melodic reduction of the principal themes, sections and fugal entries supported by figured bass.[23] According to Calvocoressi, this was one one of the few works by Saint-Saëns that Ravel admired at this time. Not only does it highlight Ravel's fascination with structure and harmonic events, it gives an insight into the manner in which he studied his elders.

Ravel and Chabrier

The enthusiasm and reverence of both Ravel and Viñes for Chabrier is clear from their visit to him in 1893 (to play the ailing composer his *Trois valses romantiques* for two pianos) and the strength of their response to his death. Declaring that he was 'influenced above all by a musician: Chabrier', Ravel was forthcoming about Chabrier's influence on *Pavane pour une Infante défunte* and *Sérénade grotesque.*[24] Certainly, there are traces of Chabrier's influence on Ravel's early piano writing in his predilection for dance forms, miniatures, his fascination with Spain, his attention to detail and captivating lyricism. Ravel's orchestration of Chabrier's 'Menuet pompeux' (1919), for the Ballets Russes, represents the tribute of a mature composer; he adds to the harmonically based original a multi-layered texture, highly varied in its range of solo timbres (including bassoon, clarinet and muted horns) and enlivened with percussion instruments, including his favoured *tambour de basque.* His intention to reorchestrate parts of *Le Roi malgré lui* in 1929 'because of certain imperfections in this inspired orchestration' indicates an awareness that he had not only consolidated Chabrier's style, but surpassed him technically.[25] Although Ravel wrote to Mme Bretton-Chabrier to gain permission, the project unfortunately came to nothing.

By way of contrast, *A la manière de ... Chabrier* was written at Casella's request as a light-hearted pastiche. Ravel's decision to adapt a famous Gounod melody (from Act III of *Faust*) not only represents a double tribute, but firmly links the two musicians, who he felt represented 'the sources from which the main stream of French music was derived'.[26] Ravel transforms Gounod's simple air into an introspective piano work, marking the entry of the melody 'avec charme' and 'rubato'. Although he retains most of Gounod's melody and bass line, he builds on the existing harmony, changing sevenths into ninths, adding arpeggio movement, dramatic pauses and delaying cadences. Harmonies of D^7 and E^7 become D^9 and E^9 (cf. Example 1.1a and b), but Ravel avoids Gounod's A minor cadence, opting for E♭ major and delaying the subsequent return to C major. It could be argued that this pastiche involves a misreading, not only of Gounod, but also of Chabrier, in that the result does not sound out of place within Ravel's own work. Roy Howat has identified a number of crucial Chabrier traits introduced by Ravel: the falling fifth (from the ninth to the fifth degree) in the tenor line of bars 13 and 25; the two-octave doublings across

Example 1.1 Melodic and harmonic comparison
(a) Gounod, *Faust* (Act III, scene I), Siebel's aria: 'The flower song' (bars 28–33)

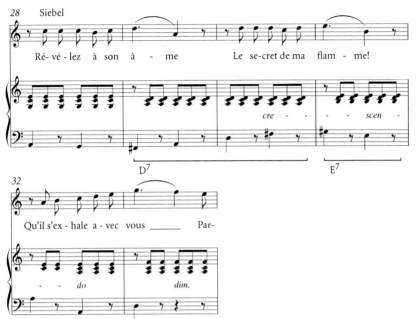

(b) Ravel, *A la manière de . . . Chabrier* (bars 26–31)

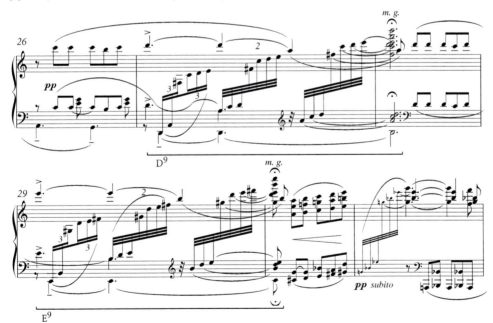

bars 22–9 (see Example 1.1b) and 35–7, recalling Chabrier's 'Paysage' and 'Melancolie'; allusions to *Caprice* in the bass figure at bar 31, and to the final eight bars of 'Sous-bois' (and Wagner's 'Liebestod') in the last three bars.[27] Such observations highlight the ease with which Ravel could move between his own and his influential predecessor's style.

Along with Debussy, Milhaud and Poulenc, Ravel was involved with reassessing Chabrier's and Gounod's contribution to French music. Although Gounod's influence was less personally felt on his music, Ravel's view that Gounod was amongst the most French of recent composers and heir to 'the French harpsichord school of the seventeenth and eighteenth centuries' indicates that Ravel envisaged French tradition as a chain of composers, with Gounod representing a continuation of the 'Golden Age' of French music; indeed, he described the 1880s as a renaissance in French music, claiming that 'Without Gounod, perhaps there wouldn't be any modern French music.'[28]

Ravel and Debussy

Ravel refused to undermine Debussy's importance, despite his own complex association with him. In Ravel's student days, Debussy was his idol; he and his fellow 'Apaches' endeavoured to attend every performance of the initially controversial *Pelléas*. In a letter to Florent Schmitt of 8 April 1901, Ravel admitted that he was working on a 'transcription of Debussy's wonderful *Nocturnes*, in collaboration with Bardac', alongside writing 'choral pieces and fugues in preparation for the competition [Prix de Rome]'; the pleasure from one task would counteract the boredom of the other.[29] *Prélude à l'après-midi d'un faune* always remained important for Ravel; when asked by Rosenthal what he would like played at his funeral, he replied: '*L'Après-midi d'un faune* . . . because it's the only score ever written that is absolutely perfect' (Roland-Manuel aptly described Ravel's arrangement of the work for four hands in 1910 as a 'homage to a man of genius').[30] Ravel, however, displayed considerable anxiety about his debt to Debussy; while he was happy to admit the influence of Debussy on his *Shéhérazade* in 'An autobiographical sketch', he refused to be regarded simply as a follower and imitator.

Ravel's need to assert his independence from Debussy, yet acknowledge his role, is evident from an interview for *The Morning Post* (1922) in which he declared himself an 'anti-Debussyist' while placing Debussy as 'the great creative influence in modern French music'.[31] In his view, Debussy lacked a certain discipline, particularly with regard to form; his comment that 'I started the reaction against him in favor of the classics because I craved more will and intellect than his music contained' gives an important clue to Ravel's independent aesthetic position.[32] His dedication of the Sonata for Violin and Cello to the memory of Debussy is apt given its formal terseness, its austere and restrained expression, and its assimilation of some of the latest preoccupations; it is a fitting example of independence based on a healthy awareness of the past and present of French music.

Ravel's orchestrations of *Danse* and 'Sarabande' in 1922, at the request of the publisher Jean Jobert, differ from his earlier transcriptions in that they are the response of a mature artist. Once more, Ravel imprints his personality onto Debussy's scores; his arrangement of *Danse* contains sustained lines and more solid textures underlined by a rhythmic incision not common in Debussy's orchestral writing.

Ravel and Satie

In 'Contemporary music', Ravel placed Satie alongside Fauré and Chabrier as a formative influence. Although Ravel's interest in Satie while a student at the Conservatoire contributed to his reputation as an anti-establishment figure, it was in fact the charge made by Satie of Ravel's being part of the establishment that exacerbated the rift between the two: Satie's public statement in *Le Coq* of May 1920 that 'Ravel rejects the Légion d'honneur but all his music accepts it' was to constitute a particular snub.[33] As a founding member of the SMI, Ravel was by 1911 in a position of power to promote Satie, and a dedicated concert on 16 January (the first of the 1911 season) signalled a wider interest in Satie's music, leading to the publication of his early works. An indication of their artistic sympathy at this point is found in Roland-Manuel's statement that by 1910 Satie 'considered Debussy as a musician of the past, [whereas] Ravel illustrated the present', while Ravel wrote in 1911 that 'Erik Satie is the originator of the present form of expression.'[34] Ravel's dedication of 'Les Entretiens de la Belle et de la Bête' from *Ma Mère l'Oye* 'to Erik Satie, grandfather of the "Entretiens" and other pieces, with the affectionate homage of a disciple', indicates a more personal realisation of indebtedness.[35] Additionally, his dedication of 'Surgi de la croupe et du bond' from *Trois poèmes de Mallarmé* can be viewed as a tribute to Satie's role as experimenter, given that it is the most harmonically advanced piece Ravel ever wrote.

Beyond World War I, Satie firmly rejected Ravel's 'deplorable and outmoded aesthetic', as he explained to Jean-Aubry in 1919; Ravel, for his part, disapproved of the faulty orchestration and lack of 'sonorous fluid' in *Parade* and the technically deficient *Socrate*, though he never attacked Satie in public.[36] The gulf between them and their supporters is reinforced by an unpublished letter of 10 September 1917 that Satie wrote to Cocteau. In this letter, Satie complained about an article that Ravel's friend, Jean Marnold, had written about him, adding 'so much the better, Auric has a point: he is, and remains, a Ravel supporter'.[37] It is somewhat ironic that Ravel in 1928 allied his aesthetic with that of Satie: 'He anticipated Debussyan impressionism . . . and was one of the leaders in the direction away from it – a direction which I myself, as I think I can say, have consistently followed.'[38] His assessment of Satie's importance did not materialise until after Satie's death. Freed from the complications of Satie's personality, Ravel credited him as a pioneering experimenter and 'the inspiration of countless progressive tendencies', who had exerted an influence on most modern French composers, but who had probably never 'wrought out of his own discoveries a single complete work of art'.[39]

Ravel and writers

Ravel also acknowledged the influence of writers: in fact he placed Poe alongside Fauré and Gedalge as his third teacher. In an interview in the *New York Times* he spoke of his American teacher, 'whom we in France were quicker to understand than you . . . [and] whose esthetic, indeed, has been extremely close and sympathetic [to] that of modern French art. Very French is the quality of "The Raven" and much else of his verse, and also his essay on the principles of poetry.'[40] An examination of Poe's *The Philosophy of Composition* (1846) and *The Poetic Principle* (1850) reveals the nature of this empathy and the extent of Poe's influence on Ravel as a student. Poe's emphasis within the process of composition on deliberate, calculated and logical planning appealed to Ravel's artisan and measured approach to musical composition and, indeed, he and his friends testified to Ravel's tendency to complete a work in his head before completion.[41] In his discussion of *The Raven*, Poe's highlighting of structure, effect and proportion had an echo in Ravel's criticism of his own *Rapsodie espagnole*: 'The orchestra's too large for the number of bars.'[42] Similarly, in both his essays, Poe advocated brevity for sustaining 'the elevation of the soul', a quality that Ravel regarded as essentially French.

Ravel undoubtedly appreciated Poe's emphases in *The Philosophy of Composition* on 'originality' and the goal of perfection. And in Poe's view, art, rather than expressing truth or conscience (the moral sense), should express nothing but beauty, tempered only by taste.[43] This advocation of art for art's sake places Poe alongside fin-de-siècle writers, such as Oscar Wilde, Walter Pater and Huysmans. Moreover, the importance Poe attached to music as 'the most entrancing of the Poetic moods' shows his proximity to the Symbolists.[44] Poe's view that setting poems to music amounted to 'perfecting them as poems' gives an important insight into Ravel's notion of 'transposing', 'translating' and 'underlining' poetry.[45] Renard recalled in his *Journal* (1960) Ravel's wish 'To say with music what you say with words . . . I think and feel in music and I should like to think and feel the same things as you'; his desire to find correspondences between the arts also indicates his attachment to Baudelaire.[46]

Ravel's recognition of his bond with fin-de-siècle literary tradition is evident from the following admission:

> Naturally, I fully realize that the influences which I underwent are partially related to the time in which I grew up. I am keenly aware that the works I love best have occasionally become outdated. This is true of *A Rebours*: I can't help but consider it of major importance, and yet I know that, justifiably, it no longer retains that importance. Nevertheless, it still rings true for me.[47]

The Huysmans novel, *A Rebours*, published in Paris in 1884, for which Ravel felt a particular affection, achieved a cult status and is a fitting example of decadence in which the hero indulges in sensation and pleasure for their own sake. And beyond this, Ravel's interest in Baudelaire, Mallarmé and Verlaine reinforces his attachment to his immediate inheritance. Indeed, in a letter to Mme de Saint-Marceaux of 20 August 1898 he described himself as 'The little symbolist'.[48] Ravel elevated Mallarmé as 'not merely the greatest French poet, but the *only* French poet, since he made the French language, not designed for poetry, poetical'.[49] In addition to setting the Symbolists, Ravel ranged widely for suitable texts, showing an interest in the past, with settings of (or scenarios derived from) Marot, Ronsard, Charles Perrault, the Comtesse d'Aulnoy and Marie Leprince de Beaumont. He evoked an imagined past in his own texts, such as *Noël des jouets* and the unaccompanied *Trois chansons* for mixed choir, and also selected contemporary writers, most notably, Jules Renard and his fellow member of the 'Apaches', Léon-Paul Fargue. Ravel's immediate heritage provided the essential context for excursions into the past and to the exotic, and despite his predilection for adopting models or evoking imaginary musical worlds, his art was precisely located in time (turn of the century) and place (France).

National consciousness and tradition

In 1924 Ravel declared, 'Unlike politics, in art I'm a nationalist. I know that I am above all a French composer: I furthermore declare myself a classicist.'[50] This careful separation between art and politics was crucial to Ravel's left-wing political orientation and to his belief in an artistic national consciousness. Artistic achievement involved a necessary blending of national and individual consciousness; Debussy was one very important manifestation of the French spirit, just as Milhaud, Auric and Poulenc represented more recent manifestations. Despite his keen interest in foreign music, he regarded national traditions as separate and incompatible; 'Schoenberg, "one of the greatest figures of the time", as a German [*sic*] followed a line of development which had hardly reacted at all on the essentially Latin nature of French music.'[51] On the other hand, he viewed Wagner's influence as disastrous and destructive, and thought that d'Indy, by following Wagner, had forsaken both his personality and tradition. He regarded much of the nineteenth century as an interruption, asserting, along with French writers such as Maurice Barrès and Charles Maurras, and musicians including Debussy and Milhaud, that the French spirit was naturally classical.

Ravel occasionally equated nationality with 'racial consciousness', but generally stressed culture, climate and language as the determinants of shared national experience, declaring in 1932 that French and Austrian nationalities were not dependent on race, but on 'a cultural community crystallized out of many different races'.[52] During his American tour he welcomed the mixture inherent in national styles, suggesting that 'it will be found that national music is usually an accumulation from many sources'.[53] Indeed, he concluded his 'Contemporary music' lecture in this vein, arguing against the notion of purity in art, a notion held by as diverse a group as d'Indy, Debussy and Milhaud.

Ravel's fear of being associated with the wrong kind of nationalism is evident from his letter to Jean Marnold on receiving an invitation in 1916 to be on the committee of the reformed SN, in which he admitted his hesitation 'fearing that this Society was too ... national'.[54] More public, however, was his refusal to join the National League for the Defence of French Music because they advocated prohibiting French public performances of contemporary German and Austrian compositions. His belief that isolation from foreign music would be 'dangerous for French composers' and would lead to the degeneration of French art testifies to a very healthy openness to music from whatever source. While he felt that nationality tied an artist to a particular tradition, it was not a reason for discrimination: 'It is of little importance to me that Mr. Schoenberg, for example, is of Austrian nationality. This does not prevent him from being an outstanding musician.'[55] Nevertheless, Ravel pledged to 'act as a Frenchman', as his determination to become involved in the War and his obvious pride in finally fulfilling this aim testify.

Musical engagement with the past

Although Ravel referred to Rameau and Couperin as classics, he very rarely discussed them in his writings, admitting only his preference for Couperin and Lully rather than the somewhat intellectual style of Rameau. Unlike Debussy, he was not involved in promoting performances of the music of this 'Golden Age' of French music, or in any of the critical editions that appeared in the late nineteenth and early twentieth centuries. Nevertheless, his interest in Couperin manifested itself in his transcription of Couperin's 'Forlane' from the fourth *Concert royal* in Spring 1914. Despite Ravel's jest that he was transcribing the dance in response to the Pope's prohibition of the tango in favour of the forlane, Messing identifies a more likely reason for Ravel's transcription in the publication of a harmonisation of Couperin's 'Forlane' by Albert Bertelin.[56] Bertelin's transcription had appeared within an article by Jules Ecorcheville entitled 'La Forlane', in the *Revue musicale de la S.I.M.* of April 1914. A comparison between Bertelin's and Ravel's transcriptions reveals that Ravel adopted a sparser texture, minimising inner movement and avoiding the regular minor second dissonance in the refrain. Ravel also preferred to keep the bass nearer the upper parts, even allowing it to rise above the melody at the start of the third couplet. Finally, in the fourth couplet (Examples 1.2a and b), Ravel avoided the tedious drone effect, choosing to decorate the texture with pianistic octave leaps.

Within a few months of making the transcription (at the start of the War), Ravel wrote to Roland-Manuel stating that he had begun a French suite: 'no, it isn't what you think: *La Marseillaise* will not be in it, but it will have a forlane and a gigue; no tango, however' – a further allusion to the prohibition.[57] Messing and Orenstein have acknowledged rhythmic similarities between Couperin's 'Forlane' and that of Ravel. Certainly, Ravel retained the rhythmic gestures, ornamentation and formal scheme of refrain and couplets from the original. There are, however, some closer parallels (cf. Example 1.3a–c). Ravel's rhythm, phrasing, articulation and key of E major correspond exactly with Couperin's refrain (cf. Example 1.3a and b). Moreover, Ravel's rhythmic exchange between the parts and general melodic shape are strikingly similar to Couperin's third couplet (cf. Example 1.3a and c). Ravel overrides his decision in the transcription to maintain a high register, achieving greater force with the antiphonal effect in the bass and closely spaced chords. Other parallels can be found between Couperin's first and Ravel's second couplet, which are alike in rhythm, melodic shape and homophonic character, and between Couperin's and Ravel's fourth couplets in terms of rhythm, tessitura and key. Despite his claim that 'The homage is directed less in fact to Couperin

Example 1.2 Couperin, *Concert royal No. IV*, 'Forlane': fourth couplet (bars 1–8)
(a) Ed. Bertelin (Source: *Revue musicale de la S.I.M.* (April 1914), 28)

(b) Ed. Ravel (Source: Arbie Orenstein, 'Some unpublished music and letters by Maurice Ravel', *Music Forum*, 3 (1973), 291–334: 331)

himself than to French music of the eighteenth century', Couperin was clearly not far from his mind.[58] Retaining the linear aspects of Couperin's style, Ravel embellished and added to his model vertically by thickening the harmonies, as he did with the Gounod/Chabrier pastiche. The most repeated section in the dance, the refrain, with its rising major seventh and chordal harmonic support, is stylistically the furthest removed from the original, indicating Ravel's ultimate control of his model. (For more on Ravel's 'Forlane', see Howat, 'Sophistication in *Le Tombeau de Couperin*': Chapter 4.)

Example 1.3 Ravel and Couperin comparisons
(a) Ravel, *Le Tombeau de Couperin*, 'Forlane' (bars 124–36)

(b) Couperin, ed. Ravel, 'Forlane': refrain (bars 1–8)
(Source: Orenstein, 'Some unpublished music', 330)

Forlane

Example 1.3 (*cont.*)
(c) Couperin, ed. Ravel, 'Forlane': third couplet (bars 1–7)
(Source: Orenstein, 'Some unpublished music', 330)

3ᵉ Couplet

In other pieces his evocation of the past is unspecific, such as the imagined past of *Menuet antique* (via Chabrier), the *Trois chansons pour chœur mixte sans accompagnement* and songs, including *Deux épigrammes de Clément Marot* and *Ronsard à son âme*, with more clichéd allusions to the past in the bare fourths, fifths and octaves. Messing argues that World War I provided the catalyst for Ravel's renewed interest in older forms and styles.[59] Although some parallels can be drawn with Debussy in this respect, Ravel remained more open to the wider European musical tradition.

Tradition beyond France

Ravel did not limit his homage to French music. Indeed, Mozart was his favourite composer and, in an interview in the Austrian press in 1932, he stated that he felt 'particularly close to Mozart . . . Beethoven strikes me as a classical Roman, Mozart as a classical Hellene. I myself feel closer to the open, sunny Hellenes.'[60] In accounting for his personal empathy for Mozart in this way, he touches on an enduring French notion that the French were heirs to ancient Greek civilisation, a view that Paul Collaer later espoused in *La Musique moderne*.[61] Ravel's preference for Mozartian Grecian greatness over the colossal in Beethoven is a further indication of the link he felt between Mozart and his own intimate French art. Mozart also constituted an important part of his training, since Gedalge based his teaching largely on his works. It may appear surprising that he made no arrangements or transcriptions of any Mozart, but he probably felt that he had nothing to add to the work of the composer whom he described as perfection.

Ravel, like Debussy, had a particular empathy towards the Russian 'Five'. Admitting that he appreciated their music for its 'otherness', he also believed in its beneficial impact on French music and its role in offering French composers an alternative to Wagner's influence. Viñes recalled their early enthusiasm for Russian music, and the theme from Borodin's Second Symphony even became the rallying call of the 'Apaches'. Ravel shows his familiarity with Borodin's style in the pastiche entitled *A la manière de . . . Borodine*. Ravel worked with Stravinsky on the orchestration of Musorgsky's unfinished *Khovanshchina* in 1913, and Ravel's version of *Pictures at an Exhibition* is better known now than Musorgsky's original, with Ravel's character very much in evidence. Rimsky-Korsakov, whose predilection for orchestrating the works of others was matched only by Ravel, became Ravel's focus when he reorchestrated Rimsky's *Antar*. The incidental music comprises sections from *Antar*, *Mlada* and the songs, Op. 4 and Op. 7. A sketch at the Bibliothèque Nationale de France consists of a piano reduction of the intended excerpts from *Antar* and the songs and scraps of dialogue from the play, giving a rare insight into Ravel's working methods.[62]

Viñes's diaries and Nectoux's study of Ravel's own music library confirm that Ravel's musical interests were always broad. Educated in the traditional piano repertoire at the Conservatoire, including Schumann, Mendelssohn, Weber, Chopin, Grieg and Saint-Saëns, Ravel never lost his interest in them, as his orchestration of Schumann's *Carnaval* and his undertaking of the complete Mendessohn piano works edition suggest. Nectoux also notes that Ravel owned the first French, Italian and German editions of Liszt, whom he admired for his pianistic and harmonic innovations and for his crucial influence on Wagner.[63] The list of other composers he admired and studied ranged from Weber, Bellini and Johann Strauss through to Richard Strauss.

Ravel treated orchestration as a technical skill slightly separate from the compositional process: while Ravel never allowed anyone to watch him composing, he was seen orchestrating. He had a similar attitude towards transcriptions, a process 'which every musical work may undergo, on condition that good taste presides'.[64] He felt more strongly, however, about interfering with the harmonies of another composer's work, arguing that Rimsky-Korsakov's corrections of Musorgsky amounted to tampering with the essence of Musorgsky's conception; Ravel also writes about the inappropriateness of being asked to complete Chabrier's *Briséis*.[65] Ravel's edition of Mendelssohn's piano works constitutes his only editorial work and represents a particular kind of tribute, undertaken for Durand during the War when German editions were unavailable. It comprises nine volumes, with just the first containing editorial comments. Ravel was explicit that he drew upon two published sources: Breitkopf and Brandus, edited by Stephen Heller; and, although he adhered to the Breikopf version, he presented Heller's suggestions as serious alternatives. Characteristically, his aim seemed to be perfecting Mendelssohn's style, based on intuition, in the absence of manuscript sources. Thus he alluded to details in Heller's version as 'more successful', 'more elegant' or 'with more delicate charm', justifying his preference: 'because they are presented by a sensitive artist, and a sincere admirer of Mendelssohn'.[66] Guarding Heller from any charge of drawing on his own inspiration, he conjectured that he must have had access to a manuscript or to corrections indicated directly by Mendelssohn. Ravel clearly faced a conflict between his goal of perfection and his practice of not tampering with a completed work.

New musical developments and neoclassicism

Ravel's comment that 'musicians who are true alike to their national consciousness and to their own individuality often appreciate compositions altogether different from their own' was at the root of his objection to the aims of the National League for the Defence of French Music,[67] and also of his defence of Jean Wiéner's 'salad concerts', which had been attacked by the critic Louis Vuillemin as 'Concerts métèques' in *Le Courrier musical* of January 1923. In his joint response with Roussel, Caplet and Roland-Manuel, in the April issue, he welcomed the performance of Schoenberg's *Pierrot lunaire*, which he had tried and failed to get performed (together with Stravinsky's *Trois poésies* and two of his own Mallarmé settings) in May 1913 by the SMI, warning against the wrong sort of patriotism 'in an area where it has nothing to gain, but every-thing to lose'.[68]

Ravel attempted to remain aware of new musical trends throughout his career, at one point setting them and after 1918, increasingly responding to them. Acknowledging that his Mallarmé settings were inspired by the instrumentation of *Pierrot lunaire*, he also admitted that, while the 'Chansons madécasses* are in no way Schoenbergian', they could not have been written without Schoenberg's example.[69] In the letter to the SMI com-mittee he anticipated the audience's response to *Pierrot lunaire*, Stravinsky's *Trois poésies* and the first two of his Mallarmé settings: whereas the Schoenberg and Stravinsky 'will make the audience howl', the Ravel 'will calm them down, and the people will go out whistling tunes'.[70] Ravel would therefore have agreed with Boulez's assertion that he, like Stravinsky, was only able to capture the most superficial elements of Schoenberg's *Pierrot* because of their divergent aesthetic stances.[71]

Ravel's interest in Schoenberg brought him close to the position of some of 'Les Six', who, along with Wiéner, were actively promoting foreign music in Paris after World War I. Ravel and the members of 'Les Six' also shared other concerns, including their recognition of the importance of Gounod and Chabrier for French music, their belief in two parallel and distinct traditions – Latin and Teutonic, and their desire to find alternatives to Debussy's inimitable art. These points are well illustrated by Milhaud's article on 'The evolution of modern music in Paris and in Vienna' that appeared in the *North American Review* of April 1923.[72] Ravel shared the contemporary fascination with jazz and interest in bitonality with Milhaud. Indeed, the jazz-inspired figure (Fig. 5; bars 52–5) from the first movement of his Concerto in G indicates that Ravel knew Milhaud's *La Création du monde*, although Stravinsky and Gershwin's influence are also in evidence. Ravel retained a keen interest in the music of 'Les Six', promoting it abroad, defending it from attacks in the press and even justifying his own rejection by 'Les Six' with the comment, 'if he [Auric] didn't knock Ravel he'd be writing Ravel, and there's quite enough of that!'[73]

In the early 1920s, Milhaud, Poulenc and Auric regarded Ravel with disdain, harshly criticising what they regarded as his 'outmoded' aesthetic. Milhaud explained that as a conservatoire student he became dismissive of Ravel, perceiving a lack of depth in his music; he also expressed his contempt for *La Valse*, describing it as 'Saint-Saëns for the Russian ballet'.[74] Most likely, he and his colleagues were also influenced by Satie's deteriorating relations with Ravel. Indeed, their view that Ravel was part of the establishment seemed to be borne out by Ravel's new status as the leading French composer after Debussy's death in 1918. Ravel, who had been close to Stravinsky in the early-to-mid 1910s, did not share the younger generation's wholehearted enthusiasm for Stravinsky's neoclassicism. Declaring his incomprehension of *Mavra* and other 'failed' works, Ravel could not understand Stravinsky's fascination with Tchaikovsky and rejection of his teacher, Rimsky-Korsakov.

Yet Ravel was clearly drawn to certain aspects of neoclassicism, insisting on relating the current preoccupations with older, enduring concerns. Ravel, Stravinsky, Satie and 'Les Six' shared the ideal of *dépouillement* (economy of means); while 'Les Six' presented it as something new, initiated by Satie, Ravel credited Debussy for championing it. It is undeniable, however, that Ravel's interest in achieving economy of means increased after the War and that in this respect he demonstrated his receptivity to new musical developments. Thus, in the Sonata for Violin and Cello, Ravel combined Saint-Saëns with traces of Stravinsky's rhythmic drive, adopting a restraint which suggests both Fauré and a more contemporary austerity.

In an interview in the *New York Times* (1927), Ravel spoke of a 'reaction . . . in the direction of our oldest traditions'.[75] Welcoming the interest in counterpoint (though surely overplaying the distinction between his and Debussy's string quartets), he argued that it was not as new as Stravinsky made it seem:

> After our extreme modernism, a return to classicism was to be expected. After a flood comes the ebb tide, and after a revolution we see the reaction. Stravinsky is often considered the leader of neoclassicism, but don't forget that my String Quartet was already conceived in terms of four-part counterpoint, whereas Debussy's Quartet is purely harmonic in conception.[76]

Although Ravel links himself with neoclassicism as a precursor, he remains separate from the 'revolution' and 'reaction'. His expression of 'delight' in the 'return to pure forms, this neoclassicism – call it what you will' was due to the fact that he had never abandoned his use of traditional forms and classicising titles.[77] Ravel's classicism, including his predilection for older dance forms and his evocation of the past, owes much to his immediate predecessors, particularly Chabrier, Fauré and Saint-Saëns. Ravel was less concerned with remaking the past than with responding to it, unlike Stravinsky, who had deliberately dissociated himself from his Russian roots and borrowed wilfully to create what T. S. Eliot described as 'new wholes'.[78]

This fundamental difference in attitude towards traditional rules is captured in their response in 1913–14 to the issue of superimposing a major and minor third: 'Ravel said, "But such a chord is perfectly feasible, provided the minor third is placed above the major third below." "If this arrangement is possible", commented Stravinsky, "I don't see why the contrary shouldn't be possible too: and if I will it, I can do it."'[79] While Ravel sometimes experimented with bitonality, his music can generally be analysed in terms of unresolved appoggiaturas, and so on, operating within a single, albeit extended, tonality. Boulez's observation that, even when succumbing to Schoenberg's influence, Ravel's harmonic language derives from Gounod and Fauré, reinforces Ravel's essential link with his immediate past.[80] Ravel's response to Stravinsky's innovations and to the allied preoccupations of the younger generation was selective, adopting textures, instrumentation and some harmonic procedures, while always linking these developments to tradition.

2 Evocations of exoticism

ROBERT ORLEDGE

Art is a beautiful lie. RAVEL[1]

My music is unequivocally French. RAVEL[2]

French musical exoticism in the nineteenth century

On 8 December 1844 Félicien David's symphonic ode *Le Désert* took Paris by storm. Although David had actually travelled to the Far East as a member of the Saint-Simonian expedition to find a female Messiah in 1833, it was his imaginative translation of his exotic musical souvenirs into an acceptable Westernised format which led to their success. In fact, had he incorporated melodic augmented seconds, rediscovered modes and Glinka's new whole-tone scale within his pot-pourri of melodrama, pedal-points, arabesques, conventional chromatic harmony and bombastic choruses in praise of Allah, all the clichés of nineteenth-century musical exoticism would have been present, leaving successors such as Bizet and Delibes with only the prospect of subtle refinement of his ideas. Even the perceptive Berlioz was bowled over by David's achievement, and surprisingly more by the musical qualities of *Le Désert* than by its then-novel pseudo-orientalism. 'A great composer has just appeared; a masterpiece has been unveiled', he enthusiastically exclaimed. 'David writes like a master: his movements are carved out, developed, and transformed with as much tact as science and taste, and he is a great harmonist. His melody is always distinguished, and he orchestrates extraordinarily well.'[3] The same accolade would have been far more justifiable had it appeared after the first performance of Ravel's *Shéhérazade* songs in May 1904, and if he never passed judgement on David's 'masterpiece' and had little respect for Berlioz as a composer, Ravel knew better than anyone that authenticity was far less important than imagination and technique when it came to a successful exotic representation.

If he needed an example of this, Ravel would have needed to look no further than Louis Bourgault-Ducoudray's *Rapsodie cambodgienne* (1882), in which the practical application of the composer's ethnomusicological research had less impact than his lectures and writings on the subject. Indeed, Berlioz's reaction to the Chinese musicians whom he heard at the Great Exhibition in London 1851 (when acting as a member of an international jury on musical instruments) suggests that it was extremely unlikely that genuine authenticity would ever have created a favourable impression with a Parisian audience, and he related their music to contemporary European practices at their worst. 'The melody', he complained, 'which was altogether grotesque and atrocious, finished on the tonic, like our most undistinguished sentimental songs; it never moved out of the initial tonality or mode . . . Nevertheless, the ludicrous melody was quite discernible, and one could have written it down in case of real need.' His final conclusion, after listening to a wider range of exotic musicians, was that

> Chinese and Indian music would be similar to ours if it existed; but that, musically speaking, these nations are still plunged in a state of benighted barbarianism and childish ignorance where only a few vague and feeble instincts are dimly discernible; that, moreover, the Orientals call music what we should style cacophony, and that for them, as for Macbeth's witches, foul is fair.[4]

This view, of course, was coloured by mid-nineteenth-century French perceptions of Empire, whose expansion went hand in hand with the growth of a superficial exoticism acceptable to bourgeois audiences back home: filtered, as it were, through rose-tinted opera-glasses. The perception of Western superiority in art and culture, which ethnomusicological research in the second half of the nineteenth century was often tailored to encourage, was coupled with a widespread view of Eastern degeneracy in which the savages were rather less 'noble' than those of Rousseau in the eighteenth century as a result of their resistance to French conquest. Their chief fascination was a prurient one arising from the reported beauty and lassitude of their women, and as men bought the opera tickets, it is no surprise that harem scenes and exotic dances featured widely in operas, usually regardless of specific nationality. As early as the mid-eighteenth century, Dr Johnson had famously described imported Italian opera as 'an exotic and irrational entertainment',[5] and whatever advances operatic exoticism made beyond the customary 'Turkish music' in the nineteenth century, his description could equally well apply to Ravel's *L'Enfant et les sortilèges* in 1925. Indeed, it was the exotic as a concept that appealed to Ravel as much as opera's capacity to incorporate fantastic situations. We can also see him taking advantage of other aspects made possible through opera: the ability of stage sets and costumes to make almost any music seem exotic; the gradual acceptance of the term exotic to incorporate virtually any country outside France (the concept of 'otherness'); the growing synonymy between exoticism and eroticism; and the concomitant desirability of alluring, sensuous and luxuriant orchestral textures.

The Paris Exhibition of 1889

But as the nineteenth century progressed, fear of the strange or foreign diminished and exotic objects became a part of everyday life. The wealth which accompanied the growth of the French Empire led, for example, to a vogue for collecting Japanese prints and artefacts from the 1880s onwards, and the succession of Expositions Universelles in 1867, 1878 and especially 1889 brought the realities of Empire to the Parisian doorstep. Thus it was that Debussy, Ravel, Satie and other composers found all they needed to broaden their musical horizons without having to resort to travel which they could not afford or did not want to undertake. In 1889 Ravel was only fourteen, but the Exhibition introduced him both to the music of the Javanese gamelan orchestra and that of the Russian 'Five'. It did not matter to him that the gamelan was assembled from available musicians from various regions,[6] for it was the novel 'defective' modes, layered ostinato textures and repetitive rhythms that he stored in his mind for future use in works like the *Shéhérazade* overture and *Ma Mère l'Oye*. As he told an interviewer in 1931: 'I consider Javanese music the most sophisticated music of the Far East, and I frequently derive themes from it: "Laideronnette" from *Ma Mère l'Oye*, with the tolling of its temple bells, was derived from Java both harmonically and melodically.'[7]

In 1889, Ravel also heard Rimsky-Korsakov conduct his *Capriccio espagnol* (1887) at the Trocadéro Palace, and remained a lifelong admirer of his music and, above all, of his orchestration, which had an enduring influence on his own. If Ravel added greater musical depth to his orchestral masterpieces than Rimsky-Korsakov ever achieved, and proved himself an orchestral magician rather than a mere conjurer, then the true lesson of the *Capriccio espagnol* was finally put into practice in *Boléro* in 1928. For, as Rimsky-Korsakov rather immodestly proclaimed in his memoirs: 'The *Capriccio* is a brilliant *composition for the orchestra*. The change of timbres, the felicitous choice of melodic designs and figuration patterns, exactly suiting each kind of instrument . . . the rhythm of the percussion instruments, and so on, constitute here the very *essence* of the composition and not its garb or orchestration.'[8]

Ravel's Basque heritage, Spain and folksongs

Obviously, works like Chabrier's *España* (1883) and *Habanera* (1885) also had an impact on the succession of Spanish evocations that run through Ravel's oeuvre from his own 'Habanera' (1895) onwards, and it did not worry him in the least that he never actually visited Spain until 1911, several years after he had finished his *Rapsodie espagnole* and his opera *L'Heure espagnole*. For he had his beloved mother Marie's Basque heritage to draw on (as well as his close friendship with the pianist Ricardo Viñes), and both of them were born in Ciboure in the Basses Pyrénées. She 'used to lull me to sleep singing guajiras', he told André Révész in 1924,[9] so when their characteristic dance rhythms and irregular metres reappear in the 'Chanson romanesque' (the opening song of *Don Quichotte à Dulcinée*), we can see just how good Ravel's memory was over a period in excess of fifty years. Trying to account for Ravel's 'subtly genuine Spanishness' when Ravel had told him 'that the only link he had with my country was to be born near the border', Manuel de Falla explained the mystery in 1939 by saying that 'Ravel's was a Spain he had felt in an idealized way through his mother.'[10] This was quite different from 'the truth without the authenticity' that Falla had earlier found in Debussy's 'La Soirée dans Grenade', which recreated the atmosphere of Andalusia 'in a similar way to the images reflected by moonlight on the limpid waters of Alhambra's many pools'.[11] And of course both Falla and Ravel knew that Debussy had borrowed the score of Ravel's 'Habanera' in 1898 and used its rhythms, harmonic effects and even its insistent C♯ pedal in 'La Soirée' in 1903. In turn, Falla also explained that when Ravel 'wanted to characterize Spain musically, he showed a predilection for the *habanera*' because it was 'the song most in vogue when his mother lived in Madrid',[12] though in fact Ravel himself did not visit Madrid until 1924.

In addition, it could be said that Marie Ravel helped make her devoted son into a true folklorist and was thus the source of his natural predilections for a truly international musical 'otherness' and a consistently modal melodic approach. For Ravel accumulated an extensive library of folksongs from other nations and made sensitive harmonisations and orchestrations of some of them during his career, preferring them to be performed in their original tongues. He began by orchestrating twelve Corsican folksongs in November 1895 for the unusual, but colourful, combination of string quartet, harmonium, harp, mandoline, celesta and guitar.[13] These songs were performed at the first concert at which Ravel conducted in Paris in March 1896. Between 1904 and 1906, he harmonised eight Greek folksongs from the island of Chios (three of which have been lost),[14] adding an extra one, *Tripatos*, in 1909. He transcribed the first and last of these *Cinq mélodies populaires grecques* for orchestra, while the other three were orchestrated by Manuel Rosenthal. The following year, Ravel harmonised a series of popular songs from Spain, France, Italy, Belgium, Russia and Scotland, plus a 'Chanson hébraïque', for a competition organised by the Maison du Lied in Moscow. The 'Chanson hébraïque' was later orchestrated in 1923–4.[15] Two further Hebrew melodies followed in 1914, the first of which ('Kaddisch') is a liturgical chant, and he wrote his own folk-like texts for the *Trois chansons* for mixed choir shortly after this. We find Ravel asking Jean Marnold for information about the folksongs of the Valois region in July 1916,[16] though nothing came of this project. Neither, sadly, did he set any Basque folksongs, though he struggled in 1913–14 with a piano concerto on Basque themes called *Zaspiak-Bat* (The Seven Are One). According to Domenico de' Paoli, with whom Ravel discussed the project in 1922, this was to be a single movement with seven episodes, each using a popular theme from a different Basque province.[17] The concept of representing Basque unity in music proved too much even for the ingenious Ravel, though he did use an asymmetrical theme from *Zaspiak-Bat* to open his Piano Trio in 1914, which he described as being 'de couleur basque'.[18]

Travels abroad

Although Ravel loved foreign travel, he did not indulge in a great deal of it before his later concert tours, which his disorganisation turned into a nightmare for the artists involved.[19] But to recover from the effects of the scandalous 'affaire Ravel' after his abortive fifth attempt to gain the Prix de Rome in 1905, he embarked on a tour of France, Holland, Germany and Belgium with his friends Alfred and Misia Edwards aboard the yacht 'Aimée'. Typically, as he told Mme de Saint-Marceaux: 'During all of this time, I didn't compose two measures, but I was storing up a host of impressions, and I expect this winter to be extraordinarily productive. I have never been so happy to be alive.'[20]

His letters home also show that Ravel would have made a vivid and accomplished travel writer. Here he is describing his native Ciboure to Ida Godebska in 1911:

> And to think that you could have decided to come here, where the ocean front is lined with acacias! And those gentle green hills, covered from top to bottom with oak wreaths, trimmed in the Basque manner. And above all this, the Pyrenees, with their enchanting mauve color. Moreover, there is the light: it's not like the relentless sun found in other parts of the Midi. Here, it is delicately brilliant. The people feel it; they are agile, elegant, and their joy is not vulgar. Their dances are nimble, with a restrained voluptuousness.[21]

Ravel was equally good with the chocolate-box scenery of Switzerland when he accompanied his father there in 1906,[22] and, despite the hectic concert schedule on his triumphant American tour in early 1928, he still found time to describe Los Angeles (and the train trip to reach it) to his brother Edouard, as follows:

> A brilliant sun; a large city in full bloom, with flowers which grow in
> greenhouses in France, and tall palm trees which grow here naturally . . .
> The trip from San Francisco to Los Angeles was very pleasant, and I spent it
> almost entirely on the rear platform: eucalyptus forests, tall trees which
> might be taken for oaks, but which are in fact hollies; variegated
> mountains, which are rocky or magnificently green. It's annoying to think
> that I'll soon be back in the cold weather.[23]

As far as the exotic Orient was concerned, Ravel was fascinated by it but
never managed to get there. In 1905, almost certainly in recompense for
his official treatment during the 'affaire Ravel', he was offered the
possibility of a diplomatic mission by the Minister of Fine Arts, which had
been the 'brilliant idea' of his attaché, a M. Gaveau. This post was to be
mostly based in Paris, but with the possibility of foreign travel, and when
Ravel met the Minister he 'couldn't resist telling him of my desire to go to
the Orient, which he took note of. Naturally, on the way home, I began to
regret having spoken so thoughtlessly.'[24] Nothing came of the mission, but
the potential that it might happen caused the worried Ravel to have exotic
dreams. As he told Ida Godebska in the same letter, he had

> visited Madame Benedictus, whose brother was recently appointed a
> counselor to the court of appeals of . . . Pondicherry!! That set off ecstatic
> epistolatory impressions: an exotic atmosphere, motley crowds, palaces,
> elephants, monkeys, gazelles, Ceylon, Jakarta, darn it! The effect was soon
> felt: this morning I emerged from the train station in Constantinople, on
> to a terrace overlooking the Bosphorus, and as I was leaning over to gaze
> upon a marvelous site, I was awakened. I uttered some inhuman grunts,
> and wanted to go back to sleep, but that proved impossible.

The aesthetic problem facing French composers of exotic music had, of
course, been neatly summarised by Ravel's fellow 'Apache' Tristan Klingsor
– the pseudonym of Léon Leclère (1874–1966). 'Le Voyage', one of
Klingsor's *Shéhérazade* poems that Ravel did not set in 1903, concludes
with the lines:

> For the dream is more beautiful than the reality,
> For the most beautiful countries are those one does not know,
> And the most beautiful voyage is that made in dream.[25]

Charles Koechlin, for instance, was actually more troubled by this concept
than his friend Ravel ever was, and often referred to this passage in his
writings. But, in retrospect, it is impossible to say that works of greater
quality were produced by those who visited their exotic sources of
inspiration with this in mind (like Chabrier, Delage, Koechlin, Roussel and
Saint-Saëns) than by those who preferred to rely mainly on their imaginative powers (like Bizet, Debussy and Ravel). All one can really do is to agree

with Danièle Pistone's conclusion that: 'In its descriptive form, exoticism will only prove to have been a chapter in our culture, but, in its flights of the imagination it retains an eternal appeal.'[26] Thus when Ravel did finally visit Morocco in 1935, and Boris Masslow, the Director of Fine Arts, proudly showed him round the Embassy in Fez and its sumptuous gardens, the conversation ran as follows: '"What a setting, *cher maître*, to inspire you to write an Arabian work." To which Ravel briskly replied: "If I wrote something Arabian, it would be much more Arabian than all this!"'[27] However, despite the fact that Ravel preferred to remain near Paris, close to his friends, and invariably took his holidays in France when the choice was left to him, he did retain an inner desire to satisfy his exotic curiosity at first hand. As late as 1931 he told an interviewer that 'I yearn to see the country of the gamelan ... Like Debussy and other contemporaries, I have always been particularly fascinated by musical orientalism.'[28] In the end, though, the farthest he travelled was to Iceland (in 1905) and the USA, and the use of jazz in his Sonata for Violin and Piano predates his American tour.

Exotic theatrical projects

Ravel's oriental fascinations also feature prominently in his list of incomplete theatrical projects, and he began and ended his career planning operas based on stories from *The Thousand and One Nights* of Arabian legend. In 1898, his first known orchestral work was an *ouverture de féerie* to a projected opera *Shéhérazade*, which shows how much he was then influenced by Debussy and the Russian Nationalist school (see also Russ, 'Shéhérazade': Chapter 6). As Roger Nichols observes: 'The cut of the main B minor theme recalls the Borodin of the Second Symphony and the brass fanfares, answering each other tritonally from C major to F♯ major, those of *Boris Godunov*. From Debussy came probably the opening phrase, with its sharpened fourth and flattened seventh, as well as the frequent whole-tone scales.'[29] This phrase, as Ravel explained in his programme note to the first performance in May 1899, was 'the theme of *Shéhérazade*, played by an oboe',[30] and it was perhaps his own, rather less magical equivalent of the languorous flute opening to Debussy's *Prélude à l'après-midi d'un faune*, which he adored for its miraculous spontaneity. Certainly, the 'classical plan' he adopted was unsuited for a work which tried too hard to be sectionally fluid and technically impressive simultaneously, and he later condemned it as 'badly constructed and crammed with whole-tone scales. There were so many of them in it, in fact, that I had enough of them for life.'[31]

In fact, odd whole-tone passages do occur in his later works – for example, in the leads into the main themes in the first movement of the String Quartet (before Figs. 1 and 10) – but, by and large, this was one of the ways in which Ravel sought to differentiate his music from that of Debussy, preferring the acidulous sounds created by diminished octaves, secondary ninths, raised dominant elevenths and, in the 1920s, bitonality. In 1923, when Edouard Mignan sent him a copy of the *Rapsodie* for harp that he had based on the opening theme of the minuet from his *Sonatine*, Ravel commented on the 'paradoxical . . . way your numerous whole-tone scales accompany the theme, written by the one contemporary composer who has never used the whole-tone scale'.[32] Despite this inaccuracy, it shows that Ravel still remained determined to avoid the primary means of invoking an instant exotic atmosphere adopted by so many of his lesser contemporaries.

After his unfortunate taxi accident in October 1932, Ravel returned to *The Thousand and One Nights* for a *pantomime arabe* for Ida Rubinstein called *Morgiane*, based on the tale of Ali Baba and the Forty Thieves. Despite his acute difficulties in putting his ideas down on paper, the exotic scenery he saw on his 1935 trip to Morocco inspired him to sketch some ten pages of melody and figured bass for his project. This, however, was the way Ravel usually began his works, as far as is known, for he invariably destroyed all evidence of their secret gestation, only permitting them to appear, as if by an oriental miracle, in their perfected forms. The sketches for *Morgiane* were also the last notes he composed.

In between these two projects came plans in 1914 to write a ballet for the Alhambra Theatre in London to a scenario by the renowned artist and lithographer Georges de Feure (the pseudonym of Georges van Sluijters (1868–1928)), who had written *Le Palais du silence* for Debussy the previous year.[33] Ravel's letter to de Feure of 19 June 1914 asks for a similarly lucrative contract and states that: 'The areas which I believe would most conveniently suit this project would be an exotic subject, or a French or Italian festival set in the eighteenth century.'[34] The idea of commissioning a ballet from Ravel probably dated from 2 March 1914 when someone from the Alhambra Theatre saw the performance of the ballet score that Ravel had arranged for Nijinsky and his troupe from Schumann's *Carnaval* at the nearby Palace Theatre.

De Feure then duly sent Ravel what he thought were his two most suitable existing scenarios, for copies of these were found in his library when it was transferred from Montfort-l'Amaury to the Bibliothèque Nationale de France in the early 1970s.[35] The first was *Le Masque terrible*, based on Poe's fantastic and gripping tale *The Mask of the Red Death*, which bore the stamp of the Alhambra Theatre and the words 'received 17

March 1914'. The other was the more exotic *Les Jardins d'Antinoüs,* signed and dated by de Feure: 'Londres, l^er juin 1914'.[36] This was set in an enchanted garden on the banks of the Nile and ended with the tyrant Antinoüs' suicide in the same river. Quite why Ravel rejected these librettos is unclear, for the exotic setting and sensuality of *Les Jardins d'Antinoüs* might well have appealed to him, and Poe was indisputably amongst his favourite authors. We can only conclude that finishing his Piano Trio (and other work) assumed greater priority for Ravel in 1914 and that after the traumatic intervention of the War he never returned to de Feure's ballet projects.

Also found in Ravel's library was a libretto by Marcel Aubry for a fantastical opera in five acts entitled *L'Or* – 'a sort of musical comedy recounting the adventures of a gold-prospector across America and Japan, and ending in Paris with a very conventional moral: money does not bring happiness'.[37] Again there were exotic aspects, and perhaps Puccini's success with *The Girl of the Golden West* in 1910 might even have encouraged Ravel to consider this libretto seriously. He is also known to have been interested in writing incidental music for James Elroy Flecker's oriental drama *Hassan* in May 1920, though in the end it was performed in London in 1923 with music by Delius. Lastly, at the same time as *Morgiane,* Ravel also wanted to return to the author of *L'Heure espagnole,* Franc-Nohain (the pseudonym of Maurice-Etienne Legrand (1873–1934)), this time to '*Le Chapeau chinois* . . . with an operetta-like orchestra'.[38] If Ravel, like Debussy, thus left a trail of unfinished theatre projects across his career, it can be seen that even more of them were concerned with exoticism and that most of them reflected Ravel's lifelong interest in things oriental.

Exoticism at home

To keep exoticism in his mind and to compensate for not seeing the Orient at first hand, Ravel carefully arranged a Chinese salon at Montfort-l'Amaury when he moved to 'Le Belvédère' in 1921. An unnamed interviewer who came to visit Ravel at home in 1931, observed: 'We feel as if we are in a Chinese curio shop, in which a century of playful exoticism has been exposed.'[39] Undoubtedly the whole house was a deliberate mishmash. 'The style is half Pompeian, half Empire', the same interviewer continued, and the oriental aspects in the house were equally mixed. There was 'a Japanese vestibule', Ravel's beloved Siamese cats, and visitors

> had to admire his Japanese lawn made up of thousands of little blue
> flowers, his dwarf trees . . . and all the strange plants which had gone
> towards 'japanizing' his garden. Ravel chose them meticulously, like his

harmonies. His love of things Japanese corresponded to his taste for what was precious and perfect. There was even a tiny room in the house full of assorted Japanese objects; and he was delighted by his friends' astonishment when he proudly announced: 'All this . . . is fake!'[40]

We have already come across the concept that Ravel could create exotic music that could surpass the genuine article in its calculated effect on a European audience, and his delight in collecting artificial artefacts was an essential part of his creative process. Indeed, Ravel once told the writer M.-D. Calvocoressi that he was '"artificial" by nature':[41] the *trompe-l'oreille* was as important to him as the *trompe-l'œil*, as both were achieved through refined taste and technical perfection.

Exoticism by other composers

It is thus perfectly understandable that Ravel should have been critical of the lack of perfection in others. When it came to exoticism he looked to two areas in particular: the orchestration, and the substitution of descriptive clichés for imaginative recreation. Reviewing the *Tableaux symphoniques* ('Première partie: Thèbes') of Ernest Fanelli (1860–1917) in 1912, Ravel criticised 'the overly dense atmosphere at the beginning of the first part ['Devant le Palais de Tahoser'], the strident whining of the lammergeiers [vultures], and the slave's lament in the distance, despite its somewhat conventional orientalism'.[42] Even if the work was notated bitonally in 1883 (see Example 2.1) and many saw its extraordinary harmonic combinations as forerunners of Debussy's 'impressionism', Ravel remained unimpressed by Fanelli's novelties. Ravel noted that Liszt and Dargomïzhsky had got there first with the whole-tone scale anyway, and if others found the roots of Debussy's achievements variously in Satie, Musorgsky and Rimsky-Korsakov, then Debussy still remained 'the most important and profoundly musical composer living today'. As for Fanelli's exoticism *per se*, Ravel's point was that the textures were overloaded and that its effects all went on for too long. The 'whining' vultures ('gypaètes') similarly wheeled overhead during most of the opening scene (represented by swelling and diminishing repeated ninth chords or the tremolandos in Example 2.1). And long bass pedal-points and the slave's chromatic arabesque (the top line in Example 2.1) could both be found in David's *Le Désert*, which was clearer and less static. In fact, Ravel considered that Fanelli's main contribution was the effect he achieved 'by the most picturesque orchestration alone, which would have amazed the audience, had the Colonne Orchestra performed this symphonic poem [strictly] in time.'

Example 2.1 Fanelli, *Tableaux symphoniques*, 'Première partie: Thèbes' (bars 44–7)

'Dans l'intérieur du palais'

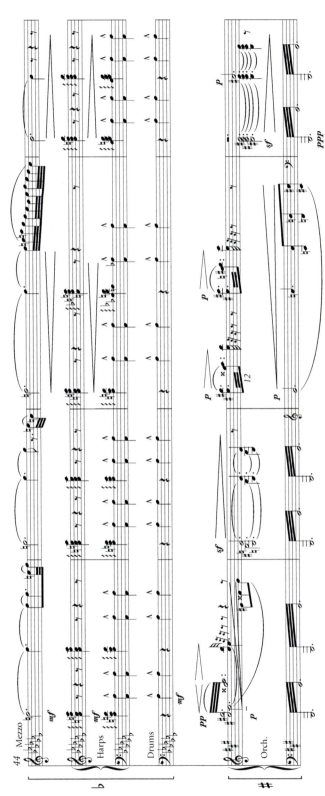

When it came to Camille Erlanger's opera *La Sorcière*, Ravel hated the over-declamatory vocal writing, which he blamed on Wagner's influence, and found the scenery ingeniously picturesque but lacking in style. Odd effects came in for praise, like 'the voice mingling harmoniously with the ringing of bells' early in Act II, but overall the music fell short of the imaginative opportunities provided by Sardou's melodramatic text, and 'the Spanish and oriental atmosphere' could have been 'taken advantage of with greater abandon'.[43]

Earlier, at a Société Nationale concert in 1909, Désiré-Emile Inghelbrecht's symphonic poem *Pour le jour des premières neiges au vieux Japon* had received its first performance, along with new works by Marcel Orban, Pierre Bretagne, Pierre Coindreau, Henri Mulet, Florent Schmitt, Blanche Lucas and Paul Le Flem. Ravel's friend Cipa Godebski had had to miss the concert, but Ravel told him the next day that his mumps had proved a blessing in disguise. 'Oh! those rotten musicians!', he complained:

> They can't even orchestrate, so they fill in the gaps with 'Turkish music'. Craftsmanship is replaced by fugal diversions, and themes from *Pelléas* make up for the lack of inspiration. And all of this makes a noise! from the gong, tambourine, military drum, glockenspiel and cymbals, used at random. Inghelbrecht holds the record, with an additional xylophone and Chinese bells. Well now! in Japan . . . it could just as well have taken place in Lithuania.[44]

When it came to exotic works that he did admire, Ravel looked for inner life, with real inspiration and musicality rather than descriptive surface garb. Falla's opera *La Vida breve* may well have made frequent use of 'certain melodic turns which are characteristic of Andalusian song', but 'it would be wrong to conclude that . . . local color alone accounts for the importance of this work . . . one discovers a sincerity of expression, as well as an abundance and freshness of inspiration which are thoroughly delightful'.[45] Similarly, he found Alfred Bruneau's symphonic poem *Penthésilée* (Queen of the Amazons), completed shortly after Fanelli's *Tableaux*, full of 'character, vigor, and . . . music',[46] and when it came to Stravinsky's *Le Rossignol* at the Ballets Russes, Ravel was lost in admiration. Of course, the mechanical nightingale had a lot to do with it, for Ravel had a similar one which he loved to demonstrate to friends.[47] But the second scene sent him into the same sort of orchestral ecstasies that Debussy had found in 'le Tour de Passe-Passe' sequence in the first tableau of *Petrushka* two years earlier.[48] In 1914, Ravel wrote:

> It would be difficult to convey through words or imagery, the roaring tumult, disturbing, but always musical, at the beginning of this scene, the orchestral enchantment of this strange and powerful march whose Far-

Eastern quality engenders a more profound feeling, truly, than that of simple curiosity, and the uncommon charm of the mysterious timbres which depict the mechanical nightingale.[49]

This for Ravel was the true Orient encapsulated in a musical masterpiece and, of course, it was only made possible by the continuing presence in Paris of Dyagilev's Ballets Russes after their brilliant opening season in 1909. More than any other single factor, it was Dyagilev's perspicacious commissions from the foremost composers of the time that kept exoticism alive in Paris; that is, if we take exoticism to imply cultural 'otherness'. Ravel was among the first to be approached for a new ballet in 1909, though it was not until June 1912 that *Daphnis et Chloé* reached the stage at the Théâtre du Châtelet (being twice postponed while Ravel struggled to perfect the final 'Danse générale').

Distancing, translations and the *Chansons madécasses*

Daphnis et Chloé paradoxically brings to the fore the concept of distancing in Ravel's oeuvre. Just as his exotic and fairy-tale works were all created from sources he had accumulated in Paris, so Ravel distanced himself still further from his creations by choosing literary sources from the past as their bases. This arose both from his love of French tradition (the *culte du passé*) and pastiche composition, and in many ways the resulting eclecticism of works like *Le Tombeau de Couperin* and *La Valse* became inextricably bound up in his engagement with cultural 'otherness'. As Roger Nichols says: 'He insisted on the importance of a composer's personal consciousness being rooted in a national consciousness and on the imitation of models as a sure way of giving that personal consciousness a well-regulated expression.'[50] An additional factor was that French was the only language in which he was fluent. Thus, when he came to writing *Daphnis,* he turned to Amyot's eighteenth-century translation of Longus' Greek original to create his 'vast musical fresco';[51] when he composed *Ma Mère l'Oye,* he turned to the seventeenth- and eighteenth-century children's stories of Charles Perrault, the Comtesse d'Aulnoy and Marie Leprince de Beaumont, even though the musical model for 'Les Entretiens de la Belle et de la Bête' came from Satie's *Gymnopédies* of 1888. And when *The Thousand and One Nights* were involved his starting point was the French translation by Antoine Galland, dating from 1704–17.

Even in the *Chansons madécasses,* Ravel's most deeply personal statement in a thoroughly modern idiom, his source was a collection of exotic Madagascan poems, first published in 1787 by Evariste-Désiré de Parny. These allowed him to introduce 'a new element, dramatic – indeed erotic, resulting from the subject matter of Parny's poems'.[52] Eroticism and exoticism naturally go hand in hand, but while both terms might well be applied to a voluptuous early song like 'Asie', it seems that the restraint and linear approach imposed by the combination of voice, flute, cello and piano forced Ravel both to crystallise his thoughts and to expand his erotic imaginative resources when he set the *Chansons madécasses* in 1925–6.

In the opening song, the falling solo cello line accompanying the waiting lover first evokes his yearning anticipation of his mistress Nahandove's arrival, the phrases becoming arch-shaped, like the curves of her body, as the point of contact draws nearer ('Voici l'heure'). At the same time, the repeated use of the same pitch range reflects the constancy of their love, and the arch shapes expand on the vocal expressions of her name with supreme economy of means. An increase in speed and rhythmic activity and the piano entry lead to the climax of Nahandove's arrival, but at the point of physical contact ('repose-toi sur mes genoux'), the slowing tempo and repetitive accompaniment subtly suggest the familiarity of their clandestine meetings as well as their gently undulating bodily delight. The lover almost murmurs his sexually explicit words of adoration, without any resource to conventional Romantic arpeggios or vocal climaxes.

In the central song, 'Aoua!' (Example 2.2), Ravel is far less restrained and for once bares his soul in a volcanic display of violent passion that has no parallel in his other music. The dissonance and piano textures would not have been possible without the *Trois poèmes de Stéphane Mallarmé*, which in turn were influenced by Schoenberg's *Pierrot lunaire*. In 1913, however, the dynamic level never exceeded *mezzo-forte*, whereas here the terrors of the real world hit the listener *fortissimo* at the start in a sinister atmosphere of total chromaticism. The poem may date from the eighteenth century, but, as Roger Nichols says: 'The story of the white men's treachery and defeat appealed to Ravel's liberal instincts and he forgot his policy of *dépouillement* in striving to give them expression.'[53] For once the fairy-tale distancing is forgotten, and without any apparent regret. (For further discussion, see Kaminsky, 'Musical narrative in the *Chansons madécasses*': Chapter 8.)

Gypsy music and jazz

The same could perhaps be said of Ravel's recourse to the real worlds of gypsy music and jazz in his quest for cultural 'otherness'. *Tzigane*, which Ravel simply called 'a virtuoso piece in the style of a Hungarian rhapsody',[54] was written just before 'Aoua!' in 1924, but is as different from it as chalk from cheese. Several reviewers commented on the artificiality and

Example 2.2 Ravel, *Chansons madécasses*, 'Aoua!' (bars 1–5)

cold-bloodedness of this undeniably brilliant piece of pastiche whose technical effects outshine those of its models; it has never been among Ravel's most successful works and its last-minute completion for Jelly d'Aranyi taught him a lesson he did not forget. 'Art' for Ravel may have been 'a beautiful lie',[55] but lies need more careful telling and preparation than the truth if they are to be convincing.

Example 2.3 Ravel, Sonata for Violin and Piano, 'Blues' (bars 11–18)

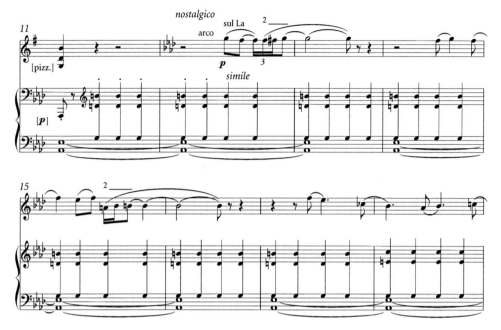

In the case of American jazz, which came to Paris through imported records during the Great War, it was the blues that most appealed to Ravel. In the slow movement of his Sonata for Violin and Piano of 1923–7, he sought to create 'stylized jazz, more French than American in character perhaps, but nevertheless influenced by your so-called "popular music". Personally I find jazz most interesting: the rhythms, the way the melodies are handled, the melodies themselves. I have heard some of George Gershwin's works and I find them intriguing.'[56]

Certainly, there are no signs of the conventional chord progressions associated with the twelve-bar negro blues, and Ravel's first melodic paragraph (bars 11–27) occupies the sixteen bars more usually found in the popular songs of Gershwin or Jerome Kern, finishing with a circle of fifths pattern typically spiced up with sevenths, ninths and judiciously spaced bitonality. Indeed, bar 11 onwards (Example 2.3) employs, like the introduction, Ravel's favoured semitonal key combination of A♭ and G major; the syncopation is mild (again in the character of Gershwin's sanitisations of authentic rough jazz), and the most recognisable features to a jazz musician would be the stylised imitation of the banjo in the accompaniment and the way that Ravel seeks to 'bend' the notes of the violin line (*à la* Joe Venuti?), with the emphasis on the flattened third and seventh degrees of the scale. The way that this 'bending' is transferred to the accompaniment in bar 26 belongs more to the big band effects of Paul Whiteman and his

Orchestra. And being as eclectic as he was, the gentle linear modality of the first movement of the Sonata is the closest that Ravel came to the world of his friend Charles Koechlin, with the finale cast as a combination of a fantastic waltz with a violin *perpetuum mobile*.

The influence of stylised jazz can also be felt in the outer movements of Ravel's Concerto in G, even if the strange syncopations, delayed harmonies and fantastic decorations of the slow movement cause it to feel the most exotic of the three (and its opening theme was somehow modelled on the 'Larghetto' of Mozart's Clarinet Quintet).[57] But the most successful eclectic amalgam of jazz with different types of 'otherness' can be found in his fairy-tale opera *L'Enfant et les sortilèges*, for once composed to a contemporary libretto by Colette. 'What would you think of the cup and teapot, in old Wedgwood – black – singing a ragtime?', he asked her in its initial stages.[58] Elsewhere in the final version, slowly and meticulously perfected by 1925, we find a grotesque minuet for two armchairs (Fig. 17), a foxtrot for the Chinese Cup (Fig. 28), a folksong for shepherds and shepherdesses (Fig. 51) and the Cats' duet (Fig. 97), and this is just within the first half of the work. Had the libretto called for something Spanish, Ravel's happiness would perhaps have been complete.

Exoticism versus exotic music, and exoticism on the stage

It will have become apparent by now that exoticism has a wide range of interlocking associations and that it found its ideal exponent in the calculated art of Maurice Ravel. Deriving from the Greek word *exō*, meaning outside, exoticism can include anything 'introduced from a foreign country' as well as incorporating the 'outlandish', the 'romantically strange, or rich and showy, or glamorous' and the erotic.[59] And Ravel, it should be observed, indulged in exoticism far more often than he wrote specifically exotic music. As Thomas Cooper observes:

> Many questions concerning the purpose of exotic music, like that of the French Empire itself, have remained largely unanswered ... However, musical exoticism goes further than merely expressing superiority over the native. It can be seen, along with many other manifestations of Western representations, as a demonstration of power over the subject ... The exercise of this power is not simply political in its effects, however. In granting the Western observer the ability to move at will through the exotic domain, observing the scene without the limitations of culture or custom that restrict the natives, the exotic genre is conferring pleasure to a high degree ... The combined threat and allure of the 'other' is one of the qualities which gives it its power over the Western imagination.[60]

Ravel was therefore wise to avoid direct contact with the Orient and the descriptive clichés that came to involve so much exotic music in the nineteenth century. It was only very occasionally that he permitted himself to become personally involved with the white man's burden, as we saw with 'Aoua!', where for once he allowed a certain amount of the 'sincerity' that he otherwise declined to reveal. Instead, Ravel composed from within his own Western imagination with a Western audience in mind, maximising the allure of his compositions through his modal melodies, piquant harmonies and evocative orchestration, only occasionally emphasising the threats and dangers of the unknown that lay beneath its sensuous surface. And whatever the 'otherness' in question, he could truthfully state at the end of his career that 'My music is unequivocally French':[61] French in its techniques and French in the earlier literary translations that he used as he distanced himself in time and space from his customised exotic end-products. Indeed, Ravel could find all the inspiration he needed from his personal effects in Montfort-l'Amaury or from the multifarious cabaret acts he could see in Montmartre.[62] His career was perfectly placed to develop the explorations in musical exoticism associated with the expansion of the French Empire in the nineteenth century to their logical zenith in a Paris that became the cosmopolitan focus for fashionable artistic '-isms' in the twentieth. Ravel was also particularly fortunate that Dyagilev's Ballets Russes chose Paris as their main home and stimulated a desire for the exotic during most of his career. Other companies sprang up in imitation; the Paris Opéra put on more ballets, and Ravel accordingly arranged these from existing piano works (for example, 'Alborada del gracioso' from *Miroirs*, arranged in 1918) and also created new ones to satisfy public demand.

In so doing, he showed a special interest in their stage effects. Before *Ma Mère l'Oye* was produced as a ballet at the Théâtre des Arts in 1912, Ravel was solving problems involving the little Negroes and the three drop curtains,[63] and we find him backstage at the premiere on 29 January 'to animate the fervor of my birds, pagoda slaves, and little Negroes'.[64] This interest applied to his operas too. In *L'Heure espagnole*, 'I added some grotesque automatons: some dancers, musical marionettes, a soldier, a cockerel, [and] an exotic bird',[65] and we have already seen him contributing to the scenario of *L'Enfant et les sortilèges*, in which 'The fantasy of the poem would have served no purpose had it not been sustained, indeed accentuated by the fantasy of the music.'[66] Here, Ravel's enduring fascination with the world of children and the sense of almost naive wonder that he was able to retain were vital ingredients behind the success of his opera, which called for 'melody, nothing but melody'.

The horizontal versus the vertical

This brings into question the extent to which Ravel's exoticism was created more through horizontal than through vertical means. Like Debussy, Ravel often referred to the primacy of melody in his art and he worked more in terms of extended melody than his rival 'impressionist'. Yet this summary (and invariably erroneous) epithet was commonly applied to innovations that were harmonic rather than melodic, and in which orchestral texture played an inseparable role. And if we take Roland-Manuel's points that the same type of gapped dorian mode melody (without the second degree) that appears in early works like the *Menuet antique* and 'D'Anne jouant de l'espinette' also recurs in the first movements of the Sonata for Violin and Cello and the Concerto in G (in various transpositions), or that the pentatonic scale can just as easily occur in an ostensibly non-exotic work like the Concerto for the Left Hand (Fig. 25) as it can in 'Laideronnette, Impératrice des Pagodes',[67] then we can see that the vertical aspect is arguably the more important, and that context is everything. Many of the Spanish works which cross Ravel's entire career show a preference for the phrygian mode of Andalusian flamenco music, yet context makes the central dances of the *Rapsodie espagnole*, for example, very different from the final song of *Don Quichotte à Dulcinée*.

Indeed, Ravel, like Debussy, wrote very little absolute music, and even a work like the Sonata for Violin and Cello has modal elements which might be deemed exotic, as we have seen. In the case of *La Valse*, the 'apotheosis of the Viennese waltz' *à la* Johann Strauss, Ravel's desired 'impression of a fantastic, fatal whirling'[68] and the effects of hallucination are clearly linked with the dervishes of oriental fame. Similarly, the ostensibly absolute appearance of the Piano Trio did not stop Ravel evoking a 'Basque colour' at the start, or creating his ingenious musical equivalent to the Malayan palindromic verse form of the *pantun* in its Scherzo. Even boredom and monotony have associations with the Orient, and not only because its authentic music appears so to Western ears. Ravel experiments with these concepts in very different ways in 'Le Gibet' from *Gaspard de la nuit* and *Boléro*. The former piece, of course, provides other links with the Orient in its persistent bell effects and sinister atmosphere, even if its source was the nineteenth-century prose poems of the Frenchman, Aloysius Bertrand, to which Ravel had been introduced by his main Spanish catalyst, Ricardo Viñes!

So it is extremely difficult to come to any irrefutable conclusions about Ravel's evocations of exoticism except to say that his talent was one of metamorphosis and that he was more concerned with imaginative interior fabrication than the realistic portrayal of external events. Just as he could make Musorgsky's *Pictures at an Exhibition* sound more exotic through his orchestration, or write 'an orchestral transcription for the piano' in his virtuosic evocation of the mercurial dwarf 'Scarbo',[69] so he treated exotic effects as musical objects to be transformed at will in his 'original' compositions, whether or not their titles suggested exoticism. If various threads run across his career – like the dance, the *culte du passé,* Spanish evocations and deliberate artificiality – then exoticism embraces them all and in one form or another pervades his entire output. And it is a tribute to Ravel's eclectic genius that he somehow managed to gather the various strands of musical 'otherness' together within a clear and appealing style that was both French and unmistakably his own.

3 Musical objects and machines

DEBORAH MAWER

Ravel was a decorative artist of the highest order, defining and elaborating musical objects and images which exert a continuing fascination. HOPKINS[1]

But over all would be the triumph of the machine, the vast monster that man has created to do his bidding. What a noble inspiration! RAVEL[2]

An important part of Ravel's compositional aesthetic is bound up with objectification, crystallisation and detachment, ideas that connect with Symbolist notions of imagery, Cubist notions of spatial and temporal planes and, beyond World War I, with the basic tenets of neoclassicism. Musical machines or mechanisms represent a particular embodiment of this aesthetic, and so this chapter probes Stravinsky's commonly invoked image of 'the most perfect of Swiss clockmakers'.[3] Although ideas of musical objects and machines are closely related (even interlocked), for the sake of clarity, and in keeping with the artificial subject-matter, they are here explored successively rather than simultaneously.

Ravel's objectivity and 'l'objet juste'

Beyond the elusive essentials of inspiration and imagination, composition for Ravel involved a life-long striving for the highest technical achievement: 'conscience compels us to turn ourselves into good craftsmen. My objective, therefore, is technical perfection.' Ravel then goes a step further: 'The truth is one can never have enough control. Moreover, since we cannot express ourselves without exploiting and thus transforming our emotions, isn't it better at least to be fully aware and acknowledge that art is the supreme imposture?'[4] As a subsidiary non-musical pursuit, Ravel also had a passion for collecting meticulously honed objects at his small house in Montfort-l'Amaury: glass ornaments, figurines, clocks and mechanical toys.

Various early writers have discussed Ravel's fondness for objectivity and artificiality. As early as 1907, Louis Laloy disputed the naturalness of *Histoires naturelles* and later celebrated Ravel's conjuring with artifices: 'his mind is a sorcerer which, even when emotional, still beguiles with a prestigious skill'.[5] In 1913, Calvocoressi reported that many writers, including Debussy, objected strongly to a 'dryness' and 'artificiality' in

Ravel's music.[6] It was, however, Roland-Manuel's article in the dedicated issue of *La Revue musicale* (April 1925) that first foregrounded Ravel's 'aesthetic of imposture', while the main credit for developing this idea beyond the composer's death should go to Vladimir Jankélévitch, who discussed Ravel's love of problem-setting and -solving by quoting Nietzsche's adage 'to dance in chains'.[7] Around the same time, Laloy claimed that 'Nobody has pushed as far the art of substitutions, alterations and unforeseen convergences, to the extreme limit where the chord at the point of rupturing still remains in balance, and always submits to the rational principle of tonality: everything surprises and everything is explicable.'[8] It is of course only a small step from the possible to the impossible, and so to fantasy. Jankélévitch styled Ravel's home 'the pavilion of imposture' – a neat counterpart to Le Corbusier's 'pavilion of the new spirit' – and saw Ravel as concerned with forging objects, 'especially those objects which feign life. A master in objects . . .'[9]

In formulating a definition of Ravel's 'l'objet juste', we must accept that in music, as distinct, say, from sculpture, we are already adopting a metaphor (or perhaps extending the Symbolist concept of *correspondances*) – at least, apart from the score, we are not dealing with physical objects. Even so, something is still being made that exists in space and time; and, beyond an implicit interpretation of the main musical dimensions as horizontal and vertical (sequence and simultaneity?), Bill Hopkins regards the large-scale unfolding of time as equivalent to depth.[10] Obviously, other interpretations are feasible: Edgard Varèse considered the third dimension to be dynamic fluctuation and somewhat after Proust, who saw time as a fourth dimension, he perceived his fourth as 'that of sound being projected like a beam of light with no hope of being reflected back'.[11] In essence, a musical object – an artefact or device – is a fixed, passive entity, as distinct from a motive which engenders organic growth and development. An object might be an unchanging component of a larger motive or phrase. Objects extend from single pitches (C$\sharp$, as Ravel's 'germ' in 'Habanera' from *Sites auriculaires*; B$\flat$, repeated 235 times in 'Le Gibet' from *Gaspard de la nuit*), through distinctive intervals (the tritone in *La Valse*, or third in *Boléro*), a 'cell', or chordal construct (as in 'Soupir' from *Trois poèmes de Stéphane Mallarmé*), to more complex large-scale ostinatos ('La Vallée des cloches' from *Miroirs*, *Frontispice* and *Boléro*). An important criterion is that the object should be presented in relief from its surroundings, positioned with some detachment or abstraction, so that we clearly perceive its identity. Igor Stravinsky famously remarked that 'when I compose an interval I am aware of it as an object', and for Ravel the signature interval, objectified across his repertory, is the perfect fourth, often used in descent or with the two pitches in parallel.[12]

Example 3.1 *Daphnis et Chloé*: solo horn theme (Fig. 2⁻³)

A basic premise of Hopkins is then that a musical object is essentially 'synoptic' – in his use of the term as 'perceivable from a single standpoint' – and that its main means of extension, or movement, is created through time by simple sustaining, or repetition. It might, though, still be possible for the temporal dimension to simulate rotation of an object (through inversion, reversion, or exact sequence), as though Ravel and ourselves, as the dual subjects – creator and receiver – are able to view the object from more than one perspective. Think about the love-theme on the horn in *Daphnis et Chloé* (Example 3.1: Fig. 2⁻³) whose prominent fifth interval is presented firstly in descent: G–C (*y*) and then, repositioned a fifth higher, in inverted ascent: G–D (*y′*), followed by a further decorated descent. Seemingly, we have two views of an object; furthermore, an object with possible symbolic meaning, where one presentation may be associated with Chloé and the other with Daphnis.[13] So there is a sense here of the object as a sign that embodies both the signifier and the signified, accepting that its 'meaning' is never fixed or universal. Clearly, whatever the status of these limited operations of rotation, an ill-defined meeting-point must exist between an object that receives simple, external manipulation and a motive with its own internal dynamic. We might argue that this is just a matter of semantics, but fundamentally it is a question of the degree of fixedness of the musical material.

Musical objects associated with Symbolism and Cubism

Despite Ravel's claim to follow an opposite path from Debussy's pursuit of symbolism,[14] it is still worth charting his exploration of musical objects with associated, possibly symbolic, meaning. Headed by Chopin's pronouncement that 'Nothing is more hateful than music without hidden meaning', an article by Ravel suggests that the requirement for the musician is 'To thrill to the linking of two chords, just as one would to the linking of two colours. In all the arts, the subject is of primary importance, for everything flows from it.'[15] Where musico-literary comparison is concerned, things are less straightforward. Jacques Attali, for instance, is adamant that 'Quite unlike the words of a language – which refer to a signified – music, though it has a precise operationality, never has a stable reference to a code of the linguistic type.'[16] Certainly, any associations that arise are culturally and temporally defined and result in multiple interpretations depending on the experience of composer, performer and listener. Then again, our context is founded on the artistic principles of Symbolism and Cubism, and our interest is primarily in the composer's associations. Artists of 'la Belle Epoque' (1885–1914), and the years immediately preceding, were fascinated by new ways of viewing space and time, focused on simultaneity. Symbolist poetry, especially, thrived on multiple images and suggestions, consequent ambiguities and a fascination as much with the sound-patterns of words as with their meaning. The wealth of literary names beyond Baudelaire included Mallarmé, Verlaine, Proust, Valéry, Cendrars and Apollinaire; painters numbered Sonia Delaunay, Picasso, Braque and Metzinger. Undoubtedly though, the single most important influence upon Ravel was the mid-nineteenth-century American writer Edgar Allan Poe; Ravel was spellbound by *The Raven* and empathised with Poe's description of its evolutionary process as presented in *The Philosophy of Composition* in objectified and mathematical terms.[17]

Miroirs held a special constructive significance for Ravel, as noted in 'An autobiographical sketch'; its very title suggests Symbolist *correspondances* and ambiguities between the aural and the visual, between supposed reality and reflected simulation, between external and internal. Ravel identified especially with a quotation from Shakespeare's *Julius Caesar*: 'the eye sees not itself / But by reflection, by some other things'.[18] 'La Vallée des cloches', in particular, features small musical objects repeating at varying rates which evoke bells (the final one, at bar 50, referred to by Ravel as 'la Savoyarde'),[19] while the larger structure projects the geometric planes that were to become so beloved of Cubism: a means of grappling with fractured time and space so as to create an illusory solid object (see Example 3.2). Implicit here, and developed later, is that the idea of an object may be extended from small-scale examples to encompass a complete piece, or work. This larger-scale concern is signalled by the additional stave (as a precursor of *Frontispice*) that facilitates the simultaneous layering of horizontal planes, extended in time by varied ostinato configurations. Parallel fourths and octaves suggest the overtones of the harmonic series, as bell-like reverberations; the bells mark and fragment time, and also carry their own ecclesiastical associations. The fourth interval especially constitutes an object with an additional resonance in evoking the distant past – of organum, perhaps. Bells appear widely in early Ravel: for example, the *Ballade de la Reine morte d'aimer*, 'Entre cloches' from the synaesthetically suggestive *Sites auriculaires* and 'Le Gibet' from *Gaspard*.

Example 3.2 *Miroirs*, 'La Vallée des cloches' (bars 1–6)

The Symbolist case *par excellence* is the *Trois poèmes de Stéphane Mallarmé*, whose music has been examined from various linguistic stances by writers including Robert Gronquist and Michel Delahaye. Gronquist aims to apply musically what Theodor de Wyzewa has said of the poems: 'Each one of his lines was intended to be at once a plastic image, the expression of a thought, the enunciation of a feeling, and a philosophical symbol.'[20] Delahaye meanwhile connects with the synaesthetic colour-theories of Skryabin and Kandinsky, mentioning Ravel's engagement with *correspondances*: 'numerous are those who have been obsessed by the problem of correspondences: Baudelaire, Rimbaud, Ghil . . . then Ravel, who knew *Les Fleurs du mal*, the Baudelairian theory of the universal analogy, the famous verse of the sonnet of the Correspondances'.[21] Beyond strict definitions of Symbolism, several of Ravel's works have been viewed symbolically both by his contemporaries and more recent writers, generally without the composer's approval. *La Valse* has been interpreted as denoting the fall of the Habsburg Empire or the wider demise of high European culture beyond World War I, while *Boléro* has been seen (especially in French musicology epitomised by Marcel Marnat and Serge Gut) as symbolising torment, madness and death.

Ravel's pieces distinguished by 'sur le nom', the *Menuet sur le nom d'Haydn* and *Berceuse sur le nom de Gabriel Fauré*, offer clear examples of symbolic objects of homage, as a 'free adaptation of the Renaissance "soggetto cavato" (a "carved-out subject")'.[22] The discrete lettered devices embedded in the musical fabric have indisputable signification. Writing to Jules Ecorcheville in a letter of 12 September 1909, Ravel's use of imagery neatly demonstrates his conscious objectification: 'The minuet is tailored.'[23] And, as a connected matter, Ravel's own monogram has his initials conjoined and presented in geometric lines, set mainly at right angles – decidedly constructivist! (His signature shares this stylisation, as for instance in documents from the Dossier Ravel at the Bibliothèque Nationale de France.) While hardly of direct musical significance, this compressed utterance highlights the composer's objectified thinking.

Reminiscing about his childhood, Ravel says that 'The only subject that interested me a little was mathematics, to the great joy of my father, who was an engineer';[24] and this numerical curiosity is well embodied by the fantastic character of Arithmétique in *L'Enfant et les sortilèges*. Several works, including 'Oiseaux tristes' and 'Alborada del gracioso' from *Miroirs*, the Sonata for Violin and Piano, sections of *Le Tombeau de Couperin* and the whole of *La Valse* seem to involve workings-out of the Fibonacci series (0, 1, 1, 2, 3, 5, 8, 13, 21 etc.), as the progressively closer whole-number approximations of the proportional ratio known as Golden Section ($\approx 0.618/0.382$).[25] And, on the resulting shapes of these architectonic works, if Stravinsky produces 'rhomboids, scalenes, trapeziums, or trapezoids – shapes somehow stretched or shrunken into asymmetry and arranged in unpredictable combinations',[26] then Ravel specialises in distorted or broken circles (developed from the closed forms of dance), ellipses and, as the ultimate implication of Golden Section, the spiral.

One intriguing example of numerical objectivity, with more speculative symbolic overtones, involves the miniature *Frontispice* which prefaces a philosophical introspection on World War I by the Italian poet Canudo, entitled *S.P. 503, Le Poème du Vardar*. Ravel's piece, requested by Canudo, first accompanied an extract of the poem, 'Sonate pour un jet d'eau', in *Les Feuillets d'Art* of 1919 (accessible at the Bibliothèque Nationale de France); it then reappeared with the full poem in 1923. As observed by Orenstein (who edited the Salabert edition in 1975), Jean Roy and Tobias Plebuch,[27] Ravel evokes the poem's water imagery and exoticism, portraying birdsong in remarkable anticipation of Messiaen; aspects of numerology, while acknowledged by Plebuch, have however been less explored. Although reconstruction of the chronology of *Frontispice* in relation to the poem is incomplete (Ravel and Canudo had first met as early as 1905), it is hard to ignore the musical preoccupation with 'five' and 'three' and that of the titular designation 'S.P. 503'; if unrelated, they constitute a striking coincidence. Canudo states in an explanatory preface that '*Le Poème du Vardar* carries the numerical designation of the postal sector of my [combat] Division like a coat of arms.'[28] And, whatever future research reveals about the extent of liaison and precise order of events, Ravel's numbers certainly relate time and space fundamentally as $3 \times 5 = 15$ bars. (Canudo's zero might suggest the possibility of variable function between the surrounding integers: multiplication, addition and palindromic reflection, as well as denoting certain absences.) In the published score, five staves, 'progressing' vertically from flats through naturals to sharps, are played by five hands (three players) in metres of 15/8 (i.e. 3×5; $3 + 5$) and 5/4. A five-pitch ostinato, using thirds, presents as continuous triplets (D♯–E–G♯, F–A–D♯ etc.), augmenting at bar 10 into notes of three semiquavers' duration (Example 3.3: L.H. of Piano I). Bar 6 reveals the fifth voice entirely in thirds, while bar 11 onwards presents a succession of five-beat triads, with melodic thirds and harmonic open fifths (see again Example 3.3). Ostinatos of differing lengths create a kaleidoscopic effect, with occasional metarhythm when they coincide to create larger-scale accentuations.

The irony of any such symbolism would be that it could be linked to something so seemingly banal as the equivalent of a present-day postcode, though of course the 'S.P. 503' designation itself might be seen as a powerfully bleak symbol for the depersonalising atrocities of World War I. Indeed, Ravel's likely original intention to present *Frontispice* on pianola, as suggested by Rex Lawson,[29] nicely maintains this depersonalised objectivity and, together with the mechanised ostinato presentation, clearly links up with the machinist fascination.

Neoclassicism and 'l'objet (re)trouvé'

That Ravel saw composition as involving objectified craftsmanship is already evident, and is further supported by his comments on the Sonata

Example 3.3 *Frontispice* (bars 10–11)

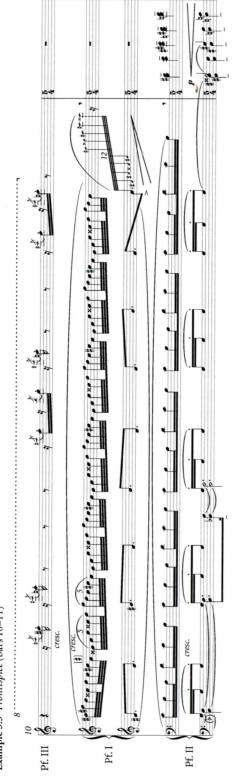

for Violin and Piano (rather as Stravinsky on his Octet): 'I had already determined its rather unusual form, the manner of writing for the instruments, and even the character of the themes for each of the movements before "inspiration" had begun to prompt any of these themes.'[30] That such a view accords with a neoclassical aesthetic founded on abstraction, manipulation and reconstruction, whose prime mover was Stravinsky, will soon be apparent. Ravel himself reputedly viewed the artistic dilemma post-World War I through a constructivist metaphor: 'The solidly-built edifice philosophy and art had constructed began to totter, and thereupon began what is customarily referred to as the "crisis in Art".'[31] Neoclassicism is just one expression of this modernist crisis, and, as Scott Messing acknowledges, the increasing importance assigned in the nineteenth century to iconic 'objects of the past', as upholders of a canon, strongly invited twentieth-century challenge.[32] For further thoughts on neoclassical objectivity, including its own duality in projecting the present partly through the past, consider Pieter van den Toorn:

> Whether a musical object be Baroque, Classical, or, as in the cases under consideration here, neoclassical, the issue of its appreciation remains unchanged. That issue concerns, on the one hand, the immediacy of aesthetic contemplation, that which is sensed and felt, and, on the other, the musical tradition (or social conditions, possibly) that are alleged to enter into that immediacy.[33]

Explicit here is that, as well as illuminating a component or aspect of a work, the image of an object may, more unusually, describe a whole music work. Beyond Ravel's music, many writers have examined the philosophical arguments that support or refute the abstract music work as object. Issues of ontology come to the fore, as does the need to differentiate further between objects and concepts ('closed' and 'open'). Space permitting, we could engage with the contemporary views of Theodor Adorno who, in his search for artistic truth, perceived a complex mediation between (collective) Object and (individual) Subject directed by the socio-historical concerns of German Idealist philosophy.[34]

Underpinning this extension of the argument for our purposes is the view that the score acts in part as a symbol for the larger music work, and that performance plays a crucial role in projecting the time-dimension and sonorous being of such an object. The propositions of thinkers like Richard Wollheim who advocated greater separation between an object/work ('type') and its performance ('token') now seem unduly synthetic; on the other hand, Lydia Goehr's detailed philosophical critique of music works as objects merits close study, even though in fact she favours a rather different way of thinking.[35] Beyond these universal considerations, not all

Ravel's works have equal candidacy for object status, which seems best determined on the strength of individual constructivist credentials.

Ravel's own advice to his pupils elucidates *his* general views on sourcing and responding to musical 'objets trouvés': 'If you have something to say, this something will never emerge more distinctly than in your unintended unfaithfulness to a model';[36] thus he concretises musical experience through imagined or actual usage of a model or paradigm. And in a teaching capacity, Ravel did use models from Mozart, Chopin, Saint-Saëns, Rimsky-Korsakov and Richard Strauss. Equally for himself, certain 'objets trouvés' functioned as models, almost templates, for other members of a family of connected objects, so linking with wider issues of intertextuality. Regarding small-scale correspondence focused on rhythm, Frank Onnen selects two striking examples, firstly between an ascending phrase of dotted rhythm in thirds from Chabrier's *Trois valses romantiques* and one from *Valses nobles et sentimentales*; secondly between the reiterated figuration of Chabrier's *Bourrée fantasque* and that in the 'Toccata' from *Le Tombeau de Couperin*.[37] Larger-scale instances include Debussy's Quartet and Saint-Saëns's Trio Op. 18 as inspirational models for Ravel's own embodiments. (The initial melodic material of Ravel's Trio also has a likely forerunner in that of his own early Sonata for Violin and Piano.) As a specific reference by Ravel to an earlier source, it is worth noting his explanation of a 6/5 chordal construction in *Valses nobles* through allusion to the opening of Beethoven's Piano Sonata Op. 31 No. 3.[38] A further example, as a three-work relationship observed by Boulez, concerns 'trajectories' from the source material of Schoenberg's *Pierrot lunaire*, through Stravinsky's *Trois poésies de la lyrique japonaise* and Ravel's *Trois poèmes de Stéphane Mallarmé*.[39] Of course, to use models is not synonymous with imitation; Ravel highlights rethinking and reconstruction when he talks of the 'blues' in 'Contemporary music': 'these popular forms are but the materials of construction, and the work of art appears only on mature conception where no detail has been left to chance. Moreover, minute stylization in the manipulation of these materials is altogether essential.'[40]

Work-concepts in Ravel's music exhibit fluidity of genre; his resulting objects may be reshaped, refinished, or viewed from a new instrumental perspective, as with the re-creation of 'Habanera' from *Sites auriculaires* in *Rapsodie espagnole*, and the piano and orchestral versions of 'Alborada'. (In part this is because Ravel tended to compose in short piano score and to orchestrate separately.) The phenomenon is also relevant to ballet, which is already a multifaceted (collaborative) creation, the more so when concerned with projecting myths that have their own intrinsic plurality. (While one pragmatic reason for any composer of staged works to produce multiple versions is simply to aid diffusion, revisiting works nonetheless occupied Ravel more than many of his contemporaries, with the obvious exception of Stravinsky.) In this way, *Daphnis et Chloé* presents as a composite object which includes the full ballet (1912) with its orchestral score; the orchestral suites (1911, 1913); the solo piano version (1912); the early piano version (1910) and an instrumental version of the choral section (1914), albeit that the last two are compromised facets, or views, of the object. Beyond its Schubertian (and Beethovenian) model, *Valses nobles* comprises the piano original, its subsequent orchestration and the full ballet realisation entitled *Adélaïde ou Le Langage des fleurs*. *La Valse*, with its early gestation as *Wien*, exists for solo piano, for two pianos, for orchestra (1920) and as the full balletic spectacle (1929 onwards).

Furthermore, Ravel's music is characterised by continuing themes of homage, national dances, 'jazz', musical machines, bells and so on, which also cross generic boundaries: again, the notion of a collection of connected objects offers a useful metaphor. (More conceptual, or goal-directed, ideas may be better served by Boulez's term 'trajectories'.) This is rather as for Stravinsky's ragtime pieces, where 'These impressions suggested the idea of creating a composite portrait of this new dance music.'[41] Ravel's most striking 'composite portrait' – the creation, exploration and destruction of mechanised (often high-speed) dance – runs through 'Feria', the 'Danse générale-bacchanale' of *Daphnis et Chloé*, *La Valse* and *Boléro* (discussed below and in Chapter 7).

The machinist phenomenon

Even if only an artifical dividing line separates Ravel's broad fascination with objects from his particular love of objects set in high-speed motion and subjected to extreme, mechanised repetition,[42] his machinist writings make a distinct contribution. In addition to Symbolist and Cubist activity, 'la Belle Epoque' witnessed astonishing inventiveness: the diesel engine, the early Ford car, gramophone disc, X-rays, radio telegraphy and the movie camera, in the early to mid-1890s alone.[43] Technological endeavour was symbolised by the Eiffel Tower, built for the 1889 Paris Exposition which also featured a 'Galérie des machines'. This love of machines – sources of noise and velocity – was developed by the Italian Futurists: Francesco Pratella and Luigi Russolo (resident in Paris in the 1920s), author of 'The art of noises' (1913) and composer of *The Awakening of a City* (1914). After the cataclysm of World War I, the machine emerged as a quasi-religious icon of modernity; Theo van Doesburg, founder of the Dutch journal *De Stijl* (1917–28), saw factories as new cathedrals, while Le

Corbusier's article on 'Le Purisme' in *L'Esprit nouveau* (1921) hailed mechanical selection as the successor to natural selection.

Stravinsky's experiments connected Paris and the radical Bauhaus in Weimar, with *Fireworks* staged as a Futurist production by Giacomo Balla in 1917. Paris espoused the machinist aesthetic with huge enthusiasm: relevant composers and works include Darius Milhaud, *Machines agricoles*; Arthur Honegger, *Pacific 231*; George Antheil, *Ballet mécanique, Airplane Sonata*; Sergey Prokofiev, *Le Pas d'acier* and of course Ravel's *Boléro*. The player-piano offered a special focus for experiment as a music-producing and -reproducing machine unlimited by human fallibility, as with Stravinsky's Etude for Pianola (1917) and possibly Ravel's *Frontispice* (1918). Beyond Paris, Varèse (resident for much of his life in the United States) was one of the most revolutionary thinkers associated with mechanisation, whose experimentation led to new concepts of musical sound and a foreshadowing of electronic music.

In painting, theatre and ballet, Fernand Léger's ideas proved especially innovative and powerful. The machine connected 'Art and the Everyday' (in the words of Nancy Perloff); its exponents delighted in modes of transport whose mechanisms exhibited both interior and exterior motion, and in the popular institutions of the circus, fairground, music-hall and cinema. Beyond France, dramatic film portrayal, such as in Fritz Lang's *Metropolis* (1926) and Charlie Chaplin's *Modern Times* (1936), also attested to the dehumanising and catastrophic potential of factory life. Artists were social commentators, both on technological triumph and on mass industrialisation, depersonalisation and drudgery.

A fascination with engineering was also inherent in the legacy of Ravel's father, a civil engineer of Swiss origin whose profession was later taken up by Ravel's brother, Edouard. Pierre Joseph Ravel designed a railway from Madrid to Irún and in 1868 patented a steam generator; he later invented 'a really useful two-stroke internal-combustion engine and a spectacular though less useful circus-act [with a somersaulting car] called the Whirlwind of Death'.[44] Ravel's *La Valse* and *Boléro* share this readiness to engage in risk and potential destruction, while his own fascination with motor vehicles is shown by a letter to Maurice Delage (6 February 1926), written in Oslo, when he enthuses that 'There are all kinds of vehicles: trolleys, cars (with chains), sleighs, skis . . . '[45]

A further dimension concerns Ravel's revisiting of childhood imagination, often approached through life-feigning mechanical toys. An internalised microcosm (the enchanted garden of *Ma Mère l'Oye*) speaks with powerful innocence to the real world beyond, suggesting a parallel with the naive art of Henri Rousseau (1844–1910). Ravel's musical toys include the mechanical cricket in *Histoires naturelles* 'which went tick-tock like a timepiece' and the malfunctioning clock in *L'Enfant et les sortilèges*; he also had, 'like Satie, a particular predilection for out-of-tune pianos or old quavering gramophones . . .'[46] Ravel aptly summarises his early connection with machines: 'Well, in my childhood I was much interested in mechanisms . . . I visited factories often, very often, as a small boy with my father. It was these machines, their clicking and roaring, which, with the Spanish folk songs sung to me at night-time as a *berceuse* by my mother, formed my first instruction in music!'[47] The ultimate convergence of these machines and Spanish songs was surely to be *Boléro*.

Ravel's writings on machines

A useful introduction to Ravel's views on machines is provided by Edouard Ravel's letter to Jacques Rouché of 19 February 1940, three years after Ravel's death:

> My brother admired everything which was mechanical, from simple tin
> toys to the most intricate machine tools. He would thus spend entire
> days . . . in front of street vendors' stalls, and was delighted to come with
> me to factories or to expositions [exhibitions] of machinery. He was happy
> to be in the midst of these movements and noises. But he always came out
> struck and obsessed by the automation of all these machines.[48]

The key element is an overall 'admiration', implying tribute as in Ravel's relationship to the past, which is sometimes tempered by a troubled preoccupation with the inhuman automation of factories. Edouard continues: 'He never spoke to me of his plans for scenarios, but often, when passing Le Vésinet, he showed me "the Boléro factory".' The Parisian suburb of Le Vésinet was famed for its heavy industry, while the context for Rouché's enquiries was a factory-based production of *Boléro*, staged at the Opéra in 1941, with designs by Léon Leyritz. (In fact René Chalupt suggests that Ravel did see and approve Leyritz's work in progress.)[49] So the *Boléro* factory was not merely imagined, though the label may have been attached retrospectively.

Ravel's main writings on machines appeared in English around 1932–3, and the most extensive quasi-manifesto is 'Finding tunes in factories'.[50] Although classified as an article, the style of this piece is more like newspaper journalism. Various subtitles read as soundbites or editorial additions and the ensuing short paragraphs function mainly to whet the appetite rather than to detail a comprehensive aesthetic stance.

Ravel's premise is that the artistic scope in pastoral evocation is not limitless. This offers a partial *raison-d'être* for his own machinist aesthetic;

it also suggests that nature and technology exist in some kind of balance. Under an initial subheading, 'Inspiration from noise', Ravel embraces a modernist outlook: 'In our search for fresh inspiration we cannot overlook the appeal of modern life.' Traffic and mechanical sounds may or may not be euphonious, but both have strong musical potential. Ravel, the grand old master, then speaks for France and prophesies the future of European music: 'Unquestionably the mechanics of this age will leave their imprint on music that will be handed down through generations, and more and more of our composers will find inspiration in what some now regard as mere noise.'[51] The tone accords with the scale of the content: 'great music' and 'mighty engines'. His thinking about the relationship between music and noise, and the legitimacy of both as sound, may be related back to Russolo (whose 'noise intoners' had intrigued Ravel at a Parisian exhibition in 1921); historically, Ravel points out that battles, so fruitful a source of inspiration in the nineteenth century, inevitably involved their share of violent noise.

The next subheading, 'Business man as hero', considers the industrial magnate as a modern-day Napoleon. Ravel then changes tack by imagining 'The strange, disordered sounds of a great motor vehicle pulling up a steep hill [a reminder of his father's traction engines?]', which, although they may not be beautiful, still offer non-literal musical scope, just as 'The song of the nightingale in the forest is very different from the musical interpretations that have found their way into our scores.'[52] This remark may allude to Stravinsky's *Le Rossignol*, itself the subject of an earlier article by Ravel;[53] equally, representations of birdsong feature in Ravel's own music. (Despite Ravel's endorsing a more sophisticated evocation of machinery, statements elsewhere still suggest the appeal of a more primitively literal response.) A somewhat grandiose declaration on artistic truth ('To set such sounds to music is true art') then receives a more lowly explanation: 'Of course the music does not necessarily suggest the noises, but it can tell in music the story of the machine and interpret the machine's works.'[54] Unfortunately, 'story' has rather childish connotations in English, doubtless unintended, while 'works' suggests both the internal workings and productivity.

Sometimes Ravel's comments seem slightly contradictory: the third section salutes a 'Beauty in industry' which is not really substantiated by what follows (or what has preceded), although this may just be the result of a poor editorial interpolation. Nonetheless, the idea nicely confounds the expected beauty of the old natural order. Beauty, including that of craftsmanship, was after all fundamental to Ravel. Ravel suggests that the factory may constitute 'the entire being of thousands of workers' and of course he too functions within variously sized and defined worlds of reality and make-believe. His somewhat onomatopoeic writing reflects the repetitive motion of the machines that he describes: 'Throughout the day its mighty engines turn and turn and turn. Clanging bells punctuate its ordered progress, piles of finished goods pay tribute to the mechanism and to the greatness of the brain that conceived it.' The literal language of 'clash' and 'clang', 'thunder' and 'rumble' is almost comical, but more compelling is the setting up of stark contrasts which indicate awareness of the dark underside of mechanisation: bustle and void; cacophony and silence: 'where a few hours before was noise and toil is stillness and desolation'. This angle is arguably more typical of an Eastern European approach – man as automaton imprisoned in a factory; we think of Prokofiev's 'Fabrika' in *Le Pas d'acier* (the premiere of which Ravel heard), and this music may well have influenced the ostinatos in *Boléro*. Paradoxically, cheap mass production excluded elite craftsmanship (the subject of Ravel's perpetual striving), and yet, in their different ways, both the factory and the craftsman sought productive perfection.

In the following section on 'Music of machines', Ravel declares how much musical potential lies in a factory setting. Again, we might see a possible contradiction in that, while exclaiming that 'musicians have not yet captured the wonder of industrial progress', Ravel clearly acknowledges the contributions of Honegger (*Pacific 231*), Mosolov (*Zavod* [Iron Foundry], of which Ravel had a Pathé recording) and Schoenberg (presumably the grotto scene from *Die glückliche Hand*). In fairness to Ravel, maybe he is simply advocating more of the same; furthermore, this writing dates from the years during which he was increasingly incapacitated by his terminal brain disease. Despite any compromising element, the next sentences contain Ravel's important pronouncement that 'My own *Boléro* owed its inception to a factory. Some day I should like to play it with a vast industrial works in the background.'

Remarks about 'An airplane symphony' convey Ravel's fervour for machinist projects which are partly tributes to human endeavour; unfortunately, the broad coverage and superficiality of treatment suggests an unmerited casualness. In just four sentences Ravel proposes projects on the airplane, a liner and railways;[55] the content and tone is strikingly similar to Pratella's 'Technical manifesto of Futurist music' (1912), which sought mechanical realisation of 'the musical soul of crowds, great industrial complexes, transatlantic liners, trains, tanks, automobiles and aeroplanes'.[56] Whether or not Ravel had read Pratella's manifesto, the main Futurist projects were certainly publicised in the foreign press before World War I. That Ravel's propositions, especially the airplane symphony, were not just opportunistic journalese is, however, made clear by references elsewhere. Orenstein mentions a letter to Manuel de Falla (6 March

1930), where Ravel talks of a project on '*Dédale 39*, which as you can guess is an airplane – and an airplane in C'; similarly, an unpublished letter to Manuel Rosenthal indicates plans for *Icare*, a symphonic poem inspired by flight. Sadly, it appears that neither work was ever sketched.[57] Nonetheless, Ravel realised some of these ideas domestically at his brother's home in Paris: 'The bed, however, is an ordinary built-in sleeping-car berth, or better still the cabin bed of a luxury liner', while '"A bit like Dekobra," I observed, as we sat down on the curious but comfortable steel armchairs, constructed from authentic airplane parts.'[58]

The final exultant paragraph proves telling in characterising Ravel's relationship to machines and to a machinist aesthetic:

> But over all would be the triumph of the machine, the vast monster that man has created to do his bidding. What a noble inspiration! Surely one that will in future years be felt by hundreds of our composers, who will bring into being music that will faithfully and beautifully reflect the spirit of the age in which machinery struggled to lighten the burdens of man.[59]

Comparison may again be made with Pratella's belief in 'the domination of the machine and the victorious reign of electricity'.[60] Despite limited acknowledgement of the negative side of machines as representing control, Ravel cannot hide his almost childlike wonderment. Even the expression 'vast monster' embodies admiration and is swiftly sanctioned by the notion of nobility. Once more, Ravel adopts the grand prophetic mode, appropriate enough given the machinist connection with Futurism, while the final thought emphasises his simple faith in the essential 'goodness' of the machine and his belief that the balance of power lay with man.

In looking to characterise further Ravel's machine aesthetic, an unsigned interview of 1932, entitled 'Factory gives composer inspiration' (clearly the basis of Ravel's article of 1933), offers additional insights. Ravel was asked whether 'typewriters, lathes and saws' might take the place of standard orchestral instruments. Referring to Satie's *Parade* (1917), Ravel responded that 'it has already been tried in one of the Russian ballets, where a typewriter being tapped was a legitimate instrument of the orchestra'.[61] More significant is his rejoinder that, were this to become standard practice, it would not be 'art'; the artistic challenge would be to convey machine sonorities through conventional means, or to create musical sounds through machines. This aestheticising response is largely opposed to Russolo's earlier vision of an orchestrated factory of noises: 'the motors and machines of our industrial cities will one day be consciously attuned, so that every factory will be transformed into an intoxicating orchestra of noises'.[62] Similarly, Ravel's stance contrasts with that of Antheil, who, in the mid-1920s, predicted the imminent demise of the symphony orchestra, to be superseded by a transformed orchestral machine.[63]

Ravel then hints tantalisingly at another potential project, expressed in the words of the interviewer:

> in these days of cacophony it might be quite an original idea for the orchestra to start, say, in C major, and then, through a series of discords the instruments should divide, some going up a semitone at every three or four bars, while others went down in the same way, eventually ending in perfect harmony two octaves apart.[64]

Ravel reputedly saw such a formula (rather in anticipation of Bartók's *Music for Strings, Percussion and Celesta* of 1936) as establishing new patterns of consonance and dissonance. Certainly, this concept would have created a suitably mechanical, predetermined structure even if not wholly novel. Milhaud, among others, had used similar ideas in his Fifth Chamber Symphony of 1922;[65] furthermore, moments of *La Valse* also hint at this construction, when (beyond Fig. 93), from a chord of E^7, the upper line ascends chromatically: D–G, while the bass descends: B♭–F♯, thence to G. Once more, we see Ravel's fondness for mechanised structures founded on a 'neutral' C, the intended pitch-centre of the unrealised *Dédale 39* and of *Boléro* (though Nichols has discovered that at one stage the piece was in D major). Although Ravel always had more ideas than those which he was able to realise – on occasion perhaps a failure of courage though at other times an indication of lucidity – it is especially poignant that these machinist notions, expressed so vigorously in the early 1930s, were to remain latent largely because of his progressive illness.[66]

In seeking appropriate imagery for machinist readings of Ravel's music, a letter to Delage (5 July 1905) proves illuminating. Ravel describes a huge foundry 'on the Rhine towards Düsseldorf' that employed 24,000 men, exclaiming: 'How can I tell you about these smelting castles, these incandescent cathedrals, and the wonderful symphony of traveling belts, whistles, and terrific hammer blows which envelop you? . . . How much music there is in all of this! – and I certainly intend to use it.'[67] This statement might be thought to anticipate *Boléro*, though Orenstein usefully mentions the unfinished opera *La Cloche engloutie*, of which the librettist, A. F. Hérold, said: 'The scenes which occur in the factory of Henry the founder were to have been of striking power. Ravel did not envision a small artisan's workshop; he imagined a huge factory, equipped like the most grandiose one sees today, and he would have utilized the innumerable sounds of hammers, saws, files, and sirens.'[68] In addition to these images, we might adapt ideas from Russolo's 'The art of noises' with its six, loosely defined, classes of noise that included rumbles, explosions and crashes; whistles and snorts; murmurs and whispers; screeches; elemental percussion; and shouts, screams and howls.[69] While we should guard against over-literal representation, these sources offer a collection of machinist imagery which might enhance readings of Ravel's music.

Musical mechanisms and *la machine infernale*

How might a composer relate to machines? He could simply be an illustrator; a celebrator of invention as a modern act of homage (Darius Milhaud, *Machines agricoles*); a promoter of new musical definitions that include noise (Varèse, *Ionisation*); an advocate of machines as performers (Stravinsky, Etude for Pianola; Ravel, *Frontispice*); or an exponent of musical mechanics to convey properties of machines, especially movement (Honegger, *Pacific 231*; Ravel, *Boléro*). This last category, most important to Ravel, often employs what Derrick Puffett has called the 'ostinato machine':

> a composite ostinato in which each of the separate strands pursues its own harmonic/rhythmic course, together creating a dense polyphonic structure. The 'machine' metaphor is apt because such structures tend to assume a kind of autonomy, unfolding alongside, or even in opposition to, whatever mode of organisation prevails for the piece as a whole; there is a constant risk that the machine – *la machine infernale*? – will get out of hand.[70]

Indeed the destructive potential is intrinsic to Ravel's conception of the machine, especially after World War I, and the machinist imagery suggested above could facilitate working through various oppositions in the music: of the controller versus the controlled, fixed/free, motion/stasis, stop/start, construction/destruction. Examples of Ravel's machines include the Sonata for Violin and Cello, whose deceptive mechanistic facility cost him dearly: 'It may have an air of nothingness, this machine for two instruments: there is nearly a year and a half of toil in it.'[71] The finale ('Perpetuum mobile') of the Sonata for Violin and Piano provides another good illustration, while an alternative view of *Frontispice* could highlight an archetypal 'ostinato machine' whose complex of competing fixed elements threatens to overthrow the free.

The 'Introduction' to *L'Heure espagnole* offers the most concentrated depiction of mechanisms (see Example 3.4): a multiplicity of clocks that epitomises Stravinsky's 'Swiss clockmaker'. This work shares the contemporary fixation with portraying time, which is not homogeneous and may

Example 3.4 *L'Heure espagnole*, 'Introduction' (Fig. 1)

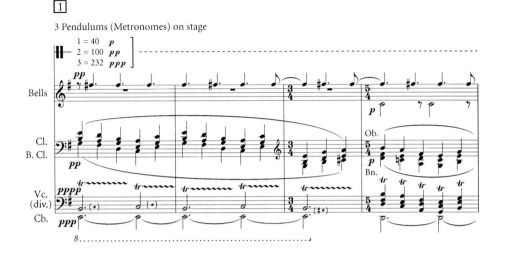

be ironised, trivialised and made to misbehave. The opening – Puffett's 'ostinato machine run riot' – uses a 5/4 metre, though, unusually for Ravel, bar-time periodically contracts and augments. Against this metrononic background, several clocks tick and chime at different registers, timbres and rates (the three specified 'pendulums' coincide every fifteen seconds). Mechanised melody is reduced to repeated scalic or monotone figuration, while rhythmic patterning undergoes gradual diminution. Among mechanical toys are featured an automaton trumpet-player (on horn), marionettes dancing to childhood tunes and birds. Later, in Scene XV (with Gonzalve hidden in the large clock), a myriad of intricate mechanisms, whose pitch dimension is again restricted, sound in 3/4 metre in varying durations and textures: staccato ('sautillé') and smooth (harmonics, glissandos). As in so many of Ravel's machinist contexts, at climactic points like in Scene XVII (Fig. 89, 'Animé'), the musical substance reduces to chromaticism in surging descent and ascent. (For the main discussion of *L'Heure espagnole*, see Langham Smith, Chapter 9.)

In returning to Ravel's 'dance-machine' trajectory, we focus now on the obsessional destructiveness of *la machine infernale*. 'Feria' from *Rapsodie espagnole*, which marks the starting-point, suggests fiesta and festival, but also fairground. And in French views of the fair, the machine was certainly writ large:

> the fair seizes us with all its tumult. The huge site is a formidable factory, where the sounds of instrumental arrangements, carriage shafts and brass [bands] are almost covered by the steam-whistles, the rolling of the merry-go-round, the barrages from the shooting-galleries, the grating of the turnstiles, the stall-holders' calls and the cries of the crowd.[72]

An expectant rhythmic background is set up within a brisk 6/8 metre, over which the circus's brassy orchestra is explored with muted metallic effects on trumpets (Fig. 4), intensified by horns *bouchés* and *en dehors* (Fig. 5). Surging figurations, coloured by harp and string glissandos, simulate fairground rides (Fig. 6ff.); intricate, repeated triplet patternings suggest an unstoppable merry-go-round (Fig. 9). Intensifying diminution and dissonance hint at risk beyond revelry. The reprise features increased competition between the simultaneous mechanisms, with the horns especially active, while the ending reveals the hallmarks of the cataclysmic 'dance-machine'. As earlier in the piece, Ravel shortens his main ostinato from one bar to half-a-bar for doubled momentum (Fig. 30). A four-bar build-up (Fig. 31) then offers the paradox of movement yet stasis, as rhythm stutters uncontrollably on fixed pitches within a quickening tempo, while the final condensed climax (Fig. 32) comprises a fierce chromatic explosion followed by the briefest consonant flourish. (See also Russ, '*Rapsodie espagnole*: modality and form': Chapter 6.)

This large-scale 'dance-machine' trajectory continues with the chromatic descent–ascent figurations and rhythmic stutterings that end *Daphnis et Chloé* (Fig. 220), where, 'Like Prokofiev, Ravel found untold delight in coaxing from the orchestra an almost automatic kind of drive'; with *La Valse* comes further intensification: 'the sheer mechanics of the score seem more frenzied than . . . in any of his earlier works, including even the Bacchanale from *Daphnis*. They look forward to the hysteria-inducing devices of the *Bolero*.'[73] And beyond, perhaps, to the suppressed subterranean tensions of the Concerto for the Left Hand.

In conclusion, some differentiation between musical objects and machines aids discussion since, while all machines are objects, not all objects are machines. Moreover, since Ravel's obsession with destructive mechanisms is most prevalent after World War I, there is a broad chronological evolution. Concern with the object is rooted in 'craft' which may enjoy a distinct classical legacy; the object also acts as a vehicle for confronting wider questions of distance and detachment. Essentially, the consciously positioned object is an anti-romantic inversion or reflection of the subject. Whatever the broader philosophical arguments about the musical object, Ravel's engagement with the notion is compelling: 'As a promoter of musical objectivity he paved the way for Stravinsky and the whole anti-Romantic school which flourished in the 1920s and early 1930s.'[74] Exploration of the machine shares this detachment and fragmentation, and so reveals a particular depersonalising mask and another dimension to imposture. Paradoxes persist since although machines represent predictability and mundane reality, they also possess awe-inspiring grandeur as giant monsters in fantastic fairy-tales of Futurism. The machinist focus foregrounds Ravel's writings which, at their most extreme, hold common ground with the views of cultural critics such as Adorno (writing in *Musikblätter des Anbruch* from 1925) in regarding technology – particularly phonograph recording, film and radio – as a crucial means of securing a musical future.

In practice, musical objects and machines often merge. *Frontispice*, for example, suggests a possible symbolic object which projects its geometric planes in part through Puffett's 'ostinato-machine'. José Bruyr neatly claimed that the object and machine jointly offered access to all Ravel's music: 'He then shows me his treasures: Viennese crystal, bibelots brought back from Arizona ("Doesn't it look like a Picasso?"), a delightful minia-ture village from a toy box for a fairy godchild... But it suddenly strikes me that the mechanical toy and the surrealist tableau thus placed side by side illuminate all of Ravel's oeuvre.'[75] The truth is surely more complex. If arguments for regarding a significant facet of Ravel's music in this way are extended to encompass his complete oeuvre, they become too diluted to maintain their potency. Moreover, while it is apt to explore Ravel's cerebral precision, his aesthetic also embraces more nebulous (and typically French) charm, sensibility and instinctiveness. Fundamentally, Ravel argues for the balance between intellect and sentiment, between knowing and feeling, that he perceived in Poe's *The Raven*; in the words of Olin Downes, 'Fantastic as you please, but always form, form, form...'[76]

PART II

Musical explorations

4 Ravel and the piano

ROY HOWAT

Ravel, that master of tender irony, has left in his wake two supreme ironies: of being viewed as archetypally French, and of his musical forms often being viewed as conventional.[1] French though he was, his temperament, humour, expression and technique are all distinct from French habits and stand out, by their incisiveness and bursts of raw sensuality, even from his contemporaries Fauré and Debussy. Besides the technical daring inherited from his Swiss-born engineer-inventor father, the foreign element that most strongly colours Ravel's character and music is the Basque-Spanish heritage of his mother. In a letter of 1911 to Joaquín Turina, written from Spain, Ravel signs himself off, 'A thousand friendly greetings from your (or my) motherland', and his letters from the Basque region or to relatives there are peppered with Basque phrases as well as Basque forms of place names.[2]

Viñes and the early piano music

Ravel's closest and most influential childhood friendship, from the age of thirteen, was with Ricardo Viñes. A month older than Ravel, Viñes arrived from Barcelona with his mother in 1887 to study in Bériot's Conservatoire class (which Ravel joined in 1889); apparently it was the two mothers who first met, in 1888, with Mme Ravel delighted to discover a fellow-Spanish-speaker.[3] In their teenage years, Viñes introduced Ravel to the prose poems of *Gaspard de la nuit* and then, in 1907, introduced him to Manuel de Falla (just before Ravel repaid Viñes handsomely for that introduction to *Gaspard*); above all, it was Viñes whose brilliant and subtle piano playing first brought a whole series of piano masterworks to the public. How many of those works, Ravel's, Debussy's and others, would exist as they do without the enthusiastic stimulus of Viñes, and the knowledge that he could quickly assimilate whatever was put in front of him?[4] It was also Viñes who (as seen below) helped to maintain a current of musical stimulus between Debussy and Ravel in later years when the two composers were no longer in personal contact.

From his late teens comes Ravel's first surviving piano music, the unpublished *Sérénade grotesque* of about 1893. Its overtly Spanish idiom

Example 4.1 Ravel and Chabrier comparison
(a) Ravel, *Menuet antique* (1895), bars 56–8

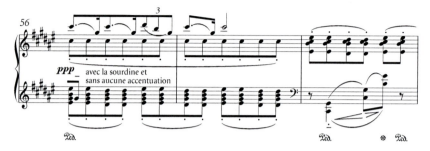

(b) Chabrier, *Pièces pittoresques* (1880), 'Menuet pompeux' (bars 74–6)

includes one idea strong enough to be reused twelve years later in 'Alborada del gracioso' (bars 7–8 and similar).[5] Already, the *Sérénade* shows that lifelong Iberic penchant for semitone clashes, notably in the main dance section from bar 15; almost exactly the same clash (F♯ against E♮) announces the opening chord of its successor, the *Menuet antique* of 1895. This title is unabashed about its ancestry, for the second part of the piece's central section strongly echoes the equivalent moment in Chabrier's 'Menuet pompeux' (1880), a special favourite that Ravel later orchestrated (Example 4.1a and b).

Ravel was adamant that much though he admired Debussy, his own musical language came largely from Chabrier.[6] (Chabrier's idiom, too, is coloured by the influence of his childhood Spanish music teachers, even before his long adult visit to Spain.) Nonetheless, it is not hard to hear where Debussy's influence strikes: for example, the *Pavane pour une Infante défunte* of 1899 (Example 4.2a) revels in a succession of parallel ninth chords taken almost verbatim from Debussy's 'Sarabande'(Example 4.2b) – another piece which Ravel later orchestrated – as it had briefly appeared in print in a supplement to *Le Grand Journal* of February 1896.[7] Even there, though, Chabrier is not far away, for Act II of his opera *Le Roi malgré lui* (1887) features both diatonic and chromatic successions of ninths (Example 4.2c). As can be seen in Example 4.2d–e, Ravel's, Debussy's and Chabrier's chains of ninths all simply 'ellipticise' classical logic by taking

Example 4.2 Ravel, Debussy and Chabrier comparisons

(a) Ravel, *Pavane pour une Infante défunte* (bars 25–6)

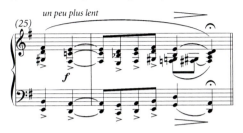

(b) Debussy, 'Sarabande', 1896 version (bars 11–12)

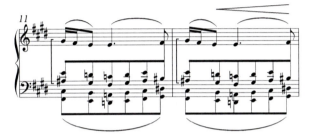

(c) Chabrier, *Le Roi malgré lui*, 'Fête polonaise'

Harmonic logic

(d) Ravel–Debussy

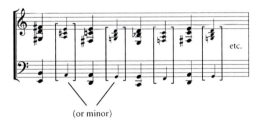

(or minor)

(e) Chabrier

Example 4.3 Debussy, *Pour le piano*, 'Sarabande' (bars 63–5)

each resolution as read and replacing it with the next questioning ninth chord. Chabrier's example in particular echoes the rising chromatic sequence of sevenths in bars 61–2 of Chopin's *Nouvelle étude* in D♭, which again follows the logic of Example 4.2e. Such harmonic ellipsis quickly became an essential part of Ravel's musical thinking.

Another chain of parallel chords from Debussy's 'Sarabande', the more diatonic sequence shown in Example 4.3, also becomes an element as Ravelian as Debussian, as can be heard very clearly in Ravel's *Sonatine* of 1903–5 and his 'La Vallée des cloches' (cf. the bracketed falling fourths in Example 4.3). Ravel having been thirteen years Debussy's junior, it is easily assumed that he started by emulating Debussy before finding his own voice. Closer acquaintance suggests the contrary: that his understandable admiration for Debussy added an extra dimension, one that he assimilated and developed so quickly that it soon concealed its model and even started to stimulate the older composer.

Sites auriculaires

This creative interaction is well illustrated by the famous 'Habanera' incident: Ravel is reported to have lent Debussy an unpublished manuscript of his 'Habanera' from *Sites auriculaires* (1895–7) for two pianos and then been annoyed when one of its most characteristic moments was echoed in Debussy's 'La Soirée dans Grenade' from *Estampes* of 1903 (Example 4.4a and b). Several more details are needed to complete the perspective. In April 1901, two years before 'La Soirée', Debussy composed his two-piano habanera *Lindaraja* but left it unpublished, perhaps embarrassed by a more extended, if patchy, resemblance (across bars 117–41) to Ravel's 'Habanera'. By 1903, with Ravel's 'Habanera' still unprinted, Debussy may simply have tired of holding back fertile ideas. Perhaps he also saw that the critical moment in 'La Soirée' in any case took its harmony equally from his own *Prélude à l'après-midi d'un faune* of 1892–4 (the piece's only

Example 4.4 Ravel and Debussy comparison

(a) Ravel, 'Habanera' (bars 13–14)

(b) Debussy, *Estampes*, 'La Soirée dans Grenade' (bars 23–4)

anacrusis: Fig. 3) – a work Ravel loved unreservedly. Had Ravel overlooked this, or was he feeling territorial about the added Spanish rhythm? Even here, though Ravel could not have known it, Debussy had a prior claim, for the same harmony appears, attached to a *seguidilla* rhythm, in Debussy's then unpublished *Chanson espagnole* of 1883 (bars 4 and similar). Nonetheless, the fact remains that neither *Lindaraja* nor 'La Soirée' would probably exist in its present form without Ravel's input – not least because of the implicit link in 'La Soirée' to Debussy's new friend Viñes, who, at Ravel's urging, had introduced himself to Debussy in 1901.[8]

'Entre cloches', the less known companion-piece to 'Habanera', also has an exotic element not visible in the piece's published edition: Ravel's manuscript beams the opening bar's quavers $3 + 3 + 4$, suggesting a Latin American flavour perhaps blended with elements of Basque *zortzico*.[9]

Pavane pour une Infante défunte

Spain resounds equally in the *Pavane pour une Infante défunte* (1899), a mischievously ironic title possibly dreamt up together with Viñes (did they know Alkan's satirical *Marcia funebre sulla morte d'un papagallo?*), and chosen almost entirely for its euphony. In terms of spoken metre the title suggests a truncated alexandrine starting, typically for Ravel, in mid-phrase and with each mute 'e' unpronounced (in defiance of declamatory convention, thus anticipating the *Histoires naturelles*). The music reflects this, opening with a two-bar phrase that sounds as much like a consequent as an antecedent because of the five-bar phrase that follows. As various anecdotes attest, the main challenge in performing this piece is to catch its sensuous tenderness while avoiding mawkishness or lugubriousness.

Ravel's pianistic traits

The blatant major seventh that flits across our ears at the end of *Jeux d'eau*, matching the piece's opening, prompts a tally of how many of Ravel's solo piano pieces open or close (or both) with a prominent minor second or major seventh clash: *Sérénade grotesque* (ending), *Menuet antique*, *Jeux d'eau*, the *Sonatine* (ending); 'Noctuelles', 'Oiseaux tristes' and 'Alborada del gracioso' from *Miroirs*; 'Ondine' and 'Scarbo' from *Gaspard de la nuit* (1908); *Menuet sur le nom d'Haydn* (1909), every one of the *Valses nobles et sentimentales* (1911) and five of the six movements of *Le Tombeau de Couperin* (1914–17) – in sum, almost three-quarters of all his solo piano pieces, plus the two-piano 'Habanera' and the outer movements of the Concerto in G. (The rogue major seventh at the end of the 1905 Prix de Rome fugue underlines this Ravelian hallmark.) To obtain a comparable tally from Debussy we would have to count whole-tone clashes instead, though the few semitonal occurrences that do emerge revealingly echo Ravel – the start of 'Poissons d'or' in 1907 relative to the end of the *Sonatine*, and the preludes 'Le Vent dans la plaine' and 'La Sérénade inter-rompue' relative to 'Scarbo' and 'Alborada del gracioso' (plus a sudden flurry of semitone clashes in the second book of *Préludes*).

Jeux d'eau

All this supports Ravel's famous protest to Pierre Lalo in which he defends the initiating role of *Jeux d'eau* (1901) in twentieth-century piano writing. Comparison of the last two pages of this work with those of Debussy's 'Pagodes' (composed a year after the publication in 1902 of *Jeux d'eau*) lends further weight: each piece presents a three-layered texture with stylised rippling arpeggios at the top, a slower-moving pentatonic melody in the middle and a bass line descending slowly stepwise to the tonic (like Debussy, Ravel had listened to the gamelans at the 1900 Exposition Universelle, as the second page of *Jeux d'eau* confirms). There is an equally telling difference: 'Pagodes' ends, as it began, with a relatively consonant added sixth as its blue note and a 'ritardando' into its final 'gong', in con-trast to Ravel's more biting major seventh and unequivocal 'sans ralentir'. (The end of 'Jardins sous la pluie' provides further comment on this, letting the major seventh slide down to the fifth *à la* Chabrier as at the end of Ravel's *Pavane*.) From this and many other examples, we may establish subtle distinctions between the two composers' approaches. Most appropriately, in a French Television interview of 1969 with Bernard Gavoty, the pianist Jacques Février, a lifelong friend of Ravel, differentiated between 'un poète voluptueux' (Debussy) and 'un classique sensuel' (Ravel).

Once again the influence worked in both directions, for the language of *Jeux d'eau* surely reflects the house performance Ravel heard in 1900 (with Debussy at the piano) of *Pelléas et Mélisande*.[10] At the same time *Jeux d'eau* shows its independence through ubiquitous details like the added piquancy of the dominant elevenths in bar 4 that drop by minor thirds (the whole-tone basis of each chord thus creates the maximum semitone clash against the next chord); by the Lisztian tritone cadences at bars 32–5 (a device Debussy was still to exploit cadentially, as at the end of *La Mer*); and by the cadenza's mixed C and F♯ triads (a favourite Ravel cocktail, traceable to the central part of Chabrier's *Bourrée fantasque*).

Like the *Pavane*, *Jeux d'eau* and its successors exploit Ravel's prosodic trait of adding asides, as it were, in the form of grace-note figurations that interrupt and fall outside the indicated metre. Related to this is his way of starting pieces or major musical statements as if in mid-phrase (like the truncated alexandrine of 'Pavane pour une Infante défunte'). An obvious example is the gruff opening cadence of the 'Rigaudon' in *Le Tombeau* – a descendant in this respect of Chabrier's 'Tourbillon'. Gentler examples like 'Ondine', 'Le Gibet', and even to some extent *Jeux d'eau*, leave us aware that the piece has started rather than is starting (any lingering by performers on the first note is thus counterproductive). Another simple way of starting in mid-phrase is to open with a harmonic clash. Prosodically, all this relates not only to the innovatory vocal writing of the *Histoires naturelles* and *L'Heure espagnole*, but also to descriptions of Ravel's characteristic gestures when pronouncing witty asides.[11]

The other striking innovation in *Jeux d'eau* is its implied instrumental compass: Ravel's bass A in bars 49–50, 55 and 59 is an ersatz for the nonexistent G♯ below the piano's normal range, as also happens in the finale of the Piano Trio. 'Une barque sur l'océan' explicitly notates this 'phantom' G♯ at bars 44 and 92 (see Peters Edition, also bars 39 and 41). 'Scarbo' (bars 15, 334 and 395–409) and the final bar of the Concerto in G stretch down to an implied G (or F𝄪). Astonishingly, a century later only one major piano maker, Bösendorfer, has met the challenge, probably not even with Ravel in mind. (One wonders, though, if Ravel knew some French pianos from the time of the 1851 London Exhibition, whose basses extended to that low G.)

Ravel also exploited what was available as much as he stretched beyond it, and his writing strongly reflects the Erard pianos that were his norm. Besides their lighter, shallower touch (facilitating lightly repeated notes

Example 4.5 Ravel and Chabrier comparison
(a) Ravel, *Miroirs*, 'Noctuelles' (bars 47–50)

(b) Chabrier, *Pièces pittoresques*, 'Idylle' (bars 20–2)

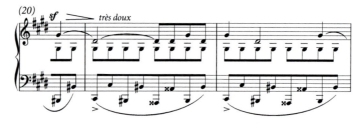

and sophisticated glissandos), a now rare quality is the distinct colour of each register (partly the result of Erards up to the 1900s or even later being straight-strung long after other makes had adopted cross-stringing). On most present-day pianos no special resemblance is evident between the opening page of *Jeux d'eau* and that of the 'Menuet' in the *Sonatine*; but play each on an Erard of the period, and their strings of sevenths in the tenor register immediately stand out. (For more on *Jeux d'eau*, see Woodley, '*Jeux d'eau*: recordings of Cortot (1923) and Perlemuter (1973)': Chapter 10.)

Miroirs

The instrument itself also accounts for some essential differences in flavour between Ravel's *Miroirs* and Debussy's contemporary piano *Images*: as is well documented, Debussy enjoyed writing for the more sensuous (but arguably less sensual) sonorities and deeper touch of the Bechstein, Blüthner and Pleyel.[12] Ravel's resulting jazzier bite is most evident in 'Noctuelles' (for example, bar 72) and 'Oiseaux tristes' (bar 20), as well as through the characteristic strings of sevenths in the central part of 'Noctuelles'. One of the most expressive moments of 'Noctuelles' also reveals the depth of Chabrier's influence, with rocking melodic fourths accompanied by simple note repetitions and a chromatic pendulum (Example 4.5a and b). The same relationship can be observed in the second system of the 'Pavane de la Belle au bois dormant' from *Ma Mère l'Oye*, originally composed for piano duet across 1908–10.

Besides the ubiquitous falling fourths that link all five *Miroirs*, 'Une

Example 4.6 *Miroirs*: motivic connections
(a) 'Une barque sur l'océan' (opening figure)
(b) 'Alborada del gracioso' (opening figure)
(c) 'Alborada del gracioso', central section (bars 73–4)

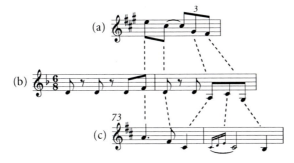

barque sur l'océan' and 'Alborada del gracioso' reveal a more specific melodic link lurking under varied rhythms (Example 4.6a–c). 'La Vallée des cloches' suggests an influence on Debussy's 'Et la lune descend sur le temple qui fut', from the second set of *Images* of 1907 (bar 6, relative to bar 12 of 'La Vallée').[13] There is some implicit documentation for this, for Viñes's diaries tell us of an afternoon *chez* Debussy in February 1906 when, after they had worked on the first series of *Images*, Debussy asked to hear Ravel's new *Miroirs*. (Some weeks later Viñes delighted Ravel in turn by playing him 'some Debussy'; this gives a possible gloss to the oft-remarked melodic affinity between 'Le Gibet' and the central part of 'Hommage à Rameau' of 1905.)[14]

Ravel's dissatisfaction with his orchestration of 'Une barque', despite the apparently orchestral nature of the original, contrasts strangely with his successful later orchestration of the brilliantly pianistic 'Alborada del gracioso' (see also Russ, 'Ravel's transcriptions of his own music': Chapter 6). Reasons are not hard to find. The rolling piano arpeggios of 'Une barque' lose much of their dynamism when orchestrated inevitably as tremolandos. Additionally, crescendos that take the piano from *pianissimo* to *fortissimo* or *fff* in two or three bars generally leave the orchestra little time to show its dynamic range (although bars 28 and 29 of the original are extended in the orchestral transcription). In short, the piece's form is so suited to the piano that orchestration really calls for some restructuring.

Ravel's orchestration of 'Alborada', undertaken twelve years later, answers this by almost doubling the length of the piece's final crescendo (bars 213–18 in the piano version). *La Valse* and *Boléro*, conceived with an orchestra in mind, corroborate this from the other side, for their long orchestral crescendos inevitably overstretch the piano's dynamic range in their solo or duo transcriptions. (To be fair to Ravel, those piano versions were primarily meant for domestic use or ballet rehearsal, unlike the unproblematic piano duo version of *Rapsodie espagnole*.)

Debussy's *L'Isle joyeuse* (1904) compares interestingly here in view of Ravel's reported (and pianistically apt) description of it as 'an orchestral reduction'. Yet Bernardo Molinari's later orchestration of the piece, based on Debussy's indications, disappoints for a similar reason to 'Une barque': that the piece's structure is essentially designed for piano. The pianistic repeated restarts of the concluding crescendos frustrate any attempt to achieve the same growth orchestrally. Comparison with the equivalent longer culminating orchestral crescendos in 'Jeux de vagues' or *Jeux*, never mind *La Valse* and *Boléro*, makes the point.

Formal and octatonic developments

Ravel's 'An autobiographical sketch' draws attention to the underlying thematic sonata scheme ('without however submitting to the classical tonal scheme') of *Jeux d'eau*, an admission which provides a vital link to the even less conventional sonata sequences of later works. Most of Ravel's larger instrumental movements exploit this, notably *Gaspard*, the outer movements of *Le Tombeau* and most of his chamber works (besides the obvious sonata forms of the *Sonatine*). Increasingly, they combine development with condensed and re-ordered recapitulation, disguising formal outlines and often suggesting an element of arch form. 'Noctuelles' and 'La Vallée des cloches' provide transitional pointers here in the way that they openly combine sonata-type recapitulations with ternary form and arch form.

From the early 1900s, the octatonic scale also plays an increasing role in Ravel's vocabulary. Consisting of alternating tones and semitones, this scale embraces combinations like the C–F♯ triads of *Jeux d'eau*, as well as triads a minor third apart and major/minor mixtures within a key. For Ravel, it also provided a welcome alternative to the whole-tone scale, as an equally effective way of undercutting tonality and moving freely between keys, with the added bonus of generous semitone clashes. (Bars 157–8, towards the end of the 'Forlane' in *Le Tombeau*, neatly contrast whole-tone with octatonic colours; see Example 4.10c below.) Example 4.7a, one of many prominent octatonic structures in *Gaspard*, shows how typically this scale accommodates Ravel's appoggiatura-based harmony: each chord fits one distinct octatonic collection, while the passage's underlying functional logic becomes clear if we resolve the top two voices up a semitone (Example 4.7b). (The result could pass for César Franck, as it also could with just the top voice taken down.) An even more spine-tingling octatonic sequence comes from bars 23–4 of 'Le Gibet', overlaying a G^7 chord with triads of E, C♯ and B♭. (Had Ravel noticed a surprisingly similar com-

Example 4.7 *Gaspard de la nuit*: octatonic structures
(a) 'Scarbo' (bars 121–3)

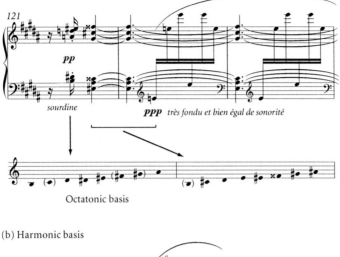

Octatonic basis

(b) Harmonic basis

bination in the first movement (bars 91–2) of Chopin's Sonata Op. 35?)[15]
Although Debussy's octatonic usage at that time tended to favour less dissonant sequences, as in 'Jardins sous la pluie' (bars 37–42) or 'Reflets dans
l'eau' (bars 20–1), examples such as 'Des pas sur la neige' and 'Ce qu'a vu le
Vent d'Ouest' do more closely reflect Ravel (compare bars 21–2 of 'Des pas
sur la neige' with bars 26–7 of 'Le Gibet').[16]

Form and motive in *Gaspard de la nuit*

The three towering pieces of *Gaspard de la nuit*, composed in 1908 and
published in 1909, relate to various models, which they characteristically
outbid in various ways. 'Scarbo' suggests a heady mix of Liszt Mephisto
Waltz, Chopin Scherzo, Saint-Saëns's *Danse macabre*, Chabrier's *España*
and Balakirev's *Islamey*, while 'Le Gibet' links to the tolling B♭ in the
'Marche funèbre' of Chopin's Sonata Op. 35. 'Ondine' echoes, not least
through its key, Liszt's *Waldesrauschen*, Debussy's 'Reflets dans l'eau' and
'Clair de lune' (both published in 1905), plus the expansive Nocturne No.
6 of Ravel's teacher Fauré. (Compare especially bars 79–80 of 'Ondine'

Table 4.1 Thematic sequence of 'Ondine'

Motive	a	b	b1	b2	c	d	e
Exposition (bb.)	0	2	10	16	22	32	45
Development	–	42, 47	–	–	–	52	(45), 50, (57)
Recapitulation	89	80	84	88	72	66	57

The motives are closely interlinked: *a* accompanies *b* and *b1*; *b1* is derived from *b* (bars 5–6), *b2* from *b* (bar 4); *c* comprises two motives permanently linked together, the first of which (bar 22) is an intervallic augmentation of *b2*; and *d* repeats the second element of *b1*. Bar 88 also refers back texturally to bar 55. The opening incomplete bar is counted here, as in the Peters Edition, as '0'.

with bars 30–1 of 'Clair de lune', bearing in mind 'les mornes rayons de la lune' in the opening stanza of Bertrand's poem.)

The basic texture of 'Ondine', however – a long entrancing melody spun out over rippling harmonies – looks back to models like Schubert's *Impromptu* in G♭ (D. 899 No. 3) and Chopin's *Etude* Op. 25 No. 1 in A♭ – until that sudden cackle of laughter on the last page gives at least Ondine's game away. The laughter may also be Ravel's, for the piece suggests a parody of Chopin's *Etude* in A♭ in the same special sense that several paintings of Edouard Manet (one of Ravel's idols) are known to be parodies of classical masters.[17] Besides the textural affinity between the two pieces, the parallel becomes exact at the *appassionato* climax of each piece, where for a beat 'Ondine' (bar 66) quotes directly from Chopin's *Etude*, a semitone higher (and with hands an octave farther out). The musical parallel continues, for Chopin's *Etude* then gradually subsides with a texture of octaves echoing quietly across the right hand, just as 'Ondine' does at bars 75–8, before ending in a sudden flurry of arpeggios that equally suggest a ripple of laughter and a shower of spray.

'Ondine' and 'Le Gibet' push even Ravelian sonata form to the verge of unidentifiability. 'Ondine', really a sonata form by stealth, conceals its outlines by closely interlinking its themes, virtually reversing their final order of return, and dovetailing the development section into both the exposition and the recapitulation (see Table 4.1). Only in retrospect can it be seen that, by bar 47, a characteristic Ravel development section (alternating two operatically contrasted themes) is already under way, and that, in bars 57–65, development turns imperceptibly into recapitulation. The latter aspect is quietly underlined by the enharmonic tonic at bar 57, the only sounding tonic between the piece's first four and last three bars. (Additionally, the added seventh at bar 57 links to the sevenths at both bar 14 and bar 2; bars 14–15 differ crucially from bars 2–3 by omitting the tonic except as a final passing note.) At the end, Ravel emphasises the arch shape by embedding the piece's opening figuration: G♯–A–G♯–G♯–A–G♯ –G♯–A in the arpeggios of the last three bars.[18]

'Le Gibet' also masks its quietly climactic development section (bars 28–34, mainly exploiting the 'sigh' from bar 7), starting it within a crotchet of the piece's half-way point and then leading it straight into an abbreviated recapitulation of bars 12–24. A final recapitulation of bars 1–11 in reverse thematic order again leaves us with a strong sense of arch form. Surprisingly little attempt has been made to analyse this piece's ingenious tonal basis: essentially, how Ravel manages to keep us on tenterhooks for so long at such a slow tempo. A strong clue lies in Debussy's closely related prelude 'Voiles' of a year later, whose B♭ bass ostinato sounds the same rhythm as the bell of 'Le Gibet', almost as if to set us on the scent. Since Ravel's piece is structurally the more recondite of the two, it makes explanation easier if we start with 'Voiles'.

The one clear tonality in 'Voiles' is E♭ minor (the piece's pentatonic climax and the repeated cadences that follow), since the surrounding whole-tone passages *ipso facto* can define no key. Under the whole-tone surface, though, the arrival at E♭ minor is firmly prepared, for the preceding two-and-a-half pages constantly reinforce the dominant seventh: B♭ (bass pedal), D and G♯/A♭. Even at the crucial cadence (bars 41–2), Debussy veils the tonality by holding it in second inversion (like the ending of 'Le Gibet'), and by chromatically splitting the 'leading-note', D, to E♭ and D♭, rather than resolving it in the prosaic classical manner.

Ravel's ploy is a variant of this. Although 'Le Gibet' appears to divulge its E♭ minor tonality from the outset by its key signature, the repetition of B♭ and the first chord, where is the tonic chord? Where are any identifiable concords? A search soon reveals why and how this piece holds us in suspense (in keeping with its title). Ravel's tonal strategy here has two strands. The first is his constant use of appoggiaturas, a technique he later described relative to *Valses nobles*.[19] The first harmonic entry merely implies the piece's tonality (bar 3), leaving us waiting for the appoggiatura, F, to resolve up to G♭. Half a bar later G♭ duly arrives, but the rest of the texture moves in parallel, thwarting the resolution. Each time the melody and texture return to home position (bars 4 and 5), back comes that unyielding appoggiatura, F. In bar 15 comes another chance, now with an upper A♭ appoggiatura; again the subsequent parallel chord motion thwarts the resolution. This continuing quiet drama ends the piece in reverse: bar 46 returns us to the A♭ appoggiatura, bar 47 resolves it to G♭ but renders it ineffective by removing the rest of the tonic harmony and, when the latter returns in bar 48, the crucial voice has meanwhile continued down another degree to F. We are back where we started, and the piece fades out just as it faded in.

Example 4.8 *Gaspard de la nuit*, 'Le Gibet'
(a) Bars 6–7

(b) Bars 10–11

Ravel's second strand of tonal strategy, more Moorishly chromatic, is centred on F♭, a semitone from the (implied) tonic and a tritone from the B♭ ostinato. Bars 6–7 emphasise both relationships, letting the F♭ bite into some of the piece's very few consonances (Example 4.8a – cf. also bar 32 of 'Scarbo').[20] F♭ goes on to haunt much of the piece, sometimes spelt as E, sometimes acting as a sort of 'second-degree' appoggiatura to F (as across bars 6–7 and 11–12, and then in reverse at bars 28–9). From this comes one of Ravel's subtlest coups at bars 10–11, which repeat bars 6–7 but with F♭ now added to the first chord of bar 10 (Example 4.8b). This new voice, moving in parallel with the others, results in two fleeting E♭ minor triads (bars 10–11) – but in contexts that rob the chord of its tonic value, forcing it into the role of appoggiatura to the following diminished chord. Ravel compounds this ironic reversal of classical functions by alighting for just one quaver on E♭ major – almost like a final ray of hope then dashed by the following minor and diminished chords.

Around this, like a ghost scene, unfold the motions of classical sequence. The first tonal excursion prepares a tonic cadence (via the dominant ninth at the end of bars 12, 13 and 14), only to be balked by the persistent A♭ (and F) at bar 15. Bars 17–19 repeat the sequence a fourth higher, as if to move to the subdominant, A♭ minor, only for bar 20 to take off with other ideas above the A♭ bass resolution. Bars 35–9, as condensed recapitulation of bars 12–19, balance this by preparing implicitly a

Table 4.2 Thematic sequence of 'Scarbo'

Motive	a	a1	b	b1	c	d	e
Exposition (bb.)	1	32, 110	52	65	80	94	121
Development	314	–	215	–	–	256, 318, 345	289, 303, 366
Recapitulation	395	386	431	437	448	–	477
Coda	617	580	593	–	–	–	586, 602

All motives are closely related by an abrupt rising semitone or tone, creating audible motivic continuity across transitions like bars 210–15 and 377–87. As in 'Ondine', development and recapitulation are so mixed that the labels above are more for convenient reference than for exact definition.

cadence to a dominant, Bb minor (Chopin's 'Marche funèbre'?), only to be balked again at bar 40 by our Fb that stubbornly refuses to resolve to F. On the way there, we hear the only other Eb minor triads of the whole piece, robbed again of their tonal function by the persistent bass C underneath. The whole structure is as uncompromising as the gallows, and if the analytical language above keeps veering towards the picturesque, it is because of how strongly the piece's form acts out its story. It also gives an apt context to the strong echo of *Tristan und Isolde* at bar 12. (For more on 'Le Gibet', see Woodley, 'Casadesus's recordings of "Le Gibet" (1922 and 1951)': Chapter 10.)

The form of 'Scarbo' is equally programmatic, acting out the poem's recurring insomniac fantasy, combined with a progressive tightening of thumbscrews that gradually accelerates the piece to no less than twenty-seven times its opening speed![21] Ravel's expansive sonata form (see Table 4.2), more explicit than in 'Ondine' or 'Le Gibet', brings the piece to three powerful *Mephisto*-esque culminations, the first two a tritone apart on F♯ and C (bars 204 and 366). Only at the final one in B major (bar 563) is the tonal function of the previous two defined retrospectively (dominant and Neapolitan, or phrygian supertonic).

Those keys are carefully prepared by the second of the piece's three main motives (Example 4.9a; bars 52–4), an idea that would unambiguously divulge the closing tonality were it not for the irritant of the mirrored semitonal appoggiaturas, G and F; if only they would resolve to F♯ ... 150 bars later, the exposition's culmination at last achieves this resolution (Example 4.9b; bars 203–6) – only for the C♯ above it to split into C and D, restarting the process (Example 4.9c; bars 215–16). This, in turn, is finally resolved at the last climax (Example 4.9d; bars 561–3): the descending bass line picks up the same C and D as its last two notes, before resolving them this time downwards to B – only for the F♯ above to split into

Example 4.9 *Gaspard de la nuit*, 'Scarbo': motive *b*
(a) bars 52–4
(b) bars 203–6
(c) bars 215–16
(d) bars 561–3

F and G, taking us back to where we were at bar 52. The bass approach to the final climax sums this all up: by following a complete octatonic octave descent of A–G♯–F♯–F–E♭–D–C–B, it first retraces the approach to the piece's first climax (A–G♯), continues down as if to the C of the second climax and finally sinks that extra 'dungeon step' to B.

All this can hardly have been lost on Debussy: his first book of *Préludes* makes repeated structural use of chromatic semitone splits of the type seen here in 'Scarbo', and his obvious harmonic fascination with *Gaspard* emerges equally from the quotation of bars 24–5 of 'Le Gibet' in bars 29–32 of the fourth of his *Six épigraphes antiques* of 1914.[22] Stravinsky's *Petrushka*, too, resonates with both the first and last page of 'Scarbo', in the former case via Ravel's explicit intention for the D♯ tremolandos to sound 'comme un tambour' – 'like a drum'.[23] (Anyone in doubt about Ravel's early impact on Stravinsky need only compare the end of 'Kashchei's dance' from *L'Oiseau de feu* with the end of *Rapsodie espagnole*.)

Another essential feature of 'Scarbo' is its mix of waltz and flamenco (most dramatic from bar 314). A stormier cousin of the fourth of the *Valses nobles*, the waltz in 'Scarbo' launches itself from the top of the second page (the 'quelle horreur' motive), followed by the flamenco or *jota* element from bar 51 (mixing rhythms from Chabrier's *España*[24] and the Scherzo of Chopin's Sonata Op. 35). Recognition of this alternation (with more waltz from bar 65 and new flamenco material from bar 94) is vital, for the *jota* material, far from being a speed test for repeated notes, continues the waltz tempo, and any dislocation of tempo between them shreds Ravel's larger-scale play on speed. The link to Chabrier reaches its focus at the dominant pedal that launches the approach to the final culmination. From bar 478 onwards Ravel's left-hand figuration comes note-for-note, at the same tempo, and in one case in the same key, from the equivalent points in a *jota* and a waltz: *España* (in Chabrier's two-piano arrangement) and the 'Fête polonaise' from *Le Roi malgré lui* (in Chabrier's piano reduction).[25] The links are so thematically and structurally close that Chabrier's excellent metronome indications in his two-piano version of *España* can work just as usefully for 'Scarbo' – 80 as the basic tempo (the first page's quaver and the second page's bar), with a slight kick up to 88 for the culminating crescendo (bar 477 onwards).

Operatic and orchestral resonances

The dark-edged operatic humour that can then emerge from 'Scarbo' should not surprise us, especially given Ravel's love of Mozart. Even if *L'Enfant et les sortilèges* postdates all of Ravel's solo piano music, knowing his operas is arguably as vital to playing his piano music as the equivalent in Mozart. 'Scarbo' opens and ends with a clear case, the rising semitone-plus-fifth that dominates the second half of *L'Enfant,* from the Cats' duet (Fig. 97) onwards (to the supremely apt words 'Où es-tu?' at the start of the 'Valse américaine': Fig. 107). Among many other examples, both *A la manière* pieces of 1913 come to life as miniature operatic scenes; in 'Laideronnette' of *Ma Mère l'Oye* (from bar 33) we can almost hear Arithmétique from *L'Enfant,* jabbering 'Quatre et quat' dix-huit!' (Figs. 80 and 93); and the ravishing Garden Scene of *L'Enfant* (Fig. 100 onwards) is the key to several of the *Valses nobles et sentimentales* – notably the seventh, the only one lacking a clear tempo marking, for which the closely related 'Danse des Rainettes' (Fig. 113 and Fig. 123^{-5}) provides the excellent indication of $\downarrow = 208$.

Reference between *L'Enfant* and the *Valses nobles* (acknowledging also the orchestral score and balletic scenario, retitled *Adélaïde, ou Le Langage des fleurs*), has another use, for, unlike even *Gaspard* – which almost plays itself from the score once its technical hurdles are mastered – the *Valses nobles* require a high degree of operatic and orchestral voicing, well beyond what a score can indicate.[26]

Sophistication in *Le Tombeau de Couperin*

Probably the most vital orchestration for pianists is that of the 'Forlane' in *Le Tombeau de Couperin,* the suite in classical style ('Prélude', 'Fugue', 'Forlane', 'Rigaudon', 'Menuet' and 'Toccata') composed across 1914–17, then partly orchestrated in 1919 and subsequently produced as a ballet. Alfred Cortot went so far as to argue that this music found its definitive form only in Ravel's orchestral score,[27] and comparison of the two (structurally identical) versions of the 'Forlane' quickly reveals the orchestral score's more accurate indication of breathing, articulation and sometimes voicing, by means of added rests and shorter slurs. A more specific warning for performers concerns the metronome indications commonly printed in *Le Tombeau:* absent from early prints, they were apparently added after Ravel's death by Marguerite Long.[28] Besides two obviously over-slow indications (for the 'Fugue' with its subtle glint of jazz, and the 'Menuet'), her very fast indication for the 'Toccata' risks over-stressing both it and the performer, especially at the low dynamics which Ravel indicates for most of the piece.[29]

An interesting perspective here comes from one of the most popular toccatas in French piano repertoire of the time, Daquin's 'Le Coucou'. Besides the shared key of E minor, 'Le Coucou' provides a natural tempo (at the piano) that carries effortlessly across to Ravel's 'Toccata'. Extending the link to Debussy broadens this perspective farther, for not only is E minor the key of one of Debussy's most popular toccatas, 'Jardins sous la pluie', but the opening bar of his 'Toccata' in *Pour le piano* also strongly recalls a repeated cadential gesture in 'Le Coucou' (bar 23). Incidentally, surviving second proofs of *Le Tombeau* (in the archives of Durand, Paris) show that the 'Prélude' was once entitled 'Prologue', that Ravel originally supplied then removed some fingering (shades of Debussy's *Etudes*), and that several of the tempo indications were added only at proof stage.

The apparently classical outlines of *Le Tombeau* form only a thin veil over its compositional sophistication. Is the opening key of the 'Prélude' E minor or G major? Bars 1 and 3 suggest the former, bars 2 and 4 the latter. The first-time repeat bars opt clearly for G major, yet the piece ends in E minor. The rest of *Le Tombeau* plays on this dichotomy (notably the opening of the 'Toccata'), resolving it only with the final triumphant E major of the 'Toccata'. (The orchestral suite adds a further twist by ending in C with the 'Rigaudon', retrospectively giving a different cadential value to the E minor and G major of the preceding movements.) Ravel matches this with similar plays on metre. If bars 1–2 of the 'Prélude' obviously follow a strong–weak or antecedent–consequent sequence, repeated in bars 3–4, what about the equivalent-looking bars 11–12? The *agent provocateur* here is bars 9–10: by attaching itself thematically to bars 7–8, bar 9 throws bar 10 (a reprise of bar 2) into an antecedent role towards bar 11 (a reprise of bar 1), and similarly bar 12 towards bar 13. The Suite is full of such touches, like the feint treble entry at bar 43 of the 'Fugue' that makes the real entry a bar later sound like a consequent, and this knife-edge ambiguity plays a constant part in holding our rhythmic and structural interest.

This whole technique involves a wider context. In 1975, Brian Newbould showed how the 'Pantoum' of Ravel's Piano Trio follows the structure of Malayan *pantun* poetry.[30] Many French poets were attracted to this genre; a famous example is Baudelaire's 'Harmonie du soir' (a poem best known to pianists for its third line, 'Les sons et les parfums tournent dans l'air du soir'). The basis of a *pantun* poem is two-fold: each four-line stanza is made up of two contrasted couplets, and the second and fourth line of each stanza reappear as the first and third of the next stanza. The poem thus maintains two alternating strands of narrative (like Ravel's 'Pantoum'), and the two 'consequent' lines (lines 2 and 4) of each stanza become antecedent lines in the next stanza, in a constantly dancing form. Ravel's technique in *Le Tombeau* consistently follows this second aspect.[31] (Additionally, a *pantun* often starts and ends with the same line – though not 'Harmonie du soir' – and this invites comparison with the major seventh that starts and ends *Jeux d'eau*, the mirrored start and close of

'Ondine' or 'Le Gibet,' or the identical start and close of the 'Rigaudon' in *Le Tombeau* and the finale of the Concerto in G.)

At first glance the eight bars that open the 'Menuet' of *Le Tombeau* seem a clear antecedent–consequent 4 + 4 sequence. But there is a cadential finality hidden in bar 4 that reverses the classical norm (in which the consequent provides the conclusive cadence, as in bars 1–8 of Mozart's 'Jupiter' Symphony). Ravel plays on this at the close of the opening section of the 'Menuet' (bars 29–32), where the melody of bars 1–4 accordingly returns, but now as a closing consequent. As the recapitulation moves into the coda (bars 101–6), Ravel follows this through by quoting the antecedent–consequent melodic line of bars 1–6, but in a consequent–antecedent setting, thus gracefully carrying the music over the join into the coda.

The recapitulation of the 'Menuet' uses the same technique on a larger scale, by combining the last line of the 'Musette' (as consequent) with the opening melodic eight bars of the 'Menuet' (as structural antecedent). When Ravel did this almost twenty years earlier at the same point in the *Menuet antique*, the device was essentially a feint, heralding the obvious recapitulation; here the combined melodies are a structural *fait accompli*: we subsequently arrive, as we think, at the moment of recapitulation (bar 81), only to discover that we are already eight bars into it.

The 'Forlane', notated throughout in 6/8 metre, applies the same play within the bar, by opening with a first beat that can equally be heard as an upbeat to the accented dissonance on the half-bar; the phrasing and accentuation of the next seven bars maintain this ambiguity. Seven bars from the end (bar 156ff.), Ravel makes the point explicit by recapitulating the piece's opening beat as a notated anacrusis; in between he exploits the ambiguity in ways that create a constant rhythmic intrigue. Ravel's precedent here is the Couperin 'Forlane' that he transcribed, whose strong beat sounds throughout on the half-bar (for further comparison of these forlanes, see Kelly, 'Musical engagement with the past': Chapter 1). Ravel's 'Forlane' does the same throughout the first and second episodes (bars 29–54 and 63–95, counting first- and second-time repeat bars consecutively, as in the Peters Edition).

Between those two episodes comes an abbreviated ritornello, consisting of the metrically ambiguous bars 1–8 of the 'Forlane' with one playful addition: halfway through the ritornello (bar 59) Ravel points up its inherent metrical ambiguity by adding an imitative left-hand entry at the half-bar. All this allows the metrical momentum of the preceding first episode (the strong beat sounding on the half-bar) to carry itself through effortlessly to the second episode. The second episode promptly adds variety by completing its short first part with a hemiola effect of two sounding units of 9/8 metre from bar 67, beat 2, through to bar 70, beat 1 (Example 4.10a). This

Example 4.10 *Le Tombeau de Couperin*, 'Forlane': metrical sophistication
(a) bars 66–71

(b) bars 92–101

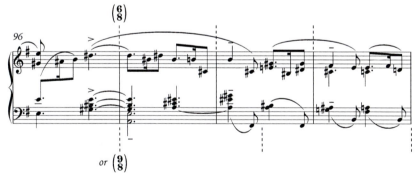

Example 4.10 (*cont.*)
(c) bars 155–62

decorative effect reveals its structural purpose at the end of the episode (Example 4.10b; bars 92–101): the momentum of the recapitulated hemiola now continues over into the ritornello, both bridging the transition and swinging the music back into synchronisation with the barline. Some pleasing ambiguity continues, not least because the music allows a continuing impression of 9/8 metre (from bar 92, beat 2) through to the left hand's imitative entry four bars later (bar 100). Thereafter, the music settles back audibly into 6/8, though without defining clearly which is the strong beat. Ravel lets this ambiguity persist through the final episode and coda, until the piece's last six bars (bars 157–62) finally settle the matter – by sounding clearly in 9/8 (Example 4.10c).

The 'Rigaudon' leads us a different dance again by alternating phrases of varying lengths with its opening two-bar cadential gesture. Everything sounds unpredictably irregular, and only a counting of bars reveals that, in fact, the larger bar groupings all conform to multiples of sixteen or twelve. The piece's central section varies this again, by giving left and right hand different bar groupings (the left hand clearly starts with two 4 + 4 + 8 groups, but not the right hand). The right hand's fourth bar in this section, for example, sounds equally as an antecedent to its fifth bar; its twelfth bar audibly links sequentially through to three bars later, though the starting point of the sequence is indeterminable; and on the heels of that sequence comes a pair of hemiola-like sounding 3/4 metrical units (bars 50–2). Most surprisingly, the totality adds up to an innocent-looking sixteen-bar group (followed by another one with a different internal structure again). Subtlest of all, it proves impossible to divide each sixteen-bar group into viable smaller groupings.

These 3/4 metrical patterns can be compared to *pantun* in two ways. Firstly, they turn weak beats (consequents) into perceived strong ones (antecedents) and vice versa. Secondly, the embedded 3/4 patterns in the 2/4 background parallel the the three-line repetitions embedded in the couplet sequence of a *pantun*. The closest musical ancestor, though, is Chabrier, whose piano piece 'Tourbillon' runs in constant four- and eight-bar groups disrupted internally by hemiolas and other more irregular metrical divisions. Equally pertinent, Chabrier's 'Danse villageoise' (from the same collection of *Pièces pittoresques*) opens with an eleven-bar phrase that is indivisible into viable smaller elements (for example, bars 1–4 initially suggest a four-bar group until bar 5 retrospectively turns bar 4 into its antecedent).

Motivic and geometric extensions

A related rhythmic play informs the earlier 'Alborada del gracioso' from *Miroirs*, and helps explain an intriguing anecdote, according to which Ravel once showed Maurice Delage how the piece's structure was 'as strict as that of a Bach fugue'.[32] The piece's first section opens out in three expanding paragraphs, bars 1–11, 12–29 and 30–70. Motive *a* begins the piece and almost immediately (at bar 5) forms an antecedent to the consequent motive *b* (Example 4.11a). Motive *b* then opens paragraph two as antecedent to the consequent *c* (Example 4.11b), which accordingly opens paragraph three as antecedent to the consequent *d* (Example 4.11c). Motive *d* in turn reappears immediately after the piece's central section, as an antecedent to launch the recapitulation at bar 166 (Example 4.11d). This enchanting surprise, after several bars that lead us to expect a regular reprise in D major, is therefore built absolutely logically into the sequence.

Figure 4.1 ('Motivic appearances') shows the ingenious geometry of this sequence. The initial planting of motives as consequents (or as a structural close at bar 22), measured by constant completed units of 6/8 metre, sets in motion a sequence of numbers (5, 8, 13 and 21) that follow the Fibonacci series, as a close approximation of Golden Section.[33] The return of the motives as antecedents then sets off the same proportional sequence on a larger scale, following the numbers of the related Lucas series (11, 18, 29, etc.), and also involving the return of motive *a* as a structural close at bar 22. In this way, the beginning of paragraph three at bar 30 divides the whole extract by Golden Section, as does the entry of the

Example 4.11 *Miroirs*, 'Alborada del gracioso': motivic development
(a) Motive *a* (antecedent), bars 1, 3 (5, 7)   Motive *b* (consequent), bars 6, 8

(b) Second paragraph
Motive *b* (antecedent), bars 12, 13   Motive *c* (consequent), bar 14

(c) Third paragraph
Motive *c* (antecedent), bars 31, 32   Motive *d* (consequent), bar 33

(d) Recapitulation
Motive *d* (antecedent), bar 166

flamenco sub-episode at bar 43; the beginning of paragraph two at bar 12 marks a similar Golden Section (11 : 18 units) on the way to paragraph three. As it progresses, the sequence is compressed from the theoretical Lucas numbers of 47 and 76 to an actual 46 and 74 (and from a theoretical 34 to 32.5); far from invalidating the proportional logic, this makes dramatic sense of the piece's increasing urgency.[34] This proportional structure extends throughout the piece, and is even allowed for in Ravel's changed dimensions in the orchestral version; it also adds an interesting gloss to his repeated mention of a childhood liking for mathematics.[35]

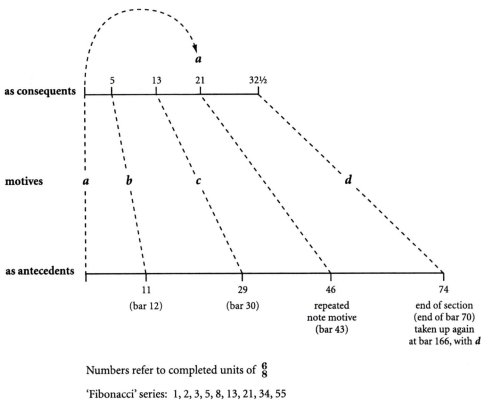

Numbers refer to completed units of $\frac{6}{8}$

'Fibonacci' series: 1, 2, 3, 5, 8, 13, 21, 34, 55

'Lucas' series: 3, 4, 7, 11, 18, 29, 47, 76

Figure 4.1 *Miroirs*, 'Alborada del gracioso': motivic appearances

How characteristic this is of Ravel's thinking can also be seen by comparison with 'Ondine' from *Gaspard*. As already seen in Table 4.1 above, motives *b1* and *b2* in 'Ondine' are consequent offshoots of *b* which promptly return as antecedents to launch new melodic waves. We begin to sense some of the ways in which Ravel, in 'Ondine', managed to spin out such a long, apparently seamless melody so resistant to cut-and-dried analysis.

Ravel's later years

Ravel's lack of solo piano music in his last twenty years may be attributed to two main factors: firstly, his more traumatised post-war years were generally less productive than his supremely fertile first decade (characterised pianistically by *Jeux d'eau*, the *Sonatine* and *Gaspard*); secondly, he tended to focus his remaining energies on works for larger forces – of mixed instrumentation – often including a dramatic or textual dimension: the concerted chamber music of the *Chansons madécasses*, the ballet projects of *La Valse* and *Boléro* and the operatic triumph of *L'Enfant*.

This absence of later solo piano writing prompts a brief mention of his two piano concertos composed across 1929–31. That he gave a single hand more notes to play in the Concerto for the Left Hand than both hands in the Concerto in G is no surprise; the contrasting characters of the two concertos also relate to two distinct threads of his earlier piano writing, the classical traits of *Le Tombeau* against the more romantic figurations of *Miroirs* and *Gaspard*. The rising waves of arpeggios in the first solo entry of the Concerto for the Left Hand, for example, recall 'Une barque sur l'océan' from *Miroirs* and even the early Sonata for Violin and Piano of 1897.

Pianists may note Ravel's careful beaming of the piano part at two strategic locations in the Concerto in G. In the opening page of the 'Adagio', Ravel's left-hand beaming in constant quaver pairs guards against any 'oom-pah-pah' effect (the gentle undercurrent of 6/8 metre here echoes a similar effect in Chabrier's song *Tes yeux bleus*). The other place is the first solo entry of the finale, where Ravel's beaming marks out exactly the melody the solo bassoon has to play when launching the movement's recapitulation 153 bars later – a factor that bears importantly on tempo.[36] This parallel – plus the four bars of introduction in each case before the solo takes off – disguises another structural coup, for although the movement's binary outline incorporates an entirely restructured second half (blending development into reprise), it still manages to divide exactly into 153 : 153 bars (at Fig. 14).[37] This becomes part of a larger geometry, for the finale's dimensions can be measured directly against the preceding 'Adagio', by a tempo equivalence of $\flat = 72$ in the 'Adagio' to bar $= 72$–6 in the finale (taking Perlemuter's suggested tempo). Six bars of the finale thus correspond to one of the 'Adagio' – a suggestive figure since the finale's total of 306 bars is conveniently a multiple of six. If the total length of the finale is mirrored backwards from the end of the 'Adagio', by counting back 306 quavers or 51 bars, it takes us exactly to the main turning-point of the 'Adagio' at bar 58 (Fig. 4). Whether this was planned or fortuitous, it can do performers no harm to be aware of such a large-scale rhythm.

Vlado Perlemuter has often opined that a major reason why Ravel's piano music holds its place so well in the repertoire is its formal strength.[38] The more we observe the music, the more richly this observation resonates.

5 Harmony in the chamber music

MARK DEVOTO

Ravel's popular, if somewhat misleading, identification as an 'impression-ist' composer depends on three categories of his achievement: orchestral music, piano music and vocal music, including operas as well as songs. His chamber music is of another stripe, revealing another all-important side of his musical persona: it is classically based absolute music, without ties to texts, literary references or descriptive titles. In this regard as in so many others, he is like Debussy, but, while Debussy's chamber music frames his career at beginning and end, Ravel's chamber music follows his career throughout, providing significant landmarks at different stages.[1]

Ravel's chamber music, like his piano music, inclines to formal variety, yet always as concisely and precisely as the classical masters whom he so much admired. One never finds the formal adventurousness and only seldom the textural experimentation that characterise the musical 'impressionism' of his most radical piano works like *Gaspard de la nuit*. Yet the essential wholeness of Ravel's personal style is never in doubt; the highly individual melodic idiom and the integrity of his harmonic lan-guage are unified between the chamber music and all the other works, in continuous evolution from the beginning of his maturity to the end of his career.

In its instrumentation and instrumental sound, Ravel's chamber music is often a reflection, though of course on a smaller scale, of his search for large timbral dimensions, as though the colouristic richness of his orches-tral works could find an effective tableau in a chamber setting. The String Quartet and the *Introduction et allegro* have striking passages of very full and brilliant sound that one can easily imagine in a full orchestration (a point endorsed by the Tortelier orchestration of the Piano Trio). The *Trois poèmes de Stéphane Mallarmé* (1913) certainly counts as a chamber work in which the resources of the 'impressionist' orchestra are recreated with just nine players, but the dynamic range is small, and the instrumental colours mobilised with great subtlety in support of the highly expressive harmony. The contrast thirteen years later with the *Chansons madécasses* could not be sharper, with voice supported only by flute (doubling piccolo), cello and piano; this work – the very antithesis of 'impressionist' heterophony – shows variously a spare linearity, a percussive density and a thin, almost vanishing texture. The large-scale counterpart, orchestrationally speaking, of the *Chansons madécasses* is the opera *L'Enfant et les sortilèges*, completed the previous year (1925), which is a panorama of Ravel's orchestral styles. The resplendent richness of *Daphnis et Chloé* forms part of the sound of *L'Enfant*, but so does a chamber music-like vocal support: the two oboes with solo double-bass harmonics at the beginning (up to Fig. 2); the Princess's song in two-part counterpoint with a solo flute (Fig. 63^{-3}); unaccompanied string solos with clarinets before the Cats' duet (Fig. 95). At one point, the Mother's voice is accompanied by a solo string quartet (Fig. 4), as dramatically and stylistically striking an instrumental function as the solo string quartet that appears fleetingly in the second movement of Mahler's Fourth Symphony.

Early Sonata for Violin and Piano

This student work, a single movement of 1897, was first published only in 1975, during the Ravel centennial year. It shows the twenty-two-year-old Ravel as a less accomplished composer than Debussy was at the same age when he won the Prix de Rome. As a sonata form it suffers from a disproportionately long and slow-moving development section; by way of compensation, the recapitulation is nicely varied and abbreviated. The harmonic language, on the other hand, is already original and well developed, with many harbingers of Ravel's later work. Most striking is the A minor tonality alternating with major, regularly inflected with the dorian raised sixth, F♯, and the phrygian/Neapolitan flattened second, B♭. Orenstein has pointed out the melodic resemblance of the opening melody to a passage in the first movement of the Piano Trio, composed seventeen years later;[2] the harmonic resemblance is even more remarkable. At the same time, the very identification of A minor in this work points to Ravel's obsession, one might even say, with a characteristic A minor style that recurs in the 'Pavane de la Belle au bois dormant' of *Ma Mère l'Oye*, the Sonata for Violin and Cello, the Scherzo movement of the String Quartet and the Piano Trio.

Harmony and tradition in the String Quartet

Even the very title of Debussy's masterpiece of 1893, 'First String Quartet in G minor, Opus 10', had proclaimed an allegiance to the classical tradition in chamber music, and this may well have impressed Debussy's fellow composers in the Société Nationale de Musique (SN) even if they were not to realise that Debussy had never before and would never again use opus numbers. In 1893, of course, Debussy was nearly ten years out of the Conservatoire but still relatively unknown. Ten years later, the twenty-eight-year-old Ravel, a late bloomer at the Conservatoire, found much to admire in Debussy's brilliant manipulation of sonata form and four-movement cyclic procedures. As Debussy's had done ten years before, Ravel's String Quartet (1902–3; rev. 1910) served to establish his reputation decisively at the beginning of his public career.

The outward features of Ravel's modelling on Debussy's Quartet are obvious enough: the flying pizzicato in the Scherzo; the beginning of the third movement in the key of the second, with an early modulation to a remote main key; the pervasive cyclic treatment of themes.[3] Yet, today, it is the mere fact of Debussy and Ravel writing string quartets at all, ten years apart, that causes the two works to be paired so frequently on the same recording. (César Franck's String Quartet in D major, a cyclic model for Debussy's Quartet, is the only other French string quartet composed a quarter-century on either side of 1900 that is widely performed today.) Debussy supposedly said to Ravel, 'Don't change a single note of your Quartet', but this remark, if true, was surely more than a flattered response to sincere imitation, because Debussy, even recognising Ravel's obvious admiration, certainly would also have recognised how independent, and how different from his own, was Ravel's Quartet.

In dedicating the Quartet 'to my dear master Gabriel Fauré', Ravel acknowledged his debt in the music itself; the first eight bars of the first movement could easily have been composed by Fauré.[4] Nevertheless, the beginning of the Quartet reveals much about Ravel's classical sense of harmony, and it is above all in harmony, even with a modern vocabulary, that Ravel shows the classical ancestry that marks his mature style. Much more strongly than in Debussy, Ravel's music is characterised above all by classical triad-based root progression and bass line, notwithstanding the abundant appearances of non-classical succession, with parallel chords, remote juxtapositions and chords whose essential structure is complicated by non-harmonic notes.

The opening bars (Example 5.1) can be heard as a succession of separate root functions changing every crotchet, with sevenths and ninths entering or leaving more or less without regard to classical stepwise resolution; but this would be a narrow view. In practice, one hears this mellow passage as harmony regulated by the primary tonal chords of I, IV and V and by the inexorability of the 'voice-leading'[5] in the second violin and cello, in parallel tenths. The melody line in the soprano, with its abundance of small skips, shows the freest voice-leading in this texture; when the tonic note appears relatively infrequently in the melody, it is not as part of the tonic triad.

Example 5.1 String Quartet, I (bars 1–4)

Example 5.2 String Quartet, I (bars 55–7)

The second theme, beginning at bar 55 (Example 5.2; Letter D), is treated even more characteristically. The underlying harmony is the tonic of D minor, but the melody, typically for Ravel, stresses something other than the tonic degree in a succession of repeated small motives; here the emphasised tone is E, the ninth above D; D itself appears in this melody only in passing. When the same melody appears in exactly the same register in the recapitulation (from bar 183), it is harmonised in F major, the two bass notes, C and F (instead of A and D), and the E now the seventh above F. Examined in isolation, this melody might well be heard as defining A minor with a phrygian flattened second (B♭), but this beloved aural image does not appear with A minor harmonisation in this Quartet.

Other characteristic harmonic devices of Ravel's mature style make important appearances in this movement. One is the inverted ninth sonority. A few paradigms will show the principle of several related sonorities (Example 5.3). In form *a*, we see an ordinary diminished seventh chord whose seventh, G, is replaced by an appoggiatura, A; the A, on the other hand, is identical with the missing root of the complete ninth chord. Because the ninth in this sonority, B♭, is now below the root, we call it an inverted ninth chord, drawing attention to the fact that this position is normally prohibited in classical harmony. Rewriting the third of the chord, C♯, enharmonically as D♭ (form *b*), we now have the diminished

Example 5.3 Chord forms

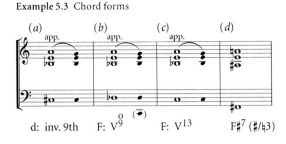

seventh chord in a different key, F, in which the missing root is C, and the A
is an appoggiatura to the fifth of the chord. If the D♭ appoggiatura ninth is
replaced in this chord by C, the true root, then we have an ordinary dominant seventh with appoggiatura thirteenth (form *c*). Substitute for this
bass a new root a tritone below, F♯, and a dominant seventh (as of B)
results, with mixed major and minor third, B♭ being rewritten enharmonically as A♯. All four of these related harmonies are found in connection
with variant statements of the main theme in this movement. Form *a* is
hinted at in bar 46, form *b* at bar 25, form *c* in bar 2 and form *d* in the *fff*
climax of bar 119. (Forms *c* and *d* can be combined in alternation in a
descending chromatic sequence over a circle-of-fourths bass; the result,
beloved of jazz composers, has one of its earliest appearances at bar 25 of
'Le Gibet'.)[6]

The secondary focus on A that we have noted in connection with the
second theme of the first movement becomes a primary focus in the
second movement, 'Assez vif – Très rythmé', where the A focuses the vigor-
ous 'natural-minor' theme. (The term 'natural minor' equates essentially
to the aeolian mode although it does imply a greater retention of tonal
function.) A fandango style is apparent in the guitar-like strumming, but
also in the phrygian flattened second, B♭, that adjoins the A minor
harmony from time to time. Secondary thematic material appears almost
at the outset with an abrupt shift to C♯ minor (dorian inflection); both
themes are extensively developed in the contrasting Trio section as well as
in the Scherzo proper.

The third movement, 'Très lent', is also the most wide-ranging in form,
with the main sections of a simple ternary form surrounded and inter-
spersed with recitative-like episodes, beginning with the A minor still
echoing from the previous movement. The first main section, in G♭ major,
recalls Fauré's *mélodie* style; it is answered by a cyclic reminiscence from
the first movement. After another fantasia-like episode, the mutes are
removed and the second main section appears, an expressive *cantabile* in
Ravel's beloved A minor with a dorian raised sixth, F♯, and an accompanimental pattern arpeggiated across the four strings of the first violin. (The

Example 5.4 String Quartet: melodic comparisons
(a) IV (bars 186–8); I (bars 1–2)

(b) IV (bars 69–71); I (bars 55–6)

fortissimo climax of this section, 'Modéré' and 'passionné', is another of Ravel's aural images: almost note-for-note, this same melody and harmony reappears in *Daphnis et Chloé*, at the moment where Lyceion drops her second veil.) F♯ major harmony makes a significant appearance in this A minor section, forming a tonal connection with the returning G♭ major that closes the movement.

The finale of Ravel's Quartet is the longest of the four movements in terms of bars (272). Once again, the A minor centring predominates over the nominal F major, beginning with the main rondo theme in 5/8 (a theme that resembles the main gesture in Debussy's finale). Contrasting subsections in 5/4 and 3/4 introduce subsidiary themes that, in both shape and harmonisation, recall first-movement material, as shown in the comparative illustrations of Example 5.4a and b. Even while ceding melodic primacy to the recurrent A, it is F major that achieves supremacy as the overall tonality. When the main rondo theme returns at the end, it centres on F, and the A is left for the uppermost voice of the final F major triad. (See also Woodley, 'String Quartet: comparison of recordings': Chapter 10.)

Bifocal tonality in the *Introduction et allegro*

For sheer amiability and relaxed sensuousness, no work by Ravel surpasses his *Introduction et allegro* for flute, clarinet, string quartet and solo harp. This all-important emblem of the harpist's soloistic repertory was written, according to Ravel's own testimony, in just a few days in 1905, on commission from the Erard Company, renowned manufacturer of pianos and harps. Again it is worth comparing Ravel's work here with Debussy's: in this case with the *Danse sacrée et danse profane* for harp and string orchestra, written in 1904 for Gustave Lyon and the harp class of the Brussels Conservatory, and frequently paired with Ravel's in recordings. Debussy's dances are restrained and even austere, but no less sensuous in their subtlety, without so much as a hint of the harp's most characteristic gesture, the glissando; Ravel's is a brilliant virtuoso piece, making full use of the technical and timbral resources of the harp, with a lushness of colour that never becomes excessively emotional. In the small ensemble of seven players, Ravel was able to achieve a remarkably full instrumental sound, carefully employing arpeggios, multiple stops, colouristic changes and registral extremes in a way that would have done credit to a much larger group.

The *Introduction et allegro* is a good illustration of Ravel's mastery of bifocal tonality of relative major and minor, in which the G♭ major of the first theme of the 'Allegro' and the E♭ minor of the second theme are constantly associated and contrasted. The two keys are especially suitable for the pedal harp, particularly in a context that supports E♭ natural minor and a black-key pentatonicity. In a natural-minor context, E♭ minor only seldom receives tonicising support from its own dominant. Thus the listener's perception of G♭ major versus E♭ minor is constantly changing, often depending on whether the one or the other key-note is in the bass or in the melody, and constantly tending to associate the two keys aurally as a single 'superkey'.[7]

The sections of the 'Allegro' are well defined by these two keys and effectively developed, but the formal outline is closer to a three-part form than to a sonata form. The G♭ major first theme begins at bar 26 (Fig. 2), the E♭ minor second theme at bar 78 (Fig. 6) and, in lieu of a development, a third theme (based on bar 1 of the 'Introduction') in a slower tempo at bar 100 (Fig. 8) which combines with the first theme. This third theme, with muted strings, is like an interior slow movement of the type so favoured by Franck and his descendants; this in turn is followed by an intensification of the third theme alone in a single key, leading then to a tutti climax and a long cadenza for solo harp; only then does the first theme return in a formal recapitulation.

The climactic *fff* at bar 200 (Fig. 17), a succession of appoggiaturas over a diminished seventh chord, is another example of Ravel's favouring the inverted ninth sonority in structurally dramatic situations. We saw it at bar 119 of the first movement of the String Quartet, but Ravel had already used it in a startling chromatic cascade in bar 5 of 'Asie' in his *Shéhérazade* songs; in another year he would make a similar outburst the centrepiece of 'Oiseaux tristes', with important echoes in 'Alborada del gracioso'.

Example 5.5 *Introduction et allegro* (bar 328ff.; Fig. 28)

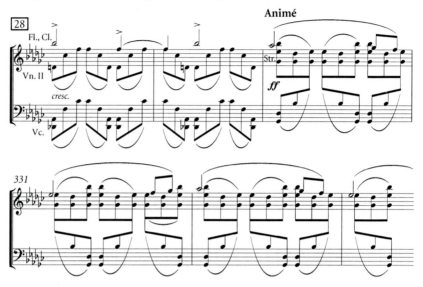

In the coda, the association of G♭ major and E♭ minor is strengthened by the simultaneous combination of their dominants, as illustrated by Example 5.5 (Fig. 28). The dominant root of G♭ wins out in this duel of inverted ninth versus dominant thirteenth, D♭ moving decisively to the G♭ bass, but the E♭ in the melody nevertheless remains strong. (We might compare these bars with bars 24–5 of the first movement of the String Quartet.)

The Piano Trio: modality and form

Ravel's Piano Trio, completed in 1914 and dedicated to André Gedalge, is often held to be the summit of his achievement in chamber music, as well as the last work that he composed in his most productive years, before his experience in the Great War permanently changed his life. On the other hand, as Orenstein points out, Ravel pushed himself to finish the Trio more quickly than he would have wished,[8] and it is thus not surprising that the result is uneven in quality. But, if the last two movements do not consistently show Ravel's best level of inspiration, the first two enthral the listener with their mastery and invention. The harmonic language includes some remarkable new discoveries, and no other work of Ravel's (except *Daphnis et Chloé*) shows such a variety of explorations in rhythm and metre.

The published score of the Trio does not have a key designation, but the first movement nevertheless represents a classic manifestation of Ravel's beloved A minor. The 8/8 metre, 'Modéré', uses a modification of the Basque *zortzico*, a dance in irregular metre but characteristically featuring 5/8 with dotted second and fourth quavers;[9] Ravel uses this pattern, adding a quaver plus a crotchet at the end of each bar. The favoured sonata form of Ravel's chamber music is easily perceptible, but with some notable deviations, of which the most important is that the entire exposition is in A minor, with no more than momentary modulations.

With the second theme thus in the main key (bar 35; Fig. 4), Ravel offers a sharp contrast with the beginning of the development in a remote key, D♯ minor, at bar 60 (Fig. 7). The succession of events soon makes it apparent that this is no real development, but rather the actual recapitulation which has begun in the 'wrong' key. The climax of the movement, across bars 77–81, is only an extension of the earlier climax (bars 20–1), but the extension brings the two main themes together contrapuntally. When the second theme of the recapitulation follows, at bar 83 (Fig. 10), it is harmonised first subtly, and then decisively, in C major; we will recall that Ravel did exactly the same kind of thing in the first movement of the String Quartet, with the second theme harmonised first in D minor and later, untransposed, in F major.

Ravel's 'Pantoum' is modelled on the *pantun*, a Malay verse form that has been adopted by several Western writers.[10] Formally, the 'Pantoum' is a straightforward scherzo and trio, but with special tonal and rhythmic features. The A minor beginning, 'Assez vif', has significant echoes from the previous movement: the natural-minor mode is frequently inflected with a phrygian flattened second (B♭) in the first eight bars, and with a dorian raised sixth (F♯) in the next four, cadencing in bars 11–12 on an A major triad, similarly to bar 4 of the first movement. If the very idea of an Oriental verse-form suggests something exotic, that exoticism is reflected in the vivacious 3/4 metre in irregular rhythm, which is marked by unpredictable groupings of two and three beats. The piano's accents alternately match the pizzicato chords in the strings or fight with them; a third variable is the groupings of repeated quavers, which are sometimes modified by changes from bowed notes to pizzicato, or from squeaky harmonics to natural pitches. At the beginning, this bouncy dialogue continues through three four-bar phrases, and then there is a sudden shift: a new theme appears, a distinctive melody in the strings in regular rhythm, with the piano entirely in an accompanimental role in a waltz-like texture. The modulation is to F♯ (bar 13; Fig. 1), but in a special mode that might be called 'natural minor/major', a favourite of Ravel's which features major third degree, minor sixth and seventh degrees: F♯, G♯, A♯, B, C♯, D, E, F♯.[11]

What follows is an intensive development of these two themes with dazzling skill through a highly complex harmony. The tonality is constantly shifting but always diatonically organised; the chromaticism appears in a fine assortment of piquant appoggiatura chords freshly adapted from the *Valses nobles et sentimentales*. The ornamented ii–V–I progression in No. VI of the *Valses nobles* is reborn with additional appoggiatura 'spice' in bars 47–50 (Fig. 4) of the 'Pantoum', and even more so at bars 67–74 (Fig. 5). This is followed at bars 75–80 (Fig. 6) by a circle-of-fourths sequence entirely in appoggiatura chords. Eventually, the scherzo reaches its climax in A, in the 'natural minor/major' (bar 105; Fig. 9).

The trio section follows at bar 125 (Fig. 10^{+5}), with the ostinato motive from the first theme still jingling steadily on A in the strings, while the key changes to a pellucid F major, and the piano changes to 4/2 metre with the strings remaining in 3/4 metre. (Eight bars of 3/4 match three bars of 4/2; bars are numbered here according to the 3/4 bars throughout.) The piano's new melody in this trio section is in an organ-like chordal style that Ravel would use again in the 'Musette' within *Le Tombeau de Couperin*.

The return to the scherzo overlaps with the end of the trio section, the strings taking the 4/2 melody as the piano resumes the brittle 'Pantoum' theme, but the remainder of the movement is anything but a strict 'da capo'; the two themes are developed in ever-changing ways. Whereas the piano previously pecked out the first theme in single notes, it now hammers out this material in close-position triads and seventh chords. The various phrases of the first section reappear abbreviated, in different orderings and with new extensions, until the climax of bar 105 is recapitulated at bar 256 (Fig. 21) with even greater bravura, the piano adding the first theme contrapuntally to the texture. And so the 'Pantoum' forms the crown of this last of Ravel's pre-war works. Only rarely in later years would his inspiration be so intense and, simultaneously, so fearless.

The 'Passacaille' begins 'Très large' with an eight-bar melody, a single line in the bottom register of the piano. The curious resemblance to the beginning of Debussy's 'Jimbo's Lullaby' (from the *Children's Corner* suite of 1906–8) is related to the entirely pentatonic structure of the melody, but if this melody were transposed to the black keys, the tonic would be on G♯. The cello repeats the melody at bar 9, the piano supporting it in crotchets in the kind of two-part texture that Ravel often handled so expressively. When the violin takes it up eight bars later (Fig. 2), with a Fauré-like chordal accompaniment, the melody already begins to vary in the second bar; its original form is not restored until the end of the movement. A new theme, introduced at bar 33 (Fig. 4), is developed to a broad climax, with some short motives from the original theme added to the texture. Of that most rigorous and relentless of forms, the Baroque passacaglia, the only remaining traces in this movement are the stateliness of the crotchet bass and the eloquent cantabile of the melody. The return of the original melody in the violin at bar 65 (Fig. 8) includes the same counterpoint of bar 9, this time in the cello, with both instruments muted; the piano dies away alone at bar 88, with a fermata leading *enchaînez* to the final movement.

Ravel's 'Final' ('Animé') is a significant disappointment in comparison with the other movements of this Trio. Where the repeating modified *zortzico* rhythms of the first movement were well proportioned and lyrically effective, here the free succession of 5/4 and 7/4 metres merely serve to drag the melody along. The texture of the entire movement is burdened with too many notes, especially in the piano, which is forced to alternate between running arpeggios or muscular *fortissimo* gestures in the manner of a Rakhmaninov concerto. It is fair to note that Ravel runs the same kind of risks in the often heavy piano texture of the other movements, when in many instances he seems to have had Brahms's chamber music as a model for piano writing; but, in this finale, the ear tires quickly of trills, tremolos and the overall too-massive sound.

Nevertheless, much of Ravel's characteristic best comes through in this movement: majestic harmony in parallel triads, fine instrumental colour and a relentlessly repeated main theme – almost pentatonic – that is similar to the second theme (bar 49ff.) in the finale of the String Quartet. Orenstein points to the trumpet-like flourish of parallel triads beginning at bars 58–9 (Fig. 7) which are telescoped at bar 67, in a short passage that recalls the end of *Daphnis et Chloé* (see the trumpets at Fig. 221 of the ballet score);[12] similar gestures occur in the finales of the Sonata for Violin and Piano and the Concerto in G.

Intensity and austerity: the Sonata for Violin and Cello

The Sonata for Violin and Cello, originally called Duo, was begun probably in 1920 as a memorial to Debussy, with the first movement published that year in a supplement to the Debussy memorial issue of *La Revue musicale*. The remainder of the Sonata was complete by 1922; at one point, dissatisfied with the scherzo movement, Ravel discarded it and wrote an entirely new one in time for the first performance in April of that year.

This least known of all of Ravel's mature chamber works is in some ways his most radically different: a work of the greatest melodic and contrapuntal intensity because of the spare, sometimes mechanistic, linearity of much of the instrumental texture, and a work in which he begins to extend the boundaries of tonality and to experiment with harmony more closely related to Bartók's style than to Debussy's. This resemblance is significant, for it was in 1922 that Bartók visited Paris on tour with the violinist Jelly

Example 5.6 Sonata for Violin and Cello: minor/major treatment
(a) I (bars 1–3, repeated)   (b) II (bars 1–4, repeated)

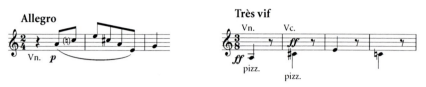

d'Aranyi, accompanying her in his first Violin Sonata; Ravel and Bartók became personally acquainted at this time, though he certainly knew some of Bartók's music before the meeting.

At the same time, characteristic features of Ravel's style persist as prominently in this Sonata as in any earlier work. The four-movement structure is identical with that of the Piano Trio. Once again we find a pervasive and idiosyncratic handling of A minor that constantly and freely associates the minor and major tonic triads and the minor seventh degree; this is apparent in the opening motives of both the first and second movements (Example 5.6a and b). The way that A minor is defined in this Sonata has abundant echoes in Ravel's earlier works, especially the Piano Trio, as we have seen. The natural-minor scale is preferred, the relative major (C major) is a readily available alternative focus and the dorian raised sixth (F♯) appears frequently.

The first movement, 'Allegro', is remarkable for its extreme melodic cohesiveness; the flow of crotchets and quavers proceeds uninterrupted to the end without pause and, except in the middle section which functions as a development, without any change in tempo. The opening motive, shown above, is first utilised as an accompaniment figure to the first theme; yet this first theme is not what Ravel chooses to develop during the course of what is a very tightly knit sonata form. As if to compensate for the intensive use of the major/minor pattern, the recapitulation brings back this first theme with a new accompaniment consisting of the violin's open strings plus middle C, directing the ear away from A minor and more towards C major, but still effectively combining the two keys (bars 176–80; Fig. 11).

A transitional theme beginning at bar 47 is very angular, with nine pitch-classes in twelve notes, but it effectively leads to G, the dominant of the second key, as can be seen in Example 5.7. The second theme, first appearing at bar 69, is easily recognised in C major, preceded by eight bars of dominant harmony. In the recapitulation, however, the strength of the expected C major is attenuated and varied by combination with the opening accompaniment pattern, freely moving among distantly related triads in the bass, forming polychordal harmony with the well-established C major above, as in Example 5.8 (bar 228ff.; Fig. 14^{-1}).

Example 5.7 Sonata for Violin and Cello, I: transitional theme (bars 47–52; Fig. 3)

Example 5.8 Sonata for Violin and Cello, I: recapitulation (bars 228–33; Fig. 14^{-1})

By the end of the movement (bars 273–5), the order of major and minor third as presented within the initial pattern (see again Example 5.6a) has been reversed. It is this latter pattern that reappears cyclically in the fourth movement, beginning at bar 135; more importantly, the arpeggiating A triad with major and minor third becomes the principal motive of the second movement (see again Example 5.6b), which we will recall was the last to be composed.

In the second movement, 'Très vif', Ravel once again shows his fascination with exaggerated use of pizzicato in A minor, as in the String Quartet and the Piano Trio. Yet this movement, like the fourth movement, ends in C major. The C major is blended with the A major/minor across bars 17–48, and the ostinato harmonies of these bars are brought back near the end of the movement (bars 445–504) to prepare its last two chords: A major and C major. In between, there are several sections of simultaneous mixed key signatures suggesting bitonality, but these are tonally less complex than they look. The appearance of simultaneous B minor and F minor at bar 316 is essentially a diminished seventh chord inflected by the major/minor motive (see Example 5.9).

The B♭ minor melody over an ostinato of C, D (♮) and A at bar 97 is very close to the combination of 'bell chords' that Musorgsky used in the Coronation Scene of *Boris Godunov*, but the mixture of instrumental colours, plucked *fortissimo* notes with lightly bowed harmonics, makes this relationship difficult to hear. (The pitches of the melody itself, though

Example 5.9 Sonata for Violin and Cello, II: apparent bitonality (bars 316–19)

Example 5.10 Sonata for Violin and Cello, II: semitonal combination (bars 142–8)

not the tempo, sound like an echo of two prominent melodies in Stravinsky's *Le Sacre du printemps*.) The combination of major and minor triads differing by a semitone results in a harsh sound, familiar to Bartók but new for Ravel, as used later across bars 142–8 (Example 5.10).

Generally, the notation in two simultaneous different keys in this movement results in a sense of polychordal harmony in which one or the other key momentarily predominates, rather than two perceptible keys at the same time. More complex and more subtle bitonal harmony is a later development in Ravel's music, notably in *L'Enfant et les sortilèges*.

The third movement is practically identical in form to that of the Piano Trio: a slow crescendo from the low register to a first climax, then followed by a bigger second climax in the high register and a slow descent back to soft dynamics in the low register. The opening melody is perhaps the clearest and most eloquent example in all of Ravel's work of his predilection for spare two-part counterpoint, typically in 4/4 metre with walking crotchets and pairs of quavers. This expressive *bicinium* exhibits a familiar tonal approach: A natural minor with much use of the dorian raised sixth, F♯, and frequent side-steps into C major.

The movement builds slowly, rising very gradually in register. Ravel even stipulates that the melody is to be kept on the lower strings wherever possible, so that the brightening of instrumental colour will be delayed. For a long time, F♯ is the only accidental sign, and much of the time it is not even accidental but integrally dorian; then more foreign notes are introduced into the counterpoint, and the texture more saturated with quavers, until the first climax is reached. Quavers dominate the texture from bar 25

Table 5.1 Sonata for Violin and Cello, IV: thematic outline

Bars	(Figs.)	Material
1–63		Main theme, quasi 7/4 (2/4 + 2/4 + 3/4), with some unvaried 2/4
63–99	(5–9)	First *X* theme
100–59	(9–14)	Second *X* theme, including reminiscence of first movement theme
160–7	(14–15)	Main theme
168–230	(15–19)	*Y* theme, F♯ minor, then A minor
231–86	(19–24)	Main theme, beginning on A
286–312	(24–6)	*Z* theme (from transitional theme, first movement), chromatic, close fugato à 2; stretto with inversion at bars 295ff.; initial motive of main theme added at bar 302
313–20	(26–7)	Main theme and *Y* theme combined; from bar 316 to the end (bar 388) entirely in 2/4
320–31	(27–8)	*Y* and *Z* themes combined, completed by first movement major/minor accompaniment figure
332–60	(28–32)	Stretto of *Z* theme, harsh trills and double-stops, concluding with accelerating major/minor figure
361–88	(32)	Stretto of first half of main theme alternating with *Z* theme, *ff*, ending with C major triad

to the end of the movement. The next resources of intensity are an increasing tempo beginning at bar 34, which coincides with an increasingly chromatic angularity in the melodic lines, with major sevenths and diminished octaves predominating.

These intervals are characteristic in Ravel's harmony from the beginning of his maturity; to see them emphasised in the melody, or in a spare two-part texture, represents a new departure in this work, though they were to become a special resource in the *Chansons madécasses* (1925–6) and the Sonata for Violin and Piano (1923–7). By the time of the Sonata for Violin and Cello, Ravel had already visited Vienna for concerts at Schoenberg's Society for Private Musical Performances (in 1920),[13] and had doubtless absorbed more of Schoenberg's music than he had in 1913 when, although modelling the instrumentation of his *Trois poèmes de Stéphane Mallarmé* on *Pierrot lunaire* on the basis of having seen the score, he had in fact not yet heard that pathbreaking work. Indeed, he had to wait until January 1922, right in the middle of his culminating effort on the Sonata, when Darius Milhaud conducted the French premiere of *Pierrot lunaire*, and it is not surprising that the Sonata includes melodic gestures suggestive of Schoenberg's second-decade atonality.

The rondo fourth movement, which is also the longest, marks the climax of a Hungarian style in this Sonata. The sections are given in Table 5.1. As in the other movements, the tonality is loosely organised around A minor and C major, with the harmony often non-triadic but dominated by the open strings of the two instruments. Subsidiary keys include D dorian and F♯ minor, both relatively clear, and other keys which are more fleeting, sometimes suggesting momentary bitonality.

The chromatic Z theme, taken directly from bars 47–50 of the first movement, marks the beginning of a 'grand mélange' in which most themes of the movement appear in stretto and combination in rapid succession, in an increasingly strident texture of multiple stops. The mixed tonalities of the last fifty or so bars are perhaps not fully convincing, but there seems to be no doubt that Ravel has mastered Bartók's percussiveness, in technique if not in spirit. Ravel may have had Bartók's violinist Jelly d'Aranyi in mind in composing this movement, but it was the spectacular *Tzigane* that he eventually wrote for her, two years later, whereas the violinist at the first performance of the Sonata for Violin and Cello was Hélène Jourdan-Morhange, for whom Ravel later composed his Sonata for Violin and Piano.

Tzigane, rapsodie de concert

Completed in 1924, the *Tzigane* is Ravel's last essay in the Hungarian style. The original version, for violin and piano – with or without the unusual 'luthéal' attachment that created a cimbalom-like sonority – was arranged by Ravel soon after for violin and orchestra (2[picc.]-2-2-2, 2-1-0-0, triangle, glockenspiel, cymbals, celesta, harp, strings). Some of the Hungarian-style thematic material in the *Tzigane* sounds as though left over from, or derived from, the Sonata for Violin and Cello. The major/minor triadic harmony is prominent, though not as a melodic motive (see, for example, bar 46). The opening G-string motive is very reminiscent of Liszt's *Hungarian Rhapsodies*, and Ravel's own Duo has a comparable figure. (So, too, the snarl at 'Was willst du, fremder Mensch?', in Strauss's *Elektra*, a work that Ravel probably admired more than he actually liked.) As another instance of Ravel's own traits, his favoured tonality of A minor is again in evidence, centring the solo violin melody that begins the fast section, 'Moderato' (bar 76), and cadencing to the main key of D minor only at the end of the second phrase.

The long unaccompanied cadenza at the beginning of the *Tzigane* occupies nearly half of the total time of the piece. Very free and recitative-like in form, it includes almost casually the principal thematic elements heard later in the work; its virtuoso features here consist principally of intense high-position work on the G string, together with octaves and

Example 5.11 Sonata for Violin and Piano, I (bars 49–53)

other multiple stops, tremolos and arpeggios. Harmonics and further fireworks are left for the fast section: a more dazzling assembly of left-hand pizzicato had not been heard since Paganini's *Hexentanz*, while the whirlwind of semiquavers would make a later appearance in the 'Perpetuum mobile' of Ravel's mature Violin Sonata, his final chamber work.

Sonata for Violin and Piano: mechanised rhythm and blues

Ravel's Sonata for Violin and Piano (1923–7) in three movements is, next to the Sonata for Violin and Cello, the least known of his chamber works and, like its counterpart, it breaks new ground. The instrumental style, especially, marks a significant departure from the Piano Trio of thirteen years earlier in which heavy textures and a late-Romantic conception of piano writing with abundant octaves and booming bass carried the day. In the first movement of this Sonata, a light and even ethereal texture predominates, much of it in the piano's high registers; the often spare linearity is presented with a two-part or even monophonic texture in the piano, but with a continuity that never weakens.

The sonata form of the first movement is elusive and very free. The opening theme in the piano is six bars long, but only the first two bars of it (in a lydian-inflected G major) reappear regularly for development. Other motives appear in quick succession: a bitonal 'chirp' at bars 10–11; a whole-tone succession of parallel major triads at bar 12; and a major/minor motive at bars 34–5 (Fig. 2^{+2}), arpeggiating an inverted ninth chord. A loosely defined second-theme region begins at bar 47 (Fig. 3^{-6}) with vibraphone-like diminished octaves; when these become diatonic (major) sevenths at bar 51, one is aware that in an earlier work Ravel might have written a similar melody harmonised in parallel seventh chords rather than the bare intervals favoured here in the piano part (Example 5.11).

The *espressivo* violin melody above this texture defines a clear E minor, an appropriate second-theme key; yet this melody never appears again. Its

Example 5.12 Sonata for Violin and Piano, I (bars 152–3)

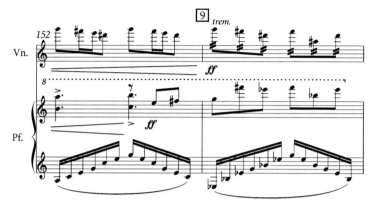

harmonisation at bars 55–84 (Fig. 3^{+3} to Fig. 4) is exclusively in the piano's right hand, with parallel perfect fifths in the manner of Ravel's most pronounced parallel-fifths essay, the song *Ronsard à son âme*. The end of this extended passage comes to a slowing point where F♯ leans on E in the upper violin – apparently a codetta – but now, in the piano, the parallel fifths are doubled and an organum-like new theme appears. The A minor harmony suggests the subdominant of E or supertonic of G, and the listener wonders if there will even be a development.

This question is tentatively answered at bar 96 as the G major (lydian-inflected) first theme returns in the piano, but over an E♭–B♭ drone, a remnant of the recent organum-like theme. The violin holds onto its F♯–E, and then the development begins in earnest. New short motives arise out of fragments of the first theme, but all the earlier motives receive attention through a variety of keys. The climax of the development is approached through Ravel's favourite supertonic ninth chord, incorporating both a strong root function and the ambiguity of subdominant and submediant within its span (compare, for instance, the climax of both the 'Prélude' and the last page of the 'Menuet' in *Le Tombeau de Couperin*). It resolves deceptively, however, to an E♭ major/minor chord (G♭ notated enharmonically as F♯), with G forming the melodic climax (Example 5.12; bars 152–3).

Another surprise: yet another new theme appears, at bar 165 (Fig. 10), in the low register of the piano over a D pedal while the violin's E♭ major/minor tremolo continues; this prepares the recapitulation of the first theme in the piano, with a clear dominant-to-tonic cadence. But the newest theme, now in the violin (bar 173; Fig. 11), accompanies the first theme in the piano. It is the frequent appearance and disappearance of new thematic material that makes this continuously melodic and forward-moving movement difficult to reconcile with a familiar sonata form.

Nor does the recapitulation proceed as the same ordered succession of

Example 5.13 'Jazz' comparisons
(a) Ravel, Sonata for Violin and Piano, II (bars 8–9)

(b) Ravel, *L'Enfant et les sortilèges*, foxtrot (Fig. 28, bars 7–8)

(c) Milhaud, *La Création du monde*, fugue (Fig. 11^{-1})

events first heard in the exposition. After the first theme, various motives reappear in the piano, but the pedal-point passages and harmonic ostinatos are omitted and a much more regular bass sustains the texture, while the violin moves more slowly – in 3/4 metre against the piano's 9/8 – in an entirely new melodic line. The motivic substance of the piano is increasingly dominated by the first six or seven notes of the first theme. The climax of the recapitulation, at bars 201–3 (Fig. 14^{-2}), is satisfying in its melodic continuity and as a V–I cadence, but we are left wondering what has been recapitulated. The coda that follows provides some answers: the organum theme in parallel fifths, at bars 86–9 (Fig. 4^{+2}), supports the violin's oscillating F♯–E, which becomes F♯–G at bars 223–5 (Fig. 15).

Ravel's dating of 1923–7 for the Sonata, at the end of the published score, suggests a period of gestation that had lengthy interruptions. On harmonic grounds, one might hazard a guess that it was the second movement, 'Blues', that was composed first. This is more a French than an American blues, but it comes complete with blue notes, slow rag rhythms and 'bent' pitches. The abundance of dotted rhythms includes a motive recycled from the foxtrot in *L'Enfant* (Fig. 28); without dots, one recognises it as a jazz 'lick' that Ravel could have borrowed from Milhaud's *La Création du monde* of 1923 (see Example 5.13a–c for a comparative view).

Much of the violin part consists of pizzicato chords, becoming more intense as the movement progresses. The prolonged back-and-forth strumming across the four strings that worked so well in the string ensemble within *L'Enfant* (Figs. 31–7; as well as in Gershwin's Concerto in F and Debussy's 'Ibéria') is of less resonant effect in a solo instrument, with disconcerting reminders of a ukulele, but it is well relieved by the feline glissandos in the violin cantilena (which Ravel marks 'nostalgico': Fig. 1^{+2}).

Example 5.14 Sonata for Violin and Piano, III (bars 29–32)

Another echo of *L'Enfant* is in the bitonally notated beginning, with a G major triad (a hold-over from the first movement) in the violin above an Ab–Eb pedal in the piano. This not really perceived as true bitonality; rather, it is equivalent to a major triad on the leading-note positioned over the tonic and dominant, a harmony that was used long before Ravel, though it appears prominently at the beginning of the 'Valse américaine' (Fig. 107) in the Garden Scene of *L'Enfant*. In the 'Blues', the same sonority – in various spacings and transpositions – reappears at intervals throughout the movement, and its persistence prompts the listener, in retrospect, to recall it as a subtle harmonic motive from the first movement (it emerges first at bars 10–11 of the first movement, then again at bars 17–22 and 28–9).

A likely apocryphal story has Ravel remarking that he was inspired to compose *Boléro* after having spent a summer in the neighbourhood of a sawmill. Few composers who dared to experiment with extreme mechanicity in their music were able to bring it off as successfully. (After a performance of *Boléro* many of the soloists get to take a bow, but it is the relentlessly constrained snare drummer who probably deserves it most.) In the mechanised 'Perpetuum mobile' of the Sonata, Ravel keeps the violinist playing relentlessly across bars 15–194; the part ranges far and wide with a variety of bowing styles, but shows a marked preference for repeated notes on the G string. Certainly, it is the violin that sustains the energy of the movement, but it is the piano that provides the structure as a modified sonata form.

The first distinct theme is the melody on the piano in parallel triads that begins at bar 29 (Fig. 2), as shown in Example 5.14. This is comparable to the fanfare in the finale of the Piano Trio and to another melody in the finale of the Concerto in G. All the other themes in this movement are recycled from the previous movements: the diminished octaves of bars 47–51 of the first movement reappear in the third at bar 52 (Fig. 4); two themes from bars 67–9 (Fig. 5^{+4}) and 78–80 (Fig. 6) of the 'Blues' are transformed into bars 55–60 (Fig. 4^{+4}) of the finale. The major/minor theme at bars 34–5 of the first movement reappears as a kind of *valse sentimentale* across bars 93–6 (Fig. 8^{+5}) and 101–4 (Fig. 10^{-4}) of the 'Perpetuum mobile'. The exposition ends with a climax in B major at bars 79–84 (Fig. 7); the development then begins in Ab major, rather puckishly recalling the A♭ major tonality of the introduction, and proceeds through modulating sequences: B♭ minor, C minor, A minor and finally E major. The abbreviated recapitulation begins at bar 139 (Fig. 13), the parallel-triad first theme now combined with the jazz bass. When the climax of bar 79 is recapitulated at bar 155 (Fig. 14), it is merged with the earlier cadential harmony of bar 46: blue notes and all.

The tonality of the 'Perpetuum mobile' reveals both its unity and its continuity with the movements that preceded. The opening fourteen bars are an introduction, nominally in A♭ major as a structural hold-over from the 'Blues' (just as its opening chord was held over from the first movement). When the violin's *moto perpetuo* gets under way in G major, the accompanying harmony (rooted on G) includes elements of the F♯ major triad as appoggiaturas. Thus we have once more the motivic/harmonic relationship that was so prominently displayed earlier, and that will be featured again repeatedly in this movement, indeed forming the complete cadential harmony of the last eight bars. (Nor is this the end of it; Ravel's fondness for this sonority, based in G major, appears again in full strength in the finale of the Concerto in G.)

Thus Ravel's last chamber work shows a remarkable heterogeneity of moods, from the inner-directed, even exploratory sound quality of the first movement, not quite like any other work of his, to the experimental and sometimes stark blend of jazz, dance and *concertante* elements that engaged his interests repeatedly in the 1920s and up to the end of his career. The *Chansons madécasses* (1925–6) may also be reckoned with the two sonatas as a chamber work that particularly favours the long melodic line in its instrumental as well as vocal function, and where instrumental colour, though still transparent and masterful, is less striking than the expanded harmonic language. All these stylistic features emphasise Ravel's development away from the lush *art nouveau* 'impressionism' of his pre-war works that – excepting the special case of *Boléro* – are still his most famous achievements.

6 Ravel and the orchestra

MICHAEL RUSS

Innovation in orchestration and genius in the handling of shape and colour are generally undervalued in broadly analytical studies of music, even in work on early twentieth-century music where, arguably, these factors were increasingly used to grant the coherence that pitch relationships were no longer able to provide. Pitch-centred analysis of modernist music has tended to regard music as independent of its medium, and has helped to build an aesthetic that treats works that depend on colour and shape, Ravel's *Rapsodie espagnole* for example, as less significant than those that directly confront the problems of tonality's supposed demise. Furthermore, the popularity of such pieces has meant that analysts have been denied their crusading role: they have not had to invoke complex methods to help secure the place of these compositions in the canon. Given the scope of this chapter, analyses must be brief, and will often give explications of form, thematic interconnections and post-tonal harmonic structures in the time-honoured way, but there will be a little more attention to register, shape and colour than normal, indicating the essential rather than secondary role of these parameters in Ravel's music.

Shéhérazade (overture)

Ravel's first orchestral work, *Shéhérazade, ouverture de féerie*, was conducted by its composer in its first and only performance until recent times on 27 May 1899.[1] It was the first of only four orchestral pieces that did not begin their lives as piano works or as ballets. I will consider these in the first part of this chapter and then proceed to Ravel's transcriptions.

In its treatment of the orchestra *Shéhérazade* is assured: 'I was satisfied with the orchestration. It was generally found to be picturesque.'[2] In its use of repetition and ostinato, block juxtaposition, climaxes achieved through building up layers, and its piquant modal and whole-tone harmony, it reveals a composer following a decidedly modernist agenda driven by encounters with exotic music and Russian music in particular (see also Orledge, 'Exotic theatrical projects': Chapter 2). Unfortunately, Ravel attempted to cast his materials in a sonata form and then made himself a hostage to fortune by drawing attention to this in a programme note. The critical response was damning: the overture 'is composed of a series of very brief fragments ... attached to each other by extremely weak bonds. You have ten measures, or fifteen or thirty, which seem to present an idea; then brusquely, something else happens, and then something else again. You don't know where you're coming from or where you're going.'[3] Ravel incorporates a couple of modifications to his sonata form, engaging, for example, in a simultaneous recapitulation of the two main subjects at *fortissimo* dynamic (Fig. 19). But, despite the weight of brass given to the transformed version of the first subject at this point, it loses out to the second. Furthermore, at the end of the piece, Ravel merely recalls the introduction verbatim.

There are some skilful thematic transformations, but *Shéhérazade's* problem remains that the materials are not well suited to their functional roles. The introductory 'Shéhérazade' theme, an attractive idea in B minor with raised fifth in the oboe, recalling the opening of Debussy's song 'La Flûte de Pan',[4] might as well be regarded as his first subject. This exotic dance (bar 25) is followed by a whole-tone idea in the trumpet announcing the arrival of the second subject: Ravel's 'Persian melody' (Fig. 7^{+8}). In practice, this is an entirely diatonic melody in F♯ minor presented over a dominant pedal; any Eastern exoticism is superficial and flows via Rimsky-Korsakov and Borodin. The 'Intermezzo' from Borodin's *Petite suite* comes to mind (at Fig. 7^{+14}), though the effect of this idea as an outburst of pure melody amongst more picturesque and fragmentary sounds is rather similar to Rimsky-Korsakov's *Antar* theme, which Ricardo Viñes and Ravel spent many hours playing.[5] A direct influence of Rimsky-Korsakov's *Shéhérazade* may be heard in tritonally juxtaposed fanfares (Fig. 2). Some may trace these chords back to Musorgsky's *Boris Godunov*,[6] but they surely come by way of the second movement (bars 108–49) of Rimsky-Korsakov's work.

The development transforms and fragments many ideas from the exposition, employing novel instrumental combinations and techniques. For example, the opening of the Persian theme is restated by piccolo and flute accompanied by an ostinato in low horn, celesta and harps – one of which plays harmonics (Fig. 8^{+9}); the cellos play *à volonté* (Fig. 13^{+2}); and there is an antiphonal juxtaposition of bassoon trio plus side drum against clarinets, horns and tambourine (Fig. 14). Percussion is much used, with each little section having its own distinctive instruments, from the triangle and tambourine at the beginning, to the timpani dyads at the close of the piece. When percussion and wind momentarily disappear to leave pure string sound for the reprise of the latter part of the second subject (Fig. 20), the effect is telling.

Although Ravel criticised his work for its excessive whole-tone scales and strongly Russian flavour,[7] its problems really stem from a mismatch

Example 6.1 Scalic forms: common fragment
(a) 'Andalusian' scale   (b) Octatonic I

between structure and materials. The block juxtapositions are crude and the larger-scale control of register and shape insufficiently refined. The ensuing *Rapsodie espagnole*, however, is much more successful in this respect and in its control of large-scale rhythm.

Rapsodie espagnole: modality and form

A product of Ravel's Spanish year (1907), first performed in March 1908, *Rapsodie espagnole* marked a considerable step forward in his orchestral writing. While it was drafted in a version for piano four hands,[8] this music (excepting the 'Habanera' which is an orchestration of the earlier two-piano work) is conceived with the full range of orchestral shapes, colours and registers in mind and is unconstrained by traditional formal procedures.

Four pieces make up the *Rapsodie*. The 'Prélude à la nuit' and the 'Malagueña' are closely linked and the final piece, 'Feria', incorporates the ostinato of the 'Prélude'. The third piece, 'Habanera', fits in remarkably well since, as Ravel pointed out, it contained the 'germ of several elements' in his later works.[9] It seems, for example, to share certain Andalusian harmonic relationships with the first two pieces: some phrygian flattening of the second degree, plus use of both major and minor thirds. These relationships can be related to an Andalusian scale which in the 'Prélude' and 'Malagueña' is built on A (Example 6.1a), and in the 'Habanera' on both the tonic F♯ and dominant.[10] 'Feria' is more concerned with C major and mixolydian diatony, together with some acoustic and pentatonic writing. The work's principal tonal centres are A, F♯ and C; rearranged they form a chain of minor thirds.

Rather than set forms, the 'Prélude' and 'Malagueña' are best discussed as gestures, interruptions and shapes. The 'Prélude' is dominated by its ostinato, a descending four-quaver idea derived from the Andalusian scale, forming a two-beat grouping against the triple metre (Example 6.2a). The ostinato creates articulative gestures when, for example, it falls away to a single octave and declines in dynamic (Fig. 2^{-2}), or, after similarly ebbing away, it is restored on a strong downbeat (Fig. 4). Soon after (at Fig. 5), it is temporarily emasculated by the removal of its first note. The principal dra-

Example 6.2 *Rapsodie espagnole*, 'Prélude à la nuit'
(a) Ostinato   (b) Fig. 7, bars 1–5

Example 6.3 *Rapsodie espagnole*, 'Malagueña': motives *w* and *x*
(a) Fig. 6, bars 1–5

(b) Fig. 12, bars 1–4

matic interruptions are the clarinet and bassoon cadenzas towards the end which open wide registers after the ostinato has been reduced to virtually a single note. Wave shapes are also significant, most obviously the octave transpositions of the B♭/A♭ dyad (Fig. 3). Melodic materials are minimal and are closely linked to the ostinato; perhaps the most remarkable passage is where the principal theme is heard in heterophonic combination with the ostinato from which it derives (Fig. 7; cf. Example 6.2a and b).

The 'Malagueña' has four distinct parts. The first is built from ten repetitions of a three-bar ground bass (slightly modified towards the end), plus some chromatic 'whirring' in flutes and cor anglais. The second provides an example of Ravel using secondary parameters to shape a substantial passage. Statements of the main theme (Example 6.3a; Figs. 6 and 8) in streetwise brass are separated by sophisticated, almost Mahlerian, strings. In each statement, harmonic, dynamic and timbral qualities are fixed. To propel the music, Ravel then energises short crescendos by rapid harmonic rhythm and a strongly functional bass; at the core are four-part horns with a powerfully directed wave figure. Simultaneously, he precipitates a collapse: a straight-line descent from the high f♯^{3} established by the violins. Reducing in texture and dynamic, the music falls through five octaves and the harmonic motion is frozen by pedals. Only a few low instruments are left (Fig. 10^{-2}). The music is immediately reinvigorated by the

'Malagueña' theme, unmuted and with castanets, and by the tonal shift to D♯ (a diminished fifth from the tonic). A strongly directed upward motion in parallel harmony (a slower, more dramatic version of the harp glissando that precedes so many downbeats in Ravel) takes us to the climax which, in turn, is cut off as we reach the third phase: the gypsy song in the cor anglais. Vocal elements were essential to the fandango and malagueña and one form of the latter included a 'vocal improvisation and cadential flourishes, sometimes extending to nearly two octaves'.[11] This description neatly fits what happens here and the harp and lower strings' glissandos capture the sound of a band of strummed instruments with remarkable authenticity. The final section (Fig. 13) overlaps with the conclusion of the cor anglais melody (Example 6.3b; Fig. 12) and restores the ostinato from the 'Prélude', a variant of which is combined with the ground bass of the 'Malagueña'. The final cadence is a reorchestration of that of the 'Prélude', the link strengthened by the return of the celeste.

By the time Ravel composed this work he was thoroughly familiar with the octatonic scale (as the String Quartet demonstrates), probably through studying Rimsky-Korsakov's music. Octatonic writing is most explicit in the clarinet and bassoon cadenzas of the 'Prélude' which employ octatonic scales III and I, respectively.[12] The two-clarinet cadenza with its tritonal opposition to the accompanying chord surely helped suggest to Stravinsky his more astringent octatonic clarinet duo in Petrushka's cell, though Stravinsky combines C and F♯, like Ravel in *Jeux d'eau*.[13] The ostinato figure is common to the octatonic and Andalusian scales as the passage between the cadenzas, entirely referable to scale I, demonstrates (cf. Example 6.1b and Example 6.2b). Octatonic scales (also referable to collection I, which excludes the tonic, A) make an obvious appearance in the woodwind at the end of the 'Malagueña' (Figs. 13–14) as a type of 'dominant' preparation for the arrival on A (Fig. 14).

At the head of the 'Habanera' score is the date 1895, lest we think that Debussy got there first. Ravel's 'Habanera' sounds a C♯ pedal for much of its duration; against this, chords sound (often dissonantly) and wisps of melody are heard. Ravel would have explained the strong dissonance as arising from pedals and/or unresolved appoggiaturas, but the sounds take on a life of their own independently of the 'voice-leading'. The key, F♯ minor, is constantly challenged by the dominant and at times the two seem in equilibrium. The tonic version of the Andalusian scale is strongly evident in the move to a ♭II⁷ over the C♯ pedal (bar 2) and in the progression from F♯ minor to major that ends each main section. The dominant scale-form is evident in the opening move to D⁷ and at bar 9, where a phrygian melody begins with a C♯ major/minor chord.[14] The 'Habanera' is in two parts; the second begins as a reworking of the first, but with the intro-

Example 6.4 *Rapsodie espagnole*, 'Feria': motives *y* and *z*
(a) Bars 4–5

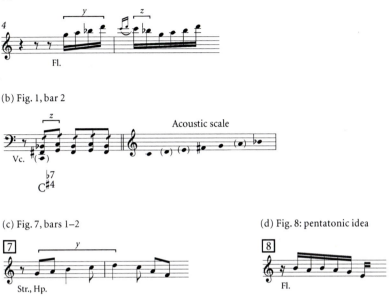

(b) Fig. 1, bar 2

(c) Fig. 7, bars 1–2

(d) Fig. 8: pentatonic idea

ductory chords omitted. During the second section, a brief shifting of the pedal to E sets off the piece's longest, most seductive phase. This is not a habanera to dance to; it is, to paraphrase Dyagilev on *La Valse*, more 'a portrait' of a habanera.

The orchestral score follows the piano one closely and enhances its exotic effect. The opening illustrates Ravel's sensitive allocation of instruments to particular attack points. The two main elements are assigned to upper strings (with their evocative harmonic on the second beat) and clarinets in octaves, but a four-part wind chord, an eight-part harp chord and contributions by cor anglais, bassoon, muted cello and viola give each attack point its own weight and colour, adding a pointillistic layer to the score.

'Feria' shows Ravel at his wildest. The ternary form with improvisatory quasi-vocal middle section reminds us of 'Alborada del gracioso'; its outer sections are founded on a tiny collection of minimal ideas (Examples 6.4a–d and 6.5a–c). These move within a narrow compass and are combined and repeated to form layered ostinatos in which each idea is associated with a particular timbre and register, and with percussion that draws out distinctive, often Spanish, rhythms. These ostinatos are propelled by kinetic energy, not by harmonic forces. Sectional articulation is achieved by secondary parameters: waves and ebbings away of sound. Just before Fig. 1, the flute's opening idea (Example 6.4a) is interrupted by a wave: an up–down glissando in the harp plus natural string harmonics.[15]

Example 6.5 *Rapsodie espagnole,* 'Feria': motives *w* and *x*
(a) Fig. 4, bar 1

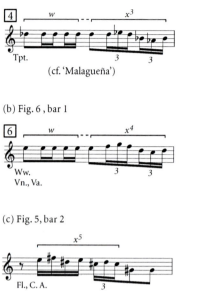

Tpt.

(cf. 'Malagueña')

(b) Fig. 6 , bar 1

Ww.
Vn., Va.

(c) Fig. 5, bar 2

Fl., C. A.

Both outer sections set forth the main ideas and lead to giant 'ostinato machines' (to use Derrick Puffett's phrase); they reach climaxes which repeat motive x^4 with the prefix *w* deleted (see Example 6.5b). Stopping such pantechnicons is not easy; conventional cadential closure is not an option and the ostinatos generate an almost dangerous momentum. The signal for their end is the same in both cases: a forcible statement of motive *y*, in the horns and trumpets (Fig. 11^{-2}) and in the woodwind (Fig. 26^{-2}). Each time, a B♭ disrupts the C diatony and a huge shimmering chord appears which collapses in just a few bars to leave a few low quiet sounds. The first section ends here, but the final one begins again and builds yet another ostinato. Harmonic forces are also employed now: the arrival on C is made more dramatic via the Neapolitan C♯(D♭). A sudden shift to a whole-tone chord (A♭, B♭, D, F♯) sets off a huge wave-like surge, including glissandos and a trombone snarl, before the tonic is restored and the piece ends.

This music has many mechanical properties. Deborah Mawer puts forward an attractive argument for the sounds of fairground machinery having an influence here (see 'Musical mechanisms and *la machine infernale*': Chapter 3). An imaginative ear might liken the opening flute idea to a wheel on a squeaky axle, but the weirdest mechanical sounds are heard in the central section which ticks and whirs like a giant clock, while the long cor anglais and clarinet solos suggest a spring unwinding (this was the year in which much of *L'Heure espagnole* was written). The prominent tritones in the bass (Fig. 13ff.) remind us of another clock: the one that caused Boris Godunov to hallucinate, as do the strange four-part violin glissandos (Fig. 15^{+5}). A return to the ostinato and main theme of the 'Prélude' momentarily creates the illusion that time has reversed.

Overcoming difficulties: the Concerto for the Left Hand

Over twenty years elapsed before Ravel's next purely orchestral essay during which he completed many fine transcriptions and balletic projects. In March 1929, Ravel visited Vienna for the Austrian premiere of *L'Enfant et les sortilèges* and also heard the Austrian pianist Paul Wittgenstein (1887–1961), who had lost an arm because of a war injury, play 'a concerto for the left hand alone by Richard Strauss'.[16] Wittgenstein commissioned a concerto from Ravel, with which the composer was busily engaged during summer 1929 alongside the Concerto in G. The first performance took place in Vienna in January 1932 with Wittgenstein as soloist and Robert Heger conducting; Ravel conducted the Paris premiere in January 1933. The relationship between Ravel and Wittgenstein, who wanted to make alterations, was strained and led to the famous outburst: 'Performers must not be slaves!' to which Ravel replied 'Performers *are* slaves.'[17]

The Concerto for the Left Hand is a darker work than the Concerto in G, but not unremittingly so. Roland-Manuel's reference to 'the dying gasp of a lost soul' or Marguerite Long's apocalyptic vision are surely, as Gerald Larner suggests, going too far.[18] Comparing the concertos, Ravel observed that the outer sections of the Concerto for the Left Hand are 'nearer to [the style] . . . of the more solemn kind of traditional concerto'; but there are many similarities too, not least in the incorporation of 'a good many jazz effects'.[19] Jazz, machines and circus all play a role and the almost comic and tragic intermingle in a sometimes bitter and ironic way.

Ravel remarked that the 'fear of the difficulty . . . is never as keen as the pleasure of contending with it'.[20] The difficulty here was to produce a work which appeared to be close to the nineteenth-century piano warhorses (a tradition for which Ravel, paradoxically, felt little sympathy), giving the 'impression of a texture no thinner than that of a part written for both hands', yet avoiding the accusation of being written '"against" the piano'.[21] In this Concerto, Ravel is not so much participating in the nineteenth-century tradition as viewing it from a distance. For technical guidance he turned to, amongst other things, Saint-Saëns's *Six Etudes for the Left Hand* but, as he acknowledged, they do not confront the biggest problem: 'to maintain interest in a work of extended scope while utilizing such limited means'.[22] While the sounds seek to conceal that the pianist has only one hand, we all know the truth: the fact is boldly declaimed in the title and Ravel strongly resisted attempts to arrange the Concerto for two hands. The idea is not to make us unaware of the difficulty but, rather, amazed by the deception, just as in a good conjuring trick.

Ravel conceals the limitations of the pianist multifariously. In the first subject (Fig. 4^{+4}), the length of the first beat gives enough time for the hand to move down and provide bass support. In the second (Fig. 8^{+6}), Ravel exploits the momentary gap between the attack points of the quaver and triplet quaver to generate a duple melody with triplet counterpoint. In the final cadenza, we find this again and also have the gap between the two parts filled with hemidemisemiquavers (Fig. 50^{+21}). In its concluding bars, the single hand plays in octaves while accompanying itself with demisemiquavers and providing a bass pedal!

There is here a demonic virtuosity which we associate with some nineteenth-century virtuosos. The build-up to the pianist's entry is substantial, and his arrival ('the coming of a conqueror')[23] is marked by cascades of demisemiquavers doubled in exotic fourths and fifths. We are reminded of Stravinsky's first conception for the unfinished *Konzertstück* that eventually became *Petrushka*, described in a French publication just before Ravel begun work on his Concerto: 'I saw a man in evening dress, wearing his hair long: the musician or the poet of Romantic tradition. He sat himself at the piano and rolled incongruous objects [*des objets hétéroclites*] on the keyboard.'[24]

As with Liszt's Piano Sonata and Schoenberg's First Chamber Symphony, Ravel's single movement draws together the contrasting moods of a multi-movement structure. An introduction precedes a sonata form whose development section is replaced by a mechanistic scherzo. Ravel gives the pianist maximum exposure: a cadenza-like solo exposition of the first subject, sole charge of the exposition of the second and an extensive cadenza which serves also as part of the recapitulation. A tiny coda then returns to the material of the scherzo. The opening 'Lento' and lyricism of the second subject compensate for the absence of a slow movement.

The outer sections and central scherzo are polarised in that the depths of the opening are matched by the heights of the scherzo where both E♭ clarinet and piccolo (which also feature strongly in the Concerto in G) have prominent roles. The introduction, exposition and recapitulation display elements of growth and transformation, and their broad tonal structure is conventional. The introduction is founded on E which progresses through A to D at the start of the solo exposition; the second subject is in the mediant, F♯, with leanings to B minor (with both keys using dorian raised sixths). By contrast, the scherzo bursts onto the scene like some giant machine, employing block juxtaposition, transposition and much repetition (its opening major/minor tetrachord prevails for ninety-four bars). Things happen suddenly without anticipatory crescendos, glissandos or ascents; tonal relations fit together like cogs. The principal centres of the scherzo are a major third apart: E (Fig. 14), G♯ (Fig. 23), C (Fig. 27), dividing the octave symmetrically and moving from a tone above to a tone below the work's tonic. Within the areas on E and C are short cycles of minor thirds: E, G, B♭ appears twice as a point of melodic focus (Figs. 17–19 and Figs. 21–3) while a complete rotation, C, A, F♯, E♭, C, emerges after Fig. 27.

Setting melodic material in different orchestral and harmonic contexts is an important feature. The main ideas are stated in bold wind colours, the strings confined to providing backgrounds and reinforcement. At the opening, the contrabassoon anticipates the first subject and its characteristic dotted rhythm against a dark background of cellos and basses. This idea makes its next big appearance in the solo piano (Fig. 4^{+4}) and, a little later, is taken up by the cor anglais accompanied by strings and rippling chords in the piano. These recolourings are matched by varied harmonic contexts such that the first two notes of this melody are heard as E: $\hat{1}$–$\hat{2}$ (beginning), D: $\hat{3}$–$\hat{4}$♯ (piano exposition), B♭: $\hat{5}$–$\hat{6}$ (cor anglais at Fig. 10^{+1}).

Even more striking is the treatment of the horn idea at the close of the contrabassoon's melody (Example 6.6a; Fig. 1^{+2}) which is transformed into the main theme at the centre of the scherzo. Critics have interpreted its first appearance variously: 'a syncopated blues tune' (Larner); 'a lament' (Long); 'an anguished complaint' (Myers); 'sneering' (Nichols).[25] Ravel, it seems, only wanted its jazz features to become apparent in the scherzo: 'A special feature is that after a first part in this traditional style, a sudden change occurs and the jazz music begins. Only later does it become evident that this jazz music is really built on the same theme as the opening part.'[26] The winding of this material around two minor thirds and its dark initial presentation also suggest a Russian flavour. Detached from its harmonic context of C, its scale is G dorian (Russian minor) with a missing fourth (i.e. a 'gapped' scale: Example 6.6a). The idea is dramatically and dissonantly stated in the trumpet and trombone with its opening B♭ presented as the ninth of the dominant (Example 6.6b; Fig. 3); at the end of the recapitulation it is heard against G major with its B♭ then sounding like a 'jazzy' flattened third.

This material is repeatedly reorchestrated (*Boléro*-like) in a long build-up of forces (Fig. 28ff.): 'A new element suddenly appears in the middle, a sort of ostinato figure extending over several measures which are indefinitely repeated but constantly varied in their underlying harmony.'[27] While the major/minor harmonic background is rotated through minor

Example 6.6 Concerto for the Left Hand
(a) Fig. 1, bars 2–6

(b) Fig. 3, bars 1–2

(c) Figs. 28–35: dimished seventh framework

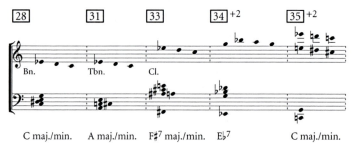

thirds creating a complete octatonic collection: C (Fig. 28), A (Fig. 31), F♯ (Fig. 33), E♭ (major only, Fig. 34^{+2}), C (Fig. 35^{+2}), the melodic idea is not transposed from C dorian (Example 6.6c). When the harmony returns to C, the melody appears stridently, doubled at the diminished octave – a doubling that emerges out of the clash of major and minor thirds. After appearing to restart, the chain of minor third transpositions is broken with strong rhetorical effect (Fig. 37) when a fifth-progression, A–D, is followed by the blues theme in D, again doubled at the diminished octave.

The scherzo also introduces three ideas not heard elsewhere. The first is a descending series of parallel triads, heard in the trumpets (Fig. 14^{+2}) and subsequently in piano, which interject unpredictably like products falling down a chute. Initially, the triads are E phrygian against E major/minor harmonies beneath; since the E phrygian scale is synonymous with C major, a link is formed, not only with the progress of the scherzo, but with juxtapositions of these centres elsewhere. The second is the scherzo's principal theme (Example 6.7): an energetic toccata-like 'stomp' (written in the

Example 6.7 Concerto for the Left Hand, central section: principal theme (Fig. 17, bars 1–2)

piano's tenor register to maximise sonority) which is major-scale diatonic with sharpened fourth and flattened seventh – essentially the 'acoustic' scale. Acoustic writing is evident elsewhere, not least in the solo exposition of the principal theme (Fig. 4^{+4}) which begins in D major with raised fourth; nine bars later the next phase of the theme begins on C (the flattened seventh). The most overt usage occurs when, over an E pedal, a C acoustic scale climbs through the orchestra (Fig. 13). The third idea employs yet another scale, the pentatonic, in flute and piccolo (Fig. 25). Pentatonicism is also evident in the fourths of the opening ostinato and the cascades of fourths and fifths when the piano enters. As an alternative to these pentatonic, acoustic, octatonic and modal relationships, we might link the major/minor thirds, sharpened fourths and flattened sevenths to the unwieldy 'blues' scale. But this would over-emphasise the jazz influence and undervalue the way in which these inflections have their sources in various kinds of harmonic activity with different origins.

The Concerto in G and jazz

Work on the Concerto in G began in 1929, but was interrupted by the Concerto for the Left Hand until later in 1930; due to his weakening condition, it took Ravel another year to complete. The first performances of the two works took place less than a fortnight apart in January 1932, but Ravel's plans to take the Concerto in G on a world tour never materialised.

When Ravel declared: 'I set out with the old notion that a concerto should be a divertissement',[28] he was, in a sense, acknowledging that his Concerto stands alongside rather than within the canon; he was placing his work with those that entertained rather than pushed musical development forward. Ravel's concertos are among the most popular works from the second quarter of the twentieth century, yet their admission to the canon has always been a little grudging. In his study of the twentieth-century concerto, Paul Griffiths slips in Ravel by way of jazz after a long exploration of Stravinsky, and Laurence Davies cannot help remarking that the concertos were 'composed with a dreadful creative fatigue perched . . . on the composer's shoulder' and that the finale of the G major concerto 'falls below Ravel's best standards.'[29]

Musicology is wary of declaring as 'canonic' works which set out to

Example 6.8 Concerto in G, I: opening motives *x*, *y* and *z* (bars 1–2)

entertain rather than those which confront the audience with what it might find unpalatable as a necessary part of discovery and self-expression. Parts of Tchaikovsky's output have also suffered from this 'Zivilisation'/'Kultur' dialectic; Taruskin's words about Tchaikovsky's 'Rêves d'enfant' (1879) might apply to much of Ravel: 'This exquisitely realized composition is one of Chaikovsky's palpable masterpieces – if, that is, the idea may be entertained of a masterpiece of instrumental color, orchestral texture, and harmonic contrivance.'[30] Like Tchaikovsky, Ravel idolised Mozart precisely because 'What Mozart created for the enjoyment of the ear is perfect . . . Beethoven, however, overacts, dramatizes, and glorifies himself, thereby failing to achieve his goal'; 'Mozart is absolute beauty, perfect purity.'[31]

The Concerto calls for an orchestra of chamber proportions and, like a Mozart concerto, employs prominent soloistic woodwind, though in Ravel's case this extends to piccolo, cor anglais and E♭ clarinet. Furthermore, Ravel specifies thirty-two string-players to balance the wind section. Theatrical, grotesque and chameleon-like treatments of instruments are evident. Extremes are favoured, as demonstrated by the E♭ clarinet at the start of the finale, the bassoon solo (Fig. 9) and horn solo (Fig. 25) in the first movement. Considerable virtuosity is required in the wind parts: the bassoons in the finale (beyond Fig. 14) are at the limits of their capability.

The first movement is in sonata form. Two structural parallels exist between this movement and the Concerto for the Left Hand. Firstly, both developments are replaced by mechanical sections; in the Concerto in G this consists of a toccata built on the opening idea and the E♭ clarinet idea from the transition. Secondly, both recapitulations begin with a powerful, much abbreviated, reminder of the first subject, while the second is recapitulated within the piano cadenza. In the Concerto in G, this is preceded by an extremely evocative reworking of the transition in the harp, whose sonority is then imitated by woodwind and horn. The coda returns to the toccata style of the development.

The principal subject begins pentatonically and during its fifteen bars, despite its limited supply of rhythms, not a single bar is repeated. The opening bar-and-a-half contains three motives (Example 6.8): *x* is

Example 6.9 Concerto in G, I: motive *y* (Fig. 5, bars 1–2)

Example 6.10 Concerto in G: motive *z*
(a) Fig. 1, bar 1

(b) Fig. 4, bars 1–2

(c) Fig. 5, bars 4–6

Example 6.11 Concerto in G, I: motives *y* and *z* (Fig. 7, bars 1–4)

significant in the main theme and its developmental derivatives; *y* appears in the transition where it is attached to a 3̂–2̂–1̂ voice-leading descent (Example 6.9; Fig. 5) creating a figure similar to the opening of the slow movement (Example 6.12 below); *z* is prominent throughout the exposition (Example 6.10a–c), particularly in the second subject where it appears in multiple forms combined with *y* (Example 6.11; Fig. 7). The second subject also begins pentatonically.

At the opening of the work, the combination of G and F♯ triads is not strictly bitonal since we do not hear this as anything but G major, with F♯ as a dissonant colouring. Ravel had been using such combinations since the 'Habanera' (bar 14), while in the 'Blues' and 'Perpetuum mobile' of the Sonata for Violin and Piano triadic combination a semitone either side of G major was exhaustively explored. Many hear the influence of *Petrushka* in this passage; the connection is as much a matter of theatre as harmony. The crack of the whip and the jaunty piccolo tune (scored low in its compass so as to suggest a fife), with an accompaniment (including piano) that is really a long percussion roll, generate expectancy. More characters enter, including braying horns and the full wind band, all of whom suddenly exit as the curtain rises to reveal the main act (Fig. 4), whose exotic credentials hail from Spain and America.

In much of the exposition the rate of harmonic change is slow and melodies unfold over static harmony. When Ravel wishes to move to a new section or idea he often announces this with music that proceeds directly up or down and may support with more rapid harmonic change. These 'energising' passages take several forms. Just before Fig. 2, for example, rapid contrary motion allied to a crescendo, harp glissandos and percussion rolls, leads to a strong downbeat and repeat of the opening material. Conversely, a strong upward motion allied to parallel harmony (Fig. 3^{+4}) then leads to an anti-climax; the music rapidly collapses and the cor anglais lags behind as the others leave the stage. At Fig. 17, a long dramatic ascent in the solo piano leads to the recapitulation, and, at the very end, rapid downward parallel motion closes the work.

As the music proceeds we are increasingly aware of jazz influences in the cut of ideas: Fig. 4 reminds us of the solo entry in Gershwin's Piano Concerto in F and the second subject (Fig. 7) links directly with Gershwin's *Rhapsody in Blue*.[32] The foxtrot rhythm in the left hand of the piano part (Fig. 5^{+4}) together with wood-block and cymbal (Fig. 6) also help to establish the Broadway atmosphere. Both of Gershwin's works had been performed when he visited Paris in 1928 and Ravel had visited America and met Gershwin just before. Ravel underplayed the jazz elements: 'In certain respects this Concerto is not unrelated to my Violin Sonata. It has touches of jazz in it, but not many.'[33] As in the Concerto for the Left Hand, many of the harmonic preoccupations which we call 'jazzy' followed on from Ravel's own innovations. The music of Figs. 4–7 could be related to a blues scale; equally, it could be the result of phrygian, Andalusian and dorian alterations to second, third and sixth degrees of the natural minor, already common in Ravel. Furthermore, the harmonic language of American popular music took something from French music at the beginning of the century.[34]

Two remarks by Ravel always come to mind with the wonderful melody that begins the second movement: 'a melody that recalls Mozart, the Mozart of the Clarinet Quintet . . . the most beautiful piece he wrote' and

Example 6.12 Concerto in G, II: opening melodic shape (bars 1–3)

'That flowing phrase! How I worked over it bar by bar! It nearly killed me!'[35] This melody recalls Mozart more in spirit than in thematic shapes, but it is a supremely beautiful and scrupulously crafted artefact; that it took considerable effort is not surprising. Mozart's melody (from the 'Larghetto' of the Quintet) is a remarkable outpouring of some twenty bars; no bar is repeated exactly but the rhythmic shapes of the first two bars are a constant guide. Ravel builds an even longer, thirty-four bar, melody from his opening shapes, again without repeating a single bar. Both Mozart and Ravel build their melodies over pulsating quavers: Mozart's is directed by its strongly functional harmony, Ravel's by its descending bass.

The 'archaic lyricism' of Satie's *Gymnopédies* also hovers over this melody,[36] mainly through the constant employment of mild harmonic dissonances that cannot simply be regarded as inessential or colouristic. This is music to delight the connoisseur. When, for example, the piano holds A against G♯ just a bit longer than it should (Example 6.12: bar 2), we relish the way that eighteenth-century harmonic syntax and twentieth-century colour are held in perfect equilibrium. Similarly, from bar 7, we enjoy the tension between the descending series of parallel ninths that form the harmonic skeleton and their underplayed resolutions. Reducing this music to a consonant triadic framework along the lines of the analyst Heinrich Schenker is possible, but much would be lost in the process. Reduction to a mildly dissonant *Gymnopédie* would more accurately represent its spirit.

The left hand's pulsating quavers persist through this ternary movement, including its more tonally mobile central section. The reprise of the main theme is ten bars shorter than the original and is a 'Glinka variation': melody, harmony and piano left-hand are unchanged, but the music is exotically recoloured using one of the most evocative of orchestral sounds, the cor anglais, with a new, purely decorative, background. The piano right hand plays an unbroken chain of demisemiquavers until we reach the tiny coda. This is not an exercise in virtuosity, it is there purely to delight.

Circus and jazz are obviously to the fore in the finale and musical progress is more a matter of theatrical gestures than the following of a strict form. Nevertheless, a sonata form can be traced. A group of terse ideas which includes the opening four chords, the E♭ clarinet's squeal and a trombone glissando forms the first subject; the 'stomp' which begins in the piano (Fig. 7) constitutes a transition and the 6/8 march section, with its tritonally opposed opening fanfares, a second subject. The development (Fig. 14) is really a long written-out crescendo in which the main ideas are repeated almost ostinato-like, and the bassoons are asked to do more than they should. The reprise (Fig. 20) is much abbreviated.

The finale is in G major, but is coloured with F♯ from the outset. When the E♭ clarinet enters, it is notated in G♭ major against the orchestra's G major. This idea and its tonality come directly from the 'Perpetuum mobile' (Fig. 2) of the Sonata for Violin and Piano, as becomes even clearer when the piano takes it up at the recapitulation. Similarities can also be traced to *L'Enfant et les sortilèges*. The E♭ clarinet idea (Fig. 1) resembles the moment when the Child pricks the Squirrel with his pen (just before Fig. 10), and the second subject (at Fig. 7^{+7} and later stages of the development) recalls the compound-time celesta accompaniment to the Chinese Cup (Figs. 31–3).

Ravel's transcriptions of his own music

Transcription is routinely ascribed a lower place in the scale of musical values than original composition, reflecting a generally held view that the medium is less significant than the work. Even though Ravel's decisions are those of genius and his choices sound inevitable and supremely convincing, the fact that many of his orchestral works began their lives as piano pieces leads too easily to the view that the piano version represents the 'true' work, its later instrumental version an attractive variant – the public face of the more private piano utterance (see also Mawer, 'Neoclassicism and l'objet (re)trouvé': Chapter 3). But such a view seems unjust. An alternative is to view his transcriptions as brilliant and truly creative interpretations, clarifications, even analyses of their originals. The orchestral creation becomes an equal but more explicit realisation of the original, able to use its greater resources to reveal what can only be latent in a piano rendition.

Ravel's transcription technique was strict; indeed, this was part of the challenge. But he does not simply dress the originals in pretty colours. Instead, he clarifies shapes, adds appropriate effects, energises and adds weight in a way not possible with the piano. Through the careful provision of dynamic and attack markings, percussion parts and the careful apportioning of orchestral forces, Ravel provides a layer of large-scale rhythmic differentiation previously left entirely to the pianist. The symbiotic relationship between the piano and orchestral realisations of certain of Ravel's work-concepts is illustrated by the way that his piano scores often imitate instruments and voices, and his orchestral ones sometimes recreate piano sounds, while translating pianistic into orchestral virtuosity.

Ravel's orchestrations are of short pieces or collections that he can characterise distinctly. Several are associated with ballets. Each transcription creates its own sound-world: the waves of flutes and strings in 'Une barque sur l'océan'; the horn, pizzicato strings and woodwind in octaves in the *Pavane pour une Infante défunte*; the guitar-like string band and singing bassoon in 'Alborada del gracioso'; the biting dissonance in trumpets, woodwind and strings that begins the *Menuet antique*; or the folk band sounds captured in *Tzigane*. Three transcriptions will now be considered briefly.

Ravel's orchestration of 'Une barque sur l'océan' was performed once in 1907 and then withdrawn. Critical opinion has tended to support Ravel's decision, placing the blame more on the piano original than the quality of the transcription: 'banal' (Hopkins), 'pretentious, unsuccessful' (Davies).[37] This piece is really just a barcarolle plus some squalls big and small; it lacks the power and majesty of Debussy's *La Mer*, which received its first performance just before Ravel began his orchestration. Nonetheless, 'Une barque' contains several two- or three-bar wave figures which can be effectively orchestrated, not least at the beginning. Here, the blurring suggested by 'Très enveloppé de pédales' in the piano score is recreated by a complex orchestral texture in which the chord is both sustained and presented in arpeggios with various rhythmic values simultaneously. Blurring is also evident when a pentatonic glissando assigned to the celesta is obscured by two flutes playing arpeggios in different rhythmic values (Fig. 8). Glissandos are the natural territory of the harp (as at Fig. 13) but, typically, when a harp seems the obvious choice (Fig. 23), Ravel substitutes the celesta. In Vlado Perlemuter's piano score, Ravel actually wrote 'comme une harpe' at this point![38] A magical and entirely characteristic moment comes towards the end when a siren call is built on a blues-like conflict of D major/minor scored for muted trumpet, string harmonics and glockenspiel.

By the time that he came to orchestrate 'Alborada del gracioso' Ravel's technique was highly refined and he found that transcription came more readily than original composition. Commissioned by Dyagilev for a composite ballet that also included Ravel's transcription of Chabrier's 'Menuet pompeux' performed in London in 1920,[39] 'Alborada' was first performed as an orchestral piece in 1919.

As a piano piece 'Alborada' is more successful than 'Une barque'. As an orchestral showpiece it is beyond comparison. Ravel makes the original even more entertaining through the wholesale exploitation of orchestral means. This energetic work is propelled by strongly directional harmony and Spanish rhythms, the subtleties of which are drawn out by the orchestra, particularly the percussion section. The trick is to translate the pianistic energy into the orchestra without losing its special tautness. The initial imitation of the guitar in the piano score is marked 'sec, les arpèges très serrés'; in the orchestration, the harp playing close to the soundboard and carefully arranged pizzicato strings successfully reproduce this effect. Sharply drawn musical shapes, whether blocks moving within a narrow compass energised by their own internal rhythms (as at the opening), or the many varieties of glissando (including the trombone's final snarl) leading both to climaxes and anticlimaxes, or the wave shapes and ebbings away or collapses, lend themselves to orchestral treatment. In particular, the juxtaposition of blocks of sound becomes much more sharp-edged in the orchestral version (Figs. 3 and 4).

Rapid triplets on a single note separated by a glissando (Fig. 5) presented an interesting challenge to Ravel's transcription technique. Although this could have been easily accomplished by the strings, Ravel replaces pianistic virtuosity with a muted trumpet triple-tonguing and extremely rapid flute figuration assisted by harps, to which a pair of hand-stopped horns and a cymbal add subtlety. As the passage is restated, a crescendo is built through the addition of a second trumpet and horns. The ebbing away of the climax to a single horn is striking. Spectacular woodwind writing also features elsewhere, notably in the flutter-tonguing (after Fig. 25). At the centre of 'Alborada', the bassoon plays the role of the jester. In an attempt to replicate the sounds of the extreme treble of the piano, the accompaniment is scored for twenty-four-part strings: many playing multiple stops, some arco, others pizzicato, some harmonics, others 'sul tasto'. A percussive edge is afforded by the xylophone, cymbal and drum.

Nearly thirty years separate the original *Menuet antique* and its transcription; the piece reflects Ravel's love of both dance and the antique. Eighteenth-century techniques appear most obviously in the cadences and sequential harmony, but Ravel's musical language extends just beyond classical acceptability. We can explain the opening cluster in eighteenth-century terms as appoggiaturas, but not its accentuation and *forte* markings and its astringent orchestration with trumpets a semitone apart (reminding us of neoclassical Stravinsky). The orchestral forces, slightly larger than those of the Classical era, produce sonorities that take eighteenth-century ones as their starting point, but extend them, as in the rich, deep woodwind writing which begins the middle section, or the pompous cadences of the outer sections.

Transcriptions of music by others

In evaluating Ravel's reworking of other composers' music we face the ever-present question of the ethics of transcription:[40] how far may one composer legitimately alter another's work? But this is not the place for detailed engagement with this question: suffice it to say that good orchestration may be likened to good interpretation. It must be judged by what it draws from the original work, the new insights it brings and the service it does for the original. Musorgsky's *Pictures at an Exhibition* would possibly not have gained its place in the musical canon, even as a piano work, had it not been for Ravel's transcription.

Ravel's orchestrations of works by others contain nothing to match *Pictures*. The first extant transcription is of Schumann's *Carnaval*, made for Nijinsky in 1913 following his break with Dyagilev, and described by Taruskin as 'unaccountably clumsy';[41] certainly these orchestrations, of which only the 'Préambule', 'Valse allemande', 'Paganini' and 'Marche des Davidsbündler contre les Philistins' remain, contribute little to Schumann's original. Ravel may have felt Schumann's aesthetic was too distant from his own. As a young man, he refused to consider Schumann if he was to play duets with Jacques-Emile Blanche;[42] he later described Schumann's music as 'sentimental' and reflecting 'the life of the German bourgeoisie in the nineteenth century'.[43] The orchestration simply translates from one medium to another with a loss *en route*; it takes from Schumann giving nothing in return.

In orchestrating other composers' works, Ravel sticks closely to the originals except for a tendency to simplify expressive markings and add those of dynamic and attack. Some markings disappear in the orchestration of Chabrier's 'Menuet pompeux', the ninth of his ten *Pièces pittoresques*. Orenstein rightly links this piece with Ravel's *Menuet antique*, and the two pieces share several features, notably their archaic cadences.[44] There are also similarities in the wind and brass writing, although their sound-worlds are distinct. Ravel comes close to 'sending up' the outer sections of Chabrier's piece, intensifying the feeling of small-town ceremonial pomposity through use of the wind band, to which string portamento at the cadences adds a touch of humour. The writing in the central section is much more delicate.

Musorgsky/Ravel, *Pictures at an Exhibition*

Pictures at an Exhibition was commissioned by Sergey Koussevitzky in 1920 and completed in the first half of 1922, during a period when Ravel produced his finest transcriptions. Koussevitzky apparently requested an orchestration in Rimsky-Korsakov's manner, but, as Nichols observes, Ravel 'avoided . . . the temptation to make the *Pictures* sparkle and vibrate *à la* Rimsky. Much of the sound has a roughness and solidity that we find nowhere else in Ravel's output.'[45] Ravel could not, however, escape Rimsky-Korsakov's influence altogether: unable to obtain Musorgsky's original score, he had to make do with Rimsky's edition.[46] While Rimsky-Korsakov left the bulk of Musorgsky's work intact, he was responsible for several significant alterations: the most important was the removal of Musorgsky's *fortissimo* at the beginning of 'Bydlo' and the substitution of the crescendo so effectively orchestrated by Ravel.[47]

The programme is indispensable to the piano original. The work was not published in the composer's lifetime and only performed to his friends, all of whom had seen the pictures of the late Victor Hartman that had inspired Musorgsky's music; it was in many ways a private utterance between friends. Ravel's transcription turned the composition into a much more public work which used the orchestra to create a more self-reliant structure. Nonetheless, the subjects depicted – the promenading composer, the lame gnome, children quarrelling, 'Baba Yaga' and so on – could not have failed to appeal to Ravel; furthermore, these were all subjects viewed through the filter of a piano work by a composer who, despite his subjects from France, Italy and Poland, never stepped outside Russia. But the attractions were probably not entirely to do with the subject-matter. Musorgsky's score depends largely on contrasts (registral, dynamic and antiphonal), whether in the solo and chorus at the beginning, the choirs and bells at the end, or the low and high of 'Catacombs', 'Cum Mortuis', 'Samuel Goldenberg and Schmuÿle'; these must have given Ravel great pleasure to orchestrate.

Ravel added a whole layer of articulative and dynamic markings, the successful implementation of which is often dependent on the large body of percussion and instrumental combinations that are carefully measured out and interlocked. But it is also the individual instrumental choices that make Ravel's orchestration work. The saxophone in 'Castello' and the muted trumpet for Schmuÿle's whinging both sound so right that the solutions adopted by others who have orchestrated this work simply pale by comparison.

Transcriptions of Debussy

Two orchestrations of early Debussy were made just after *Pictures* at the request of the publisher, Jobert. Ravel, in a letter to Debussy's widow requesting permission to make them, described the 'Sarabande' as 'very orchestral'.[48] Debussy's marking 'Avec une élégance grave et lente' informs Ravel's orchestration: the stark block chords with parallel fifths and octaves are displayed in bare woodwind. The unmuted trumpet and tam-tam make telling contributions even though the latter only sounds twice, in combination with harp homophones (emphasising the essentially percussive role of the harp in Ravel).

Hand-stopped horns play an important role in the 'Sarabande', but it is in *Danse* that this instrument comes into its own. It appears hand-stopped in dialogue with harp and pizzicato strings (Fig. 8), a duo of horns play their favourite fourths and fifths (Fig. 12) and, moreover, at the beginning, it is the horn that takes the tarantella theme (this piece was originally called the *Tarantelle styrienne*). The tempo here is frantic: although Debussy's marking is 'Allegretto', Ravel adds the metronome mark ($\downarrow$. = 132). This is a fine orchestration in which Ravel makes explicit the light and shade suggested by Debussy's piano textures and harmony; the passing reference to *Tristan* (Fig. 21) is appropriately highlighted by his treatment. *Danse*, like all Ravel's transcriptions, is music at its most civilised, music which, while being respectful to the original, is superbly crafted and wonderfully entertaining.

7 Ballet and the apotheosis of the dance

DEBORAH MAWER

Ballet is the most lavish and unpractical kind of dancing. Steps are embellished at every point with little angles of the shoulder or head, decorative arm movements, beats and flourishes of the ankles or feet. MACKRELL[1]

Dance, that is to say stagnation, movement on the spot, the whirling action which, instead of being unleashed on the world, surges back on itself, finds its finality within itself, tramples and turns around. JANKÉLÉVITCH[2]

This chapter serves to point up the significant position of ballet within Ravel's smallish oeuvre, and the idea of dance forms as a way of connecting between music and choreography, focused on movement, phrases (*enchaînements*) and patterning. Additionally, these two arts share an interest in animating space and time; as Mackrell comments, 'Space isn't simply a neutral area where the dance takes place. Like the stillness between movements, it's part of the dance itself', and 'It is rhythm too that allows choreographers to play with Time – to drive it forward, freeze it or make it race.'[3] Although music and choreography exist as autonomous arts, they may still come together for greater collective effect. Despite our main focus on the musical portrayal of dance, ideas from classical ballet and flamenco will influence analytical readings of *Daphnis et Chloé, La Valse* and *Boléro* (works whose main embodiment is as ballet rather than as piano music). The first quotation heading this chapter is used to encapsulate Ravel's highly stylised and varied approach to dance (exemplified by *Daphnis*); the second quotation suggests the obsession intrinsic to closed dance forms which leads to Ravel's 'apotheosis of the dance' as a glorified ideal, followed by its destruction in *La Valse* and *Boléro*. (For more on the 'dance-machine' trajectory, see Mawer, Chapter 3.)

Ravel's sizeable ballet repertory, spanning 1909–28, comprises *Ma Mère l'Oye* (Mother Goose), *Daphnis et Chloé, Valses nobles et sentimentales* (retitled *Adélaïde, ou Le Langage des fleurs*), *Alborada del gracioso, Le Tombeau de Couperin, La Valse* and *Boléro*.[4] Ballet offered Ravel a multidimensional projection of dance; visual spectacle of exquisite elegance and beauty; a vehicle for fantasy and opportunity for distancing and detachment: 'Ballet not only contrives to display the body in the most pleasing and harmonious arrangements, it also rarely chooses to express raw emotion. Love, cruelty and madness are conveyed through the most decorous of dance metaphors.'[5] Above all, it was Ravel's fascination with dance, itself a unifying vehicle for his wide-ranging explorations of classicism and exoticism, that led inexorably to ballet.

Ravel's debt to dance has long been acknowledged. Both Jankélévitch and Jourdan-Morhange noted his extensive enquiries from 'ancient dances' (menuet, pavane and forlane), through 'romantic dances' (waltz) and American dances (foxtrots, 'two-steps' in *L'Enfant et les sortilèges*), to Spanish dances (habanera, bolero and malagueña).[6] Jankélévitch presented Ravel's use of dance as a mask that enabled indirect expression and even falsehood in the feigning of indifference, the handling of allegory and contradiction. As an enclosed, often microcosmic, form, dance perhaps matches Ravel's own need for internalisation and self-imposed limitation. His dance is ubiquitous and its connection to physical movement, as choreography, inherent. Supporting the idea of *correspondances* between reality and imagination, Jankélévitch argued (using objective imagery) that 'Dance is the isolating envelope for his dream',[7] while a final image from criticism of the 1920s presented Ravel as Rameau, 'sacrificing above all to the god of the Dance'.[8]

The pre-war context

The impetus for the Ballets Russes (1909–29), founded by Sergey Dyagilev (1872–1929), stemmed from the exposition of new ideas on ballet and aesthetics – superseding those of the aged Marius Petipa – in a publication called *The World of Art*. This magazine was edited jointly by Dyagilev, Alexandre Benois (1870–1960) and Léon Bakst (1866–1924), all of whom later collaborated in projects with Ravel. Around the same time, Mikhail (Michel) Fokin (1880–1942), trained at the Imperial Ballet, gained prominence for his forward-looking views on choreography:

> He believed that ballet should aim for a greater naturalness, just as Noverre had advocated in the eighteenth century, and felt that every ballet should have a style of movement suitable to its theme, country and period. He wanted to reform the long mime interludes and let movement convey the dramatic content and he wished to use the *corps de ballet* as part of the action instead of in its decorative role.[9]

Across 1906–8, Dyagilev capitalised on the West's interest in the East by encouraging artists such as Anna Pavlova (1881–1931), Thamara Karsavina (1885–1976), Bronislava Nijinska (1891–1972), Vaslav Nijinsky (1888–1950) and Fokin to display their talents in Paris. Although the Opéra maintained a modest company, Parisian ballet had lost much of its former popularity and was perceived as jaded and formulaic; thus the French capital was hungry for the originality and technical skill of the

Russian dancers. The astounding success of the opening performance on 18 May 1909 of dances from Borodin's *Prince Igor* and Tcherepnin's *Le Pavillon d'Armide* contributed to a momentum which resulted in Dyagilev's setting up a permanent company in Paris, securing Karsavina as 'prima ballerina' and Nijinsky as 'premier danseur'. Dyagilev's products of 1910 and 1911 – Rimsky-Korsakov's *Shéhérazade*, Stravinsky's *L'Oiseau de feu* (The Firebird) and *Petrushka* – exerted a particularly powerful influence upon Ravel.

Ma Mère l'Oye and *Adélaïde*, Ravel's first completed ballets, provided further experience of artistic collaboration (that for *Daphnis* having begun as early as 1909). The former, with certain additions to (and reorderings of) the piano duet movements, was first performed under Jacques Rouché's directorship at the Théâtre des Arts on 29 January 1912. Gabriel Grovlez conducted, sets and costumes were by Jacques Drésa and choreography by Jeanne Hugard. Highlighting dance, Ravel remarked that 'I wanted everything to be danced as much as possible. Dance is a wonderful art, and I have never been more keenly aware of it than through observing Mme Hugard arrange the choreography.'[10] *Ma Mère l'Oye* presents an attractive childhood fantasy rather than *Daphnis*'s fantasy of another age; additionally, the work enjoys a magically opulent exoticism. 'Laideronnette', especially, with its tolling temple bells, explores the scalic sonorities of Java. *Adélaïde*, discussed further below, was first performed at the Théâtre du Châtelet (like *Daphnis*), on 22 April 1912 by the troupe of Natasha Trouhanova. Ravel himself conducted the Lamoureux Orchestra, with sets and costumes by Drésa and choreography by Ivan Clustine.

Analytical aside

Before the first analytical reading, a brief aside on musical language and analytical approach seems apt (this also offers something of a summary for Chapters 4–6). Ravel employs a broad modality, as an extension of traditional tonality, which includes ionian (major), lydian, dorian and aeolian ('minor') modes, as well as pentatonic, whole-tone, chromatic and octatonic collections. As Orenstein and Philip Russom have acknowledged,[11] beyond chords with added thirds, pedal-points, appoggiaturas and harmonic substitutions, Ravel viewed his music within structural levels governed by a melodic 'voice-leading' (directed linear motion from one pitch to another) not so dissimilar to that of the music theorist Heinrich Schenker. In one of several short analyses of his own music, Ravel reduces part of *Valses nobles* to suggest larger-scale 'prolongation' (structural continuation of pitches which underlie more superficial embellishments); conflicting accidentals in 'Oiseaux tristes' are not problematic when they operate at different levels (ornamental pitches equate to 'fore-ground diminution'), while implicit resolutions of appoggiaturas are denoted by parenthetical pitches.[12] As Russom notes, 'Certain basic organizational schemes stand out in our study of the RSCs [Referential Scale Collections] in the horizontal dimension, namely: linear progressions, neighbor motions, arpeggiations and sequences. In Ravel's bass lines, these patterns are arranged so as to direct motion toward a particular bass note which asserts its priority as the tone center.'[13] Ravel's awareness of these ideas will be borne in mind in the readings below, each of which is presented chronologically to aid listening with a score, or study prior to a ballet production or concert performance.

Reading dance in *Daphnis et Chloé*

Following an extended gestation, *Daphnis et Chloé* ('symphonie choré-graphique') was premiered by Dyagilev's Ballets Russes at the Théâtre du Châtelet on 8 June 1912. Pierre Monteux conducted, choreography was by Fokin, with sets and costumes by Bakst. Nijinsky and Karsavina danced the title roles some ten days after, and rather overshadowed by, Nijinsky's erotic premiere of Debussy's *Prélude à l'Après-midi d'un faune*. Indeed, *Daphnis* shared the programme with Debussy's *Prélude*, Rimsky's *Shéhérazade* and Weber's *Le Spectre de la rose*.

Ravel's view of the myth, as told in Longus' Greek 'romance', was coloured by his reading of it through an eighteenth-century French intermediary, Jacques Amyot. His often quoted aim was to paint 'a vast musical fresco, less concerned with archaism than with faithfulness to the Greece of my dreams, which is similar to that imagined and painted by French artists at the end of the eighteenth century'.[14] For Ravel, it was a pastoral idyll of classical purity and innocence, symbolised perhaps by the small Hellenistic figurines around his home at Montfort-l'Amaury. Significantly for a dance-orientated reading, Calvocoressi remarked:

> I also remember that the very first bars of music which Ravel wrote were inspired by the memory of a wonderful leap sideways which Nijinsky (who was to be Daphnis) used to perform in a *pas seul* in *Le Pavillon d'Armide*, a ballet produced by Diaghilev that very season; and that they were intended to provide the opportunity for similar leaps – the pattern characterised by a run and a long pause, which runs through Daphnis' dance.[15]

Artistic fusion through ballet was not, however, without its problems. Ravel was unsupportive of Fokin's striving for a more literal archaism, in terms of Greek pagan dance with an erotic physicality, so that *Daphnis* might 'recapture, and dynamically express, the form and image of the ancient dancing depicted in red and black on Attic vases'.[16] Equally, the dancers failed to appreciate the 5/4 metre of Ravel's 'Danse générale', though such metric challenges must have soon paled in comparison to those of Stravinsky's *Le Sacre* (1913). Nonetheless, increased synthesis and choreographic sensitivity on Fokin's part were noted by Louis Vuillemin, writing in the *Lanterne* (21 June 1921) on the later Opéra production: 'Gestures and steps, group entrances, general dances, are truly complementary to the symphonic episodes.'

The first feature which strikes the listener to the ballet music, rather than just the suites ('Nocturne', 'Interlude', 'Danse guerrière'; 'Lever du jour', 'Pantomime', 'Danse générale'), is how important dance is as a unifying vehicle; the music is evidently only part of a multi-dimensional creation. Putting aside Pierre Lalo's indictment in *Le Temps* (11 June 1912) that *Daphnis* 'is lacking the first quality of ballet music: rhythm', our reading looks to vindicate Emile Vuillermoz's view (supported by Louis Laloy and others), that 'Maurice Ravel's score is a ballet score' and that his dances 'have a surprising dynamism and an irresistible impetus'.[17] Of the eighteen subsections of the ballet, no fewer than eight are extensive dances, constituting well over half of the performance duration. In exploring the nature and role of dance in *Daphnis*, our main emphases are on melody, rhythm and metre:

> The rhythms and melodies of a score can't strictly be separated from its structure, yet in some dances we're aware of them as unusually compelling elements in the dance [choreography]–music relationship. When rhythm strikes us in this way, it's because the movement isn't just riding along with the counts of the music, but seems to be grappling with it, like some elemental force.[18]

The 'Introduction' (up to Fig. 5) sets the scene dramatically and musically as Ravel's motivic exposition: muted stacked fifths proceeding in slow common time (Jankélévitch's six-note 'frontispiece') suggest a primeval awakening of the past, then complemented by a series of harmonic double-fourth 'objects' on horns. The first melody on flute sets up inevitable association with Pan and, indeed, this is the nymphs' theme (Example 7.1; Fig. 1). Its initial D$\sharp$ secures a lasting tritonal relation with the bass on A which may support a lydian or whole-tone inflection; equally prevalent are descending melodic fourths. Affinity between the horns' material and that of the wordless chorus, which now accompanies with reiterated double-fourths, constitutes one of several instances of ambiguity, substitution and equivalence in *Daphnis*, convincingly explored by Danielle Cohen-Lévinas in association with Symbolist *correspondances* or synaes-

Example 7.1 *Daphnis et Chloé*, 'Introduction': flute theme (Fig. 1, bars 1–4)

Example 7.2 *Daphnis et Chloé*, 'Danse religieuse' (Fig. 5, bars 1–5)

thesia.[19] A solo horn response to the flute statement presents the love-theme of Daphnis and Chloé, objectified by the fifth interval (see Example 3.1: Chapter 3). Complementary fourth/fifth objects (*x* and *y*) act in almost all the thematic material, appearing in descent or ascent (*x* or *x*'), as prefix or suffix, singly or in combination, and in simple or decorated forms (see Examples 7.1 and 7.2, and later Examples 7.3, 7.4 and 7.5). The large-scale bass of the 'Introduction' comprises an octave descent from the modal 'final' on A, whose 'unfolding presents a complete whole-tone referential scale collection'.[20]

Dances in *Daphnis* loosely exemplify four types, or tendencies, which are not mutually exclusive and may be used in combination: ritual, high-speed, character-portraying and exotic dances. (On 'exotic dance', see also Russ, '*Shéhérazade*': Chapter 6.) Dance firstly expresses a deep-rooted pagan spirituality in the mysterious 'Danse religieuse' ('Modéré': Figs. 5–15), shown in Example 7.2, suggesting an extended lineage from some legendary primordium. Such ritual dance (type 1) may offer a means of exchange between everyday and heightened spiritual existence – between mortality and immortality; reality and unreality. This is dance to propitiate the nymphs as pagan deities, with a later incarnation in Stravinsky's *Le Sacre*: 'In Spring, at the edge of a sacred wood, young men and girls come to make offerings to the altar of the Nymphs.'[21] There is greater momentum now with fluid triplet contours, initially subdued, that repeatedly build to a tutti climax; a lydian melodic inflection is maintained, together with some pentatonicism. The *corps de ballet* function here to reflect and comment upon the main action as would a Greek chorus, though André Levinson found the massed, ritualised effect problematic: 'These dancing Hellenes, barefoot or in sandals, throwing their knees up high, sauntering

Example 7.3 Melodic/motivic comparison
(a) *Daphnis et Chloé* (Fig. 29, bars 4–7)
(b) *La Valse* (Fig. 5, bars 1–4)

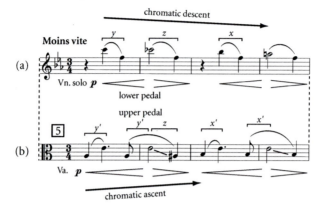

around in pairs or forming sculptural groups and processions in simulation of ritual mime, are intolerable, like any vulgarisation of great art and almost inscrutable sacred objects.'[22]

An initial 'Danse générale' ('Vif': Figs. 17–29) brings together the *corps de ballet* and soloists, and is later transformed for the finale. This is high-velocity dance (type 2) which celebrates the excitement of speed and may progress to 'risk', mechanisation and potential cataclysm. Metre is articulated and characterful: 7/4 subdivided as $3+4$ (as in the finale of Stravinsky's *L'Oiseau de feu*); texture is now more differentiated between smooth and staccato qualities. From an introductory portion (focused on Db), the dance develops (on Gb) and leads to its presentation proper (back on Db); its intervallic hallmark is again the falling fourth. Another brief scene ('Moins vite': Figs. 29–32) introduces on solo violin the legato waltz-theme associated with Chloé (Example 7.3a), and surely a catalyst for *La Valse* (Example 7.3b): the intervallic similarities and (partial) inversional relationship are striking. The diminished fifth (z) suggests tension, conveying an unfulfilled yearning within a chromatic voice-leading descent of 'sighs': C–Cb–Bb–A.

Dance is also used for musical and dramatic character portrayal, as an operatic aria without words; thus it has a role in acting and semblance. Circumscribed forms facilitate clear characterisation. Chloé (a shepherdess), Daphnis (a shepherd) and Dorcon (a goatherd) each feature in their own 'character dance' (type 3), using the second balletic sense of the term: 'Dancing based on the classical steps performed primarily to define an individual'.[23]

A brief 'Danse grotesque de Dorcon'('Très modéré': Figs. 32–41) assumes a heavily accented 2/4 metre, with crude octave reiteration in the

Example 7.4 *Daphnis et Chloé*, 'Danse légère et gracieuse de Daphnis' (Fig. 43, bars 1–3)

Example 7.5 *Daphnis et Chloé*, 'Lyceion danse' (Fig. 57, bars 1–3)

bass on E and humorous melodic characterisation by three bassoons, so presenting the unlikely suitor as a clumsy laughing-stock. By contrast, the 'Danse légère et gracieuse de Daphnis' ('Assez lent': Figs. 43–51), shown in Example 7.4, is founded on the 6/8 metre of the barcarolle, with pitch-structure also much more sophisticated. The ternary design articulates a progression from a centricity on F to one on F♯, featuring octatonic modality (Figs. 47–8), and back again. Nijinsky's 'sideways leap' is conveyed by arpeggiated pizzicato interjections between the lilting flute phrases. Beyond the fourth/fifth hallmark (*x* and *y*), this dance explores issues of time and space amid imaginative timbral effects. Cohen-Lévinas notes a confounding of expectation when the second-beat resolution of the initial rhythmic stressing is delayed by the pause 'in mid-air'.[24]

And so the heroic, would-be lover, Daphnis secures his kiss from Chloé (Figs. 51–3), while the disgusted Dorcon appropriates and sullies Chloé's waltz-theme within his own 2/4 metre – a pathetic likeness. After a re-hearing of the love-theme (Figs. 53–4), Daphnis falls into an ecstatic dream-like state which again suggests *correspondances* (and possible Freudian association). In the ensuing episode with his temptress, Lyce[n]ion ('Très modéré': Figs. 57–60), whose music is quoted in Example 7.5, dance offers a vehicle through which to legitimise the erotic, often via the exotic (types 4 and 3 combined). Again, one theme masquerades as another in deceptive semblance: the far-reaching variant of the love-theme on solo horn suggests unavoidable connection between love and lust (cf. Examples 3.1 and 7.5). Lyceion also assumes the 6/8 metre (and flute) of the slumbering Daphnis in her refined dance whose modality blends G minor and B♭ major, spiced by pentatonicism and chromaticism. As Cohen-Lévinas says of *Daphnis* as a whole: 'The work no longer offers a definitive face, but rather its likeness.'[25]

Following Chloé's abduction by pirates (Figs. 61–70), a transitional 'Nocturne' ('Modéré': Figs. 70–4) sees the statues of the nymphs – flute, horn and clarinet – come to life, mirrored by harmonic subterfuge which combines G♯ (minor) and D^7, then E (minor) and B♭^{7}, in *Petrushka*-like fashion with a similar underpinning octatonicism. The 'Danse lente et mystérieuse des nymphes' (Figs. 74–83), heralded by the wind machine, balances the early 'Danse religieuse'. In empathy with Daphnis, the nymphs also adopt a 6/8 metre whose rhythmic identity is intricate and fluid. Beyond the fixed falling fourths, pitch-structure too is flexible, with semitonal activity and trills, though broadly contained within a D♭ lydian mode. Dance here affords Daphnis spriritual solace in his sorrow. Stravinskian harmonics cue a mystic episode where the nymphs lead Daphnis (in re-awakened reality) to invoke the assistance of Pan (as supernatural unreality), whose form emerges from an immense stone (Figs. 78–82). An 'Interlude' (Figs. 83–8), set for unaccompanied SATB choir, offers a poignant extemporisation on Chloé's theme with the bass-line initially assuming an unworldly whole-tone identity.

Beyond introductory fanfares and chromatic flourishes, Part II consists almost entirely of dance. The fine 'Danse guerrière' *à la* Borodin ('Animé et très rude': Figs. 92–104) expresses the primitive celebrations of the plundering pirates in Dorcon's vulgar 2/4 metre. This savage, energetic dance (type 2) minimises melody with a percussive tritonal bass pounding beneath continual semitonal figuration. Within the overall modality of *Daphnis*, the centre on B here acquires the status of an alternative dominant. Back in a modality of A lydian, the central section (Figs. 104–22) features the piccolo's exotic melody with its augmented second and tritone: the alluring but dangerous 'diabolus in musica'. This exotic/erotic dance (type 4), bearing some resemblance to Stravinsky's 'Dance of the Firebird', suggests the promiscuity of the pirates who want to rape Chloé.[26]

Direct juxtaposition highlights the heroine's anguished response in the 'Danse suppliante de Chloé' (Figs. 131–3; 133–9), with its unusual fluctuating tempo. Additionally, the intervals of her theme are expanded for emotional heightening and expressed in the remote context of G♯ minor (five sharps, as used by the nymphs), later balanced by five flats (Fig. 136). Falling fourths abound in the cor anglais motif which suggests Chloé's thinking of Daphnis (Figs. 133, 139). This dance denotes the centre of the work as classical ballet, in terms of its focus upon the prima ballerina.[27] Mysterious and awesome sonorities, foregrounding the tritone C–G♭/F♯, then mark Pan's entry as the *deus ex machina* who rescues

Chloé from her tormentors (Figs. 144–53). The enharmonic changes suggest musical masquerading (*trompe-l'oreille*) between opposed states.

Part III begins with the famous 'Lever du jour' (Figs. 155–70), founded on D major (subdominant) with a prominent added sixth, and also featuring melodic pentatonicism. This dawning symbolises the lovers' reunion; musically, it involves the gradual restoration and intensification of the love-theme. The ensuing 'Pantomime' (Figs. 172–87), based on F♯, was an important convention of classical ballet, though generally anachronistic by the time of Fokin's reforms.[28] In thanksgiving, Daphnis and Chloé mime the story of Pan's intense, unrequited love for Syrinx, and so finally they dance together, though only briefly under assumed roles as yet another quasi-Symbolist 'equivalence'. As Larner points out, 'Most extraordinary of all, Daphnis and Chloé are denied the amorous *pas de deux* which any choreographer and any other composer would have considered basic to the whole enterprise.'[29] Nonetheless, Chloé does finally fall into Daphnis's arms, at which point the love-theme reappears, suggesting at least a symbolic consummation at the emotional peak of the work (Figs. 187–92) which concludes on the powerful supertonic, B major.

Finally, the 'Danse générale' (Fig. 194ff.; type 2) in 5/4 metre, on a restored if chromatically obscured final of A, leads seamlessly into the irrepressible Bacchanalian celebrations – Fokin's choreographic 'whirlpool' – whose compositional demands took Ravel over a year to resolve. Although Ravel made no secret of Rimsky's influence (as at Fig. 196), 'This last episode – which is twice as long as in the 1910 version and immeasurably more dangerous in its use of a pagan five-in-a-bar metre rather than a civilised three-in-a-bar – remains one of the most exciting passages in the choral and orchestral repertoire.'[30] Descending fourths persist, reinforced as double-fourth objects on E♭ clarinet, then paralleled by trumpet, lastly writ large by woodwind tutti (Figs. 200–2). Beyond restating the main materials, this dance dissolves melody into waves of chromaticism so as to focus on the sheer rhythmic drive and ultimate breakdown of repeated formulae, as a development from 'Feria' (*Rapsodie espagnole*). Metric diminution compounds the effect, reducing from 5/4 to 3/4 and ultimately to 2/4.

The stature of this work is beyond doubt. Rollo Myers expresses a consensus when he states that 'The score of *Daphnis* is one of the richest in the whole repertoire of ballet and shows clearly the influence of the Russian Ballet aesthetic with which the whole of civilized Europe was permeated in those years before the first world war.'[31] More particularly, *Daphnis* comprises an astonishing collection of dances: Ravel's 'composite portrait'. Dance is employed imaginatively for various purposes (divided above into four main types), but therefore does not have the single-minded, devastating intensity of the post-war dances.

The post-war context

The First World War, the death of his mother and poor health clearly impact on the post-war ballets. *Le Tombeau de Couperin*, with its dual homage to friends killed in the War and to a broader eighteenth-century French past, received its staged premiere with the newly inaugurated Ballets Suédois on 8 November 1920. Désiré-Emile Inghelbrecht conducted, Jean Börlin created the coquettish choreography and Pierre Laprade designed the sets and costumes: 'This delicate and charming evocation of the eighteenth century was something of a light relief for Rolf de Maré's aggressively avant-garde company.'[32] Discussion of *Le Tombeau* has typically promoted its objective basis to the extent of viewing the dances as receptacles: 'It was unremarkable that he [Ravel] should have taken readily to the disguise of Neoclassicism in *Le Tombeau de Couperin* for piano or orchestra (1917–19), where the forms of a French Baroque suite are made to hold self-contained ideas of characteristic finesse.'[33]

Although *Adélaïde* (*Valses nobles*) is a pre-war work, its relevance here is within a trajectory of essays on the waltz which extends from *Gaspard de la nuit*, through *Ma Mère l'Oye*, moments of *L'Heure espagnole* and *Daphnis*, to its culmination in *La Valse*. From a celebration of Schubert's own *Valses nobles*, Ravel proceeds to the ultimate rethinking of waltzes of the Strauss family. Both works delight in nostalgia, with James Harding highlighting in *Valses nobles* 'the tangy harmonies and unexpected accidentals which flavour the nostalgia generated in these wonderfully expressive dance movements'.[34] On the larger trajectory, the creation and destruction of dance, which directs this whole chapter, it is worth recalling Constant Lambert's assertion that 'There is a definite limit to the length of time a composer can go on writing in one dance rhythm (this limit is obviously reached by Ravel towards the end of *La Valse* and towards the beginning of *Bolero*).'[35]

Duality in *La Valse, poème chorégraphique*

'I conceived of this work as a sort of apotheosis of the Viennese waltz, mingled with, in my mind, the impression of a fantastic, fatal whirling . . . Although essentially intended to be danced, it has only been staged until now in the Antwerp theater and at Madame Rubinstein's ballet performances.'[36] Ravel's apotheosis elevates Viennese dance-band music to the status of orchestral high-art music and amateur dancing couples to professional ballet-dancers. Most importantly, he elevates musical materials to their breaking-point. This apotheosis leads to 'a dancing, whirling, almost hallucinatory ecstasy',[37] and consequent ideas of dream and memory. Given the fundamental choreographic basis, it would be perverse not to consider *La Valse* in its full balletic embodiment, especially since the music's implicit concern with succession and simultaneity still owes much to Cubist views on visual representation. Ravel's own scenario prefaces the score: 'Through breaks in the swirling clouds, waltzing couples may be glimpsed. Little by little they disperse: one makes out (A) an immense hall filled with a whirling crowd. The stage is illuminated gradually. The light of the chandeliers peaks at the *fortissimo* (B). An Imperial Court, about 1855.'

Although intended for the Ballets Russes, Dyagilev's deprecating response to the score caused the final rift between the two artists: 'Ravel, it is a masterpiece ... but it is not a ballet ... It is the portrait of a ballet ... the painting of a ballet.'[38] *La Valse* received its orchestral premiere on 12 December 1920, with the Lamoureux Orchestra under Camille Chevillard (and symphonically has never looked back), but had to wait until 23 May 1929 for the Opéra production by Ida Rubinstein (1885–1960), with choreography by Nijinska and sets and costumes by Benois. The main conductor of the programme was Gustave Cloez, but press reviews such as from *Le Figaro* (25 May 1929) suggest that Ravel may have directed his own work. Unfortunately, Rubinstein and Nijinska seriously compromised Ravel's scenario in favour of an idiosyncratic, light-weight interpretation: 'We are, on the bank of the Danube, in a marble swimming pool surrounded by high, massive columns' where 'Mme Ida Rubinstein, in a silver corset and a cap with flaxen plumes, appears as a kind of water goddess of the Waltz'![39]

The characterising slant for this reading is that of duality: the existence of two levels, balancing states or planes, within various dimensions. One perspective, building on Ravel's scenario, views the work's moving in and out of focus as quasi-Symbolist *correspondances* between present and imagined past, reality and a fantastical dream-world. Musically, duality shows itself successively by the large-scale structural division close to that of Golden Section (Fig. 54), as noted by George Benjamin; harmonically, 'The narrative trajectory of *La Valse* is above all realised through a harmonic language in which the opposing forces of civilised order and destructive disorder are characterised by a range of interconnected techniques.'[40] *La Valse* offers an explosive forum for diatonicism versus chromaticism, chordal juxtaposition, bitonality and enharmonic change. Metric/rhythmic interaction thrives on hemiola, essentially 2/4 groupings within 3/4. Early thematic searchings and some later developments, which balance antecedent (ascent–descent) and consequent (descent–ascent), are characterised by two main intervals: the tritone (z) – intrinsic to the V^7–I duality of the waltz – and the ubiquitous perfect fourth/fifth (x/y).

Example 7.6 *La Valse*: melodic searching (Figs. 1–2)

Furthermore, the emerging theme (as at Fig. 5) has a former, partly inverted, existence in *Daphnis*, and its various transformations receive binary-type constructive treatment (especially Fig. 18ff.).

Musical duality may be mirrored by staging and choreography. Cyril Beaumont remarked on Nijinska's revised production of 22 June 1931: 'The curtain rises on a scene which suggests a painting by Eugène Lami, a crimson and gold ballroom lined with enormous mirrors and lit with groups of candelabra. At the far end folding doors give onto a second ballroom.' In this way, two spaces are positioned as foreground (immediacy) and background (remoteness), connected by doors that enable or deny access. In addition to the main couple, 'She' and 'He' first danced by Rubinstein and Anatole Vilzak, Beaumont alluded to a choreographic duality: 'At another stage dancers are seen in the distant room, and a very interesting form of choreographic counterpoint is provided by the dancers in the second room moving quickly in a chain, while those in the foreground slowly revolve to the languorous strains of the waltz; later the rhythms are reversed.'[41] So, in *La Valse* we find a complex of dualities in musical and choreographic domains, whose paired entities may exist in neutral balance (as likeness), in interlocked conflict (as opposition), or harmonised in at least partial synthesis.

The opening evokes an unformed primordium: Benjamin's 'birth' process. Divided, muted double basses oscillate between E–A♭ and E–F and provide pizzicato pulses: 'a heartbeat evolves, intimating perhaps that the origins of the waltz are atavistic and physiological, not merely cultural'.[42] Association with creation in Stravinsky's *Le Sacre* is ensured by the use of bassoons for the melodic searching. Essentially this introductory portion is focused on the dominant-of-the-dominant (i.e. chord V of A), but Ravel likes obscuring matters through enharmonic 'otherness' and modal flexibility, as with A♭ (i.e. G♯) and F (the phrygian upper neighbour-note of E). The bassoons present two significant intervallic objects (Example 7.6; Figs. 1–2): the tritone z', A♭(G♯)–D (suggesting E[7]), balanced and partly resolved by the perfect fourth x', A♭–D♭ (preceded by a descending sixth). Ironically, this 'resolution' is part of another seventh chord with embedded tritone: F, A♭(G♯), C♭(B), D♭(C♯); basically a semitonal contraction of the outer voices of an E[7] sonority (i.e. E–F and D–C♯).

Example 7.7 *La Valse*: main theme (Fig. 9, bars 4–11)

Mysterious building from rhythmic/melodic fragments continues (Figs. 3–4) aptly viewed by Benjamin as 'cinematically edited glimpses of future themes'. Increased focus comes with the violas' melancholic phrase: that close relative of Chloé's waltz-theme in *Daphnis*, featuring an upper pedal underpinned by a chromatic voice-leading ascent: A–A$\sharp$–B (see again Example 7.3b; Fig. 5). Harmonic support is offered by the first bass descent to D, as the final of a flexible modality which favours the flattened seventh.

An expectant trill on G$\sharp$ (large-scale lydian raised fourth) leads via the dominant to an overt D major and Ravel's letter A of the scenario (Fig. 9): 'one makes out an immense hall filled with a whirling crowd'. Vision clarifies and with it perhaps a sense of the real beginning. The waltz is formed, its theme on violas now features the reinflected perfect fourth (x'/x), with regular phrasing supported by secure harmony (Example 7.7; Fig. 9^{+4}). A process of musical intensification begins (Figs. 13–17) as 'The stage is illuminated gradually.' Violins assume the melody with new timbral warmth and impetus through hemiola, mutes are removed, texture enriched and dynamic increased. The intensity and rhythmic vivacity at the first climax (Fig. 17; letter B) – 'The light of the chandeliers peaks at the *fortissimo*' – has the immediacy of the present although this is just affectionate nostalgia masquerading as memory of 1855. Nonetheless, as false, imagined memory it is doubtless more powerful; as Stravinsky mused: 'I wonder if memory is true, and I know that it cannot be, but that one lives by memory nevertheless and not by truth.'[43]

Inevitably, the image soon fades with the next episode (Figs. 18–46), marked by thinner texture and reduced instrumentation, though still founded on D. This is Benjamin's 'suite of waltzes', though all material is closely related and ultimately derives from the two intervallic hallmarks, used as prefix, suffix and in decorated forms. The oboe melody here (Fig. 18) assumes greater importance later as a destructive agent in the corresponding recapitulatory reading, while the repeated bass formula (E$\flat$–A–D–A–C$\sharp$–A) resembles Chloé's theme in *Daphnis*, mirroring the violas' material. Distance is increased by sequential modulatory treatment (Figs. 22–6), leading to an abundance of possible Straussian rhythmic allusions within a chromaticised B$\flat$ modality (Figs. 26–9). Indeed, the elder Strauss's *Radetzky March* Op. 228 appeared in 1848 and the younger's *Tales from the Vienna Woods* Op. 325 in 1868, but to force closer association would be foolhardy and largely pointless. Ravel is after all much more interested in the fake than the real. More consequentially, since flats later acquire significance (beyond Fig. 54), it is worth highlighting a remote Neapolitan inflection on E♭ (Figs. 30–4). Other dualities include bitonality (Fig. 36) and the use of D minor as tonic 'otherness' (Figs. 39, 44). It is hard, incidentally, to ignore a motivic similarity to the Scherzo of Beethoven's Ninth Symphony, especially when presented on A (Figs. 38–9). A further episodic section (Figs. 46–50) represents the remotest region, with mysterious nocturnal qualities. This music is intricate, kaleidoscopic and fluid in its exploration of the flat key areas of B♭ and D♭ major. Dominant preparation, with trills above a tritonal bass, then builds to a *fortissimo* and signals the reprise (Figs. 50–4).

The primordial return (Fig. 54) denotes the start of the second crescendo and Benjamin's 'decay'. Whereas the first segment (exposition and central episode) maintained convention and might have predated the War, the second segment (reprise) explodes that convention and is emphatically post-war. This segment rewrites its earlier history and so creates a large-scale antagonistic duality. Initially, there is clear correspondence, albeit telescoped and with interpolated reference to the central episode. The first significant slippage (using a technique implicit as early as Figs. 1–2) is a literal pulling-down of the viola pitches from A to A♭ (cf. Figs. 57 and 5), while enharmonic change on E♭/D♯ offers a new deceptive duality (Figs. 58–9: $\hat{2}$ of D♭; $\sharp\hat{4}$ of A). Deviation continues in an increasingly dissonant harmonic climate. The Beethovenian figure returns (Figs. 63–6) with intensified internal struggle, after which tension is briefly dissipated in the Neapolitan section (Figs. 66–8). A modulatory passage then leads to the subdominant for a *fortissimo* climax (Fig. 73), punctuated by bass drum and cymbal roll.

The return of the tonic and sense of rebuilding from primitive principles suggest, albeit prematurely, a coda (Fig. 76). Two chromatic bass ascents coupled by greater harmonic change and quickening tempo soon diminish the tonic's status (Figs. 78–80, 82–5) and are mediated by a pedal-point on A♭, again semitonally 'one out' (Figs. 80–2). The climactic moment (Fig. 85) offers the most expansive, ecstatic treatment – a Lisztian transformation – of a previously subdued idea (Fig. 46), supported by bass drum, tam-tam and string glissandos. Its D minor key signature is belied by an increasing tritonal emphasis, with diminshed seventh constructs in the bass (Figs. 86–8). String passage-work derived from the upbeat to Fig. 19 brings a new urgency (Figs. 87, 89 and 91–3), while tritonal relations are intensified by the conflicting bass and treble: A♭–D versus F♯–C (Figs. 88, 90 and 93).

Marked by a striking chromatic divergence, the mechanism begins to stutter and go awry (Figs. 93–4). The bass is locked into mechanical cadential formulae (in D), antagonised by chromatic disruption in the brass and a skewing towards G in woodwind and strings. Melodic figurations are truncated, distorted and endlessly repeated, like a needle stuck at the end of a gramophone record (Figs. 94–8). The only exception is a slow-motion 'flashback' to the theme which began the central episode (cf. Fig. 97^{-2} and Fig. 18). Melody, increasingly formless again, reduces to chromatic ascent–descent and rhythmic gesture (Fig. 98: Benjamin's coda); grotesque touches include the bestial 'snorting' of the brass. Another enharmonic duality presents on B♭/A♯ (Figs. 98–9), with the sharpened fifth sustained until the last three bars, so balancing the earlier preoccupation with the flattened dominant. In its death throes, the brief 'rattle' of the penultimate bar destroys the final rhythmic vestige of the waltz's identity (a detail reserved only for the full score). Ravel's alternative, cataclysmic, reading is now complete.

Machine and flamenco in *Boléro*

'It constitutes an experiment in a very special and limited direction . . . There are no contrasts, and there is practically no invention except the plan and the manner of the execution. The themes are altogether impersonal – folk tunes of the usual Spanish Arabian kind.'[44] So Ravel explained the predetermined mechanical structure in the spirit of his father's experiments, with the Spanish Arabian reference implying the likely relevance of flamenco. *Boléro* was premiered by Rubinstein's troupe at the Opéra on 22 November 1928; Walther Straram conducted, choreography was by Nijinska, with sets and costumes by Benois. The first concert performance was on 11 January 1930, with Ravel conducting the Lamoureux Orchestra.

Ironically, despite Ravel's down-playing of *Boléro*, this work has engendered more discussion than any other; even Ravel's life has been characterised by *Boléro*.[45] Approaches range from Lévi-Strauss's early linguistic/semiotic reading, through a perceptual study of listeners' responses to repetition measured on semantic scales (for example, 'open–suppressed', 'fantastic–realistic'), to one which represents Ravel's most rigorously constructed object by means of a computer model.[46] *Boléro* inspired twenty-five recordings in the 1930s alone, including those by Ravel and Toscanini (see Woodley, 'Recordings of *Boléro*': Chapter 10); it has been associated with film (1934, 1941) and ice-dance (1984). Additionally, it has spawned many transcriptions.

An agenda concerned with the machine and flamenco – extreme objectivity coupled by cultural 'otherness' – is directed by movement and the tension of opposites, especially fixed elements versus free. Essentially, we might see the music as machinist, with imagery derived from Ravel's writings (whistles, sirens, 'traveling belts', hammers, files, and saws; see 'Ravel's writings on machines': Chapter 3), and the choreography as flamenco-inspired. Rubinstein's concept centred on 'a flamenco dancer exciting the admiration and lust of drinkers as she works herself into a frenzy on a table top'.[47] But there is more subtle interaction: 'Mme Rubinstein understood that the strength of the score was such that the dance must appear as a kind of projection on the visual plan of this radiant music.'[48] Equally, flamenco is relevant to the treatment of melody and ostinato accompaniment.

Boléro was originally entitled 'fandango': 'A Castilian and Andalusian courtship dance in triple time and moderately fast tempo; less frequently, a slow, plaintive sung melody belonging to the class of *cante flamenco* (gypsy song).'[49] Closely related, the bolero represents a more reserved version. Despite Ravel's suppposed distance from the traditional dance, he adopts the moderate tempo, triplets (which connect with the polonaise) and a modified AAB formula (AABB). Moreover, 'The entry of the voice is preceded by at least one bar of sharply marked rhythm, and short instrumental interludes separate the sung couplets.'[50] Flamenco also synthesises song, dance (*baile*) and guitar music (*toque*), and emanates from the gypsy/Moorish heritage of Andalusia. It is characterised by phrygian modality, ornamentation and polyrhythm, using hand-clapping (*palmas*), heel-stamping (*taconeo*) and finger-snapping (*pitos*); nasal vocal timbre (*rajo*) is much prized, while guitar styles include strumming (*rasgueado*), passage-work (*paseo*) and interludes (*falsetas*).[51]

Boléro is not strictly a crescendo but a series of terraced steps from *pp* to *ff*; similarly, the piece is not concerned with organic growth but with the phased depression of a lever, stopping only at inevitable mechanical failure. Its basic plan comprises two related, repeated melodic materials (AABB), of thirty-four bars' duration. Ravel himself perceived 'an analogy between the alternation of these two themes riveted one to the other and the links of a chain or a factory assembly-line [chaîne]'.[52] The AABB formula is heard four times (up to Fig. 15); internal repetitions are then removed for doubled momentum (Figs. 16–18) which prompts the final switch to E 'major' and the imminent breaking-point.

In Debussy's 'Ibéria', Derrick Puffett noted that 'Against a guitar-like, strumming background (prominent strings and harps), a solo viola, doubled by first oboe, spins out a long, improvisatory line which turns back upon itself again and again before alighting on its modal centre or

Example 7.8 *Boléro*: ostinato basis (opening)

Example 7.9 *Boléro*: melodic basis
(a) Material A, first part (bars 5–12)

(b) Material B, first part (Fig. 2, bars 3–10)

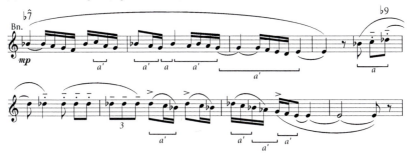

"final", F♯.'[53] *Boléro* shares this combination of a meandering melody (material A/B) and a reiterated guitar-like background: Ravel's 'ostinato machine'. The main layered elements, shown in Example 7.8, are the pulsing (basso) ostinato 1 of interlocking cogs (elaborated by promiscuous seconds on harp: beats 2 and 3 from Fig. 2) and the triplet ostinato 2 (side [snare] drum doubled by flute from Fig. 1). The repeating melodic material A/B, shown in Example 7.9, comprises ostinato 3. Ostinatos 1 and 2 span just two bars, repeated obsessively in circular motion; the unerring intonings of single pitches resemble morse-code patterings. This aspect quickly acquires a monotony (Ravel's 'drudgery'?), so that only 'ennui' temporarily relieves what would otherwise be intolerable tensions. Beyond the machine, complex counter-rhythms and cross-accentuations occur in flamenco dance, while triplets are prominent in guitar technique.[54]

Melodic material A is confined within C, with which pitch the theme has an incantatory preoccupation (reinforced by lower and upper neighbour-notes, B and D), suggesting a ritualistic dimension (Example 7.9a). Intervals expand from the seconds of stepwise motion, through thirds to the perfect fourth; in particular a small intervallic object (*a*/*a*'), the minor third, initially $\hat{6}$–$\hat{1}$($\hat{8}$), evokes the exotic and antique. Overall, the shape is an octave descent, C–C, with the first part concluding on an imperfect close, approached via the supertonic, D. The second part develops the modal interest in the supertonic and presents another voice-leading descent to C; in flamenco, too, a characteristic cadential formula comprises a strong descent (from A minor, through G and F majors ($\flat\hat{2}$), to E major).[55] As yet, the flamenco singer/dancer seems unable to characterise the material sufficiently; the flamenco perspective is compromised by the emotionally devoid machinist one. Alternatively, this could be merely an act of suppression – a musico-sexual smouldering – which certainly has a role in flamenco, as in the tango. Picture the Vienna Opera House production where, 'with an almost demonic indifference, Ida Rubinstein rotated without halting, in this stereotyped rhythm, on an immense round tavern table, whilst at her feet the men, expressing an unleashed passion, beat themselves until the blood came . . . '[56]

Material B (Example 7.9b: first part) focuses increasingly on the phrygian collection: C, Bb, Ab, G, F, Eb, Db, C, as an intervallic mirror-image of material A: C, D, E, F, G, A, B, C. The reinflection of D as Db (and B as Bb) increases harmonic tension with the bass; as Puffett observed in 'Ibéria', 'the flamenco melody itself is constantly enriched by its associations with the prevailing harmony.' Exhibiting 'a curious refusal on the flamenco's part to commit itself as to mode',[57] this material is much more pitch-inclusive and fluid in its inflections: E/Eb; A/Ab. The raised mediant, E, offers an alternative imperfect close, often tritonally associated with Bb, and sometimes founding a diminished seventh construct: E–G–Bb–Db (comprising further minor-third objects). Ornamentation is increasingly foregrounded, with triplets, accentuations and stressings in the bassoon and Eb clarinet renditions (Figs. 2–4).

By the second mechanical cycle of AABB (Fig. 4), the continually enlarging pizzicato patterns of ostinato 1 begin to resemble the strumming formulae (*rasgueado*) and accentuations of flamenco guitar. A six-stave presentation, including a superimposed quaver articulation, leads to proliferation across eight staves (Figs. 6–7) and the threat of all-consuming

Example 7.10 *Boléro*: material A, polytonal travelling belts (Fig. 8, bars 3–6)

mechanisation. Material A seeks the *rajo* timbre of the oboe d'amore (Fig. 4) although the actual sonority disappointed Ravel, while the trumpet/flute coupling first suggests parallel travelling belts and melodic mechanisation (Fig. 5). Conversely, material B maximises ornamentation as expressive characterisation: acciaccaturas, portamentos and blue pitches played by three different saxophones (Figs. 6 and 7; later by trombone, Fig. 10). Tension develops between this increasingly 'humanised' melody and its hyper-restrictive tonic–dominant accompaniment: such modal/tonal disparity is ultimately untenable.

By the third hearing, ostinato 1 has enveloped nine staves, the bass increasingly suggestive of a punctuating hammer (Fig. 8). The travelling belt complex of material A now presents polytonally on C, G and E majors, attesting to the continuing fascination with simultaneity: the grating simultaneity of factory life (Example 7.10). A subsequent bitonal presentation, organum-like on C and G (alternatively, a composite mode with lydian tendency: C, D, E, F/F♯, G, A, B, C), receives five-fold amplification in the woodwind (Fig. 9); the side drum of ostinato 2, now more dynamically evident, has the dry precision of castanets, while ostinato 1 assumes thirteen staves with fully-notated strumming effects. The *forte* dynamic marks a nine-fold proliferation of material B (Fig. 11), starting on pitches B♭, E and G, as the intermeshed cogs of a large mechanism. This material could also be seen as localised B♭ lydian although the bass-pedal on C confirms B♭ as the overall flattened seventh. Returning to Ravel's '*Boléro* factory' (see again Chapter 3), we were perhaps previously concealed behind the doors where all was heard in muted, colourless terms, but now those doors are opened and we approach a huge mechanised process. From a film perspective, beyond an initial wide-angled panorama, we are dealing increasingly with acute, close-up, camera angles.

The fourth rendition is briefly monotonal with material A warmed by violins (Fig. 12), but bitonality returns, thickened by thirds, in a 'block' harmonisation (Fig. 13); fighting against the infiltration of ostinato 1, this melodic mechanism now involves seventeen parts. Modal unity returns for material B (Fig. 14), but is again obfuscated by multiple lines starting on B♭, E and G (Fig. 15). Intensification results from the *fortissimo* dynamic, the myriad of semiquaver triplets (linking ostinatos 1 and 2) within a suffocating tutti orchestration, the removal of melodic repetition and the entry of the second side-drummer (Fig. 16).

This pent-up energy cannot be contained indefinitely. In Leonard B. Meyer's terms, the over-extended 'implication' finally receives some 'realization',[58] with the crude transposition of the whole apparatus up a major third (Fig. 18): popular song technique gone-one-better. The immediacy of effect simulates the pushing of an electric switch and signals an impending cataclysm; as Larner nicely expresses it, 'the friction between melody and mechanism finally causes ignition, the tonality lifts off from C major to E major and, as it falls back, the edifice collapses'.[59] This final cycle lasts only fourteen bars, eight of which comprise a distorted melodic variant in what is effectively an altered mixolydian mode: E, F♯, G♯, A, B, C, D, E (see also DeVoto, 'The Piano Trio: modality and form': Chapter 5); the use of this scalic collection, together with a small phrygian inflection, maximises connection with C.

The last six bars constitute the breaking-point: melody is destroyed, reiterated movement is merely impotent stasis. Drastic chromatic cacophony on saxophones and trombones might suggest the ear-piercing whistle of steam-pistons, but it better resembles a distressed bestial braying, or human wailing. As Manuel Rosenthal observed: 'in the later part of his life many of Ravel's compositions show that he had a feeling for a dramatic death – the *Boléro*, for instance.'[60] This musical outburst relates to ideas of Jacques Attali, who regards noise as a 'simulacrum of murder': 'In its biological reality, noise is a source of pain . . . A weapon of death. It became that with the advent of industrial technology.'[61] The penultimate bar denotes the final stutter, or Attali's 'rupture': the destruction of the (inhuman) mechanism and death of the (human) dance. The final melodic descent is fittingly phrygian; the only possible cadence is plagal (iv♭13–I) since there is nothing left in the tonic–dominant domain. Thus this piece is at least in part a working-out of the ambiguous relationship between man and machine that so fascinated Ravel. Despite Ravel's great enthusiasm for the machine as man's 'noble inspiration' (see again

Chapter 3), perhaps it was all along just a 'vast monster', albeit a highly compelling one.

And so these three works constitute Ravel's balletic 'dance-machine' trajectory, founded on creation–apotheosis–destruction. Each brings its own characterisation to this agenda, and our final images might be of *Daphnis et Chloé* as Ravel's expansive classical fresco, *La Valse* as a late-Romantic oil-painting and *Boléro* as a stark twentieth-century photograph.

8 Vocal music and the lures of exoticism and irony

PETER KAMINSKY

Given that Ravel's compositional output is relatively small for a major composer, his corpus of thirty-nine songs would appear to be significant by sheer size alone. However, once we discount the eight songs composed prior to the orchestral cycle *Shéhérazade* (1903) – all essentially student efforts, and the twelve folk melodies for which Ravel provided accompaniments as something other than fully composed, serious 'art song', we are left with quite a scant amount of work. How then does the genre of song figure within Ravel's oeuvre? Is its stature analogous, say, to that of solo song in Mozart, or perhaps Stravinsky – some tasty morsels obscured by works of far greater scope and quality? Or is the situation closer to Debussy, whose songs clearly are more significant and represent a critical component of his stylistic evolution?

Despite its relative obscurity, even for devotees of Ravel, the genre of song is crucial to his compositional development and achievement. Ravel himself cited among his favourite works the *Trois poèmes de Stéphane Mallarmé* and the *Chansons madécasses*. More concretely, the songs (and the operas) provide a perfect conduit for characteristic elements of Ravel's musical voice, including exoticism, irony, 'literalism' (text painting on multiple planes) and archaism.

Taken together, Ravel's published songs divide fairly neatly into three categories: individual settings, folk/ethnic settings and art-song collections. With respect to chronology and stylistic development, the songs also divide into three distinct periods. Beginning with the *Ballade de la Reine morte d'aimer* (1893), the first period consists entirely of settings of individual poets, ranging from the sixteenth-century Marot to Ravel's contemporary, de Marès. *Shéhérazade* (1903) for soprano and orchestra, Ravel's most ambitious vocal work to date, initiates the second period, whose other significant works include the cycle *Histoires naturelles* and the two popular song collections *Cinq mélodies populaires grecques* and *Chants populaires*. The final period is dominated by three cycles: *Trois poèmes de Stéphane Mallarmé*, *Chansons madécasses* and *Don Quichotte à Dulcinée*. These works, along with the 1920s settings of Ronsard and Fargue, represent the zenith of Ravel's song composition and stand among his greatest and most characteristic works.

My division of the songs into three periods assumes the notion of

Ravel's continual growth as a song composer. The idea that he reaches full maturity only with the Mallarmé settings (1913) may appear paradoxical, given his much earlier mastery in piano, chamber and orchestral genres (for example, *Jeux d'eau*, *Sonatine*, *Miroirs*, the String Quartet, *Introduction et allegro*, and *Rapsodie espagnole*, all composed prior to 1909). Beginning, however, with Mallarmé's poetry, Ravel's choice of texts and their musical expression become progressively more ambitious (at least through to the *Chansons madécasses* and *Rêves*); and his statements concerning the Mallarmé and Madagascar texts show that he was well aware of their difficulties.[1] While risk-taking and artistic maturity are not necessarily related, in Ravel's case such an equation is validated by the originality and daring of the later songs.

In tracking Ravel's artistic progress, I shall focus on his compositional choices, from the exoticism and late Romanticism of *Shéhérazade*, to the irony and literalism of *Histoires naturelles*, the confluence of literalism and Symbolism in the *Trois poèmes*, the primitivism and bitonality of the *Chansons madécasses* and the final evocation of Spain in *Don Quichotte*. Given his profound concern for texts, and based on the evidence of the mature songs, this commentary proceeds from a fundamental assumption that the text invariably motivates Ravel's compositional strategies. If the connection remains obscured, then the fault lies with the analysis rather than the song.

Early songs: foreshadowings and failures (1893–1903)

All the songs composed before 1903 represent individual settings of different poets (excepting the pair of Marot poems). For the young Ravel, these poems provided opportunities for experimentation; despite their immaturity, each of these songs establishes its own distinctive atmosphere and tone. Not surprisingly, given the harmonic inventiveness of the *Menuet antique* and *Sites auriculaires* (1895–7), the early songs all share Ravel's sophisticated harmonic language, including dissonant chord extensions (ninths, elevenths, thirteenths, flattened and sharpened fifths), post-tonal pitch collections (octatonic, whole-tone, and pentatonic), pedal-points and dissonant linear counterpoint. Also evident is the predilection for archaism through modality, parallel fifths and other devices. Many such features are already present in the *Ballade*; as Orenstein observes, 'The musical and poetic elements in this youthful work – pastiche, preciosity, modality, and the chiming of bells – indicate the path Ravel will soon follow with increasing maturity.'[2]

Notwithstanding the prescience of the *Ballade*, these early experiments counted more failures than successes. Ravel's setting of Mallarmé's *Sainte* provides a telling example; the opening five lines are given below.

A la fenêtre recélant	At the window that harbours
Le santal vieux qui se dédore	The old flaking-gilt sandalwood
De la viole étincelant	Of the viol that sparkled
Jadis selon flûte ou mandore	In the past to flute or mandore
Est la sainte pâle étalant ...	Is the pale female saint who displays ...

(trans. Orenstein)

Sainte is representative of the Symbolist poet in its attenuated syntax (with its subject delayed until the fifth line, and the entire poem comprising a single syntactical unit), complex temporality (a meditation on a faded stained-glass saint and associations arising from events and objects of the past) and highly nuanced musical references. Ravel's setting is undistinguished and dull. The opening performance directions, 'Liturgiquement' and 'sans aucune nuance jusqu'à la fin' appear naive and at odds with Mallarmé's poetry which is nothing if not nuanced. The chordal ostinato and undifferentiated texture bear Satie's influence and appear totally inappropriate (although a similar approach taken to Verlaine's *Un grand sommeil noir* (1895) is at least congruent with the sombre and monochromatic text). For Ravel's *Sainte*, the sophistication and textual complexity outstrips not so much his musical technique as his concept of song composition. (Eighteen years later he was to take on Mallarmé's poetry again with very different results.)

Other poems like *Si morne!*, the *Chanson du rouet* and *Manteau de fleurs* are so poor as to be irredeemable for musical setting, notwithstanding Ravel's occasional flashes of inspiration. (An example occurs in bars 18–20 of *Manteau de fleurs*, whose texture, quasi-octatonic harmony, registral placement and formal coincidence with the mid-point of the poem are replicated ten years later in the middle section of 'Soupir'.) Probably the most successful early songs are the *Deux épigrammes de Clément Marot*, whose modality, gentle irony and archaic parallel fifths begin to sound like the mature Ravel.

At the risk of being overly reductive, the causes of early failure are: insufficient experience, poor poetry and a lack of empathy for the subject and rhetoric of the poem. If this formula has validity, then the three essential requirements for Ravel's successful song-writing should be: sufficient technique (essentially a 'given' from *Shéhérazade* onward), strong poetry and, above all, empathy for the text. With the songs of 1903–10, this empathy becomes articulated as an attraction to the exotic and the ironic.

Example 8.1 *Shéhérazade*: exotic harmony in the introduction to 'Asie' (bars 1–11)

(a) bars 1–3   (b) bars 3–6   (c) bars 7–11

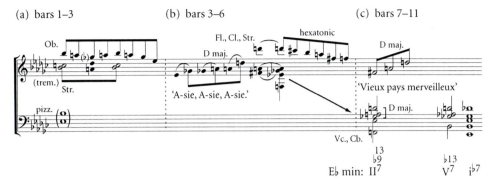

First maturity: exoticism and irony (1903–10)

Shéhérazade (voice and orchestra)

Exoticism for Ravel implies a wide variety of musical and literary interests sharing the notion of 'otherness'. In contemplating his first large vocal work, Tristan Klingsor's cycle of one hundred poems entitled *Shéhérazade*, a vivid and sometimes overheated fantasy of the Orient, was a natural choice. 'In discussing the *fin de siècle* in France, Tristan Klingsor observed that "the Orient was in the air, through Bakst, Rimsky-Korsakov, and Doctor Mardrus, who translated the *Thousand and One Nights*."'[3] Moreover, Klingsor and Ravel were friends and fellow members of the 'Apaches'.[4] The Klingsor poems chosen by Ravel range from the colourful depiction of various Asian locales in 'Asie', to the harem-like atmosphere of 'La Flûte enchantée', concluding with the languid seductiveness of 'L'Indifférent'. Together, they give ample sway to Ravel's mastery of orchestration and precision of text painting. In the recitative-like setting of Klingsor's free verse and the lush but delicate orchestration, the influence of Debussy (especially *Pelléas et Mélisande*) persists.

While a formal exegesis of the introduction to 'Asie' (Example 8.1) cannot account for its magical and evocative qualities, it can provide a snapshot of Ravel's arsenal of technical and expressive devices to date. Beginning with the string pizzicato on the root and fifth of the tonic, E♭, which gives way to a muted string tremolando, the oboe theme evokes the Orient through the ubiquitous exotic augmented second (B♭–A–G♭–A–B♭–A–G♭–E♭: Example 8.1a). This interval is then incorporated enharmonically into the vocal invocation 'Asie, Asie, Asie', within a rising D major triad (Example 8.1b). At the culminating 'Asie', the flutes, clarinets and strings cascade down the symmetrical hexatonic scale (also called

Wunderreihe) D–C♯–B♭–A–F♯(G♭)–F.[5] As D major is arpeggiated by the vocal line ('Vieux pays merveilleux' – 'Ancient wonderland') and sustained in the upper register, the lower strings add the minor seventh, F/E♭ (bar 7: Example 8.1c). In the resultant extended dominant seventh harmony on F, the root and third of D major become the thirteenth and flattened ninth, respectively. Characteristically, the chord progresses by fifth descent resolving to E♭ minor and the start of the song proper. Together, the emphasis on the augmented second and *Wunderreihe* – plus the octatonic flavouring (signalled here by combining chords of F[7] and D major) – reflects not only 'Orientalism' but, more broadly, represents Ravel's sole foray into late nineteenth-century Romanticism within songwriting.

Interestingly, after *Shéhérazade*, Ravel composed no other true orchestral song cycles (the Mallarmé songs are really a chamber work) despite the particular popularity of the medium in pre-war Paris. Given his taste for exoticism and mastery of orchestration, why should this be so? For one thing, the sheer abundance of exotic images, especially in 'Asie', and Ravel's ability to convey them musically, approach the kind of Oriental kitsch about which he spoke so disparagingly in other composers (see also Orledge, 'Exoticism by other composers': Chapter 2). Perhaps realising this, his subsequent settings tend to eschew Romantic sentiment, reflecting his apparent desire to express text 'directly' without the virtuosic veneer of a large orchestra.

In this second period, the lure of the exotic is complemented by his attraction to the make-believe world of machines, mechanical toys, animals and childhood fantasy (see also Mawer, 'The machinist phenomenon': Chapter 3). For Ravel, like Debussy, this 'magical kingdom' inspired many works including *L'Heure espagnole*, *Ma Mère l'Oye* and *L'Enfant et les sortilèges*. In each of them Ravel, sympathetic and ironic in equal measure, invests the utmost musical refinement, expressivity and even high drama in bringing his make-believe world to life.

Make-believe in *Noël des jouets*

His maiden voyage is the delightful *Noël des jouets* (The Toys' Christmas) of 1905, the only solo song for which Ravel wrote the text. Ravel's genius for text painting, thoroughly exploited in *Shéhérazade*, is joined here by his ability to convey a narrative with a few well-chosen musical strokes (Example 8.2a–e). In bars 1–2, the left-hand descending thirds, right-hand open fifths and gentle quaver rhythm convey the tenderness appropriate to the song's Virgin Mary doll and candy baby Jesus. The mechanical toys

Example 8.2 *Noël des jouets*: motive and narrative
(a) bars 3–4

Le troupeau ver-ni des mou - tons

très doux

(The painted flock of sheep)

(b) bar 12

(The rabbit drummers)

(c) bars 23–6

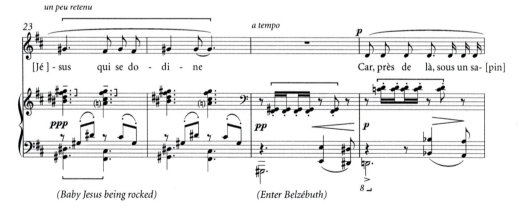

[Jé] - sus qui se do - di - ne   Car, près de là, sous un sa- [pin]

(Baby Jesus being rocked)   *(Enter Belzébuth)*

Example 8.2 (*cont.*)
(d) bar 52   (e) bar 69

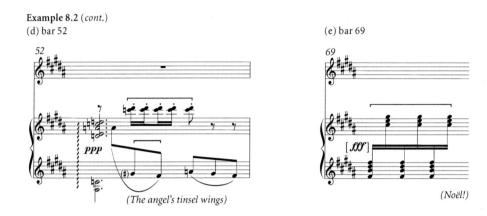

(The angel's tinsel wings)   *(Noël!)*

come to life as the right hand adds a composite semiquaver rhythm (bar 3:
Example 8.2a), interlocking with the left hand like the meshing of little
gears.

At bar 12 (Example 8.2b), Ravel introduces a motive of repeated
seconds on G♯/F♯ conveying 'Les lapins tambours, brefs et rêches, /
Couvrent leurs aigres mirlitons' ('The rabbit drummers, curt and harsh, /
Cover their squeaky tin flutes'). This motive, rhythmically prepared by the
vocal entrance of bar 3 ('Le troupeau verni' – 'The painted flock'), recurs
throughout in different harmonic contexts according to the narrative.
Thus G♯/F♯ returns 'un peu retenu' (bar 23: Example 8.2c) in the top of the
right-hand chords, the vocal line and bass fifths, portraying the baby Jesus
being rocked in his mother's arms. With the chilling entrance of
'Belzébuth, le chien sombre' (bar 25), the motive assumes its original
rhythm in the bass; its transposition (bar 26) by the devil's own tritone,
C/D, generates a contextually dangerous whole-tone scale. At bar 52
(Example 8.2d), C/D returns in the upper register (but with G♯–F♯ lurking
in the left hand), mimicking the noise of the angel's tinsel wings.

Finally, at bar 69 (Example 8.2e), the joyous ending on 'Noël' marks the
arrival of B major, with G♯–F♯ as the top notes of alternating chords.
Significantly, register and the harmonic context of the main motive mirror
the status of the creatures associated with it: Belzébuth has the ugly low
register and whole-tone harmonies, the mechanical rabbits the middle
register amid the gentler dissonance of dominant ninth chords, while Jesus
and the angels naturally have the upper register and mimimal dissonance.
Ultimately, Jesus is saved and the toys rejoice noisily (anticipating Disney's
Toy Story), reflected harmonically as the ending safely ensconces G♯ as a
neighbour-note within the tonic, B major, harmony.

While relatively unknown, *Noël des jouets* is as much a breakthrough
work for Ravel as *Shéhérazade* in establishing a characteristic voice.
Indeed, the portrait of Belzébuth, with its bass seconds, tritone and whole-

tone colouring, comes back virtually unaltered as the 'Beast Music' within *Ma Mère l'Oye*. More generally, the little song foreshadows the many settings of make-believe, beginning with *Histoires naturelles* composed a year later and culminating with his masterpiece, *L'Enfant et les sortilèges*.

Animal fantasy in *Histoires naturelles*

For the song cycle *Histoires naturelles* (1906), Ravel set five animal fables in prose by Jules Renard. It is easy to understand his attraction to Renard's naturalistic depiction of animals and nature:

> [Renard] eschews the anthropomorphic attitude of La Fontaine; his animals do not speak like humans . . . Nor is he attracted by the hierarchical classifications of the eighteenth-century naturalist [Buffon] . . . It is not, therefore, as a moralist or a philosopher that Renard approaches the world of nature, but as an observer of unusual receptivity.[6]

Ravel's attitude towards setting these texts is revealed in a conversation with Renard himself, reported in the latter's journal:

> M. Ravel, the composer of the *Histoires naturelles*, dark, rich, and elegant, urges me to go and hear his songs tonight. I told him I know nothing about music, and asked him what he had been able to add to the *Histoires naturelles*. He replied: I did not intend to add anything, only to interpret them.
>
> But in what way?
>
> I have tried to say in music what you say with words, when you are in front of a tree, for example. I think and feel in music, and should like to think and feel the same things as you.[7]

Ravel's statement uncovers his literalism, which entails a two-fold desire to suppress his own emotions and thoughts and take on those of the poet, and to translate a text directly into musical terms. Generally, the vocal line is uncomplicated, set syllabically within a limited range and changeable metre in response to Renard's prosody; Ravel, somewhat controversially, does not set the French mute 'e' as a separate syllable. His settings also reflect Renard's rhetorical shifts from narrative to brief aside (laconic, ironic or both). Musically, these shifts coincide with interruptions of the ongoing progression and texture in favour of sparse or unaccompanied recitative. A wonderful example concludes 'Le Cygne' when legato arpeggios depicting the swan on the water abruptly give way to recitative, staccato chords and the implied key of C major (the flattened supertonic of the tonic B). The shift signals the narrator's ironic realisation that the entire narrative hitherto was an illusion: instead of the swan dying in his attempt to capture the cloud's reflection in the water, he is in reality fattening up on the worms which he pulls from the mud.

Ravel's accompaniments bring to life the subject of each narrative as well as the main physical action associated with it.[8] Thus, in 'Le Paon', the peacock struts pompously to the dotted rhythms of the French overture; in 'Le Grillon', the industrious cricket rakes sand and files a blade of grass to a mechanical high ostinato; 'Le Cygne' sounds like the water music of *Jeux d'eau* and 'Ondine' with added vocal line; the subdued dynamic, rich chromatic counterpoint and slow pace create the stillness of 'Le Martin-pêcheur' (The Kingfisher); finally, the frenzied repetitions and staccato chords portray the foul temper and lethal beak of 'La Pintade' (The Guinea-fowl).

'Le Grillon' demonstrates Ravel's ability to suggest multiple levels of meaning simply by interpreting the text. The song portrays the daily life of a cricket and his attempts to put his house in order; in Ravel's best mechanical manner, the opening ostinato depicts busyness and the compulsive need for order. Musically, the conflict between order and disorder takes shape as the most fundamental structural conflict: consonance versus dissonance. In the introduction, the pitch G♯, while functionally the leading-note of the initial A minor, is dissonant in relation to the ostinato E–C. Thereafter, G♯ is invariably dissonant across varied chordal contexts; notated as A♭, however, the same pitch is consonant as the fifth of D♭ major, the tonality in which the song concludes. Metaphorically, G♯ and its attendant 'sharp' world represent the cricket's disorder; correspondingly, A♭ symbolises the 'flat' world of his security, which ultimately equates with the stillness of the trees in the moonlight. The resulting contrast between the cricket's 'human' efforts to create order and the truly natural order of 'nature' subtly underscores the implied irony of Renard's narrative.

Remaining second-period songs

Most of the remaining songs here are harmonisations of folk melodies, including the *Cinq mélodies populaires grecques* (1904–6) and the *Chants populaires* (1910). (Although the melody is Ravel's own, the *Vocalise-étude en forme de habanera* (1907) falls into the same 'ethnic' category.) Their composition reflects not only his broad musical interests, but also his chameleon-like personality – the desire to efface his own voice and take on the character of the 'other', be it Greek, Spanish, Italian, Hebraic or Scottish. Even the 'Chanson française', the second of the *Chants populaires*, becomes merely another cultural entity. Ravel's accompaniments are almost invariably tasteful and appropriately ethnic, the sole exception being the 'Chanson italienne'; skilled mimic as he was, Ravel could not cast himself as a soulful Italian tenor!

Two individual settings from 1906 round off the period: de Régnier's *Les Grands Vents venus d'outremer* and Verlaine's *Sur l'herbe*. Unfortunately, Ravel could not do much with de Régnier's ill-conceived poem except match its alternately grey and histrionic tone. The Verlaine, while a distinctly minor effort, looks forward in its preciosity and idiosyncrasy to the far more successful setting of Mallarmé's 'Placet futile'.

Full maturity: symbolism and suggestion (1913–32)

Musical *transposition* in *Trois poèmes de Stéphane Mallarmé* (voice and ensemble)

If *Shéhérazade* represents the lure of the exotic, and *Histoires naturelles* the exemplar of literalism and irony, then the *Trois poèmes de Stéphane Mallarmé* (1913) initiates a new stage marked by the revelation of inner meaning(s) of the text through its musical setting. For Ravel, the expression of inner meaning may be traced back to his deep admiration for Edgar Allan Poe. In the later nineteenth century, Poe was practically a cult figure in France, entrancing writers and musicians alike, including Baudelaire, Mallarmé and Debussy. For Ravel, the specific locus for his interest was *The Philosophy of Composition*, in which Poe explicates his composition of *The Raven*;[9] after enumerating the many technical devices leading to its creation, Poe finally reveals what is still missing:

> But in subjects so handled, however skillfully, or with however vivid an array of incident, there is always a certain hardness or nakedness, which repels the artistical eye. Two things are invariably required: first, some amount of complexity, or more properly, adaptation; and, secondly, some amount of suggestiveness, some undercurrent, however indefinite, of meaning. It is this latter, in especial, which imparts to a work of art so much of that richness . . . which we are too fond of confounding with the ideal.[10]

We probably cannot say why Ravel thought that Poe exerted so great an influence on the development of his compositional technique, but we can relate Poe's emphasis on suggestiveness and Ravel's approach to Mallarmé around 1913. About Mallarmé and the *Trois poèmes* Ravel writes:

> The aesthetic of Edgar Allan Poe, your great American, has been of singular importance to me, and also the immaterial poetry of Mallarmé –
> unbounded visions, yet precise in design, enclosed in a mystery of sombre

> abstractions – an art where all the elements are so intimately bound up together that one cannot analyze, but only sense, its effect.
>
> I have a predilection for my *Trois poèmes de Stéphane Mallarmé*, which obviously will never be a popular work, since in it I transposed the literary procedures of Mallarmé, whom I personally consider France's greatest poet.
>
> I wished to transpose Mallarmé's poetry into music, especially that preciosity so full of meaning and so characteristic of him.[11]

Unlike some literary critics who focus primarily on the ambiguity and undecidability of Mallarmé's Symbolist poetry, Ravel cites precision, abstraction and mystery as its defining elements. He also refers twice to 'transposition' (in French, the cognate *transposition*) in discussing his aesthetic goal in the Mallarmé settings. Reconsidering Ravel's previous statements on aesthetics and text setting in the light of those on Mallarmé, the notion of *transposition* appears to synthesise his own predilection for literalism with Poe's undercurrents of meaning. For the *Trois poèmes* and beyond, Ravel's lasting achievement is to plumb these undercurrents in stunningly original ways while remaining true to his literalist roots.

In March–April 1913, Ravel and Stravinsky were living in Clarens, Switzerland, working together on Dyagilev's commission to revise Musorgsky's *Khovanshchina*. Stravinsky told Ravel about a new work he had just heard, Schoenberg's *Pierrot lunaire*, whose scoring for soprano and chamber ensemble inspired Stravinsky's own *Trois poésies de la lyrique japonaise*. Attracted to this instrumentation, Ravel began work on his *Trois poèmes*, completing them by August; the songs are scored for soprano and a chamber orchestra consisting of two flutes (doubling piccolo), two clarinets (doubling bass clarinet), string quartet and piano.[12]

Given the tremendous complexity of the poetry and music comprising the *Trois poèmes*, a proper analysis would require a separate essay. Instead, I will concentrate on the opening song 'Soupir' and suggest a point of departure for its analysis.[13] While the remaining songs 'Placet futile' and 'Surgi de la croupe et du bond' differ markedly from one another and from 'Soupir' in compositional strategy, they are all related by Ravel's objective of *transposition* – particularly the extent to which the syntax and semantic content of the poem dictate compositional choices. More than any other vocal work, the Mallarmé songs demand that we begin with the poem – to establish the central tension, problem or paradox that captivated Ravel's imagination, and to discover the means both for his literal interpretation and for his attempt to transpose the text's inner meaning(s).

'Soupir' (Sigh) is the least complicated of the three poems; formally, it

divides into two halves of five lines, corresponding broadly to the inhala-
tion and exhalation of the sigh itself:

> Mon âme vers ton front où rêve, ô calme sœur,
> Un automne jonché de taches de rousseur
> Et vers le ciel errant de ton œil angélique
> Monte, comme dans un jardin mélancolique,
> Fidèle, un blanc jet d'eau soupire vers l'Azur!
> Vers l'Azur attendri d'Octobre pâle et pur
> Qui mire aux grands bassins sa langueur infinie
> Et laisse, sur l'eau morte où la fauve agonie
> Des feuilles erre au vent et creuse un froid sillon,
> Se traîner le soleil jaune d'un long rayon.

> My soul rises toward your brow, O calm sister, where there lies dreaming
> An autumn strewn with russet freckles,
> And toward the restless sky of your angelic eye,
> As in a melancholy garden,
> A white fountain faithfully sighs toward the Azure!
> Toward the compassionate Azure of pale and pure October
> Which mirrors its infinite languor in the great pools
> And, on the stagnant water where the tawny agony
> Of the leaves stirs in the wind and digs a cold furrow,
> Lets the yellow sun drag itself out in a long ray.   (trans. Orenstein)

Syntactically, the two halves are linked by the phrase 'vers l'Azur', a clue to
the semantic richness of the central image 'l'Azur' for Mallarmé.[14] In the
first half, 'vers l'Azur' culminates the images of soul, brow, sky, angelic eye
and fountain, all implying ascent (captured in the contour of the vocal line
and flute part) and suggesting an ideal of purity and freedom, or a positive
trajectory. By contrast, in the second half, 'l'Azur' has a downward and
negative trajectory associated with images of stagnation and death, reaching its metaphorical nadir with 'sa langueur infinie'.

Ravel's setting interprets Mallarmé's poem as three stages in the
progress of the sigh: the positive ascent towards 'l'Azur' (the first half), the
negative descent towards 'l'Azur' (the opening of the second half) and
the arrival at its Stygian core ('sa langueur infinie'). Each stage is translated
literally by instrumentation, pitch collection and contour (Example 8.3).
Thus Stage 1 consists of an unbroken ostinato in natural string harmonics,
rising and falling like 'un blanc jet d'eau soupire vers l'Azur!' ('a white
fountain sighing toward the Azure'); the pentatonic collection further
emphasises the purity of 'l'Azur'. These elements culminate in the vocal
highpoint on 'Fidèle' and plagal cadence in E minor. With the clarinet
dyad, G/B, acting as a pivot between the two halves of the song, Stage 2 is
projected by the strings' drooping chromaticism. The progression then

Example 8.3 *Trois poèmes de Stéphane Mallarmé:* literalism and metaphor in 'Soupir'

Stage 1: pentatonic (bars 1–17)

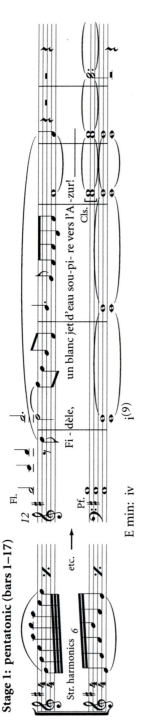

E min: iv

Stage 2: chromatic (bars 17–24)

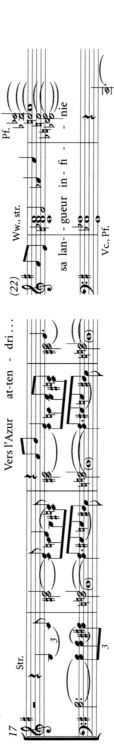

Stage 3: octatonic (bars 24–8)

chromatic (bars 31–4) ⟶ pentatonic (bar 35)

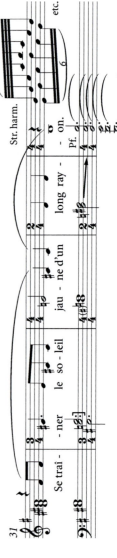

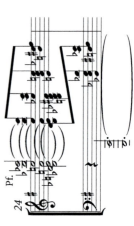

leads by fifth descent ((implied D)–G–C) to Stage 3, the strange solo piano music coinciding with '[sa langueur infi]-nie'. The passage sounds almost like Messiaen in its stratified texture, harmonic stasis and absence of tonal function. Its onset significantly coincides with the internal rhyme between 'Vers l'Azur attendri' and 'sa langueur infinie'. Not only is there a mimetic relation between the static octatonic harmonies and the image of infinite languor, but the rhyme, by associating languor with 'l'Azur', completes the negative trajectory of the latter.

If the above constitutes the literal aspect of the song, where lie the undercurrents of meaning? The answer is to be found in Ravel's creation of a music-syntactical problem based on his reading of the poem's second half. By sustaining a non-functional octatonic harmony for five bars (from bar 24), he creates a structural dead-end coinciding with 'sa langueur infinie' (thereby ignoring Mallarmé's enjambment: 'sa langueur infinie / Et laisse,'). The problem: how to progress beyond the dead-end and conclude, true to the poem and the prior musical movement. Ravel's elegant solution: turn back and retrace the previous path. Thus, after a brief holding pattern, the original pivot dyad, G/B, returns (now with C♯ and E♯ positioned symmetrically a tritone below and above). In turn, the dyad re-initiates the drooping chromatic movement (cf. bars 17–19) and its 'expiration' on E coincides with the reprise of the E minor/pentatonic collection and string harmonics (cf. bars 13–16).[15]

For Ravel, the motivation for the reprise represents far more than the desire for conventional formal closure. Rather, the formal structure itself conveys the shape of the sigh, corresponding to the inevitable progress of weary autumn towards death in the poem: 'Se traîner le soleil jaune d'un long rayon' ('[the October Azure] Lets the yellow sun drag itself out in a [single] long ray'). The untransposed path of drooping chromaticism both away from and back to E minor/pentatonic becomes the musical analogue to Mallarmé's autumnal sigh.

The remaining songs, 'Placet futile' (Futile Petition) and 'Surgi de la croupe et du bond' (Rising from the Crupper and the Leap), express opposing sides of the musico-poetic vision: for 'Placet', refinement and preciosity; for 'Surgi', the emptiness of the void.[16] One way of approaching these difficult works is to compare their use of significant musical techniques to earlier less sophisticated usage. Example 8.4 shows a technique in 'Asie' (cf. Example 8.1) and its recurrence ten years later in 'Placet futile': the construction of extended harmonies by positioning a pitch, interval or chord below a previously stated sonority. Recall that, at the opening of 'Asie', a D major (6/3) chord is sounded and then sustained in the middle register while the seventh F/E♭ enters below it, thereby transforming consonant chordal notes into dissonant extensions of an F dominant seventh

Example 8.4 'Sub-position' and dominant harmony
(a) 'Asie' (1903), bars 4–5   (b) 'Placet futile' (1913), bars 2–3 and 26–7

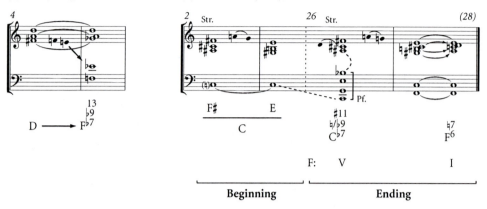

chord (Example 8.4a). In Klingsor's 'Asie' this device of 'sub-position' serves a purely colouristic purpose within the Orientalist fantasy; in Mallarmé's 'Placet futile', however, the same device carries profound structural and expressive consequences.

The most crucial difference is that in 'Placet' the process of subpositioning frames the entire piece. The song opens with the strings sounding F♯ major (6/3) moving to E major (6/3) over the bass pedal C, a progression with little sense of harmonic function; it concludes with virtually the same progression in the strings – the sixth, C♯, enriches the sonority of the E chord (Example 8.4b). Here, however, the piano positions a C dominant seventh chord below the F♯ chord creating a sharpened eleventh construct; the fifth interval, F/C, is then added below the E chord, which is treated as an appoggiatura.[17] Tonally, the progression constitutes the sole cadence in the tonic key of F major. Ravel's motivation for transforming the opening like this springs directly from the poem: the poet petitions a princess to change his current status as a chaste abbé in favour of his desired role as shepherd of her smiles. Ravel's representation of the poet's 'before' and 'after' states by means of opening harmonic ambiguity transformed into concluding tonal functionality barely hints at the richness of the song.

Example 8.5 compares the orchestration and texture of 'Surgi' with the opening of 'Asie'. Strikingly, both works begin with a pizzicato chord, followed by high violin tremolando which accompanies an expressive melody for solo wind (oboe in 'Asie', piccolo in 'Surgi'). Additionally, the flute and piccolo arpeggio in 'Surgi' (D–E♭–F♯–A–D, bar 1) parallels the vocal entrance in 'Asie'. There are, however, significant differences of tonal context. In 'Asie', we hear the initial fifth, E♭/B♭, as consonant and the tremolando C as a neighbour-note to B♭; our impression is confirmed as the introduction closes with a cadence in the tonic E♭ minor

Example 8.5 Orchestration, evocation and difference
(a) 'Asie' (bars 1–4)

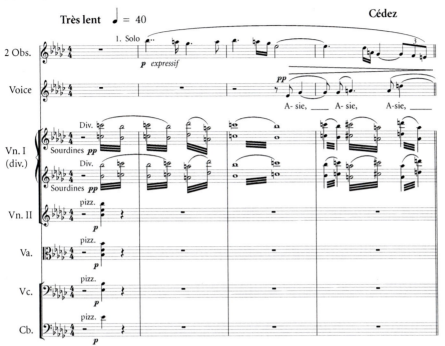

(b) 'Surgi' (bars 1–3)

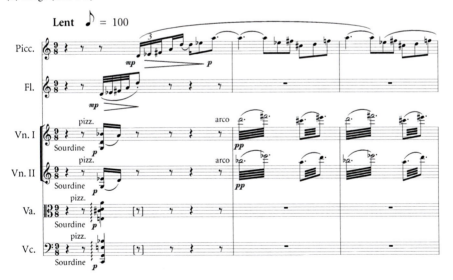

(bar 11). By contrast, the opening chord of 'Surgi', while underpinned by a C dominant seventh in the cello, contains so many dissonant notes (C♯, D, E♭ and A) that – especially in its pizzicato articulation – it sounds like nothing more than a quiet 'thump'; even its status as a recognisable chord is questioned. Moreover, unlike 'Asie', the succeeding tremolando and flute melody give little clue to any sort of pitch centricity.

Once again, the reason for these differences lies in the text. In 'Asie', Shéhérazade-as-narrator evokes a mythical Asia which nonetheless is real in representing Klingsor's and Ravel's fantasy vision. In 'Surgi', however, the very notion of representation is interrogated. The narrator attempts to evoke something from an ephemeral piece of glass (which we later learn is a vase), the evocation of which becomes a metaphor for writing the poem or, more broadly, the possibility of poetic creation itself. With its primary images involving death or stasis and its negative grammatical constructions, Mallarmé's sonnet is a prime example of his 'poetics of negation', already hinted at in the darker side of 'l'Azur' from 'Soupir'. Ravel therefore chooses to begin 'Asie' in a tonally determinate manner, but 'Surgi' in a state of indeterminacy signalled by the unapprehensible opening chord.

Considering the tremendous subtlety and difficulty of Mallarmé's poetry, the extent to which Ravel succeeds in representing shades of meaning and metaphor is remarkable. And, in Ravel's eyes, evidently unrepeatable as he never again attempted to set such refractory texts. His subsequent major vocal works, the *Chansons madécasses* and *Don Quichotte à Dulcinée*, turn away from textual complexity and return to exoticism and irony, albeit with the resources of his full maturity.

Musical narrative in the *Chansons madécasses* (voice and ensemble)

Ravel composed the *Chansons madécasses* (1925–6) for soprano, flute, cello and piano, to a commission from Elizabeth Sprague Coolidge. The prose texts for the three songs are drawn from the *Chansons madécasses, traduites en français, suivies de poésies fugitives* by the Creole poet Evariste-Désiré de Parny (1753–1814). Orenstein notes that Parny never travelled to Madagascar nor did he know the language.[18] Leaving aside questions of authenticity, clearly the exoticism of the text appealed to Ravel:

> The *Chansons madécasses* seem to me to bring a new element, dramatic – indeed erotic, resulting from the subject matter of Parny's poems. The songs form a sort of quartet in which the voice plays the role of the principal instrument. Simplicity is all-important. The independence of the part writing is pronounced . . .[19]

The composer hints here at several new musical developments: a more overtly contrapuntal style; the representation of the erotic (in 'Nahandove' and 'Il est doux') and the dramatic (in 'Aoua!'); and simplicity, especially the use of ostinato as a 'primitive' element. Whatever the psychological reasons, Ravel was not predisposed to the erotic in his music, perhaps a consequence of his ironic nature. Indeed, it was easier for him to compose a love duet for two miaowing cats in *L'Enfant et les sortilèges* than one for humans. So the erotic presented a serious challenge, requiring Ravel to adopt yet another mask in the quest for *transposition* of the text.

'Nahandove' provides a test case for Ravel's representation of the erotic, as Parny's text describes a romantic tryst between the narrator and the beautiful Nahandove. The narrative consists of seven 'verses' (literally paragraphs) comprising four stages: the anticipation of Nahandove and preparation of the 'love nest' (verses 1–2); her approach and his rapture at her arrival (3); their lovemaking (4–5); his longing and anticipation of her return that evening (6–7). Previously, in Chapter 2 ('Distancing, translations and the *Chansons madécasses*'), Robert Orledge provided a sensitive introduction to the song, focusing on the reflection of erotic desire and sensuality through musical contour, rhythm and pacing. The following account complements it by focusing on formal structure and how it reflects Parny's text in quite specific ways.

Even in setting an overtly erotic text, Ravel is as mathematically precise as Stravinsky's 'Swiss clockmaker'. Example 8.6 aligns the musical form of 'Nahandove' with the four stages of the narrative; the selected passages represent the beginning and part of the ending of each stage (Stage 3 shows the beginning only). Example 8.6 is meant to be read both horizontally and vertically: the horizontal axis approximates a *diachronic* or temporally linear reading (Stages 1–2–3–4), the vertical a *synchronic* or synoptic reading (Stages 1–3, 2–4). Proceeding diachronically, the song opens simply with the muted cello stating the principal motive, immediately followed by the voice, whose initial figure on 'Nahandove, ô belle Nahandove!' is treated as her leitmotif. In this 'anticipation' stage, the tone is hushed and relatively neutral; tonally this neutrality is conveyed by the primarily white-note modal pitch collection and, in the absence of a true bass line, only a hint of pitch centricity (A aeolian leading to E aeolian).

With her approach ('Elle vient'), the tempo quickens and the rhythmic pulse shifts from quavers to semiquavers. Intensity increases with the addition of chromatic pitches; her climactic arrival ('c'est Nahandove') is marked by texture, dynamics and register, and by the lydian-inflected cadence in C major. With the lovemaking ('Tes baisers'), the emotional temperature and tempo actually recede, while the harmony is enriched with quasi-bitonal chords, leading to a transient and highly chromaticised

Example 8.6 *Chansons madécasses*: eroticism and narrative in 'Nahandove'

Stage 1: anticipation (bars 1–3; 16–17)

Andante quasi Allegretto

A aeolian ⟶ E aeolian

Stage 3: lovemaking (bars 42–5)

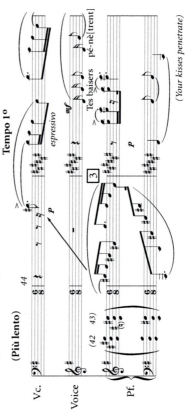

Stage 2: approach (bars 21–3); arrival (bars 28–9)

(She comes. I recognize her quick breathing)

C maj. /C lydian

**Stage 4: longing (bars 75–6);
anticipation of return (bars 79–81)**

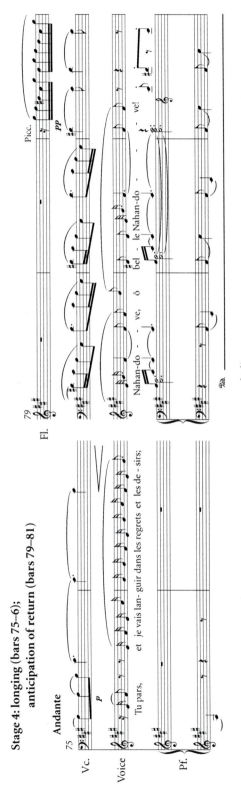

A lydian

F♯ major. Following a reprise of the opening, the music turns with understated tenderness to A major. In the aftermath of lovemaking (Stage 4), the texture is further reduced to voice and cello (on a sustained C♯), emphasising the pleasurable pang of desire ('Tu pars, et je vais languir dans les regrets et les desirs' – 'You leave, and I shall languish in longing and desire'). With the anticipation of Nahandove's return, the cello, flute and piano echo the aching sweetness of the lydian sharpened fourth, D♯, over the tonic harmony.

With the diachronic reading as a backdrop, the synchronic reading proposes that the formal structure for the song has as its foundation a two-fold transformation: the music of Stage 3 transforms Stage 1; and the 'longing' and 'anticipation-of-return' music of Stage 4 transforms, respectively, the 'approach' and 'arrival' of Stage 2. In progressing from anticipation to lovemaking, the first transformation intensifies motive, texture and harmony. Motivically, 'white' becomes 'black': the opening G–F–D–A and its transposition D–C–A–E become G♯–F♯–D♯–A♯ and D♯–C♯–A♯–E♯. Correspondingly, the linear texture turns chordal, and 'pale' harmony turns colourful. All this suggests a process of actualisation for the narrator – from the indefiniteness of imagination to the flesh-and-blood act of making love. By contrast, the progress from Stages 2–4 is one of relaxation, motivated by the simple actions of arrival and departure: 'Elle vient' and 'Tu pars'. While the vocal lines are nearly exact transpositions of each other, the agitation of her approach contrasts completely with the sated exhaustion at her departure; similarly, the climax of her arrival (bar 28ff.) modulates both mode and mood in the concluding anticipation of her return. Moreover, the addition of the caressing flute obbligato (bar 81) refers back to the black-note version of the opening motive by sounding the opening dyad of both pitch levels (G♯–F♯ and D♯–C♯; cf. bars 44–5). Simultaneously the cello's D♯–C♯ lydian appoggiatura 'blackens' the white-note figure, D–C, at the top of the piano (cf. bar 29ff.). Metaphorically, the accretion of earlier gestures literally suggests 'carnal knowledge': the narrator's concluding state of anticipation, basking in the afterglow of his lovemaking to Nahandove, radiantly transforms the earlier musical stages in the light of experience. In effect, the articulation of musical form in 'Nahandove' enacts the narrative by embracing the entire arc of the relationship, reflecting the cyclic ebb and flow of desire as naturally as the sigh in 'Soupir'.

In his quoted statement on the *Chansons madécasses*, Ravel does not mention the one element which, arguably, has received most attention from commentators: bitonality, featured in 'Aoua!' and to a lesser degree in 'Il est doux'. Ravel appeared to discover bitonality in the early 1920s, and it subsequently figures in some – but not all – vocal (and instrumental)

Example 8.7 *Chansons madécasses*: bitonality and race in 'Aoua!' (bars 6–9)

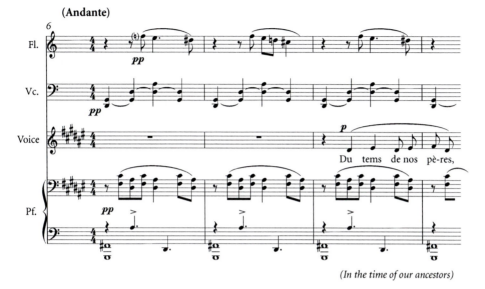

(In the time of our ancestors)

works. What then in the text motivates Ravel's use of bitonality? Part of the answer is revealed in 'Surgi', the first song with any hint of bitonality. In the middle section (bar 9ff.), the piano sounds the fifth, E♭/B♭, while the strings play a D major triad in harmonics, creating an eerie and intense effect; the bitonal chords subsequently progress through a partial cycle-of-fifths, still retaining the semitone between their roots. Significantly, the primary textual images are 'deux bouches' ('two mouths') and 'chimère' ('chimera'). Thus the former provides a literal impetus for bitonality, while the latter (defined by *Webster's Seventh New Collegiate Dictionary* as 'an imaginary monster compounded of incongruous parts') might explain the timbral and registral dichotomy.

Let us consider the opening of 'Aoua!' in the light of Ravel's literalism and bitonality (Example 8.7). Following the explosive introduction, 'Aoua! Aoua! Méfiez-vous des blancs, habitans du rivage' ('Beware of white men, dwellers of the shore'; see Example 2.2: Chapter 2), the song proper begins by setting up five ostinatos: flute, cello, right-hand piano part and, in the left-hand part, both the semibreve major seventh, G/F♯, and the descending twelfth interval, A–D. In accounting for the grinding dissonance, various commentators highlight the seventh in the bass against the D♯ minor of the right hand and voice (the flute's essentially chromatic line does not really belong to any key).[20]

A simple experiment at the piano suggests an alternative interpretation. If we isolate the parts that 'belong together' and play them in succession, then the bass G/F♯ may be interpreted not only as a major seventh but as a 'compound root' of two keys a semitone apart (like 'Surgi'). The G, therefore, would support the cello ostinato and underpin a kind of I–V in G, with the twelfth, A–D, supporting the dominant and coinciding with the fifth in the cello; meanwhile, F♯ would support the right-hand piano ostinato and the vocal line. In this reading, the operative keys are G major and F♯ major (with D♯ as added sixth), rather than G major and D♯ minor. This semitonal combination remains consistent as the harmonies progress through the second verse to A/G♯ (bars 22–4) and B/A♯ (bar 27).

A possible inspiration for such bitonal treatment is, as in 'Surgi', both literal and breathtakingly simple. The text – an angry account of white people's colonialism as narrated by a native – describes the arrival of white men, their broken promises, their attempt to impose their God and culture, the consequent war and its aftermath. In simplest terms, the 'black' tonality of F♯ major sounded by the bass F♯, right-hand piano part and – most importantly – the vocal line could represent the native people; the 'white' tonality expressed by the lower bass G and the cello ostinato could represent the white people. Unlike some bitonal works (for example, the 'Blues' of the Sonata for Violin and Piano and 'Il est doux' from *Chansons madécasses*), 'Aoua!' never resolves in favour of one key or the other; there is no final progression to equilibrium, only a return to the opening. Ravel hereby suggests that white and native peoples cannot live in harmony but coexist only in a dissonant state, though, ironically, Ravel's pessimistic view of the ending is at odds with the concluding verse: 'I have seen new tyrants, stronger and more numerous, planting their tent on the shore. Heaven has fought on our behalf. It has sent rain to fall on them, tempests and poisoned winds. They are no more, and we live, and live in freedom. Aoua! Beware of white men, dwellers of the shore.'

In the concluding 'Il est doux' (It is Sweet), the prevailing mood is one of erotic languor. The poem's narrator is a *pasha* figure in a south-of-the-equator harem scene, describing the joys of resting under a cool tree, watching the girls perform their slow erotic dance and commanding them to go and cook. Having chosen this seemingly unappetising text, Ravel conjures up the fragrance and sultriness of an idealised Madagascar through the slow undulation of the opening flute solo, the prominent major sevenths (suggesting native instruments) and the dance with its ostinatos and drum-like cello harmonics.[21] Consistent with the hazy atmosphere, the D♭ major tonality is suspended until the end, largely obscured by bitonality. Although the gently dissonant bitonality here stands in total contrast to 'Aoua!', its presence in both songs underscores a poetic duality: in 'Il est doux', the woman as 'other'. Musically, the 'male' signature of five flats (implying either D♭ ionian or C locrian) is brought into gentle conflict with the E major vocal line on 'Femmes, approchez' (bar 14), whose opening pitches, B–A, replicate the initial cello entry in harmonics. Unlike 'Aoua', the 'other' is finally resolved in favour of the tonic, D♭. Thus *her* B–A becomes enharmonically transformed in the penultimate phrase as C♭–B♭♭, resolving to A♭ over *his* tonic D♭.

Don Quichotte à Dulcinée

After the technical innovations and expressive complexity of the Mallarmé and Parny settings, Ravel's last completed work for voice and piano *Don Quichotte à Dulcinée* (1932–3, subsequently orchestrated; text by Paul Morand) signals a return to his beloved Spain and to his earlier stylised folk settings. The songs range from the tongue-in-cheek chivalry of the 'Chanson romanesque' to the austere organum-like 'Chanson épique', closing with the exuberant 'Chanson à boire' (Drinking Song). Orenstein observes that 'each song is based upon the rhythm of a Basque or Spanish dance': the first on the Spanish *quajira* alternating 6/8 and 3/4 metre, the second on the Basque *zortzico* in quintuple time and the third on the quick triple metre of the Spanish *jota*.[22] Ravel's refined art, though disguised by simple texts and ethnic flavouring, emerges through a myriad of details: the shifting phrase lengths subtly distorting the metric symmetry of Morand's poetry in the first song, the musical merging of the Madonna and Dulcinea in the second and – the crowning touch – the musical representation of the hiccup in 'Chanson à boire'!

Remaining third-period songs

The other third-period songs are the earlier *Deux mélodies hébraïques* (1914), consisting of the traditional 'Kaddisch' text and 'L'Enigme éternelle'; the *Trois chansons pour chœur mixte sans accompagnement* (1914–15) to poems by Ravel, arranged about the same time for solo voice and piano; *Ronsard à son âme* (1923–4), Ravel's contribution to the collection *Tombeau de Ronsard* (including settings by Aubert, Caplet, Dukas, Honegger, Roussel, Ravel's student Delage and his biographer Roland-Manuel);[23] and the tiny *Rêves* (1927), to a poem by Léon-Paul Fargue.

In the Hebraic songs, 'Kaddisch' presents a relatively simple accompaniment to the cantorial melismas, until characteristic Ravelian arpeggios and altered chords create a more intense expression; 'L'Enigme éternelle' anticipates the *Chansons madécasses* in its dissonant ostinatos.[24] The colourful *Trois chansons*, Ravel's sole work for chorus, manifests once more his love of children's stories and the child-like side of his character, always tinged with irony. All feature strophic folk-like settings and clever text painting. In 'Nicolette', the theme itself with falling fifths and even rhythm creates a stilted 'sing-song' effect perfectly in tune with the nursery rhyme-like tale of Nicolette, who, after refusing the entreaties of the wolf (fearfully) and the handsome page (regretfully), goes off with the 'twisted, ugly, stinking and fat' but rich gentleman. 'Trois beaux oiseaux du paradis' tells the touching story of three birds – blue, white and red (the colours of the French flag) – who bring with them the gaze, kiss and finally the heart (metaphorically) of a soldier at war to his lover; since Ravel aged thirty-nine had just enlisted and was serving in the army, this song most likely reflects his experience and deep feelings about the war. The cycle closes with 'Ronde', a 'patter' song, in dialogue, warning of the dangers of the Ormonde wood. Ravel apparently requested the help of his friends in creating the names of the monstrous sylvan creatures in the song.[25]

Despite their small proportions, *Ronsard à son âme* and *Rêves* have a rightful place among Ravel's late songs; both share the subject of sleep and dreams. The Ronsard song invites comparison with the early Marot settings of 1896–9, the two sixteenth-century courtly poets being near contemporaries. The modal Marot songs breathe the stylised antique atmosphere of the *Pavane pour une Infante défunte* composed around the same time; Ravel however takes a very different tack with Ronsard, setting the poem essentially in strict organum at the fifth, replete with *vox principalis* and *organalis*. At the conclusion, the crossing of the border into sleep is represented by the seemingly limitless stacking of perfect fifths, above and below the central C# (A–E–B–F#–C#–G#–D#–A#).[26] In Fargue's *Rêves*, Ravel's music captures the fluidity and distortion of the dream state. Beginning diatonically, the music becomes progressively more dissonant and concludes with fully-fledged bitonality, corresponding to the gradual revelation within the poem of its images as fragments of a dream.

In 1924, Ravel came as close as he ever did to articulating an aesthetic credo: 'I consider sincerity to be the greatest defect in art, because it excludes the possibility of choice. Art is meant to correct nature's imperfections ... The most interesting thing in art is to try to overcome difficulties.'[27] His statement confirms precisely those qualities that we associate with his music: the adoption of masks (which embraces melody, harmony, texture and tone – see also Mawer, 'Introduction'); artificiality; technical perfection and an almost ironically literalist approach to composition itself ('overcoming difficulties'), drawn directly from Poe and *The Philosophy of Composition*. For Ravel's song composition, his statement suggests a further undercurrent of meaning: the text itself as a mask or, more precisely, as providing a concrete pretext for his donning of a mask.

This helps to explain why Ravel's songs have no single defining musical technique or characteristic – unlike, for instance, Schubert and modal mixture, or Debussy and chromatic mediant relations.[28] Paradoxically, Ravel's consistency in song composition springs from the same source as his unabashed eclecticism, summed up by the notion of *transposition*: his compulsive desire to transform his compositional technique in order to align it as closely as possible with the tone, content and inner life of the text. The end result is not the absence of a distinctive voice that might occur with a lesser artist who chooses to wear so many hats. Instead, by illustrating most directly his mechanism of expression, the songs allow us to 'peer behind the mask' and understand a little more of Ravel's unique, sometimes bizarre, world and its musical representation. In their breathtaking imagination, artistic quality, stylistic variety and sheer ambition in setting text, Ravel's songs represent one of the most significant bodies of vocal repertoire in the twentieth century.

9 Ravel's operatic spectacles: *L'Heure* and *L'Enfant*

RICHARD LANGHAM SMITH

Among strategies for the study of the elusive Ravel is that of the ubiquitous 'compare and contrast' approach: Debussy and Ravel give insights by refraction even though their theatrical works could hardly be more different. If Ravel attended all the performances in the first run of Debussy's *Pelléas*, no wonder his two completed 'operas' are nothing like Debussy's: he knew he had to be different.

L'Heure espagnole in context

L'Heure espagnole was written between April and October of 1907, orchestrated in 1910, and described as a 'comédie musicale'.[1] It was around this time that Ravel's professional relationship with Debussy crossed the thin line from respect to rivalry. In 1906, there was the well-documented conflict with Pierre Lalo when Debussy was credited with an innovatory style of piano writing which Ravel felt he had initiated in *Jeux d'eau*. In 1907, a further accusation was the last straw, this time of Debussy's plagiarism, in 'La Soirée dans Grenade', of a harmonic 'trouvaille' from Ravel's early 'Habanera' from *Sites auriculaires*.[2] All the more reason for Ravel to distance himself from Debussy. This latter furore may have suggested that Ravel was particularly proud of his Spanish innovations. Manuel Rosenthal noted the strength of the composer's relationship with his mother, of 'basquo-ibérique' descent: there was a strong sense of his belonging to Spain, and of Spain belonging to him, as it could not have done to Debussy.[3]

So, in the wake of *Pelléas*, Ravel staked out territory elsewhere: Debussy never wrote a comic opera and Ravel never wrote an entirely serious one; Debussy wrote a full-length piece and Ravel only managed one-acters; above all, Debussy's setting of Maeterlinck has entered the musical canon whereas Ravel's best work (*L'Enfant*) is perceived as a much-loved miniature and his other (*L'Heure*) is somewhat fought shy of by promoters. This said, the comparative approach can probe the contrast between the two composers' interests in hispanicism and their varying responses to the world of the child.

Franc-Nohain and *L'Heure*

In the line of Spanish pieces from *Carmen* to those of Debussy and Ravel (via Chabrier's *España*), *L'Heure* occupies a unique position because of its fertile text. Its author, Franc-Nohain, a pseudonym for Maurice-Etienne Legrand, was born in 1873 at Corbigny in the Nièvre. Ravel had made his acquaintance in 1906 through the composer Claude Terrasse. By the age of twenty-five, Franc-Nohain had already published two collections of ironic poetry (*Flûtes* and *Chansons des trains et des gares*) and had been a favourite at the Paris Odéon in August 1904, where aspiring poets and playwrights presented evenings of their work. Here, he had been described as 'an excellent humorist, paradoxical and amusing, biting without seeming to be; making digs without it being apparent, but always hitting the mark'.[4] Three months later *L'Heure espagnole* was produced at the Odéon for the first of fifty-eight performances on 28 October.[5]

This rhymed one-acter lasted scarcely half-an-hour and was used as a curtain-raiser for a full-length play *La Déserteuse* which had been premiered a couple of weeks before and was also concerned with adultery. *L'Heure*'s premiere was only signalled by a couple of papers (*Le Figaro* did not bother) and was nowhere reviewed, overshadowed by a scandal concerning the similarity between *La Déserteuse* and another play, *Le Bercail*, running at the Gymnase. Nonetheless, *La Déserteuse* was deemed a powerful play, with moments of bad taste but moving in parts.[6] *L'Heure* might well have been chosen because its theme warmed up audiences for an evening of unfaithful wives.

The critic Gaston Carraud described *L'Heure espagnole* as 'mildly pornographic vaudeville'; although set in the eighteenth century, it exploits well-developed nineteenth-century fictions about Spain, packaging them into the mildly titillating fare which was commonplace at the Odéon.[7] Furthermore, it shares with other contemporary plays – *Pelléas* included – a distanced setting of subject-matter about the moral conduct of the Parisian bourgeoisie: the essential fodder of the boulevard *comédie*.

Spanish fictions and traits

Jobbing theatre critics uncritically accepted the stereotypical Spanish fictions, but a deeper analysis of foreign constructions of Spain was already under way. The nineteenth-century fascination for travel had thrown up a welter of Spanish travelogues, stretching back to publications by eighteenth-century travellers, for example Smollett's *The Present State of All Nations* (1768–9). This expanded into a vast corpus of material via German and English travellers as well as several Americans. French chroniclers of the country 'across the mountains' included Victor Hugo, Alfred de Musset and Théophile Gautier.

By the first decade of the twentieth century this literature was subjected to critical review,[8] and the Spanish writer Julián Juderías was soon to publish his seminal study *La Leyenda negra*: the 'black legend' which became the term describing the fictional denigration of Spain.[9] Common to many writers is the portrayal of a country locked in a time-warp behind 'civilised' Europe; a place of atrocities caused by the untamed passions of its people, rife with smugglers and brigands. Its difference was exaggerated by its inaccessibility from France ('Tras les monts', as Gautier put it), and by the well-worn mythology of the contrast between Northern and Southern Europeans: a mythology to some extent perpetuated in *L'Heure*.

A typical example of fiction confused with reality is found in the jottings of the French traveller, Pierre Léonce Imbert. Overwhelmed by the splendours of the Alhambra, he lets his imagination run riot:

> I listened and this is what I heard:
>> 'We are the girls of the Sun; fire courses in our veins: only we know how
>>> to love.
>> Come, men of the North, come and warm yourselves at our lips,
>>> Our kisses have the sweetness of Spring and the scent of roses . . . '
> They undressed and one by one unveiled the exquisite forms of their
> supple and firm young bodies . . .[10]

The mythical over-sexed Spanish female, conjured up more by masturbation than by observation, evoked a land of licence. She turns up again as Concepcion, for whom the weekly highlight is her 'Thursday off'. To some extent, this mythology may be traced back to the Spanish painter Goya, especially in France where his devotees included Balzac, Hugo, Dumas *père*, de Musset and Debussy. How appropriate then that the costumes for the premiere of Ravel's *L'Heure* should have been modelled on Goya's erotic designs.[11]

Other Spanish characteristics were based more on observation. Gautier's *Voyage en Espagne* was a celebrated, finely written travel diary. He noted, for example, the separation of women from their menfolk as they walked in the streets, a characteristic which 'already had the scent of the Orient'.[12] Further differences were their *décolletage* and their command of the language of the ubiquitous fan. In his description of the customs of Granada, where the various age-groups of the extended family spend the early hours in different corners of the courtyard of a *tertulia*, Gautier helps us to understand the roots of Franc-Nohain's portrayal of the insatiable housewife receiving several suitors. She is undoubtedly closer to a French stereotype than a Spanish one: 'In Granada, to pay attention to a married woman is unheard of, while nothing is simpler than to court a young girl. In France it is quite the opposite', remarks Gautier; Ravel himself recognised a Parisian dimension in the play which he claimed represented 'a Spain seen from the heights of Montmartre'.[13]

A further perception echoed in *L'Heure* was that of the power of the Spanish woman in a nation in which the men had degenerated, through in-breeding and emigration to the South American Spanish colonies. Contemporaneous with the writing of Franc-Nohain's play, Alfred Fouillée devotes part of his early psychological study to 'The degeneration of the Spanish character and its causes', highlighting indolence.[14] Both male degeneration and indolence are essential themes in *L'Heure*. None of the men, except Ramiro, achieves anything and none is really good enough for Concepcion, who, in Scene XVII (Fig. 84^{+3}), declares that they are unfit to represent their country:

> Oh! La pitoyable aventure!
> Et ces gens-là se disent Espagnols! . . .
> Dans le pays de doña Sol . . .

Spanish decadence and its portrayal in *L'Heure*

For James Russell Lowell, an American emissary in Spain in the 1880s, Spain was unquestionably 'unstable, frivolous and wholly reminiscent', living on the reputation of past greatnesses.[15] Hence Juderías's perception of the 'black legend' of a decadent country was disseminated not only through travellers' jottings, but also through the outside world's perception of its turbulent historical events. Spain had only briefly sustained a republic from 1873 to 1875, in the wake of uprisings by Carlist conservatives, and finally restored the monarchy. And in what must have seemed like a return to the practices of the *Grand Siècle*, the sixteen-year-old Alphonso XIII acceded to the throne in 1902, virtually an *enfant-roi*.

The strength of this view of a decadent Spain can hardly be underestimated. Could this 'black legend' account for the darkness of Ravel's orchestral introduction to what on the surface is a fairly ordinary beginning to a not-too-serious play set in a small-town shop? Such scenes typically commanded music evoking the hustle and bustle of morning trade, yet Ravel presents a series of parallel chords, increasingly dissonant, over a bass whose tonality is doubly distressed: both by semitonal trills uneasily shifting over four semitones and by the use of mutes and *sul tasto* (before Fig. 1).

Issues of time in *L'Heure*

As the curtain rises, stratified tuned percussion, followed by the sarrusophone and piccolo, hold the piece together with interlocking ticking representing the various clocks in Torquemada's shop (see Example 3.4: Chapter
3). (Their significance, incidentally, is clearly indicated in the Durand
vocal, but not miniature, score.) This extraordinary passage has attracted
much comment. And in the 'black legend', time was perhaps running out
for a country in moral decay. Certainly, the turn-of-the-century was
obsessed with time, scientifically and philosophically. World Standard
Time was only established in 1892, and the centennial celebrations naturally caused much discussion about time. Einstein's theories of relativity
(and quantum theory) date from early in the new century, while
Schopenhauer's extensive discussions of time were widely read. Recurrent
in Schopenhauer's *World as Will and Idea* were considerations of transitori-
ness, and of the relationship between time and man's quest for happiness:

> Past and future ... are as empty and unreal as any dream: but the present is
> only the boundary between the two. (Book 1 § 3)

> Every time a man is begotten and born, the clock of human life is wound
> up anew, to repeat once more its same old tune that has already been
> played innumerable times, movement by movement and measure by
> measure, with insignificant variations ... The life of every individual ... is
> really a tragedy; but when gone through in detail it has the character of a
> comedy. (Book 1 § 58)[16]

Besides Schopenhauer, the ideas of Henri Bergson also dealt with the
nature of time.

Ideas along these lines made a deep impression on post-Wagnerian
France. The coincidence of time, and the question of whether the 'now'
exists at all or whether it is the only thing that does exist, became a precoc-
cupation. The ticking clocks of Edgar Allan Poe echoed in the collective
memory, prolonged by Surrealism which frequently employed distorted
images.

Ravel saw the clocks of *L'Heure* as 'mischievous' and 'grotesque' and, in
an interview in *Comœdia*, he explained how he had reinforced their initial
presence: 'With Franc-Nohain's consent, while the clocks chime their mischievous hubbub, I added some grotesque automatons: some dancers,
musical marionettes, a soldier, a cockerel, an exotic bird, whose mechanical movements add to the illusion.'[17]

Their omnipresence ensured by the perpetual ticking, three meanings
of 'L'Heure' are explored: in French it is both the word for an hour – the

approximate duration of the action – and for 'time' in general. This is how 'time' is passed in Toledo. Torquemada's regular excursion to wind the town clocks controls the action of the play whose characters are the servants of time in this city fallen into decay. Each is more preoccupied with time than with what they are meant to be doing: Concepcion snatches her hour; Ramiro is obsessed with having his watch mended (rather than tending his mules); and Inigo, the banker, effectively appoints Torquemada to his 'regular and periodic position' and is preoccupied with time through his age – positively because of his experience, but negatively because time is a harbinger of physical decay since he is grossly fat. 'We kill time, time kills us.' Seemingly unaware of time, Gonzalve, the student, shows no sign of studying except that he spins atrociously parodistic verses. Spain is the convenient victim on which to foist this view of an effete society.

A third meaning is given by Ravel, who claims the title to refer to 'the hour of the muleteer', encapsulated in the Boccaccio quotation with which the opera finishes: 'There arrives a moment in the pursuit of Love, when even the muleteer has his turn.'

As the paraphernalia at his residence, 'Le Belvédère', in Montfort-l'Amaury proves, Ravel himself had a collector's enthusiasm for mechanical clocks. Jean-Michel Nectoux, in his commentary on Ravel's private library, discusses a play by Victorien Sardou and Maurice Vaucaire, *La Jeunesse de Figaro*, as being 'close to the spirit and familiar tone of *L'Heure espagnole*',[18] while Ravel himself identifies two roots: 'Apart from the student, who sings serenades and cavatinas in an exaggerated manner, the other roles, I imagine, will give the impression of being spoken. This is what Mussorgsky wished to do in setting Gogol's *Marriage*.'[19]

Comparison with Musorgsky (and Gogol), *The Marriage*

Ravel described *The Marriage* as the 'only ancestor' of *L'Heure* and cited the final quintet of *L'Heure* as the sole exception to the declamatory style. His justification was that 'the French language, just as much as any other, has its own accents, its own musical inflexions. And I don't see why one shouldn't take advantage of these qualities to attempt an accurate word-setting.'[20] He further described *L'Heure* as fulfilling 'my intention of renewing the tradition of opera buffa'.[21]

Musorgsky's somewhat esoteric source of 1868 merits some scrutiny.[22] Ravel was acquainted with it from the first published vocal score (in Russian) of 1907, and had considered orchestrating (and perhaps completing) it before 1911.[23] The popularity of Russian music in France, especially Musorgsky, is well known, both through academic studies and through Jean Cocteau's infamous jibe in *Le Coq et l'arlequin* (1918) that Debussy's piano music was merely 'Russian music with the pedal down'. But *The Marriage* (*Zhenitb'a*) is highly original. Musorgsky's subtitle, 'Opéra dialogué' (originally, 'An attempt of [*sic*] Dramatic Music in Prose'),[24] describes the work exactly and represents an attempt to follow a radical realist aesthetic shared by several literary figures.[25]

His description of his aims to César Cui suggests parallels with Ravel's comments about his verbatim setting of Franc-Nohain:

> In my *opéra dialogué* I am trying to underscore as vividly as possible those abrupt changes of intonation that crop up in the characters during their dialogue, seemingly for the most trivial of reasons, and on the most insignificant words, in which is concealed, it seems to me, the power of Gogol's humour.[26]

Its ironic tone parallels Franc-Nohain's technique in *L'Heure*, treating the subject of love with a light touch. It tells of a bachelor deciding to get married but opting out at the last moment by climbing through the church window. Both texts exploit the humour of seemingly trivial detail, necessitating a musical declamation in which the spoken dialogue is clearly audible. *The Marriage* also shares with *L'Heure* an exploitation of stereotypes, particularly the boringness of the bridegroom as an anonymous functionary – like Inigo and Ramiro. From Musorgsky, Ravel seems to have learnt how to handle both the off-beat entry and the varied rhythms dovetailing breaks in the speech. Franc-Nohain's work, like Gogol's, is funny, as Ravel himself commented:

> Franc-Nohain's story is delightful. I changed virtually nothing in it: the wife of the clockmaker Torquemada, in Toledo, awaits her lover, a student, and finally – I'm summing up briefly – submits to a muleteer.[27]

Ravel adds some interesting observations about the piece, including its placing in pre-existent traditions and its use of local colour:

> I have written a comic opera, which I would like to think will prove to be a fresh source of inspiration. Note that in France, this musical genre doesn't exist. Offenbach wrote parodies of opera; today, Terrasse,[28] with delightful verve, distorts rhythms and amuses with his unexpected orchestration, but it isn't the music which makes one laugh. I wanted the chords, for example, to seem funny, like puns in language. If I may put it this way, I 'heard funny' ...You should also understand that I did my utmost to make my work express Spain, and that the numerous rhythms of the jota, habanera and the malagueña will underpin my musical phrases.

Example 9.1 *L'Heure espagnole*: octatonic collections (Fig. 3, bars 1–2)

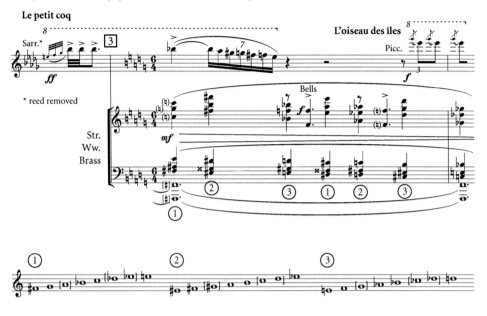

Musical humour in *L'Heure*

'Funny' is hardly the word, yet from the outset Ravel uses harmonies and sounds to project Franc-Nohain's humour, both in responding to the text (rather as Musorgsky) and in the 'Introduction' where three ticking pendulums are given specific metronome marks of ♩= 40, ♩= 100 and ♩= 232.

Ravel employs various techniques to build up the cacophony of these grotesque timepieces. Bitonality is used for the automaton whose B major fanfare, on open horn harmonics, is supported by octatonicism beneath, the accompaniment using extreme colouristic devices such as string chordal trills; muted and glissando trombones; triplet-against-duplet pizzicato cellos; and bubbling wind passages simultaneously sounding augmentations and diminutions of similar octatonic figurations (around Fig. 2). This contrasts abruptly with the clock and the musical marionettes in both harmonic field and texture as the music for these is purely diatonic and scored for celesta and harp which parodies the sound of a mechanical clock (Fig. 3⁻⁵).

Their act is cut short by the interjection of a crowing cock, given to the sarrusophone player, who has previously been growling away in his lowest register, and is now instructed to 'take the reed out of his mouthpiece, and use it as if it were a little trumpet, playing the indicated rhythm *fortissimo*, and as high as possible, without paying any attention to the notated pitches' (Example 9.1; Fig. 3⁻¹). The orchestra meanwhile erupts into an overwhelming gesture (high divided strings, tremolando, with the *oiseau des îles* – an exotic bird played by the piccolo – on top) saturating the texture with octatonic dissonance. Each chromatically descending parallel chord is a verticalisation of notes from each version of the octatonic scale (see again Example 9.1). Ironic contrast, coupled with intense dissonance, thus leads into the action of this comic mirror of tragedy, entertaining like a circus, yet precarious and decadent.

Ramiro, the 'government muleteer', enters first: a ridiculous character who claims that he needs to know the time so that he can carry out the daily parcel-post on his 'government mules'. Resounding with jokes based on fictional stereotypes, he proudly announces that his watch was 'saved from the horns of death' by a toreador uncle (Fig. 5), the implication being that all Spaniards have a relation who is a bullfighter. Here, as later, Ravel underpins the music with Spanish rhythmic and harmonic gestures. The way he does so bears some scrutiny.

Whereas an *opéra à numéros* might have been one way to proceed, Ravel's approach is, initially, to follow Musorgsky and add musical commentary in the orchestral backcloth to essentially speech-driven music. Only in Gonzalve's serenade (Scene IV) and towards the end does the dance-song – a further habanera – flow uninterruptedly to the motto which finishes the piece. The first few minutes distil the various techniques that Ravel mentions (see above). Ramiro's initial dialogue with Torquemada is underpinned by the four-note tetrachord (featuring a phrygian, flattened second: E, D, C, B) which became the hallmark of Spanish folk-music, as shown in Example 9.2 (Scene I). Although Spanish regional folk-music used many other tetrachords, it was most often upon this formula which non-Spanish composers relied to evoke a hispanic flavour.

Ravel makes the music sound 'funny' in his response to textual details. At the mention of the mule-train for the parcel-post, a jaunty figure on pizzicato lower strings and xylophone is accompanied by cow-bells, with a whip-crack on the final quaver of the bar; its strength and hilarity lie largely in its brevity (Fig. 4^{+4}). The ubiquitous 'Spanish' tetrachord reappears at increased tempo to underpin Ramiro's cock-and-bull story about the toreador rescuing his watch. Flamenco-guitar rhythms are superimposed, with a totally ostentatious up-and-down chordal glissando on trombones and tuba (Fig. 6), followed by a whack on the bass drum and a sarrusophone 'fart' as Ramiro's imaginary bull falls dead. To appreciate Ravel's humour, the listener has to be tuned in to both text and score.

Both brawn and brains are ridiculed in the characters of Torquemada (who has not much of either), Ramiro (who is brawny even if deathly dull) and Gonzalve (who tries so hard to be clever that he emerges as ridiculous). Ravel again uses Spanish devices to secure humour at their expense.

Example 9.2 *L'Heure espagnole*: phrygian tetrachord (Scene I, bars 1–5)

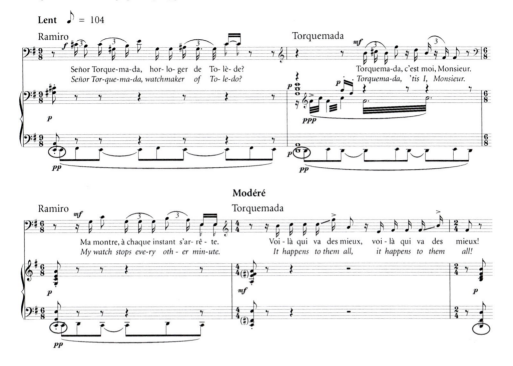

Ultimately exploiting another myth, that women are satisfied only by human seed-drills, Concepcion scorns Torquemada's 'force musculaire' (Fig. 9ff.), and thinks of stronger men, as Ravel indulges in a macho burst of tango.

Spanish pastiche and parody in *L'Heure*

Gonzalve's serenade (Scene IV; Fig. 15) is a studied piece of Spanish pastiche, including an upper and lower leading-note effect frequently found in the improvisatory passages of flamenco song (*salida*), and in guitar playing (*falsetas*); see Example 9.3a and b. However, Ravel's pastiches of Spanish styles never follow their models exactly, neither do they become set pieces. Often they are opposite in effect to pseudo-Spanish pieces which exploit the hypnotic effect of a metrical and dynamic build-up without harmonic change (such as *Boléro*). In *L'Heure*, Ravel is constantly driven by the inflections of the libretto, pausing, hesitating and changing tempo while the capricious orchestration, juxtaposing the mordant with the over-Romantic, adds to the parody.

Gonzalve's unseen entry ('dans la coulisse': Fig. 15^{-3}) indulges this frequent device of nineteenth-century *opéra-comique*. His serenade is

Example 9.3 Laparra and Ravel comparisons

(a) Excerpt from 'Cantar del Labrador' [after J. Verdú]

(Source: Raoul Laparra, 'La Musique' [1914], in *Encyclopédie de la musique et dictionnaire du conservatoire* (Paris, 1920), 2391)

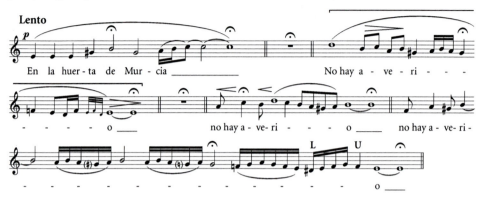

L = lower leading note

U = upper leading note

┌─── = zig-zag descent to tonic

(b) Ravel, *L'Heure espagnole* (Scene IV; Fig. 15): Gonzalve's melody (bars 1–12)

(c) Excerpt from 'Malagueña de la Madrugada' [after J. Verdú], transposed for comparison

(Source: Laparra, 'La Musique', 2390–1)

modelled on a further feature of Spanish folk-music: its tendency to use two adjacent tetrachords articulated by a dwelling on the fourth, rather than the fifth, degree. This property was recognised as a predominant Spanish characteristic stemming from several sources: the tuning in fourths of the guitar; its roots in plainsong; and from various stereotypical harmonic patterns which alternated chords I and IV.

The most accessible, detailed source on Spanish music was undoubtedly an article of 1914 by the composer Raoul Laparra.[29] Laparra had been known to Ravel since 1903,[30] and it is highly probable that Ravel knew this article whose copious examples were useful to plunder for Spanishisms, particularly in the Andalusian section. An improvisatory 'Cantar del Labrador' ('Labourer's song') features upper and lower leading-notes, used harmonically by Ravel, and also the 'zig-zag' descending pattern, used in Gonzalve's melody at Fig. 15 (compare again Example 9.3a and b). A further excerpt ('Malagueña'), transposed for comparison, is striking in its dwelling on the flattened seventh of a phrygian mode (Example 9.3c).

If pastiche was achieved through developing second-hand folk-based techniques, parody was obtained through over-emphasis: the sickly gestures accompanying Torquemada's blind belief in Concepcion's devotion to her little 'totor' (Scene II, around Fig. 7); the warping of the vocal parts with slides, especially in the more lyrical duet between Gonzalve and Concepcion (Scene IV, after Fig. 16; Scene VI, around Fig. 29); the low-register sarrusophone motive for Inigo (Scene IX; Fig. 41) and the use of a solo trombone cheek-by-jowl with lush, divided upper strings (around Fig. 44).

The final Scene XXI, after Concepcion has had her way with Ramiro (or the reverse), is a brilliant double-parody, firstly of flamenco vocal techniques and Spanish inflections, and secondly of eighteenth- and nineteenth-century operatic traditions. Here, Ravel extracts humour from the voices in combination – a device he has saved till last. Trills and swoops; cascading semiquavers punctuated by overdone harp arpeggios; staccato chordal singing; and *notes Eiffel* for everyone – all these dirty tricks constantly refer to the triplet–duplet rhythm of the habanera (Fig. 120 onwards) and marry into a virtuosic finale where the music itself carries the humour.

Comparison and transition: *L'Heure* to *L'Enfant*

This principle of musical humour was carried forward into his only other completed operatic venture, *L'Enfant et les sortilèges*. Furthermore, the overall shared ethos, sometimes identified as a characteristic of French spectacle – the treatment of potentially serious issues with a light touch – is undeniable, and there is a similar speech-driven dialogue (even if rather short-lived) between the Child and his Mother. Parody looms even larger, but, whereas *L'Heure* avoids prolonged moments untinged by humour, *L'Enfant* is at times deeply touching, evoking nostalgia and recalling a childhood which only the adult can understand. As such, the 'opera' places itself high on the list of works which at one level deal with the child within the adult. Other readings explore the transition into adolescence; the Child's gradual discovery of his own identity and the development of altruism; and, overridingly, the clash of willpower between parent and child.

Psychoanalytical perspectives on *L'Enfant*

Although she does not address the music, a most striking interpretation of the piece is that by Freud's disciple, the child psychologist Melanie Klein. She delivered a paper on the subject to the British Psycho-Analytical Society which was reprinted and widely diffused. Her interpretation must be seen in terms of her developing post-Freudian thought which over-lapped strikingly with both the work's structure and its detail.[31] One of the starting points to Klein's thought is the Child's pleasure in destruction: the sadistic impulse which is frequently directed at the objects he most desires. Equally crucial is her identification of Mother with world: thus the feelings that would have been projected on the Mother who has inflicted punish-ment are transferred to material objects.

This chapter cannot aspire to a summary of Klein's ideas in relation to her overall thought, but one or two points may be made and extended into the musical sphere. In particular, the manic, sadistic attacks that she identifies are paralleled by instrumental gestures requiring sudden bursts of unsustainable physical energy: passages of extreme rapidity, or repeated notes at very high volume. Formally, Ravel employs parody to the point where it becomes destructive of the parodied object and also explores the destruction of consonance by 'wrong-note' dissonance.

The actions of the Child, and his relationship with his Mother (and indeed his absent father), mirror Klein's thought in several ways. Naturally the Child reacts sadistically to oral deprivation: the 'dry bread' and 'sugarless tea'. Supporting Klein's theory of 'repetition-compulsion' is the fact that the Mother already has these laid out on a tray, knowing that he will disobey and incur the previously administered punishment once again and will not repent. The Armchair and the Bergère (an 'easy chair'), the first objects that the Child encounters, threaten further deprivations in an extended duet (Figs. 17–21) and may be seen as representing the unified wrath of mother and father. When they threaten 'no more pillows for his sleep' and 'no more seats for his reverie', the interpreter may identify further denials related to oral and anal gratification (the pillows associated with the Mother's breasts; the 'seat' to anal retention). The Child, for once, is powerless against these two: 'motionless and in a stupor, he sits with his back to the wall and looks on'. The parental music, though studded with grace-notes, is essentially Bachian: the counterpoint over the relentless bass is without conflict, using an antique form to convey age, authority and unflinching parental unity.[32]

Klein sees the father as an essential subtext in Colette's play: though he never appears he is represented by objects with phallic significance. 'The squirrel in the cage and the pendulum wrenched out of the clock', she writes, 'are plain symbols of the penis in the mother's body.' She goes on to ask 'what weapons does the child employ in his attack on his united parents?' and concludes that 'the ink poured over the table, the emptied kettle, from which a cloud of ashes and steam escapes, represent the weapon which very little children have at their disposal, namely the device of soiling with excrement'. Extending the idea of sadism directed towards objects of desire, it is the Teapot and the Chinese Cup, offering the oral gratification denied by punishment, which are the next objects to be attacked (Fig. 9).

Klein's admiration for Colette's piece was clearly heightened because of the later portrayal of the Child's growing out of the sadistic phase. She writes: 'In ontogenetic development sadism is overcome when the subject advances to a genital level.' This may be seen in the Child's reaction to the Princess, symbolised by his sword's inadequacy (after Fig. 68). Klein continues:

> The more powerfully this phase sets in, the more capable does the child become of object-love, and the more able is he to conquer his sadism by means of pity and sympathy . . . The profound psychological insight of Colette is shown in the way in which the conversion in the child's attitude takes place. As he cares for the wounded squirrel, he whispers: 'Maman'.

Ravel and Colette

It would be nice to think of text and music in *L'Enfant* as one of the great collaborations of the 1920s; in fact it was rather the reverse. Ravel had encountered the young Colette at Mme de Saint-Marceaux's salon in the early years of the century. Hers was a celebrated salon which counted those at the forefront of Parisian artistic life among its habitués. From a host of atmospheric memoirs, Colette's is the most evocative:

> Could I say that I really knew him, my illustrious collaborator, the composer of *L'Enfant et les sortilèges*? I first met Maurice Ravel at the house of Mme de Saint-Marceaux who used to entertain on Friday evenings after dinner. This was forty years ago,[33] and the gatherings at the Saint-Marceaux mansion, rather than fashionable curiosities, were more like a reward accorded to the musical faithful, a sort of elevated recreation, the bastion of artistic intimacy . . .
>
> A dinner, always excellent, preceded these gatherings where the mistress of the house maintained an atmosphere of 'watchful liberty'. She never insisted that everyone listened to the music, but she suppressed even the slightest whisper.

However little communication Colette sensed with her collaborator, Mme de Saint-Marceaux's atmospheric salon may have been the *sine qua non* of Ravel's second 'opera'. The richness of the clientele was incomparable: Debussy played and sang *Pelléas* there, *autour du piano*; Gounod, Massenet, Albéniz and Séverac were occasional visitors while more regular habitués included Messager, d'Indy and Fauré. Additionally, pianists, no doubt drawn by a new Steinway grand bought in 1896, included Cortot, Risler, Viñes and Blanche Selva; they partnered such instrumentalists as Casals, Thibaud and Enesco, and singers such as Maggie Teyte, Claire Croiza and Reynaldo Hahn. Celebrated literary figures also attended (such as Colette's first husband, Willy). On one occasion Ravel improvised for Isadora Duncan. Indeed the composer's close involvement may be judged from his dedication of several pieces to Mme de Saint-Marceaux and by two sketches of him by Jacques Baugnies (1874–1925), her grandson.[34] Amidst this artistic richesse, Colette and Ravel became aware of each other. Colette claimed that she recalled only the briefest of formalities with Ravel, but she described him in detail:

> Perhaps inwardly secretive, Ravel kept himself at a distance and was dry in manner. Apart from listening to his music, which I initially did out of curiosity and then from an attachment to which the slight unease of surprise and the sensual and wicked attraction of a new art added their charms, that was as much as I knew of Maurice Ravel for many years.

Colette's ear was not untrained. As an intelligent young pianist, she was ecstatic when someone brought her the German edition of Beethoven Symphonies arranged as piano duets to replace her French one.[35] Years later, clandestine witnesses overheard her playing rather beautifully. In between, she had produced musical criticism, for example for *Gil Blas*,[36] under the pseudonym of Claudine (and sporadically later under her own name).

In the same memoirs, Colette continued the story:

> One day M. Rouché asked me for a libretto for a fantasy-ballet for the
> Opéra. I still don't know how I was able to give him the libretto for *L'Enfant*
> in under a week – I who work slowly and painfully. He liked my little poem
> and suggested composers whose names I welcomed as politely as I could.
>   'But', said Rouché after a silence, 'suppose I suggested Ravel?'
>   I burst out of my politeness and expressed my approval without
> reservation.
>   'We mustn't neglect the fact', added Rouché, 'that it could take a long
> time, even if Ravel accepts . . .'
>   . . . I had no idea what the creation of a work demanded of him, the slow
> frenzy which possessed and kept him isolated, however much time it took.
> The War encompassed Ravel and silenced all mention of his name with a
> hermetic seal, and thus I got out of the habit of thinking about *L'Enfant et
> les sortilèges.*

Undoubtedly the War was one factor delaying the composition: Colette
had sent Ravel a script while he was at Verdun but it did not get through so
another had to be sent. A further factor, perhaps not unrelated, was Ravel's
poor health. This is almost all the paltry correspondence between the two
figures apart from seemingly trivial questions about how, phonetically, to
represent cats mating: 'He seemed concerned only with the "duo miaow"
between the two cats, and asked gravely if I saw any problem in his replacing the "mouao" by "mouain", or possibly the other way round.' 'Certainly',
recalled Manuel Rosenthal, 'Ravel spent a lot of time ruffling the fur of his
two Siamese cats the better to notate their purrings.'[37] The result was the
Cats' duet (Figs. 97–100), surely a highpoint of the piece.

Additionally, in February 1919, Ravel had written to Colette apologis-
ing for being such an unreliable collaborator and blaming his poor health,
at the same time reflecting on several points:

> I can truthfully say that I am working on the piece: I am making notes –
> without writing a single one – ; I am, however, thinking about some
> modifications . . . Don't worry: it's not cuts that are in my mind; on the
> contrary. For example: couldn't the squirrel's recit be developed? Imagine
> all that a squirrel could tell us about the forest, and how that could be
> turned into music![38]

Ravel asked Colette what she would think of 'the cup and teapot, in old
Wedgwood – black – , singing a ragtime? I must confess', he added, 'that the
idea of having a ragtime sung by two negroes at the Académie Nationale de
Musique [a deliberately haughty way of describing the Paris Opéra] gives
me quite a thrill.' Colette of course agreed, suggesting that the
Arithmétique section might be a polka, and referring to the work by one of

its two provisional titles, *Divertissement pour ma fille*, rejected by Ravel who pointed out that he had no daughter. Colette's three-year old daughter Bel-Gazou may, however, have been the inspiration for some of her ideas.

Readings of *L'Enfant*

However we read the work, Rosenthal has made convincing speculations about the way that Colette's libretto – written shortly after her mother's death – struck a chord with Ravel, whose relationship with his own mother was strong: 'I do not know to what extent Ravel's parents contributed to the creation of his works – he never spoke of it – but his mother occupied an enormous part of his mind.'[39] Rosenthal points out how Ravel's desk at 'Le Belvédère' faced his mother's portrait and reiterates the platitudes about boys liking their mothers, adding that Ravel (as a participant of World War I) had heard wounded soldiers crying for their mothers. Thus the 'Maman' of the beginning and end of *L'Enfant* perhaps acquired further layers of significance.

Colette's biographer, Marguerite Crosland, found a similar connection. Colette wrote the piece in 1916 (although it did not reach Ravel until 1919), the year that she published *La Paix chez les bêtes* – 'Peace among beasts'. 'Men were tearing each other to pieces', writes Crosland, 'but she believed they had established a new relationship with animals . . . one essay even contains a description of cats singing about love and war.'[40] Both artists were deeply touched by World War I, and in this sense the work may be regarded as a meeting of like minds, if not a direct collaboration.

Ravel's own commentary is, as always, restrained, but it unveils both similarities to and differences from *L'Heure espagnole*: 'The melodic element is dominant here in the service of a subject which it pleased me to treat in the style of an American musical [opérette]. The fairy-tale nature of Mme Colette's libretto allowed this freedom. It is the voice which is predominant. The orchestra, although it does not eschew instrumental virtuosity, nonetheless remains in second place.'[41] Interviewed in *Le Gaulois*, Ravel developed the idea: 'If, in *L'Heure espagnole*, the action of the play in itself required the music merely to echo each word and gesture, here, quite the opposite is the case, the lyrical fantasy demands melody, nothing but melody.'[42]

Ravel's views may be challenged to some degree because it is hard for the listener to relegate to second place the captivating sounds of the orchestra. He was open about the work's eclecticism, claiming it as a 'well-blended mixture of styles from all periods, from Bach to . . . Ravel . . . !' This he saw as going 'from opera to the American musical, passing through the jazz-band en route'.

The anonymous critic of *Le Gaulois*, perhaps drawing upon Ravel's own observations, summed up the early reception of the work, describing it as:

> a naive fairy tale, not without irony, a dream which has an element of nightmare, and if, at times, it appears to be a tiny drama, it is always a most gracious comedy; the fantastic intermingles with reality only because it is a logical consequence of it: one might say it is a very pretty series of illustrations designed and colored by miniaturists of genius.[43]

The emotional turning-point of *L'Enfant*

Not only Melanie Klein found more in *L'Enfant* than a 'pretty series of illustrations', or a collage of set-pieces. Ravel himself saw it as being 'in two parts'. The division in the composer's mind surely occurs when the Child becomes aware of something new; feels ashamed of his actions; and senses some impulse related to the altruistic: the Garden Scene (Fig. 100 onwards) 'by the little green pool' and the 'great tree-trunk covered with ivy'. Ravel marks it as a striking static moment with grainy, sustained strings and a swanee whistle (*flûte à coulisse*). Whereas the Child has previously been self-centred, he is suddenly filled with compassion, after entreaties by the Dragonfly, singing to a beautiful waltz ('Valse américaine', Fig. 107). He has now been challenged by fundamental adult feelings within: firstly by tumescent stirrings of adolescent love for the Princess (Fig. 62 onwards); and secondly by the raw spectacle of the two cats (Fig. 97), a stroke of genius on Ravel's part, for it is not just funny, it is raunchy. Thus the hinge in the piece is the Child's awakening into romantic love and his witnessing of the sex act.

Like the Fire before her (Fig. 39), the Princess is introduced by a prolonged added-note chord, here, E major over F minor, arpeggiated on the harp with a magical sustained background of horns, divided strings and muted trombones (Fig. 62). But this rich, transitional moment soon thins out into the Princess's rather serious monologue which Ravel sets in diatonic heterophony (Fig. 63^{-3}). She faces the Child with his sexuality: 'you have sought me in the heart of the rose', and climbs to a high *pianissimo* B♭ as she tells him that she has been his first true love (Fig. 64^{+4}). A sharpwards mediant shift (E♭–E major: Fig. 65), marks the beginning of the Princess's rejection of the Child who is too young: Colette cannot resist the humour of the Child 'wishing he had a sword like that of her cavalier', knowingly unemphasised by Ravel, the more to make its effect.

Example 9.4 *L'Enfant et les sortilèges*: fourth interval
(a) Cats' duet: La Chatte melody (Fig. 97, bars 1–4)

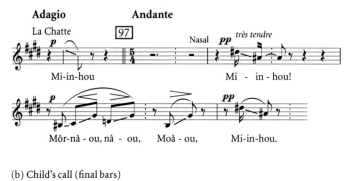

Mi-in-hou

Mi - in - hou!

Môr-nâ - ou, nâ - ou,   Moâ - ou,   Mi-in-hou.

(b) Child's call (final bars)

Ma - man!

After the exquisite *mélodie* where the Child is newly moved, filled with memories of the disappeared Princess, with only a golden hair on his shoulder to remind him of her (Fig. 74^{+5}), the action harks back to childish things (Fig. 75): to the maths which were the first issue after Maman had shut him in his room. This time the music builds up to an extraordinary climax (Fig. 92), as if something else must replace the cramming of knowledge into the Child's brain. Bitonal arpeggios (now F major over F♯ minor: Fig. 96) introduce the cats whose copulation is to be the final catalyst in the Child's growth out of self-centredness. Without reading in too much of oedipal significance, it is remarkable that the Female Cat shares the descending fourth associated with the Mother, sung for the first time at the very end (Example 9.4a and b).

Evocation of childhood

Ravel uses several deliberately naive devices to transport us from the adult world: a child improvises rather randomly in fourths and fifths at the opening (Fig. 2), and Ravel seemingly plays on their forbidden nature to evoke the Child's naughtiness. These devices return to mark the turning-point suggested above: the moment of silent reflection when the Child rediscovers his garden (Fig. 100), though now their effect is transformed as the Child's self-awareness suddenly advances beside the huge (phallic?) tree-trunk and the pool of copulating frogs.

The extraordinary sound of the double-bass playing harmonics which accompanies the pair of oboes at the opening may evoke the idea of prac-

Example 9.5 *L'Enfant et les sortilèges:* 'frenzy of perversity' (Fig. 7, bars 1–9)

tising an instrument (Fig. 1), a technique used some years before by Debussy in 'Doctor Gradus ad Parnassum' from *Children's Corner* (surely the piece that paved the way for the 'false naivety' often used for the Child's music). The potential warping of the descending perfect fourth into a tritone is exploited from the outset; as the Mother scolds the Child, the fourth of the 'Maman' motive becomes augmented (Fig. 5, then echoed by the Child after Fig. 8). The Child's first 'frenzy of perversity' (Example 9.5; Fig. 7) initiates several related parodistic techniques. A 'rude-noise' sound – as if blowing a raspberry – begins the episode, effected by a burst of rapid staccato wind notes and *fortissimo* tremolandos: techniques which no wind player could sustain for much longer than Ravel requires. The Child's first utterances, once his Mother has locked him in, are as a warped nursery rhyme: its rhythm and phrase-lengths are predictable and simple, but wrong notes are introduced, semitonally clashing with the expected cadence-note (Figs. 7–9). The semitonal clash is also used in sequence, as the Child delights in his naughtiness.

A further Debussian device is employed to release this tension, this time of the Child playing with the black notes of the piano with his right hand against a crude series of parallel white-note chords beneath (Fig. 13). Debussy had used a similar process (with hands reversed) in 'Serenade for the Doll'.

Additional musical devices

Such sophisticated naivety is spiced up with the stock-in-trade techniques of biting parody, namely acciaccaturas and *gruppetti* which Ravel employs virtuosically with varied intervals and orchestrations. Nowhere are these techniques utilised more artfully than in the duet between the Armchair and the Bergère (Fig. 17). Chordal *gruppetti* on the 'piano luthéal'[44] suggest harmonic complexity, but in fact the harmonic underlay is a simple oscillation of tonic and dominant. The voicing of the grace-note chord means that its added notes have different degrees of prominence: the major seventh and minor sixth (F♯ and E♭, respectively) are sustained, while the added major sixth (E) introduces a subtle semitonal clash within each chord. Over each intermediary dominant chord, the D is overlaid with major chords drawn from an octatonic scale, ringing into each other because of the luthéal's undamped sound.

While pedal-points and a *perpetuum mobile* characterise the Clock music (Figs. 21–8), Ravel uses a different kind of parody for the Teapot and Chinese Cup: the negro duet, to a pastiche ragtime, of which he seems to have been particularly proud (the foxtrot, Fig. 28; for a brief quotation, see Example 5.13b). Again *gruppetti* and semitonal clashes reinforce the effect, as do trombone glissandos and the use of the contrabassoon. Maybe both collaborators had Poulenc's *Rapsodie nègre* in mind when it came to the nonsense Chinese and pentatonic music for the Cup. Whatever the case, it is welded in seamlessly – a striking feature of the piece as a whole, which could easily have become too sectional – and by now we are far from the speech inflections of *L'Heure*: as Ravel pointed out, lyrical melody in the vocal parts is now paramount.

If Offenbach is not too far away from the vocal virtuosity required by the Fire, the moment of its being quelled by the Cinders is another example of a technique dependent upon orchestral colour. Eight rising chords, not exactly parallel (and with pairs bound by common notes), pull upwards over a pedal which is essentially a half-diminished chord on D: D, F, A♭, C (Example 9.6; Fig. 48). For the second moment of female apparition, this time of the Princess, Ravel employs three of the same pitches, and once again the harp is prominent (Fig. 62). (A metrical series of rising gestures, with F minor as its basis, has come to signify an important new apparition.) After the central section, discussed earlier, further set-pieces

Example 9.6 *L'Enfant et les sortilèges* (Fig. 48, bars 1–6)

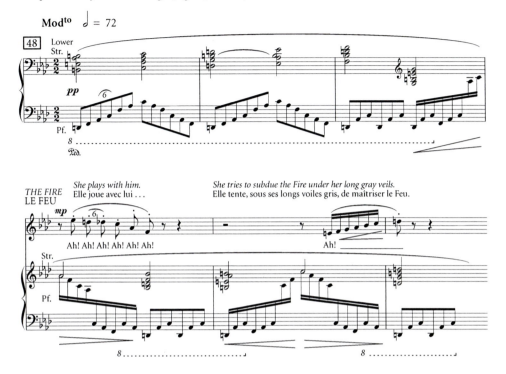

exploit the parodistic techniques initiated at the outset. The extended Dragonfly waltz (Fig. 107ff.) proceeds in the manner of the pastiche ragtime, semitonal clashes on the piano gently perfume the harmonic language which intensifies as the other animals join in (around Fig. 110).

Further enlightenment: encounter with the animals

Colette seems not to have developed the Squirrel's character in response to Ravel's request, but this encounter is a further turning-point as the Child realises that the animals have their own lives and can do without him: 'Ils s'aiment . . . Ils m'oublient . . . Je suis seul' (Fig. 135). Very tentatively, he now calls for his mother with the descending fourth of the 'Maman' motive. In a silent reinforcement of the Child's realisation that he must take on the responsibility of adulthood, the Tom-Cat licks the Female Cat's ear and plays with her affectionately before they slink off along the top of the wall. The cry, 'Maman', causes the animals to recognise him as the bad boy who had previously so tormented them and in a frenzied section, not altogether dissimilar from the Child's frenzy at the beginning of the piece, they attack him. The role-reversal is perhaps symbolised by the reversal of the black- over white-note bimodality of the Child's music: here the bass is in D♮ while the chords above consist entirely of added notes (Fig. 136^{+2}). The 'opera' ends with madrigal and fugato, as the animals themselves use the magic word 'Maman', eventually finding its downward fourth, to carry the Child back to the only person who can tend his wound.

In conclusion, this study has concentrated on different readings of the composer's two 'operas', not least because one measure of a work's durability lies in its potential for varying interpretations, both simultaneously and over time. Although this has been seen, for example, in the reception history of Debussy's *Pelléas* where each production may extract new meaning, Ravel's operas, by comparison, seem to have been too easily dismissed as lightweight. It is to be hoped that the uncovering of further layers of meaning attempted here may fall into the category of 'hidden depths', approaching less from the stance of composer – and author – intention than from the other end: the ways in which art-works acquire significance through their subsequent interpretation and reception. *L'Heure* emerges as something of a laugh, but with the exploitation of a fictionalised view of the North's view of the South shared by several late nineteenth-century operas (not least Bizet's *Carmen*), and in part based on the sense of a loss of licence and of pre-industrial ways of doing things. *L'Enfant*, on the other hand, emerges not just as a charming divertissement but as a work with psychological overtones of which neither librettist nor composer were entirely aware.

PART III

Performance and reception

10 Performing Ravel: style and practice in the early recordings

RONALD WOODLEY

Composers do not always know what is best for their music; they may hold copyright in the dots, but not, fortunately, a monopoly on their interpretation. It is naive to presume that any recording involving the composer will automatically set a qualitative benchmark: apart from anything else, performance – especially early recorded performance – does not spring fully formed like Athene from the head of Zeus, but is always subject to the practical vagaries and contingencies of players' availability, schedules, temperament, (lack of) rehearsal time and the technical limitations of the young recording medium. Yet it is too easy to overplay the scepticism. All intelligent performers know the importance of internalising the music, and appreciate that satisfying sense of the music re-emerging from deep within them, rather than feeling their hands and body functioning as mere thoroughfares between brain and instrument. And from the evidence of many early recordings of Ravel, for the best musicians working with and around the composer – unlike us – the sheer cultural currency and 'presence' of the music seems largely to have evaporated the need to deploy any self-conscious 'performance practice', and led to a directness in that process of internalisation which we have little hope of recapturing, but from which we still have much to learn.

There is a definite sense of loss here, and it is not simply a question of sentimental nostalgia for some golden age of music-making: frequently one comes away from listening to a recent CD of, say, Ravel's Quartet, or *Valses nobles*, or *Boléro*, after having previously been immersed in various pre-war recordings, thinking that the modern version is, frankly, rather boring. Partly this is to do with acknowledged social and economic pressures on the recording industry, with their flattening effect on musical risk-taking and self-perpetuating programming of audience and performer expectation. (The market's capacity for the occasional well-packaged, unpredictable virtuoso emphasises rather than undermines this tendency.) Partly it seems symptomatic, especially in chamber music, of late twentieth-century ideals of meticulous, non-soloistic ensemble, often reinforced by the formative orchestral training of young professionals – ideals which appear to have operated much less restrictively earlier in the century, when more soloistic freedom was expected even in orchestral playing. And finally it is to do with questions of performing style: not just the speeds chosen, but also the fine nuancing of phrasing, rhythm, rubato and tonal colouring. Here generalisations are difficult: did 'they' always play faster than today? Or slower? Did they pull the music around more? Or play straighter? The answer to all these questions is 'no'; and even where it is otherwise, the interest to fellow performers today usually lies more in the *detail* of the way the music and instruments are addressed within these gross categories than in the bald statement itself.

Sometimes misapprehensions are fuelled by the 'disciple problem', and this is true in Ravel's case. Vlado Perlemuter's book of reminiscences with the violinist Hélène Jourdan-Morhange (*Ravel According to Ravel*) contains fascinating, anecdotal evidence of his working with the composer on the piano music. But the constant emphasis on strictness, lack of exaggeration or sentimentality, elegance, doing just what the notation says, is bound up more with the construction of an aesthetic of 'purity' and a belief – perhaps on Ravel's part too – in the desirability of establishing an enduring, unsullied performance tradition, than with any simple mirroring of a past reality. And similarly with Marguerite Long's memoirs (*At the Piano with Ravel*) – a curiously annoying, self-serving book which delivers so much less than its title promises. The really interesting thing is the gap that opens up between the rhetoric of written testimony and the actual aural evidence, a gap which leads one to doubt that the transmission of 'authoritative' performing style by friends, pupils and colleagues, keeping their candle lit for the master, can ever be a transparent, value-free process.

Ravel was probably the most recorded living 'classical' composer in the pre-World War II period: according to Jean Touzelet's listing (based on his own formidable collection), over 250 separate recordings of the composer's music were issued up to 1939, though under ten of these appear to have been held in Ravel's personal library.[1] The composer himself entered the recording studio relatively rarely, and even some recordings ascribed to him on the labels, long unquestioned in the literature, have been shown more recently to be the work of others. Nevertheless, it is hard not to begin these reflections on performing style and habit with Ravel's own efforts as pianist and conductor, as well as considering those recordings by other musicians which were supervised by the composer or which received his imprimatur. (For a list of recordings consulted for this study, see Table 10.1, pp. 237–8 below.)

Ravel's own technical limitations as a pianist have long been adduced as a pretext for playing down the interpretative importance of his recordings, and the poor quality of some early transfers from piano roll to vinyl has tended to corroborate this opinion. In terms of straightforward facility in the faster passage-work Ravel's fingers do seem to have found their natural limits at what one might charitably call a sub-professional level, despite an apparently exceptional mobility in his thumbs (cf. the writing in 'Scarbo' from *Gaspard*). But in the slower, more lyrical music, Ravel's earliest recordings display some very interesting performing traits, and even if we would not wish to duplicate all of these today, they nevertheless provide valuable insights into the composer's address of the instrument, and can sometimes be read as possessing relational or structural significance within the music itself.

Ravel's piano roll recording of *Valses nobles* (1913)

A good example of this is Ravel's piano roll recording of *Valses nobles et sentimentales*, made in Paris in Autumn 1913 (issued 1914) for the German firm Welte, along with the first and second movements of the *Sonatine*. (Touzelet reports that according to Edwin Welte, in an interview for the American magazine *High Fidelity* (1958), recordings were usually made in Germany, but that 'for some "lions" like Debussy and Ravel' the technicians and equipment were sent abroad.)[2] Listening to the 1964 Telefunken transfer (in this case excellent, within pre-digital technological limits, and supervised by Welte himself seven years previously), perhaps the most striking idiosyncrasy is Ravel's almost continuous spreading of chords and de-synchronisation of left and right hands through the slower, more expressive movements. The spreads, usually strummed rather fast but nonchalantly, sound almost parodistically old-fashioned, but were clearly a normal and unselfconscious facet of Ravel's performing habit: even if they result partly from a laziness of technique, they function at times to emphasise a top note or line, and at other times to bring out a middle part. Where both hands have chords, each spread is generally treated independently (rather than played as a full bottom-up arpeggiation), and where the hands are de-synchronised, the left hand usually anticipates slightly the metrical positioning of the main beat, rather than the right hand delaying. (This seems very often a more accurate description of the phenomenon noticeable more widely in piano performance practice at this time, even though several writers today describe the habit as a right-hand delay.)[3]

In No. II ('Assez lent – avec une expression intense'), this attains a significance beyond that of surface-level detail, as the left-hand anticipation is retained even where it lies *above* the right hand. At bar 3 (Example 10.1a), the effect is to hear the high G as a grace-note to the top F♯ in the right hand. Combined with much chord-spreading from bar 9 onwards ('doux et expressif'), this relates quite precisely and structurally to the

Example 10.1 *Valses nobles et sentimentales*, II
(a) bars 1–4

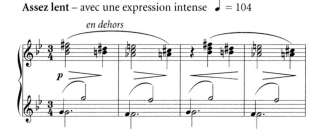

(b) bars 25–6

notated grace-notes from bar 25 onwards ('au Mouvt. (un peu plus lent et rubato)': Example 10.1b), providing a sense of pre-echo and continuity where the strict notation suggests change at bar 25. Interestingly too, Ravel does *not* actually play the notated grace-notes at bars 13–15; so, whereas the score implies an anticipatory relationship between 13–15 and 25, in Ravel's performance the relationship at 25 is back to the opening of the movement. (That the left-hand de-synchronisation in bar 3 was not a technical accident is confirmed by analogous instances at bars 19 and 35.)

A different, unnotated, rhythmical relationship occurs in his performance of No. III ('Modéré'). Here, the delicate left-hand accompanying figure, two quavers slurred into a second-beat staccato crotchet, marked *pp* 'léger' (Example 10.2a), seems simplicity itself. But Ravel places such a long agogic stress on the first quaver that the first beat of the figure – and other analogous figures – becomes effectively dotted. As well as relaying to modern ears a local curiosity of practice (one which most players today would hardly dream of emulating), this 'springing' of the first beat has the unexpected effect of linking the opening to the hemiola dotted passage at bars 48–51, which now sounds like an augmentation of the earlier crotchet-level figuration (Example 10.2b), perhaps even relating back to the grace-notes of No. II.

Example 10.2 *Valses nobles et sentimentales*, III
(a) bars 1–4

(b) bars 48–51

Significantly, although the beautifully refined and balanced 1951 recording of Robert Casadesus (1899–1972) shows no trace of this rhythmic nuance – and he had worked with Ravel on this repertoire since the early 1920s – the 1973 version of Vlado Perlemuter (b. 1904), recorded when he had himself been performing the work for half a century, again originally under Ravel's guidance, retains a distinct vestige of this agogic stress at the start of the movement. Neither performance, however, displays any trace of Ravel's characteristic chord-spreads, and only slight tendencies towards metrical anticipations in the left hand at particularly expressive moments; so even if early in their careers these habits had been present as part of a more generic pianistic culture, they clearly became ironed out with time.

Another example of an agogic stress which emphasises the gap between Ravel's reading of the musical flow and our own common perceptions occurs in No. V ('Presque lent – dans un sentiment intime'). At the beginning (Example 10.3a) a 'natural' modern tendency, taking on board Ravel's instruction to play 'le chant très en dehors', would be to regard the quaver tied over the barline as a slightly extended, languorous suspension, with the line's centre of gravity moving to the second beats of the bars and with the third beats lightened. Ravel's reading is almost the opposite: his attention is directed towards the highest notes of the phrase, the A and G♯, with the A given a distinct tenuto agogic stress, and the G♯ markedly anticipated in its metrical position in the bar. The effect seems

Example 10.3 *Valses nobles et sentimentales*, V
(a) bars 1–3

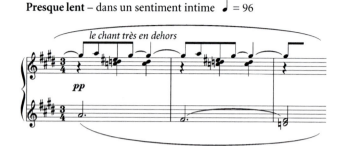

(b) Top line: approximate notation of Ravel's performance

deliberately to unbalance the slow waltz swing, and to create a new rhythmic and melodic counterpoint of which the notation gives no explicit clue (Example 10.3b).

As with the 'springing' of the first beat in No. III, there is a trace of Ravel's more layered reading of V in Perlemuter's 1973 version, though Perlemuter draws attention to this opening in terms of the need to avoid rubato: 'Above all, not that! Ravel was very insistent on this point and marked "simple" on my music.'[4] Although this is an instance of that slightly irritating disingenuousness and cultivation of artificial purity, there is no real contradiction – at a crotchet level, Ravel's playing is relatively free of rubato – but, frustratingly, the overall stance adopted by Perlemuter and Jourdan-Morhange seems to prevent them saying the most interesting things about the music. There does, though, seem more contradiction between testimony and practice in respect of the reminiscences of earlier movements fragmented and juxtaposed in No. VIII. Perlemuter claimed that Ravel demanded a unity of rhythm throughout ('In no way must the beat change when the different rhythms of the scraps of waltzes appear'),[5] whereas, even if this reflects Ravel's advice, the composer's own 1913 performance is very much otherwise, with quite radical changes of speed and mood between the fragments, which reinvoke the original statements from earlier in the work rather than create the more distanced, allusive relationship which the composer perhaps came to prefer later.

Example 10.4 *Sonatine*, I (bars 11–14)

Ravel's own *Sonatine* recording (1913)

Again, lest one think that these idiosyncrasies in the *Valses nobles* are one-off aberrations, we can see close analogies in the first two movements of the *Sonatine* in Ravel's 1913 recording.

After a rather clumsy beginning, in terms of fingerwork, and a characteristically emphatic caesura before the last quaver of bar 3, the composer subtly gradates the wind-down at bars 11–12 into bar 13 (Example 10.4). At bar 12, the first right-hand semiquaver anticipates the metrical beat, and is then slightly held over so that the remaining two semiquavers of each group spill into the next beat. (Throughout the work, wherever 'rall.' is followed by 'a Tempo', Ravel almost always plays through the barline, not grinding to a near-halt before picking up the tempo, as many players do today.) This slight *inégalité* creates a rhythm which is a halfway-house between the quaver-plus-two-semiquaver rhythm of bar 11 and the actual notation of bar 12, and leads in a rather finely nuanced way into bar 13, which Ravel plays again somewhat *inégal* with the first quaver of the accompaniment anticipating the beat and the remaining quavers under the 'agogic decrescendo' spilling forward. Perlemuter recalls that Ravel was fastidious about the last semiquaver of this and similar bars, which 'must not be played with expression; if it is "interpreted" it becomes weak and loses the rhythm which Ravel wanted'.[6] The composer's performing habit thus creates an explicit relational linkage – as in *Valses nobles* – which is present only implicitly in the score, and this is further consolidated by Ravel's slight spreading of some accompaniment chords from bar 13 onwards, linking back to the notated arpeggiations of the previous two bars. (As in *Valses nobles*, there is often little difference between Ravel's notated arpeggiations and other, notionally 'straight' chords spread through habit.) This expressive weighting of the first half of the bar then continues into the 'Un peu retenu' of bar 20 ('très expressif'), where the first, but not second, tenuto crotchet of each bar in the left hand markedly anticipates the main beat of the right-hand melody (Example 10.5), creating a further connection back

Example 10.5 *Sonatine*, I (bars 20–1)

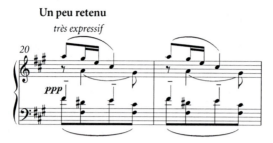

Example 10.6 *Sonatine*, II (bars 1–4)

to bars 11–12. One is reminded of Calvocoressi's report of Ravel's self-confessed indifference to 'form' as an abstract criterion, claiming 'continuity of interest' as a higher concern.[7]

The tendency to an expressive but subtle *inégalité* in Ravel's recording – a practice which seems more part of a pre-1920s tradition than generally pre-World War II[8] – continues in the second movement. Despite Perlemuter's claim that the composer required 'great exactitude of rhythm',[9] there is unexpected flexibility in the way Ravel presents the opening phrase (Example 10.6) and subsequent related figuration. There is a slight audible tendency to push forward from first to second beats in bars 1–2, followed by a barely perceptible relaxation on the third beat, creating a rhythmical spring to the middle of the bar akin to a sarabande. One might argue today that the notated accent on the second quaver of bar 4 indicates a *change* in the stress pattern from an initial strong–weak to a weak–strong at the end of the phrase, but Ravel's performance suggests that he intends more continuity, with the fourth bar of the phrase reinforcing rather than reversing the prevalent pattern. More curiously, the semiquavers of bar 3 are played in distinctly *inégal*, short–long pairings: it might be tempting to claim, again, that Ravel's technical shortcomings (and smallish hands) are to blame, but this is clearly not the explanation, as analogous but technically more straightforward passages (for example, bar 10) are performed similarly. Combined with a tendency to 'play through' semiquaver figures – especially anacrusic figures across barlines – in a way which suggests almost continuous 'arrow forward' markings, this creates a strangely unsettling experience, especially if we are expecting an elegant, ultra-poised performance with every note placed just so.

Anonymous piano recordings (1912–20)

Ravel's 1913 session was by no means the only time that his music was committed to piano roll in this early period of recording. In fact, Touzelet has collected details of significant but anonymous recordings, many from the years 1912–20, and while it has not been practicable to incorporate these here, they certainly merit future study. Among these rolls can be found the earliest recorded movements from *Gaspard*, a complete *Le Tombeau de Couperin*, and the *Menuet antique* (all 1920), *Jeux d'eau* and the *Pavane* (both *c.* 1912), *Miroirs* (*c.* 1912–14), another complete *Valses nobles* (1913) and a remarkable number of keyboard transcriptions, for example of *Daphnis et Chloé* (*c.* 1914), the *Introduction et allegro* (*c.* 1913: transcription by Léon Roques), *Histoires naturelles*, *Shéhérazade* (both *c.* 1913), other songs and the four-hand versions of *Ma Mère l'Oye* and *Rapsodie espagnole*.[10] Although the artists are not credited, and much research (archival and performance-based) will be needed before firm conclusions can be drawn, it is tempting to speculate whether Ricardo Viñes can be shown to have played any part here. It is one of the more bizarre quirks of the attributed recorded legacy that Viñes, despite his extremely close association with the composer at this time, seems to have left no solo piano recordings of Ravel's music.[11] We know, however, that he had rehearsed and performed four-hand duets with Ravel since the 1890s, as well as championing the solo music throughout Europe in the first two decades of the century. So, even if he and Ravel may not always have agreed on interpretative matters (see below), he may still have been responsible for some of these piano rolls, perhaps happy to accept anonymity, in view of his recognised dislike of the recorded medium and the creative restrictions which he believed it imposed.

Ravel's 1922 recording session

Ravel, who unlike Viñes seemed positively disposed to the new technology, signed a contract with the Aeolian Company of London on 15 May 1920, to make at least ten recordings over two years for £50 per recording.[12] Only five were finally issued, between 1922 and 1928. More intriguingly, although the

Duo-Art rolls were sold autographed and attested as performed by Ravel, at least two performances (the 'Toccata' from *Le Tombeau* and 'Le Gibet' from *Gaspard*) were in fact by the young Casadesus.[13] Only 'Oiseaux tristes' from *Miroirs* and the *Pavane pour une Infante défunte* seem incontrovertibly by Ravel, and the fifth recording, of 'La Vallée des cloches' (*Miroirs*), has not been finally identified either way, though the balance of probability favours the composer. The reason for Casadesus's ghosting of these recordings is not hard to find, though his name is kept out of most third-party correspondence. Indeed, Ravel was open about his own limitations with respect to the proposed recording programme, which seems to have included the whole of *Gaspard* (which Ravel never performed in public) and a re-recording of the first two movements of the *Sonatine*. As the composer admitted in a letter dated 24 March 1922 to Calvocoressi:

> You can reassure Mr. Mead [Alfred C. Mead, co-signatory of the Aeolian contract]: I'm presently working on 5 piano pieces (still counting the *Sonatine* as only 2), am busy finding a better pianist than myself for the 5 others, and will have everything ready for the month of June. I haven't informed him of this yet, because I don't know exactly when I will be able to go. I'm not asking Ricardo [Viñes] for 2 reasons: first, I think he's supposed to be in Spain about that time; second, I would especially like to have *Gaspard de la nuit* recorded, and Viñes never wanted to perform these pieces, in particular 'Le Gibet,' according to the composer's intentions.[14]

One factor which has probably diverted suspicion away from these ghosted performances is the poor quality of some later vinyl re-recordings, made using an incorrectly regulated Duo-Art reproducing mechanism. A classic case is the 'Toccata' from *Le Tombeau* in the 1975 Ember reissue. Although advertised as employing a 'Steinway built in 1929 utilizing the "Duo-Art" music rolls', and although three of the five recordings are reasonably convincing, the 'Toccata' and *Pavane* sound impossibly lumpy, uneven, and, in the former case, absurdly slow and amateurish. Ravel may not have been a front-ranking virtuoso, but even he would have been seriously peeved to have this rendering attributed to him. In fact, once the 'Toccata' roll is played on a properly regulated set-up, at the correct speed, a rather fluent performance by Casadesus emerges, as heard on the 1988 EMI version, using Touzelet's own Duo-Art Steinway; double confirmation is provided by Casadesus's 1951 recording (issued 1952), which even after nearly thirty years matches the 1922 version very closely in tempo and interpretative nuance.

The comparison of Duo-Art reproductive quality between the 1975 and 1988 issues of the 'Toccata' serves as a salutary lesson in analysing piano roll recordings, but it should not inhibit us from teasing out other, real musical points where we can be reasonably confident of our terms of reference. For example, the unexpectedly restless sense conveyed in Ravel's 1913 version of the *Sonatine* (movement II) finds a parallel in his 'Oiseaux tristes' from the 1922 session – a performance of extremes and active discomfiture. That the printed notation falls short of Ravel's vision is immediately clear: the composer begins the quiet tolling of bar 1 (reminiscent of the repeated B♭ in 'Le Gibet') substantially slower even than the marked ♪ = 60 ('Très lent') – in fact around ♪ = 54 – but the bird-call figuration of bar 2 is taken at almost double speed. This exaggeration of what the music is already telling us is discussed by Perlemuter: the composer had written 'plus bref' against bar 2 in Perlemuter's own copy, and the pianist comments that 'if you play strictly what's written, it loses character'.[15] Ravel's (and Perlemuter's) performance certainly bears this out; but Perlemuter does not discuss the implication for slightly later in the piece, where the bird arabesque is to be played simultaneously with the more languorous triplet-quaver inner parts (bar 8: Example 10.7a). In contrast with typical practice today, Ravel is happy to keep the bird figuration at the much more rapid tempo established at the beginning, and to accommodate the accompanying triplets (beats 1 and 4) by speeding them up somewhat, but avoiding exact vertical alignment. The effect is severely disruptive to the triplet flow set up in the previous bars, and we begin to hear the otherwise relatively harmless two-against-three quavers in bar 7 as a kind of premonition.

This destabilising influence then carries across to bar 13 – the first stirrings which lead up to the brief 'Pressez' outburst near the centre of the piece. Many pianists today would take pride in rhythmical and tonal smoothness here, but not Ravel: although the main, even quaver pulse is more or less retained, his manner with the groups of two and three semiquavers (Example 10.7b) is quite disconcerting, with agogic elongations followed by 'catch-up' shortenings in the triplet groups and spreading of the duplet dyads.[16] Again there is a further relational point here, since the right-hand figuration which then enters in the second half of the bar, generating the subsequent demisemiquaver outburst, seems to grow out of an already unsettled air, and appears less of a *subito* disruption. In Ravel's performance, too, this following 'Pressez' passage is wildly volatile, rapidly accelerating to something like ♪ = 208, and then decelerating to ♪ = 120 at the 'revenez au mouvement', and already reaching the initial 'Très lent' speed two bars before the return at bar 20. As before, we cannot simply assert that the uneven semiquavers at bar 13 result from Ravel's technical limitations, as there are vestiges of this manner in both Casadesus's 1951 and Perlemuter's 1973 recordings, even though these performances are generally characterised by much more even playing.

Example 10.7 *Miroirs*, 'Oiseaux tristes'
(a) bars 7–9

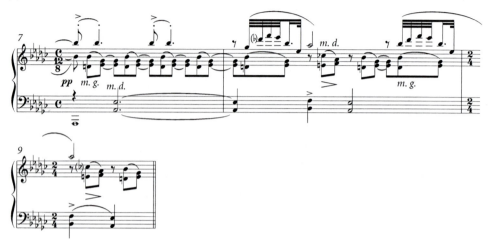

(b) bar 13, with approximate re-notation of rhythmic modifications in Ravel's 1922 recording

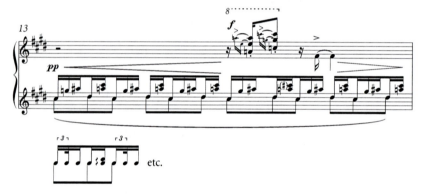

Casadesus's recordings of 'Le Gibet' (1922 and 1951)

So far discussion has emphasised a certain waywardness and volatility in Ravel's playing from the 1913 and 1922 recording sessions, as against the more restrained, 'classicising' habits apparently transmitted to Casadesus and Perlemuter. But Casadesus's (uncredited) contribution to the 1922 session reveals another interesting dimension to the evolution of interpretative practice in Ravel's music. As mentioned earlier, it is now clear that he was responsible for the 1922 version of 'Le Gibet' from *Gaspard*, attributed for many years to Ravel. There was always circumstantial evidence to doubt that this was the composer at the keyboard: his hands were simply too small to encompass the numerous awkward stretches which are managed here without spreading; and we have also seen that spreading and de-synchronisation were habitual in Ravel's playing even where there was no difficulty of stretch. But a comparison of the 1922 'Le Gibet' with Casadesus's later 1951 recording points up not only the similarities, but also the nuances of pianistic style that have changed in the thirty years between the two versions.

On the critical matter of speed, they are discrepant by only a couple of seconds in a running time of almost five minutes (Perlemuter takes over a minute longer!), and numerous details of tonal balance and emphasis suggest an overall view of the piece which has hardly altered. But two specific traits in the 1922 version stand out as symptomatic of an earlier style. The first is a tendency to over-dotting: the dotted quaver–semiquaver pairing which often occurs at the ends of bars, spilling over to the next main beat, is almost always exaggerated by the younger Casadesus, to emphasise the anacrusic nature of the semiquaver in preference to a steady, divided quaver pulse; and this is a habit which, in the early decades of the century, has been observed elsewhere by Robert Philip.[17] The second is a willingness to de-synchronise from the surrounding chords the accented, tolling B♭s which persist through the movement: usually this de-synchronisation involves anticipating the beat slightly, so that the octave B♭s stand out early in aural relief, even though this rather undermines what we read today as the solemn inexorability of the slow pulse. Casadesus clearly grew out of these two habits as there is no trace of them in 1951.

Further thoughts on performance style: anacrusis and agogic stress

As we have begun to see, it is remarkable how often changes in performing style within Ravel's lifetime, and since, are bound up with attitudes to rhythm, pulse, metre and the effects of these on detailed nuances of phrasing. In particular, the subtle kinds of agogic stress, anticipation or delay which many players felt comfortable with then have more recently become smoothed out or even reversed. Nowhere is this more apparent than in performers' approaches – both mental and musical – to the barline, to other 'main beats', and to anacrusic or upbeat figures. It is a commonplace that young players today are taught, beyond a certain basic competence, how to avoid over-emphatic first beats in much standard repertory where a particular subtlety of phrasing or longer-term contour so demands. But, equally, it is a measure of how stuck we have become – whether through interpretative insecurity, the fetishising of ensemble precision, or other insidious professional pressures – that we can still be so surprised at the flexibility of the finest players of the inter-war period and earlier. Even the term 'upbeat' seems to carry with it a certain baggage, emphasising its

Example 10.8 *Jeux d'eau* (bars 1–2)

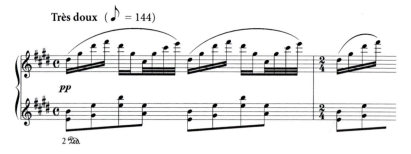

function as preparatory to, and to some extent separable from, a point of 'arrival'. When listening to these early recordings, though, one is struck by how anacrusic figures are felt as an intrinsic *part* of that arrival, and are swung across the barline without a need for any additional downbeat stress; or, alternatively, by how downbeats are slightly anticipated in a particular voice, to evoke an emphasis which does not rely on accent or dynamic level to make its point. We have already seen examples of these from Ravel's playing and from Casadesus's earlier performing style, but analogous instances – both in the piano music and in other instrumental and vocal works – are not difficult to find.

Jeux d'eau: recordings of Cortot (1923) and Perlemuter (1973)

On 1 March 1923, Alfred Cortot (1877–1962) recorded *Jeux d'eau* for the Gramophone Company. This is a stunning performance, which despite the technological limitations retains exceptional qualities of clarity and pianism, and a finely judged balance between volatility and restraint. The overall speed is rather fast, by modern standards, with the first two pages averaging nearer ♪ = 168 than the marked 144, and rising to beyond 200 at the main central climax. But it is Cortot's reading of the opening that strikes today's listener as very much of its own time. Despite Ravel's apparently unambiguous notation, which phrases the first bar in two-beat gestures ending with the demisemiquaver flourish, Cortot plays this flourish as a rapid, integrated anacrusis to the next phrase, preceded by a slight pull-back and comma (Example 10.8). The effect is to bring its fluid, exploratory qualities to the fore, and the sense of an extended improvisation with obvious links back to the Lisztian tradition is continued in the rest of Cortot's performance in a way that is rarely matched by later pianists. Indeed, although Perlemuter recalls Léon-Paul Fargue's description

Example 10.9 *Jeux d'eau* (bar 51): rhythmic nuance in Alfred Cortot's 1923 recording

of Ravel's own early performances of this piece – 'There was a strange fire, a whole panoply of subtleties and vibrations which none of us could previously have imagined'[18] – Perlemuter's own 1973 recording, made admittedly when he was quite elderly, sounds staid and doggedly tied to the notation. Cortot's version also displays other nuances of anacrusis and anticipatory, agogic emphasis mentioned previously. For example, most players today would approach the pairs of semiquavers in the second main theme with a view to placing them as evenly as possible within the metre. Cortot, however, makes a larger-scale structural point, where this theme returns, by emphasising the still-disturbed nature of the music through holding the first semiquaver – itself slightly anticipated – and then spilling forward, in a manner reminiscent of a string-player's portamento-based rubato (bars 51ff., as in Example 10.9). Then, towards the close, the thematic re-statement within a glassy, dissolving atmosphere is presented absolutely straight, but with just a hint of the same rubato effect echoed at 'un peu marqué' (six bars before the end).

String Quartet: comparison of recordings

These small-scale rhythmic inflections (which, as we have seen, can have longer-term consequences) are often heard to best advantage in particularly affecting passages in slow or moderate tempo, and an excellent locus for this within Ravel's chamber music occurs at the second subject in the first movement of the String Quartet. A comparison between the Calvet Quartet recording (December 1936) and that made with the composer's imprimatur by the International Quartet (1927) is especially instructive, since it problematises further any simple notion of chronological evolution in performing style: in some ways the Calvet version is more 'modern', but in others reflects 'older' attitudes to rhythmic fluidity.

Ravel's participation in the International Quartet recording is quite well documented, but an outline of events, based on André Mangeot's account in *The Gramophone*, is probably useful.[19] The quartet (comprising

Mangeot, Boris Pecker, Frank Howard and Herbert Withers) had toured the Ravel work, along with the Debussy and Franck quartets, across Europe for five years with great success, and, when asked by the National Gramophonic Society (NGS) to record the Ravel, they had obviously felt that they could 'wax' it without difficulty. (Mangeot had in fact known Ravel since their Conservatoire days, and always stressed the importance of personal knowledge of the composer for a performer's interpretative credentials.) At the first recording session (*c.* June 1927?), the Ravel Quartet was put on to seven sides, with Kathleen Long coming in to fill up the eighth side with the *Sonatine* (movement I). Mangeot was not satisfied with the test or 'white-label' pressings, though ('there was not enough clarity or "limpidity"; tone was not transparent enough'), and the seven sides were re-recorded. Only at this point does the composer enter the scene, as Mangeot reports that Ravel 'came to London just then to play his new violin sonata with Jelly d'Aranyi [premiered by Enesco in Paris on 30 May] and to make some piano rolls for the Aeolian Company'. This is significant, as there are no known piano rolls by Ravel from 1927; so either Mangeot was mistaken, or this recording session did not take place, or else the rolls were never actually released. In any event, Ravel came to the Aeolian Hall to listen to the latest test pressings of the Quartet, which he heard

> in a little cubicle … which was soon thick with cigarette smoke. I had the score with me, and as the records were played he marked it wherever there was an effect or a tempo that he wanted altered. It was very interesting. He is most precise – he knows exactly what he wants – how, in his mind, that quartet, every bar of it, ought to sound.[20]

The players thereupon returned to the studio, and, having rehearsed Ravel's suggestions, then recorded the work once more:

> In recording we were very particular, with a metronome and a tuning fork, to get the tempo and the pitch exactly right. We also did a thing which is I think a novelty in recording – we played in the first movement a 'fade away' (as they say in the film world) of four bars to show how the first theme is resumed after half the movement is over, and then at the beginning of the next side we played the same four bars again to convey the feeling of continuity.[21]

These new test pressings were then taken to Paris by Mangeot, and played to Ravel (on a gramophone borrowed from a friend in the Capet Quartet) at Montfort-l'Amaury. Evidently very pleased with the results, the composer penned a note, dated 18 July 1927, which effectively gave this version an authorial imprimatur: 'I have just heard the discs of my quartet recorded by the International String Quartet. I am completely satisfied

Example 10.10 String Quartet, I, second subject (bars 55–9): comparison of Calvet (1936) and International (1927) Quartets

= portamento up/down
Calvet: approximate re-notation of rhythmic nuances

with it, from the point of view of sound quality as well as the speeds and nuances.'[22] For a small, independent record company this was clearly a coup, which the NGS was keen to play up in its subsequent reports in *The Gramophone*: the Ravel records had already been advertised, ordered and in some cases paid for by subscribers, even before Ravel's involvement, and the Society had originally intended to distribute them together with recordings of the Bax Oboe Quintet (with Leon Goossens and the International Quartet) and the Dvořák Piano Quintet. The delay, however, was turned to advantage on grounds of 'authenticity': 'Members who have paid for the records and have been expecting to receive them with the Bax and Dvořák will understand that an authentic work with the imprimatur of the composer is worth waiting for in patience.'[23]

In terms of performance style, the International version, in comparison with that of the Calvet (1936), comes across as rather restrained and unsentimental. It is impossible, of course, without tracking down the undistributed white-label pressings, to be sure what effect Ravel's intervention had on the interpretation. But in the first movement's second subject, the Calvet certainly show more affectation in the kinds of dislocating anticipations and spillings-forward that we have already encountered in Ravel's early recordings. The International, meanwhile (with the composer's guidance), produce a greater evenness of rhythm, with the portamentos consistently symmetrical in the descent and ascent of the line's contour (Example 10.10). The paradox is evident: it is as though Ravel is willing a greater restraint and 'classicising' poise on the quartet's phrasing than *he* has managed in his own, earlier piano recordings.

A similar point could be made of the Galimir Quartet recording (November 1934) under a degree of supervision by the then much-ailing composer.[24] What is perhaps of longer-term historical interest is that this 'straighter' mode of playing became increasingly canonic: compare the now rather stolid-sounding Juilliard Quartet version regarded as a benchmark in the early 1970s, or the fascinating continuity of the re-formed Galimir, with Felix Galimir still as leader, issued in 1982. Back in the 1930s, various commentators with a breadth of experience began to note the change with disapproval: Henry Prunières, reviewing the original Galimir recording in 1935, writes:

> Here is a precious document which reveals to us what Ravel intended. Shall I confess that in spite of the magnificent talent of the players, this version shocks me throughout, and I prefer a thousand times that of the Pro Arte, for example? It is instructive to compare the two. One feels the Galimir Quartet to be bridled, held back on a leash; they can't do what they feel . . . Is Ravel right? I'm not convinced.[25]

In fact, the Pro Arte version (1933), of which Prunières is so approving and which sounds today very straight, forthright and grainy, is itself dismissed by Dominique Sordet in 1939 as 'careful, but cold'; she actually prefers the Galimir as 'a more lively, younger' interpretation, but, significantly, her overall vote goes to the Calvet, 'who bring together discreet emotion, spiritual fantasy and caprice with perfection of technique and recording quality'.[26]

The difficulties of defining what we really mean by a more 'modern' performing style are further exemplified elsewhere in the Quartet. On the one hand, the Calvet exhibits Sordet's 'fantasy and caprice' in the seemingly dated way the players spin their expressive melodic lines on a beat-by-beat level. But if the tendency of more recent generations has been to flatten out these local habits of rubato, there has also been an equal tendency to exaggerate other effects, such as over-inflating gestures, or anticipating changes to a slower speed, or over-emphatically 'catching breath' at a *subito pianissimo*; and there are already signs of these in the Calvet version, which are much less marked in the composer-approved International performance. Consider the 'Modéré' at Figs. 4 and 5 in the third movement of the Quartet (Example 10.11). Almost all performances today (and the Calvet), make a grand, rhetorical gesture at the cello solo; but our view of the passage and its context is radically transformed when it is heard at something nearer Ravel's marked tempo of $\quarternote = 84$, as with the International, which then makes much more sense of the added 'énergique' marking. Again, the International's approach to the repeated, accented 5/8 bars of the finale is noteworthy, with each pushing ever forward over the barline within a very fast tempo, rather than restating every bar as a five-square, self-contained gesture.

Example 10.11 String Quartet, III (bars 47–50)

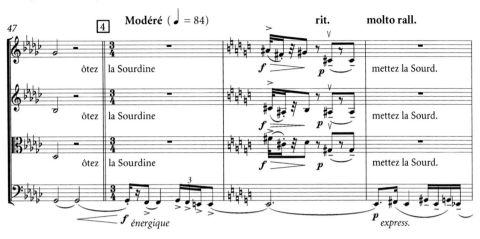

Ravel's *Introduction et allegro* recording (1924)

In so far as one can make generalisations, the evidence seems to be that Ravel preferred (or came to prefer) a way of addressing his music which emphasised forward trajectory, continuity and connectivity, maintaining controlled volatility while eschewing foreground sentimentality. Examples abound in other recordings involving Ravel. In 1923, on a visit to London, he conducted a recording of the *Introduction et allegro* for Columbia (issued in 1924). This is a performance of extremes and raw energy: the opening is very slow and characterised by the clean, straight tone of flute and clarinet (Robert Murchie and Haydn P. Draper) common at this time; but the 'Allegro' is taken at a hair-raising speed (not dictated here by time limitations of the discs' sides), producing breathtaking harp playing by Gwendolen Mason, as well as swirling over-dotting and calculatedly consistent portamento effects. (See especially Fig. 8 'Un peu plus lent', where the 'expressif' phrase is repeated four times with identical portamentos in violin 1 and viola, producing an almost sinister undermining of the surface expressivity.)[27]

Recordings of Ravel's vocal music

The freedom and exhilaration that many early performances convey is nowhere more apparent than in the remarkable singing of Madeleine Grey (1896–1979), who recorded the *Chansons madécasses* under Ravel's direction, and the *Trois chants hébraïques* (*Deux mélodies hébraïques* and 'Chanson hébraïque') with an unknown pianist (probably not Ravel) in

Paris in 1932. The rhythmic fluidity of Grey's interpretations, within controlled bounds and combined with high degrees of accuracy and musical/poetic intelligence, mirror precisely the kinds of inflection we have already seen in the instrumental music, including anticipatory and tenuto agogic stresses, spilled-forward anacruses, carefully placed expressive portamentos, and (as in 'L'Enigme éternelle' from *Deux mélodies hébraïques*) the calculated use of white, vibrato-less tone for special effect.[28] (The singer's normal voice was remarkably 'modern' in its speed and depth of vibrato.) Although Sordet was lukewarm about this recording,[29] Grey seems to have a special empathy with the semi-parlando qualities and natural speech patterns of Ravel's vocal writing, and the distance that the training process places between an individual's speaking and sung voices seems in her case to have been much less than with many of her contemporaries, without sacrifice of musical trenchancy or projection.[30]

Some similar qualities can be heard in Ravel's other favourite female singers, such as the stunningly eloquent performance of *Shéhérazade* by Marcelle Gerar (1891–1970), conducted by Piero Coppola, and the Columbia recording by Jane Bathori (1877–1970) of three of the *Histoires naturelles* (both dated 1929). The latter reveals particularly valuable evidence for deliberate, expressive non-coordination, as Bathori is accompanying herself – a remarkable accomplishment, where exact synchronisation is not only possible, but actually the easiest option. Her reception, however, by Prunières – then principal record reviewer and editor of *La Revue musicale* – was inconsistent. In October 1929, reviewing discs of Debussy and Milhaud, Prunières was unstinting in his praise for Bathori's musicality, if more circumspect on her vocal quality:

> Jane Bathori's perfect diction is wondrous in the *Chansons de Bilitis* of Debussy. To perform this music, extraordinary voices are not indispensable; above all, one must lose neither a single word nor a single note, and the performer must possess taste as much as sensitivity. These are Jane Bathori's preeminent qualities, which we should never forget have rendered such services for contemporary French music. She also sings with spirit for Columbia the *Soirées de Pétrograd* of Darius Milhaud. She accompanies herself, and with what art![31]

A few months later, Prunières was reviewing songs by Satie and Milhaud: 'I love the musicality of Jane Bathori ... but how unphonogenic her voice is! In concert, you lose not a syllable of what she sings; on record, you can't hear a thing any more!'[32] Then, in June 1930, Prunières reviewed the *Histoires naturelles* recording, conceding some improvement in Bathori's 'phonogenic' qualities, but revealing new suspicion about her idiosyncratic accomplishment: 'Jane Bathori is getting used to recording. Her latest disc of Ravel's *Histoires naturelles* is better than her previous ones. The diction is perfect, but why does she accompany herself?'[33]

Marguerite Long and the Concerto in G (1932 recording)

One recording very closely associated with Ravel is the 1932 version of the Piano Concerto in G, with Marguerite Long (1874–1966) as soloist and the composer commonly credited as conductor. The evidence, however, is now unassailable from both Long's biographer Janine Weill and an interview given to Jean-Michel Nectoux in 1982 by Jean Bérard, former artistic director of Columbia in France, that, despite the company's label 'under the direction of M. Ravel', the baton was actually wielded by the young Portuguese conductor Pedro de Freitas Branco, with Ravel supervising from the box.[34] (Ravel was generally regarded as a poor, stiff conductor with surprisingly rudimentary rehearsal technique.)[35] While there is much to admire in the fast, outer movements – particularly noteworthy are the clearly delineated, 'terraced' speed changes in the first movement, without dovetailings or anticipatory ritardandos – Long's deep understanding of Ravel's music shows itself most glowingly in the slow movement. Here, in the opening solo paragraph, we can still hear traces of that expressive de-synchronisation of the hands that was already slightly old-fashioned, and, across the long arch of melody, Long's beautifully judged placement of subtle *inégalités* and agogic stress links her performing style with a previous generation at the same time as signalling Ravel's increasingly cultivated restraint (Example 10.12). Part of the fine balance is in achieving a contained eroticism while avoiding the puritanical streak which often turns Ravel into cool formality; and part of this goal lies in understanding Ravel's particularly finely wrought use of dissonance and resolution, which teases our senses of tonal expectation and metre so deliciously. It is therefore striking how Long is not content with a clean, unblinkingly sharp presentation of the whole paragraph, but in strategic places (especially towards the end) prefers to vary the tonal palette through judicious but daring through-pedalling, followed by a clearing of the air at the next point of musical relief (see Example 10.13).

It goes without saying that the effect of Long's playing cannot be readily replicated on a modern Steinway grand without the sound becoming impossibly congested – she is clearly playing a much lighter-toned instrument in a particular acoustic with a particular sonority in mind. But such a 'close reading' of her technique nevertheless speaks eloquently of her vision of the music, and should give players today some pause for thought.

Ravel himself remained loyal to Long's interpretation. In February

Example 10.12 Concerto in G, II (bars 12–18): examples of agogic stress in Marguerite Long's recording (1932)

* = slight de-synchronisation of hands

Example 10.13 Concerto in G (bars 19–32): approximate reconstruction of Marguerite Long's pedalling (1932)

* = slight de-synchronisation of hands

1932, Henry Prunières devoted much review space to the work's premiere (14 January 1932), with Long as soloist and Ravel conducting. Of the Concerto itself, Prunières was uniformly positive, and of the slow movement he comments: 'This Andante [*sic*] is a miracle of art and sensitivity. Ravel's secret, held-back emotion allows itself to be revealed, and we are very close to being able to pull off the mask from this wonderful artist and human being, so sensitive and who takes such pleasure in affecting impassiveness.'[36] Of Long's performance, however, Prunières was almost the only critic to express disappointment: 'She played it conscientiously, with nimble fingers, and in good piano-professor fashion, without a hint of fantasy, poetry, or sensitivity.'[37] Ravel was so put out by this slur on his favourite interpreter that he replied directly to Prunières:

> Far be it from me, I'm sure, to argue against the freedom of the critical press, especially when it is writing about me. But it wasn't without a sharp surprise that I read, under your signature . . . a somewhat rash appreciation of the performance of my Concerto by Mme Marguerite Long . . .
>
> You don't like this performance – so be it – but I guess that you can't argue against *my* right, as author, to affirm that this interpretation conforms in all particulars to my own thoughts, and that it should form the basis of a tradition for future performances.[38]

Of course, by the time Ravel wrote this, he knew that the commercial recording was shortly to be issued, so his motivation was perhaps not exclusively musical.

Recordings of *Boléro*

A common refrain above has centred on a particular synergic tension set up in many early Ravel performances between volatility and restraint, between letting go and keeping in check, or between the chaste and the sensual. The *locus classicus* for this tension is surely *Boléro*, and perhaps it is at its most raw in Ravel's own recording, made for Polydor with the Lamoureux Orchestra on 9 January 1930 in Paris. Here, the composer's own limitations on the podium seem a positive advantage. In respect of speed, Ravel was right to chastise other conductors – notably Toscanini[39] – for taking the piece too fast or speeding up for cheap effect, as the most powerful sense transmitted by Ravel's version is one of resistance, probably abetted by his stiff handling of the baton. But larger issues of instrumental and orchestral performing style come into play too. *Boléro* is at some level concerned with the individual versus the collective, and the gradual but inexorable assimilation of the former into the latter. In many performances today, especially now that the work has gained such popular currency, a major problem in establishing the resistance at the outset is that we have become too knowing of what is in store. In terms of performance practice, the piece draws – consciously or unconsciously – on the knowledge that at the time of composition the individual wind and brass players in the first half were expected to take full advantage of a soloistic freedom to separate themselves from the accompaniment rhythm, sharpening the dynamic pull towards the collective in the second half. This is clearly audible in Ravel's recording, and we can perceive the same local-level rhythmic liberties being taken by his solo wind players as we have already seen elsewhere, especially crushing together some of the semiquaver grouplets in the main theme, or edging in front of the beat with slight agogic anticipations, to create momentary disjunctions with the prevailing metre.

This phenomenon is also present in the first ever recording made just the previous day for the Gramophone Company under Coppola, whose request to record *Boléro* had been granted by Ravel on condition that he attend the session. According to Coppola's account,[40] he too was censured by Ravel for speeding up in the middle, and although he implies that the fault was corrected with a retake, the eventual issue still shows a distinct increase in pulse, from about $\quarternote = 63$ to 66, at Fig. 15 – admittedly more noticeable when the sides are edited together for a CD reissue – and has reached about 69 at the close. Ravel's version actually starts a notch faster than Coppola, at about $\quarternote = 66$, but has reduced to around 60–63 by the celeste entry after Fig. 8.[41]

The concert-hall success of *Boléro* was accompanied by a more mixed reception in the British press. On reviewing the 1930 Ravel recording, the dogged anti-Ravelian W. R. Anderson dismissed the work as a 'clever novelty', while acknowledging its strong scoring, and sighed, 'Not very much of Ravel seems to be growing upon us; his is, after all, a thinnish cleverness.'[42] This level of incomprehension, while not unique, is offset by a substantial pro-Ravel article by Basil Hogarth in 1931:

> Undoubtedly the greatest of Ravel's works is the wonderful *Bolero*. This fine work has met with much formidable criticism from many unexpected quarters. Constant Lambert, famous composer of *Rio Grande*, whose own work reflects the influence of Ravel, is reported to have said that the *Bolero* reveals the French composer as a spent force. Nothing could be further from the truth; Ravel is as alive to the new influences as any. That he does not succumb to them is no proof of weakness, but of strength and will power far beyond the ordinary.[43]

Other British critics were well aware of the potential speed problem in *Boléro* soon after it entered the public domain. Scott Goddard, for example – a notable supporter of Ravel in the 1920s and 30s – compared

Table 10.1 List of principal recordings discussed[a]

Work	Company and date of recording[b]	Performer(s)	Issue or reissue consulted
Boléro	Gramophone 8 January 1930	Orch.; Piero Coppola (cond.) (Ravel in attendance)	EMI 5-65499-2 (1995: CD)
	Polydor 9 January 1930	Orchestre de l'Association des Concerts Lamoureux; Maurice Ravel (cond.)	Pearl Gemm CD 9927 (1991: CD)
Chansons madécasses	Polydor 1932	Madeleine Grey (mezzo); inst. ensemble; Maurice Ravel (cond.)	EMI 291216-3 (1988: LP)[c]
Gaspard de la nuit: 'Le Gibet'	Duo-Art 30 June 1922 (issued 1925)	attrib. Maurice Ravel (pf): actually Robert Casadesus (pf) (Ravel in attendance)	Ember GVC 39 (1975: LP)
Histoires naturelles: 'Le Paon', 'Le Grillon', 'Le Martin-pêcheur'	Columbia 1929	Jane Bathori (mezzo and pf)	EMI 291216-3 (1988: LP)[c]
Introduction et allegro	Columbia 1923 (issued 1924)	Gwendolen Mason (hp); Robert Murchie (fl); Haydn P. Draper (cl); Charles Woodhouse and Mr Dinsey (vns); Ernest Tomlinson (va); Mr James (vc); Maurice Ravel (cond.)	EMI 291216-3 (1988: LP)[c]
Jeux d'eau	Gramophone 1 March 1923	Alfred Cortot (pf)	EMI 291216-3 (1988: LP)[c]
	Nimbus July–August 1973 (issued 1979)	Vlado Perlemuter (pf)	Nimbus NI 7713/4 (1996: CD)
Miroirs: 'Oiseaux tristes' and 'La Vallée des cloches	Duo-Art 30 June 1922 (issued 1922 and 1928 respectively)	Maurice Ravel (pf) ['La Vallée des cloches' uncertain]	Ember GVC 39 (1975: LP)
Miroirs (complete)	Columbia December 1951 (issued 1952)	Robert Casadesus (pf)	Sony MH2K 63316 (1998: CD)
	Nimbus July–Aug. 1973 (issued 1979)	Vlado Perlemuter (pf)	Nimbus NI 7713/4 (1996: CD)
Pavane pour une Infante défunte	Duo-Art 30 June 1922	Maurice Ravel (pf)	Ember GVC 39 (1975: LP)
Piano Concerto in G	Columbia April 1932	Marguerite Long (pf); orch.; Pedro de Freitas Branco (cond.) [attrib. Maurice Ravel]	Pearl GEMM CD 9927 (1991: CD) EMI 5-65499-2 (1995: CD)
Shéhérazade	Gramophone 1929	Marcelle Gerar (sop); orch.; Piero Coppola (cond.)	EMI 291216-3 (1988: LP)[c]
Sonatine: movts I and II	Welte-Mignon Autumn 1913 (issued 1914)	Maurice Ravel (pf)	Telefunken HT 34 (1964: LP)
Sonatine (complete)	Columbia December 1951 (issued 1952)	Robert Casadesus (pf)	Sony MH2K 63316 (1998: CD)
	Nimbus July–August 1973 (issued 1979)	Vlado Perlemuter (pf)	Nimbus NI 7713/4 (1996: CD)
String Quartet	National Gramophonic Society June 1927	International String Quartet (André Mangeot; Boris Pecker; Frank Howard; Herbert Withers) (version approved by Ravel)	Music & Arts Programs of America CD 703 (1991: CD)
	HMV 7 February 1933	Pro Arte Quartet (Alphonse Onnou; Laurent Halleux; Germain Prévost; Robert Maas)	Biddulph LAB 105 (1995: CD)
	Polydor 1934	Galimir Quartet of Vienna (Felix, Adrienne, Renée and Marguerite Galimir) (Ravel in attendance)	–

Table 10.1 (*cont.*)

Work	Company and date of recording[b]	Performer(s)	Issue or reissue consulted
String Quartet (*cont.*)	Gramophone 4 December 1936	Calvet Quartet (Joseph Calvet; Daniel Guilevitch; Léon Pascal; Paul Mas)	EMI 291216-3 (1988: LP)[c]
	CBS 1973	Juilliard Quartet (Robert Mann; Earl Carlyss; Samuel Rhodes; Claus Adam)	CBS 72998 (1973: LP)
	Vanguard 1982	Galimir Quartet (re-formed) (Felix Galimir; Hiroko Yajima; John Graham; Timothy Eddy)	VA-25009 (1982: LP (CD reissue as VECD7521))
Le Tombeau de Couperin: 'Toccata'	Duo-Art 30 June 1922	attrib. Maurice Ravel (pf): actually Robert Casadesus (pf) (Ravel in attendance)	Ember GVC 39 (1975: LP) EMI 291216-3 (1988: LP)[c]
Trois chants hébraïques	Polydor 1932	Madeleine Grey (mezzo); anon. (pf) (Ravel in attendance)	EMI 291216-3 (1988: LP)[c]
Valses nobles et sentimentales	Welte-Mignon Autumn 1913 (issued 1914)	Maurice Ravel (pf)	Telefunken HT 34 (1964: LP)
	Columbia December 1951 (issued 1952)	Robert Casadesus (pf)	Sony MH2K 63316 (1998: CD)
	Nimbus July–August 1973 (issued 1979)	Vlado Perlemuter (pf)	Nimbus NI 7713/4 (1996: CD)

Notes:

[a] I am particularly grateful to Rémi Jacobs, Roger Nichols, Jonathan Bellman and Arbie Orenstein for making available some of these recordings. This list does not include some early, anonymous recordings of Ravel's works discussed briefly in the present chapter, or other miscellaneous recordings cited *en passant*.

[b] Full details of original international distribution, matrix and set numbers, and reissues to 1988 are given in *RR*, Appendix F. Year of issue is that of recording unless otherwise specified.

[c] This especially important set of three LPs, issued under the title 'Ravel et ses interprètes', is devoted to thirty-one historical performances of Ravel recorded between 1922 and 1944, only a few of which have subsequently appeared in CD format.

Mengelberg's recording, conducting the Amsterdam Concertgebouw, with that of Koussevitzky and the Boston Symphony (both from 1930), and unequivocally preferred the former: 'Remarkably satisfying . . . The pace is, as it should be, unvaried from beginning to end. The gradual crescendo is superbly done.'[44] Of the Koussevitzky, on the other hand, 'The weakness here is that the whole thing is taken too fast, so that the pace is continually having to be held up to accommodate one or the other instrument, and the important characteristic of the piece, its unceasing even stride, is completely lost.'[45] Sordet, however, in 1939, was less impressed with Mengelberg, and indeed Coppola too, chastising the record companies for not having yet managed a decent version of what she clearly considers one of Ravel's major works:

> one remains astonished that the *Boléro*, that masterpiece of brilliant and limpid orchestration, should cut such a lowly figure in our collections. Of the three versions [known to Sordet], the one conducted by Ravel himself is, I won't say the best, but the least bad. The one brought out by M.

Coppola is deeply mediocre, and that by M. Mengelberg is not worth much more.[46]

In conclusion: if there is a general principle, it is that it is extremely difficult to formulate general principles of historical performing habit and reception. At the level of detailed nuance, as explored in this discussion of Ravel's piano and instrumental music, the gaps between the musical assumptions underlying some early recorded practices and our own are often quite wide, and need to be pondered and internalised rather than just read about. There is much in these recordings that can genuinely inform our view of Ravel's music, as performers and listeners, if they are approached in a spirit of open enquiry rather than merely regarded through rose-tinted spectacles or fetishised as quasi-authoritative documents. It would be foolish and musically nonsensical to transplant performing idiosyncrasies on a pick-and-mix basis from these early versions and graft them on to our own playing in the vain hope of achieving some kind of historical validity. Apart from anything else, it is clearly impossible to lump together all pre-World War II practice as somehow homogeneous; and it is precisely the stylistic evolutions and modifications in Ravel performance, both in terms of general historical tendency and the development of individuals such as Casadesus, Perlemuter, and Ravel himself, that can heighten awareness of our own musical habits or presuppositions, and help us to question their basis.

11 Ravel and the twentieth century

ROGER NICHOLS

No sane commentator has ever doubted Ravel's talent. He was a wonderful technician, a superb orchestrator, a consummate stylist . . . but . . . The sense of disappointment is as often an undertow as a fully fledged current. Jim Samson, for instance, sums up Ravel's harmonic practice by saying that 'ultimately . . . the more astringent harmonies in his music are an extension and enrichment of a traditional type of tonal thinking rather than a reshaping of tonality along new, radical lines'.[1] Samson might reasonably argue that this is a neutral, non-value judgement; but in the context of a book entitled *Music in Transition* it is, I submit, easier to read it as a criticism than as a eulogy. There is surely more than a little truth in Michael Russ's contention with regard to the two piano concertos that 'Musicology is wary of declaring as "canonic" works which set out to entertain rather than those which confront the audience with what it might find unpalatable as a necessary part of discovery and self-expression' ('The Concerto in G and jazz': Chapter 6). It is, in essence, the ways in which Ravel is thought to fall short of the canonic, the 'but' of my first paragraph, that I want to examine, for what they tell us not only about Ravel but also about the twentieth century and the demands it has made of its 'serious' composers.

Ravel's musical structures

First of all, we should consider Ravel's structures (or at least, what are perceived to be such). George Benjamin (b. 1960), a Ravel lover, nonetheless confesses that

> the aspect of Ravel that I'm more foreign to is the conservatism of his structures. They work perfectly for his music, but he *is* a bit unadventurous in his structures. It's all so clear-cut and all so classical on the surface that the type of experimentation with phrase-structure and long-term structural exploration you find in German music, in the Second Viennese School, and even up to a point in Debussy, is absent there; it is quite compartmentalised, and in a way he's a miniaturist. The structures do have a certain similarity and indeed cleanness about them.
>   Now that may be on purpose, because with the harmonies being as subtle as they are, if the form became more subtle and complex, there'd be

overload perhaps, which he would have hated. But I love it in German music when you get the feeling of structures bursting out of their bounds and going into territory you could never imagine from the beginning of the piece – you find that in Beethoven, and in Brahms and Wagner also, but you don't find that in Ravel. He remains basically within his borders once he's set them up; to do otherwise would probably be contrary to his character, but I find that problematic.[2]

This feeling, that Ravel could have been more adventurous if he chose, is widespread, as is the feeling that on the occasions he did choose to be adventurous, it was in the wrong directions. Debussy was one of the first to take this line, complaining to Louis Laloy: 'I agree with you Ravel is extraordinarily gifted, but what annoys me is the attitude he adopts of being a "conjuror", or rather a Fakir casting spells and making flowers burst out of chairs.'[3]

Elsewhere in his letters, Debussy speaks of his own 'personal alchemy' and we may feel that in this context the distinction between an alchemist and a conjuror is rather a fine one. Perhaps one of the things that upset the notoriously secretive Debussy was that Ravel tends to make plain what his technical and emotional intentions are (linked, maybe, with the setting up of borders to which Benjamin alludes). At the same time, like a conjuror, he cultivates surprise within this closely defined environment.

If we are looking for a source for this emphasis on surprise, we can find it in Baudelaire's definition of the dandy (since his French is elegantly simple, I prefer to quote it untranslated). In his view, the dandy is 'épris avant tout de distinction' and embraces 'la simplicité absolue, qui est, en effet, la meilleure manière de se distinguer'; he feels 'le besoin ardent de se faire une originalité, *contenu dans les limites extérieures des convenances*' (my italics). He is motivated by 'le plaisir d'étonner et la satisfaction orgueilleuse de ne jamais être étonné'. All dandies 'participent du même caractère d'opposition et de révolte' and experience 'ce besoin . . . de combattre et de détruire la trivialité'. In short, they pursue 'le projet de fonder une espèce nouvelle d'aristocratie'.[4]

A mixture of aristocratic attitudes with aggression, and even a balance between the two, certainly helps to explain some of Ravel's music – and in the case of *Boléro*, the distaste of many may be attributable to what they hear as its too wholehearted embrace of aggression and an abandonment of the 'aristocratic' lineaments of the *Pavane pour une Infante défunte*, the *Sonatine* or *Le Tombeau de Couperin*.

There can, at all events, be no doubt over Ravel's determination to be different: witness his willingness to claim of some technical innovation 'And then, you know, no one had ever done that before!'[5] and his complaint that 'With every new endeavour, the critics throw your previous characteristics back in your face.'[6] To that extent, and with suitable caution, one may disagree with Roland-Manuel when he writes that 'as a pure craftsman Ravel was utterly different from those aesthetes who, to use Nietzsche's charming expression, always fear "that they will be understood without too much difficulty"'; though he is surely right in claiming that Ravel is not one of those 'who are eager of their own accord to give their art a significance which lies far beyond its actual range'.[7]

It is relevant to quote the only mention of Ravel in Proust's *A la recherche du temps perdu*. At the end of 'Le temps retrouvé' a young man, hearing the Kreutzer Sonata, mistakenly 'thought it was a piece by Ravel which someone had described to him as being as beautiful as Palestrina, but difficult to understand'.[8] Given Proust's sensitivity to artistic opinion in all its manifestations, we may presume that this blend of beauty with difficulty was the received judgement on Ravel's music in the salons at the end of the First World War and just after. I cannot help thinking that Ravel must have been pleased when he read it, possibly taking the reference to Palestrina as a tribute to his teacher Gedalge.

Another disconcerting factor for some, including Pierre Boulez (b. 1925), has been the perceived split between Ravel's pre- and post-war music, with *Le Tombeau de Couperin* acting as a slightly awkward bridge over the divide:

> For me what is important is works like *Shéhérazade, Miroirs, Gaspard de la nuit* or *Ma Mère l'Oye*, where he has no restriction, with a certain spontaneity. After the War, the second period is, for me, much less attractive, although very attractive from outside. He tends to be too much self-restricted, he doesn't want to go out of himself. After the Trio you don't find the same deep feeling as before, but more a kind of stylistic game, which is absolutely extraordinary. Only in the second song of *Don Quichotte à Dulcinée* does he go back to something very genuine.

Boulez and Benjamin agree about Ravel's self-restrictions and both Benjamin and Alexander Goehr (b. 1932) make the point that, whatever feeling there may or may not be in the post-war works, a piece like *Boléro* has been crucial for the minimalists. Indeed, Goehr goes further in going back:

> I think *Valses nobles et sentimentales* (which I have written imitations of several times) is a model – you can learn from Ravel something that was very unfashionable in the fifties and sixties, but could well be important: which is how you deal with something which is outwardly familiar, such as a waltz, which has a lot of 'givens' in it – and it's not just got to be three-in-a-bar, it's got to have a certain bass pattern – and you fill in the middle in a very original way.
>
> For instance, minimalist composers, stuck as they are – because once the initial impact of minimalism has been made, what does a composer

such as Glass do? – I would have thought Ravel would have been an extremely valuable model for them, because where the outward is given you go for the subtlety in the middle.

Ravel's influence in France and beyond

After this exposition of some of the problems that the twentieth century has had with Ravel, it is time for some development in the shape of a more formally organised synopsis of the influences, acknowledged and unacknowledged, positive and negative, which Ravel has exerted.

Edward Lockspeiser observed that Ravel's transcriptions and orchestrations of Debussy's music provided 'ample proof of [his] sincere devotion to Debussy. On the other hand, the name of Ravel is not once mentioned by Debussy without a note of sarcasm, irony or concern, certainly never with any sort of unreserved admiration.'[9] One explanation for this could be that, where Ravel could accept the fact of Debussy's influence on him and put his natural aggression on hold for the most part (always excepting his defence of the primacy of the 'Habanera' in the harmonic stakes and of *Jeux d'eau* in the 'impressionist' piano ones), Debussy was perhaps as anxious for a time about Ravel's influence on him as he continued to be about Stravinsky's, even if this anxiety was nowhere so openly expressed. The coincidence of the two men's Mallarmé settings was unfortunate, but already by then Ravel had given signs in *Valses nobles* that he was pursuing ends far from those of Debussy and it is hard to see that for the six years or so that remained of Debussy's composing life he was indebted to Ravel's music in any way: the quotation from 'Le Gibet' in the fourth of the *Six épigraphes antiques* (see Roy Howat, 'Form and motive in *Gaspard de la nuit*': Chapter 4) I take as the exception which proves the rule.

The extent of Stravinsky's indebtedness to Ravel is equally disputable. Among the printed sources, Eric Walter White notes a couple of possible instances: in Stravinsky's setting of Verlaine's 'Un grand sommeil noir' of 1910 (Ravel's 1895 setting was not published until 1953) 'an occasional chord of the 13th reminds one of Ravel' and in *Jeu de cartes* of 1936 'the waltz in the third deal sounds like a light-hearted skit on Ravel's *La Valse*',[10] while Stephen Walsh detects some Ravel influence in Act I of *Le Rossignol* (The Nightingale).[11] Many commentators have also noted the plagiarism of the end of *Rapsodie espagnole* in the final flourish of the 'Danse infernale' in *L'Oiseau de feu*. But, altogether, it is a fairly meagre haul. And in the last instance it is tempting to regard Stravinsky's borrowing as somewhat crudely simplistic – for one thing, where his up–down–up pattern is consistent in all instruments, Ravel slightly overlaps the three components, presenting the final C major chord as a welcome solution to threatened chaos.

To these examples, however, Benjamin makes one challenging addition:

> I don't think *The Rite of Spring* would have been *The Rite of Spring*
> harmonically if Stravinsky hadn't been friends with Ravel, because (and
> Messiaen told me this) in the twenties and thirties people thought that
> Ravel was the more modern of the two because his music was more
> dissonant. The degree of sensitivity in Ravel's polytonal, polyharmonic
> world is fabulous; and you find that in *Miroirs* and *Gaspard*. Who else was
> doing that around then? Not Debussy. And where does Stravinsky get the
> harmonic language of, say, the beginning of Part II of *The Rite of Spring?*
> That's from 'Le Gibet', I think, among other things.

In calling this view 'challenging' I am thinking especially of Richard Taruskin's warning regarding the '*Petrushka* chord': that 'by understanding the origins of Stravinsky's triadic-symmetrical octatonicism in Rimsky-Korsakov's work and teaching, one can distinguish his "*Petrushka* chord" from the ones in Ravel's *Jeux d'eau* (1901), for example, or in Strauss's *Elektra* (1908), which have very different historical backgrounds and different functional explanations, but which an analyst unarmed with historical perspective might be tempted to adduce as precedents for Stravinsky's usage'.[12] It could be that Taruskin would not adduce 'Le Gibet' as a precedent for the above passage of *Le Sacre*; the fact remains that Benjamin, as a practising composer and conductor, hears it that way.

It seems unlikely that Stravinsky's use of jazz owed anything to Ravel – apart from anything else, he got there first. Ravel's latecoming in this sphere was also commented on implicitly by Milhaud who in 1927, the year of the first performance by Enesco and Ravel of the latter's mature Sonata for Violin and Piano with its central 'Blues', stated firmly that

> the influence of jazz has already passed like a cleansing storm after which
> you find a clearer sky and more settled weather. Little by little a reviving
> classicism is replacing the exhausted gasps of syncopation. Our young
> composers are embarking on paths marked out for them by the new
> orientations of Stravinsky on the one hand and of Erik Satie on the other.[13]

No mention of Ravel . . . Milhaud admitted though that he was allergic to Ravel's music and increasingly this had come to be true of Milhaud's mentor Satie. In 1911 Satie dismissed Ravel as a 'highly talented Prix de Rome winner, a flashier version of Debussy'[14] and eight years later declined to write an article on Ravel for Jean-Aubry, saying that it 'might not be very much to your taste. The fault lies entirely with the deplorable and outmoded aesthetic professed by our friend. It would be difficult for me to water down what my thinking dictates. I love Ravel deeply but his art leaves me cold, alas!'[15]

Against Satie's complaint about Ravel being 'outmoded' (see also Kelly, 'Ravel and Satie': Chapter 1), we have to set the claim of Olivier Messiaen (1908–92) that in the 1920s and 30s people regarded Ravel as more modern than Stravinsky! The only answer seems to be that Satie and the young Messiaen moved in different circles, but it certainly serves as a warning that Ravel's standing was not an acknowledged constant across the whole spectrum of Parisian musical life.

In the case of Honegger and Poulenc, Ravel's influence has to be described as patchy. Honegger's 'Hommage à Ravel', written in 1915 and subsequently published as the second of *Trois pièces* for piano, pays lip service to the older composer in its use of modality and of Ravel's characteristic major ninth over a minor triad, but its stiff gait is most un-Ravelian. Thereafter, in the opinion of Harry Halbreich, there are echoes of *Ma Mère l'Oye* at the end of Honegger's First String Quartet (1917) and in the powerful 'De profundis' in his Third Symphony (1945–6), and the Finale of his Sonatina for Violin and Cello (1932) is close in spirit to that of Ravel's earlier essay in the medium. But by and large the two men's composing worlds were far apart, as can be judged from a denigratory remark Honegger made in 1950: 'Ravel is a little like Utrillo, who used to paint pictures from postcards.'[16]

Poulenc too was ambivalent about Ravel's music. After *L'Enfant et les sortilèges* had won him back into the fold of Ravel admirers, he went on to wax ecstatic about both the piano concertos, his epithet 'sublime' for the Concerto for the Left Hand being underlined thirteen times.[17] But elsewhere we find accusations that Ravel's music is cold,[18] that his orchestral technique is inappropriately applied,[19] and that 'neither the blues of the Violin Sonata nor the foxtrot in *L'Enfant et les sortilèges* will add anything much to Ravel's fame'.[20] His ambivalence shows itself most markedly over *L'Heure espagnole*, a work that has in general provided a focus for discussion of the technique/emotion dichotomy in Ravel's music. In 1943, he found *Mavra* 'more *démodé* than *L'Heure espagnole*' (the word 'even' is implied), but a year later, when working on *Les Mamelles de Tirésias*, he could admit: 'I've read the orchestral score of Ravel's *L'Heure espagnole* with unparalleled care, and with the piano reduction in the other hand. What a miraculous masterpiece! But what a truly dangerous example (like all masterpieces)! When you lack Ravel's spellbinding precision (as, alas, I do), you have to set your music on sturdy feet.'[21] It is hard to say whether Poulenc's praise here for Ravel's consummate technique includes any for his expressive qualities.

We can find a similar ambivalence in Messiaen who, like Poulenc, was no jazz fiend: 'I've never believed in jazz and I've always thought that the poetic and refined figure of Maurice Ravel was spoiled in his last years by this jazz influence, which really had nothing to do with his personal inclinations.'[22]

Messiaen's relationship with Ravel could provide a chapter on its own, but it is particularly interesting that, in the original French, the adjective translated as 'refined' should be 'racée', meaning 'thoroughbred, true to one's race or stock': the implication being clearly that not only was Ravel's attachment to jazz in bad taste, it was actually unpatriotic. As Roy Howat has pointed out (see Chapter 4), Ravel's Frenchness was achieved rather than inborn. But it was nonetheless how he was perceived by all but the closest of his friends, who came to recognise in him a typically Basque stubbornness, even cussedness.

Messiaen's view, like that of Boulez, was coloured by his preference for the same works: *Miroirs, Gaspard de la nuit, Ma Mère l'Oye* and *Daphnis et Chloé*. But occasionally, as Benjamin recalls, one could find cracks in the façade:

> Messiaen was rather 'iffy' about quite a lot of Ravel. He would play *Ma Mère l'Oye* on the piano and he would be in tears; *Gaspard* too. But he would try and find a flaw in Ravel – maybe that's part of the question of growing away from something you're very fond of. In *L'Heure espagnole*, you could hear him consciously finding flaws. I can't imagine him saying very nice things about *Le Tombeau de Couperin*, but one day he was in a very good mood and came into the class singing the opening of the 'Rigaudon' – and he kept on going too!

. . . which takes us back to Russ's point, quoted at the start of this chapter.

Messiaen, like all composers, tended to find in other composers' music what he needed to find: *Daphnis* was a treasure trove of irrational Hindu and Greek rhythms;[23] 'Laideronnette' fed into the *Trois petites liturgies* where, in Boulez's view, the 'side order' (the gamelan sonorities) was more interesting than the 'main order',[24] and this in turn fed into Boulez's *Le Marteau sans maître*; the coda to 'Oiseaux tristes' was metamorphosed into the opening of the 'Amen du jugement' in *Visions de l'Amen*. But perhaps the most fascinating idea that Ravel's music sparked off in Messiaen came from 'Scarbo', in the passage from bars 121 to 154 where on four occasions a short value (a semiquaver) is followed by a longer value, each one decreasing in duration: the proportions are $1 : 59$; $1 : 47$; $1 : 37$; $1 : 21$.[25] Bearing in mind that *Gaspard* was one of Messiaen's earliest possessions – he was given it between the ages of seven and ten, before the score of Debussy's *Pelléas* – we may ask whether this was the breeding ground of the *personnages rythmiques* which he was later to apply in his analysis of *Le Sacre* and in the composition of the *Turangalîla Symphony*, among other works. Over and above that, *Gaspard* remains a clear influence on Messiaen's piano writing, as a link between *Islamey* and *Vingt regards*.

Henri Dutilleux (b. 1916), born between Messiaen and Boulez and beginning his studies at the Paris Conservatoire in the 1930s, found 'Ravelism' entrenched as *the* official style and experienced considerable difficulty escaping from it. Certainly, some of his earlier works which he now prefers not to think about too much, such as the Flute Sonatina, bear some marks of Ravelian influence in their elegant modality. While yielding to no one in his admiration of Ravel's technique, Dutilleux may have been obliquely criticising his post-war stylistic games when he stated that 'an artist has a very small number of things that he has to say very firmly, and they are always the same things'.[26] On the other hand, one could equally maintain that one of the miracles of Ravel's output is that, whatever the problem being solved, the authorial voice remains constant.

Boulez has had little to say about Ravel over the years and admits that, in his view,

> for the twentieth century, of course he's not as important a figure as
> Debussy, for instance, although the comparison is maybe wrong – but
> Debussy was more inventive, from a certain point of view, trying to get
> completely out of earlier formal frames, more inventive also in the
> rhythmical aspect. But I think that without Ravel the profile of French
> music would be completely different; and that's something of patrimonial
> interest, certainly, and without him the patrimony would be much poorer.

Almost the most interesting point here is Boulez's admission that we should not be comparing Ravel with Debussy, and yet we do. Boulez admits Ravel's importance for the French composers who came after him, yet at the same time denigrates him because it is not the kind of importance (of language, form and rhythm) which Boulez particularly values. In saying that Ravel is 'not as important' to the twentieth century as Debussy, Boulez is also implying 'or to the twenty-first century and beyond', an implication which will be challenged below.

The Second Viennese School seem either to have ignored Ravel's presence, as in the case of Schoenberg, or as in Webern's example, to have taken a narrow view of his achievement – Eduard Steuermann remembered that 'Webern once did the Mallarmé songs; he adored them, especially the last, which is very close to Schoenberg.'[27] On the other hand, Joan Peyser quotes Webern asking of a Ravel orchestral piece, 'Why does he use so many instruments?',[28] which perhaps tells us more about Webern than about Ravel.

Ravel's influence in England

Ravel's influence on English music is probably a good deal greater, but even here it is hard to adduce specific evidence. Much is owed to Sir Henry

Wood, who introduced Ravel's music to Britain with commendable promptness: *Introduction et allegro* in 1907, *Rapsodie espagnole* in 1909, *Pavane pour une Infante défunte* in Manchester in 1911 (the world premiere of the orchestral version, beating the French one by ten months) and *Valses nobles* in 1913.

Among English composers, Vaughan Williams (1872–1958) benefited from his lessons with Ravel but, apart from the short-lived French fever he himself spoke of, the direct influence of the French master is small. It is confined perhaps to ideas of orchestral spacing, especially in the string writing, and to the use of models, Alain Frogley claiming that Vaughan Williams 'firmly believed in the value of modelling as a compositional training technique'.[29] Fiona Clampin suggests that Ravel's String Quartet possibly acted as a model for Herbert Howells's Third Quartet, *In Gloucestershire*, as his *Sonatine* may have done for John Ireland's *Sonatina*.[30]

Among a slightly younger generation, Arthur Bliss (1891–1975) 'at fifteen years of age . . . was immediately captivated by the French masters', including the 'cool, elegant music of Ravel – no beetling brows and gloomy looks here, but a keen and slightly quizzical look at the world'.[31] Lennox Berkeley (1903–89) in his turn studied with Ravel in Paris during the late 1920s and the same 'cool elegance' distinguishes much of his music, though not all. Ravel was an early influence too on Benjamin Britten (1913–76). By the time he was thirteen or fourteen, Britten had heard the String Quartet and been excited by it,[32] and the summer holidays of 1930 were 'largely spent studying Ravel's *Miroirs*'.[33] The astonishing orchestral sounds of the *Quatre chansons françaises* (1928) also indicate a close study of Ravel's scores.

And yet, in 1947, Percy Scholes could write that although 'some few pianoforte and orchestral pieces have become well known . . . there is not much evidence in *The Musical Times* of any really wide public acceptance of the composer'.[34] That there was however acceptance by an elite is confirmed by Norman Demuth who, writing in 1952 as a Professor of Composition at the Royal Academy of Music in London, opined that 'those who deal with young students find that when these begin to branch away from their traditional basic technique, it is Ravel who appears to give the direction'.[35]

Disentangling Ravel's music and technique

In summing up the situation at present, it is important to distinguish between the example of Ravel's music itself and that of his approach to composition. Goehr makes the point, echoed (if less challengingly) by

Dutilleux, that Ravel 'is a bit too clever to be of much influence, because you've got to be too good at it to actually do it, and people nowadays aren't characterised by their high technical abilities in this direction!'

Where influences are to be recognised, it is more in the tone and the technique than in any of Ravel's musical styles or masks, which remain too personal. Julian Anderson (b. 1967) confesses to 'tearing Ravel's scores apart to find out how it's done'; John Casken (b. 1949) muses on Ravel's 'astonishing ear for the potent magic that steers individual notes from chord to chord, for a unique orchestral resonance ... How is it possible that it all seems so effortless?' Enter Baudelaire's dandy ...

For Michael Berkeley (b. 1948), it is

> hard to think of a greater model in terms of orchestration. But of course it goes much deeper than that since the extraordinary feel and flair for scoring is always put to the service of the musical idea ... I feel that my own orchestration is profoundly influenced by the French school and in particular by an axis that is formed quite clearly in my mind by Debussy, Ravel, Stravinsky and Bartók with, strangely enough, Webern too. For I see a very strong aspirational link between the economy of Webern's little jewels and Ravel's somewhat more sumptuous but no less economical settings.

It is intriguing that so many of those who have responded to my questions about Ravel have, *au fond*, been plagued by doubt and ambivalence. Robin Holloway (b. 1943) expresses something of these quandaries:

> Maurice Ravel stands for a model of technical perfection. When younger I saw this only in terms of finish, neatness, impeccability, orchestration – something almost fetishistic, but deficient in visible/audible technical prowess *à la* Bach – fugue, canon, ritornello etc. – or *à la* Beethoven – motivic rigour, organic growth, symphonic argument or architecture. Ravel's perfection isn't measurable in terms of mastery of things that of their nature require mastery to be shown. It's more simple, yet more elusive; it can't be defined ... the mastery is of spontaneity in capturing with precision the personal predilections of a remarkably individual appetite – garlic and onions – what Virgil Thomson calls 'the discipline of spontaneity – the toughest discipline there is'.

So what happened to the *petit maître* who, we were advised in the 1960s (I speak as a student during that era), had nothing new to say to us, whose prettily voluptuous music could safely be left to tickle the ears of the bourgeoisie? Surely that 'surface' Ravel was never the 'real' Ravel. I can only applaud the common sense and humility of Peter Kaminsky's remark, in his discussion of the links between Ravel's song texts and his compositional strategies, that 'If the connection remains obscured, then the fault lies with the analysis rather than the song' (Chapter 8, p. 163 above). Ravel, it turns out, is a far more baffling, problematic and 'deep' composer than he has so far been given credit for. Added to this is the enigma of his orchestration. In many of the eulogies directed at this aspect of Ravel's craft, it is impossible to miss a sense of embarrassment, of guilt almost, that a practising composer should be singling out the sublimely sensuous instead of more 'important' things like form, motivic coherence or octatonic scales. In Anderson's words, 'Ravel disturbs with his curious mixes, with his experiments couched in traditional forms. He is unpigeonholeable. What to do with him? Like Ligeti, he is having serious fun – both are enjoying themselves at an aristocratically high level.'

And so we return, yet again, to Baudelaire's dandy who flourishes, so Baudelaire tells us (and here I dare to translate), 'especially in transitional epochs when democracy is not yet all powerful and aristocracy only partially tottering and debased'.[36]

While we must all make up our own minds as to how Ravel's music and the social order are likely to interact in the twenty-first century, the present fact, crudely put, is that Ravel's listing in the 1999 CD catalogue takes up seventeen columns – not as many as Mozart (Ravel would surely have regarded his 130 columns as only fair), but a respectable enough total when compared with those for Purcell (31), Schumann (30), Mendelssohn (27), Debussy (24), Stravinsky (15), Gershwin (12), Monteverdi (9) or César Franck (8).[37] Yet despite this basic pointer to Ravel's not inconsiderable popularity, we have barely begun to understand how his music works. Will the twenty-first century be long enough for us to find out?

ROGER NICHOLS AND DEBORAH MAWER

Ravel and the critics

ROGER NICHOLS

Like most composers, Ravel had his staunch defenders and his virulent opponents as well as one or two critics (in many ways the most interesting for us) who tried to take each of his works on its merits.

Of his defenders, the eldest was Willy (Henri Gauthier-Villars, 1859–1931) who, despite his love of Wagner, had also been one of the few early champions of Debussy's *L'Après-midi*. If he was caustic over the early overture *Shéhérazade*, this was no more than Ravel came to be himself, and his willingness to praise the 'orchestre de rêve' of *Daphnis*[1] may have been due in part to his pleasure in seeing fulfilled his prophecy of 1899 that Ravel might 'become something if not someone in about ten years, if he works hard'.[2]

Ravel's remaining supporters were men nearer his own age. Charles Koechlin (1867–1950) had been a fellow student at the Conservatoire and, as a brilliant teacher of musical technique, naturally recognised Ravel's abilities in this area and regarded him as one of France's leading composers.[3] Of *L'Heure espagnole*, Koechlin claimed that it was the work of a Japanese sculptor in ivory 'with the impeccable sureness of his accurate line and his ironic, intimate view of objects'.[4] Another friend, M.-D. Calvocoressi (1877–1944), one of the 'Apaches' and the dedicatee of 'Alborada del gracioso', became the chief music critic of *Comœdia illustré*. Even though he liked to think of himself as unusually objective, his unwavering support of Ravel prompted Debussy to dub him a 'valet de chambre'.[5]

Other defenders of Ravel included Louis Vuillemin (1879–1929), Emile Vuillermoz (1878–1960) and Henry Prunières (1886–1942). (For typical criticism, see 'Ravel's main works', Nos. 9 and 19 for Vuillemin and Vuillermoz; Nos. 16–18 for Prunières.) Vuillermoz, a fellow pupil of Fauré, wrote for a number of journals including *La Revue musicale* and *Le Temps* and was quick to emphasise the particularity of Ravel's music, especially of his word-setting in *Histoires naturelles* and *L'Heure espagnole*, while regretting the choice of subject in the latter by a composer 'for whom some of us nourish loftier ambitions'.[6] Prunières, as editor of *La Revue musicale*, was in a good position to maintain Ravel's reputation after the War, as in his enthusiastic review of the Monte Carlo premiere of

[251]

L'Enfant et les sortilèges in which he welcomed Ravel's unaggressive use of bitonality, the 'suavité céleste' of the final fugue, and the mixture of speaking and singing that leads up to it (what Ravel calls 'la déclamation plaintive, souple, presque sans timbre') which he reckoned would 'open up new horizons for opera'.[7]

Any list of Ravel's detractors must begin with Pierre Lalo (1866–1943), the son of the composer Edouard and from 1898 chief music critic of *Le Temps*. (See 'Ravel's main works', Nos. 1, 2, 4, 5, 6 and 9.) Beginning with the overture *Shéhérazade*, which moved him to hope 'that M. Ravel will not eschew unity and will turn his thoughts more often to Beethoven',[8] he conducted what can only be called a campaign of denigration. He condemned Ravel as a blind follower of Debussy,[9] as a devotee of over-complication,[10] as a purveyor of 'an awkward and aggressive affectation, mannerism and pretentiousness'[11] and as an incarnation of 'insensitivity'[12] – the 'bagatelles sonores' of *L'Heure espagnole* evoking for him Wagner's *Ring* 'seen through a microscope'. Not that these fulminations had any effect, it seems. As Roland-Manuel (1891–1966) noted in 1927, 'the corpses which Pierre Lalo has slaughtered are doing quite well'. The composer simply wrote Lalo off as 'a dilettante with good connections'.[13]

No other French critic pursued Ravel with the same determination. The composer could usually be certain of unfavourable comment from Gaston Carraud (1869–1920) in *La Liberté*: the orchestral version of 'Une barque sur l'océan' was 'a confusing kaleidoscope'[14] (Ravel's permanent withdrawal of this version suggests that he agreed) and 'the languorous rhythms' of the 'Habanera' were just so much childishness ('enfantillages').[15] Nor could Carraud find any rhythmic or melodic originality in *Daphnis*, whose instrumentation tended to obliterate 'the demarcation line hitherto set up by us, timid souls that we are, between sound and noise'.[16] Altogether more comprehensible was the mismatch between Reynaldo Hahn (1875–1947) and Ravel's more virtuosic productions. (For examples of Hahn's criticism, see 'Ravel's main works', Nos. 8 and 12.) Where Ravel inclined in the direction of Mozart, Hahn, another devotee of the older master, could follow without much trouble. But *L'Heure espagnole* left him aghast, striking him as 'a kind of transcendent jujitsu' in which the performers tried to rectify the mistakes in this 'learnedly cacophonic symphony' by missing out beats.[17]

Between these two extremes of general acceptance and rejection, two critics in particular preserved a more thoughtful, flexible approach. Jean Marnold (pseudonym of Jean Morland, 1859–1935) was both polemical and erudite: he was the French translator of both Nietzsche's *The Origins of Tragedy* and the libretto of Richard Strauss's *Feuersnot*. (For a sample of

Marnold's criticism, see 'Ravel's main works', No. 2.) After falling in love with the String Quartet and the *Miroirs* (whose impact on him he likened to that of Schumann's *Kreisleriana*),[18] in 1905 he took up the cudgels for Ravel over the Prix de Rome affaire. But his enthusiasm foundered over *Histoires naturelles* and *Valses nobles*: Renard's poetry was in the style of 'a constipated Alphonse Allais', while for him the complicated harmonies of the *Valses* were disproportionate to the essence of the exercise.[19] Only with the Piano Trio did he find himself once more in accord with the composer who, 'on a larger scale, belongs to the authentic line descended from our gentle, profound Couperin'.[20]

As Christian Goubault says, 'Jean Marnold's ideas are almost identical with those of Louis Laloy – apart from their opinions of Ravel ... '[21] (For examples of Laloy's criticism, see 'Ravel's main works', Nos. 4, 5 and 6.) Laloy (1874–1943) founded *Le Mercure musical* with Marnold in 1905 and was a powerful force in French music for many years, writing the first French biography of Debussy (who thought of him as having been 'long ago almost the only person to understand *Pelléas*') and from 1914 holding the post of general secretary at the Opéra. Unlike Marnold, he found the early Ravel 'uncertain, diffuse and often languishing'[22] and it was precisely *Histoires naturelles* that turned him into a supporter. In his important article on the work,[23] Laloy explored a number of points that were soon to become clichés of Ravel criticism. Whereas, for him, the returns of the opening phrase of the Quartet were somewhat artificial and some passages in *Miroirs*, for all their 'couleur rare', suffered from a 'surcharge ornementale', in *Histoires* he found all the qualities that had been lacking until then: 'clear construction and close linkage of all the sections, the sobriety of a continuously and exactly expressive style and, at the root of all that, unfailing inspiration and emotion'.[24] He recognised that Ravel always remained an observer, not only of nature but of his own reactions, that he was 'disposed to be entertained by what moved him'; from where it was a short journey to words such as 'ironie' and 'esprit'. But, as Laloy admitted, this article pleased neither the d'Indy faction, who regarded him as a traitor, nor those who, like Vuillermoz, nourished loftier ambitions for Ravel than that of 'farceur'.

After World War I and the death of Debussy, Ravel's reputation in France was reasonably secure. Cocteau, Satie and 'Les Six' all had their reservations about him, as did Henri Sauguet, noting that *Tzigane* had been a 'huge success, naturally, with the ladies in *pince-nez* and the gentlemen behind large stomachs', and suggesting that 'Ravel does not like the music of today. He must like it as little as we like what he's now producing.'[25] From time to time there were also diatribes against what was perceived as

Ravel's *petitesse.* Two days after a London concert of Ravel's music, including the first British performance of *Tzigane,* the critic of *The Times* (28 April 1924) wrote: 'To hear a whole programme of Ravel's works is like watching some midget or pygmy doing clever, but very small, things within a limited scope. Moreover, the almost reptilian cold-bloodedness, which one suspects of having been consciously cultivated, of most of M. Ravel's music is almost repulsive when heard in bulk; even its beauties are like the markings on snakes and lizards.'

But by then, as Roland-Manuel said, Ravel's corpse was 'doing quite well'. As for his own view of the trade of music criticism, he realised that composers had their own furrows to plough and could not be expected to be without bias. But he still found himself being astonished that the job should so rarely be put in the hands of practising composers, given that a review, 'even when it is perspicacious, is of less importance than a piece of music, however mediocre'.[26] His attitude is neatly resumed in his defence of Debussy's orchestral *Images* against the critics: namely 'M. Gaston Carraud, to whom we owe three songs and a short symphonic poem, M. Camille Mauclair, who has become known entirely through his literary and art criticism, and M. Pierre Lalo, who has composed nothing at all ...'[27]

Ravel's main works: first performances and selected criticism

COMPILED BY DEBORAH MAWER WITH ROGER NICHOLS

This listing comprises what may reasonably be regarded as Ravel's main works, supported by selected criticism. Although the aim is to present materials of musicological significance (some of which have not previously been available in published translation), the choice of content is in part subjective. (*Jeux d'eau,* for instance, could have been included here, but the Ravel/Lalo dispute is already covered elsewhere: Chapters 4 and 9.) The balance here between positive and negative reviews reflects the critical factions discussed above.

Works are ordered by the starting date of their composition; where two works were begun in the same year, entries are further ordered by their completion date. Several of the press clippings have been sourced directly from the Bibliothèque Nationale de France (including the Fonds Montpensier) by the editor, and those marked by an asterisk have been translated by the editor. For further details on the early reception of Ravel's music, see the useful documentation given in Orenstein, *Ravel,* and (in French) Marnat, *Maurice Ravel.*

1 *Shéhérazade, ouverture de féerie* (orch. 1898)

Performers	Auspices/venue	Date
Ravel (cond.)/ Orchestre de la SN	Société Nationale (SN)/ Salle du Nouveau-Théâtre, Paris	27 May 1899

> A jolting debut: a clumsy plagiarism of the Russian school (of Rimsky
> faked by a Debussyian who is anxious to equal Erik Satie) disaffects the
> audience, which, irritated besides by the aggressive bravos of a bunch of
> young claques, protests and boos. Why this cruelty? I regret it with regard
> to young Ravel, a mediocrely gifted debutant, it is true, but who will
> perhaps become something if not someone in about ten years, if he works
> hard.   (Henri Gauthier-Villars, in Orenstein, *Ravel*, 24)

> M. Maurice Ravel is still a pupil at the Conservatoire, and his colleagues
> and professsors speak highly of him ... *Shéhérazade* is explained in a
> programme note by the following prose: '... 1st part: Initial idea in B
> minor; developments – Episodic theme (muted trumpets), leading to the
> second idea (in F♯ major), inspired by a Persian melody – Conclusion of
> the 1st part. – 2nd part: development of the ... themes. – Bass pedal on the
> expanded initial idea. – 3rd part: return of the first and second ideas, heard
> simultaneously. – Return of the introduction serving as the coda.' This
> prose immediately suggests the notion of a clearly constructed work,
> composed with vigour and directed with certitude. Don't have too much
> confidence in it: if you look in the music for all that is indicated in the
> programme, you'll be hard pressed to find it. The 'developments',
> especially, are so inaudible, that one would be tempted to think that M.
> Ravel were speaking of them ironically. In reality, *Shéhérazade* is composed
> of a series of very short fragments, attached to each other by extremely
> slight links ... The harmonic workmanship is extremely curious, almost
> excessive: here M. Ravel is clearly undergoing the formidable influence of a
> musician whom one should know how to like but not imitate, M. Claude
> Debussy. And the orchestration is full of ingenious explorations and
> piquant effects of sonority. An artist may emerge from this.
>   (Pierre Lalo, 'Concert à la Société Nationale
>   de Musique', *Le Temps* (13 June 1899))*

2 String Quartet (1902–3)

Performers	Auspices/venue	Date
Heymann Quartet	SN/Salle de la Schola Cantorum, Paris	5 March 1904

> in its harmonies and successions of chords, in its sonority and form ... and
> in all the sensations which it evokes, it offers an incredible resemblance
> with the music of M. Debussy.
>   (Pierre Lalo, *Le Temps* (19 April 1904), in Orenstein, *Ravel*, 39–40)

A healthy and sensitive temperament of a pure musician is developing
here . . . a spontaneous art or the unfailing nature of instinct ensures the
communication of his thinking. One should remember the name of
Maurice Ravel. He is one of the masters of tomorrow.

(Jean Marnold, 'Un quatuor de Maurice Ravel',
Mercure de France (April 1904), 249–51: 251)*

3 *Miroirs* (pf 1904–5; 'Une barque' orch. 1906 (rev. 1926); 'Alborada' orch. 1918)

Performer	Auspices/venue	Date
Ricardo Viñes (pf)	SN/Salle Erard, Paris	6 January 1906

'Oiseaux tristes' is something extremely new, a rather extended étude (in
the sense that painters use this word) and with perfect verity of notation.
The same is true of 'La Vallée des cloches'. On the other hand, 'Barque sur
l'océan' is a veritable small symphonic poem, constructed very vigorously,
and 'Alborada' is a scherzo, a big independent scherzo in the manner of
Chopin and Balakirev. If I am not mistaken, 'Noctuelles' is a sort of étude
(this time in the pianistic sense) which is also realized in an extremely fresh
manner . . .

But what I find most remarkable in these diverse pieces are their
emotional qualities. In 'Oiseaux tristes' and 'La Vallée des cloches' there is a
great depth of feeling, of intimate feeling, totally devoid of grandilo-
quence. 'Barque sur l'océan' is once again beautiful, intense poetry. The
'humor', the frank and vivacious fantasy of 'Alborada' merit the highest
praise.

(M.-D. Calvocoressi, *Le Courrier musical*
(15 January 1906), in Orenstein, *Ravel*, 49–50)

['Une barque sur l'océan' (orch.) was] like a succession of colours imposed
on a drawing barely sketched. . . . Unfortunately the view changes every
moment. It is a confusing kaleidoscope and we cannot even tell what kind
of weather prevails on this ocean.

(Gaston Carraud, 'Une barque sur l'océan', *La Liberté*
(5 February 1907), in Nichols, *Ravel*, 44)

4 *Histoires naturelles* (voice, pf 1906)

Performers	Auspices/venue	Date
Jane Bathori (voice)/Ravel (pf)	SN/Salle Erard, Paris	12 January 1907

The *Histoires naturelles* constitute, to my mind, the work which best shows
the personality of Maurice Ravel, his particular vision of nature and this
ability to note subtle nuances of sonority, the precious gift to him from a
good fairy.

(Louis Laloy, 'Musique nouvelle', *Mercure musical
et S.I.M.*, 3 (15 March 1907), 279–82)*

In itself, the idea of setting the *Histoires naturelles* to music is already surprising . . . M. Ravel is not of this opinion because he claims to have discovered something lyrical in M. Renard's 'Guinea-fowl' and 'Peacock' . . . I have to admit that in several ways his music is perfectly adapted to the text: it is just as precious, just as laboured, just as dry and almost unmusical: a collection of arbitrary harmonies, industriously mixed, the most elaborate and over-complicated chord progressions.

(Pierre Lalo, *Le Temps* (January 1907))*

5 *Rapsodie espagnole* (orch. 1907–8)

Performers	Auspices/venue	Date
Edouard Colonne (cond.)/ Orchestre Colonne	Concerts Colonne/ Théâtre du Châtelet, Paris	15 March 1908

All of this would be quite well construed to please if there wasn't in the style of this music, in its expression, in its smallest details, an awkward and aggressive affectation, mannerism and pretentiousness.

(Pierre Lalo, *Le Temps* (24 March 1908))*

It's a very well observed Spain, but by an eye which teases, and willingly exaggerates or deforms: the Spain of Cervantes or of Goya, with more searching lines, more tortured forms, and more fantastic caprices . . . a rhapsody is not a symphony, and the art of M. Ravel, with all its concise indications and delectable findings, is repelled by the solemnity of grand constructions. The value of a work is not measured by volume, nor by weight: it is this ivory figurine which gives an impression of beauty that is denied to a giant statue of Liberty, illuminating the world.

(Louis Laloy, 'La Musique, Concerts Colonne',
La Grande Revue, 12 (25 March 1908), 397–9: 397–8)*

6 *L'Heure espagnole* (*comédie musicale*, 1907–9)

Performers	Auspices/venue	Date
Albert Carré (dir.) François Ruhlmann (cond.) M. Bailly (décor) M. Multzer (costumes)	Opéra-Comique, Paris	19 May 1911

The orchestration of *L'Heure espagnole* is charming, brilliant, idiosyncratic, diverse, full of subtle timbres and rare sonorities . . . That, for the musical material which he employs, for the chord progressions and explorations of harmonies which for him are customary, M. Ravel owes much to Debussy is a manifest fact. But the soul of his music and of his art is entirely different. M. Debussy is all sensitivity, M. Ravel all insensitivity.

(Pierre Lalo, *Le Temps* (28 May 1911))*

L'Heure espagnole, by M. Franc-Nohain, is a comedy not of manners, still less of characters, but of movements and of words . . .

Analogous to the text, the music mocks the subject-matter and itself: the vocal line alternates lyrical swoops and simple spoken dialogue; the imperturbable orchestral accompaniment is supplemented by the untimely cries of automatons; an excessive growling underlines the charge of an imaginary bull . . . the five voices unite in a final quintet where one by one, to a habanera rhythm, they create ornamented chords from their parallel trills, or else pass from one to another a motive which they transpose . . . But M. Ravel is such a pure musician that he never exceeds the limits of beauty . . . (Louis Laloy, 'La Musique, *L'Heure espagnole*',
La Grande Revue, 15 (10 June 1911), 627–8)*

7 *Gaspard de la nuit* (pf 1908)

Performer	Auspices/venue	Date
Ricardo Viñes (pf)	SN/Salle Erard, Paris	9 January 1909

For there is, and doubtless there always will be mischief in M. Ravel: his mind is a sorcerer which, even when emotional, still beguiles with a prestigious skill . . . in each of the three [pieces] the writing is so tightly woven, so meticulous, so ingenious, that each note brings with it surprise and joy. M. Ravel is a stylist . . .
(Louis Laloy, 'La Musique, Société Nationale: *Gaspard de le nuit*',
La Grande Revue, 13 (25 January 1909), 395–6: 395)*

8 *Ma Mère l'Oye* (pf duet 1908–10; ballet orch. 1911)

Performers	Auspices/venue	Date
Jeanne Leleu (pf)	Société Musicale	20 April 1910
Geneviève Durony (pf)	Indépendante (SMI)/	
	Salle Gaveau, Paris	

Ballet premiere

Maurice Ravel (scenario)	Théâtre des Arts, Paris	29 January 1912
Jacques Rouché (dir.)		
Gabriel Grovlez (cond.)		
Jeanne Hugard (choreog.)		
Jacques Drésa (décor/costumes)		

a triumph of Ravel's elegant, aristocratic, delightful, and somewhat ironic art. (Critic cited anonymously, in Orenstein, *Ravel*, 65)

nothing is less naive, less childish, less 'Stories of Mother Goose' than this attractive ballet of M. Ravel, put on by M. Drésa and presented . . . in a little temple consecrated to decadence.

(Reynaldo Hahn, *Comœdia* (2 February 1912))*

9 *Daphnis et Chloé* (ballet score 1909–12; orch. suites 1911, 1913)

Performers	Auspices/venue	Date
Ballets Russes/ Serge Dyagilev Pierre Monteux (cond.) Mikhail (Michel) Fokin (choreog.) Léon Bakst (décor, costumes)	Théâtre du Châtelet, Paris	8 June 1912

The music is more developed, richer; the thematic work is more noticeable and sustained. But it is lacking the first quality of ballet music: rhythm.
> (Pierre Lalo, '*Daphnis et Chloé*', *Le Temps* (11 June 1912))*

Much talent in this music, this is incontestable, much willpower, above all much daring: but, one has to admit, very little grace, very little charm, and above all very little inspiration.
> (Arthur Pougin (1834–1921), 'Semaine théâtrale',
> *Le Ménestrel*, 24 (15 June 1912), 187–9: 189)*

Maurice Ravel's score is a ballet score and not a symphonic poem more or less happily staged and more or less faithfully translated into the silent language of arms and legs . . . Commercially as well as artistically this ballet was a 'hit'; [but] it was necessary to secure this with more conviction . . . The thinking of the musician was absolutely betrayed by negligences of this sort and by certain imperfections of production rendering much detail of the action particularly obscure . . . His [Ravel's] dances have a surprising dynamism and an irresistible impetus . . . Thanks to *Daphnis et Chloé* the Russian season has ended in apotheosis . . .
> (Emile Vuillermoz, 'Les Théâtres', *Revue musicale
> de la S.I.M.*, 8/6 (15 June 1912), 62–8: 66–8)*

Performers	Auspices/venue	Date
Mikhail (Michel) Fokin: Daphnis (and choreog.) Vera Fokina: Chloé Philippe Gaubert (cond.) Léon Bakst (décor/costumes)	Opéra, Paris	20 June 1921

As for *Daphnis*, M. Fokine at the same time as representing the role of the shepherd, directed the choreography and movements of numerous characters. He revealed in this delicate task an accomplished knowledge of the score. Gestures and steps, group entrances, general dances, are truly complementary to the symphonic episodes.
> (Louis Vuillemin, 'La Semaine musicale',
> *Lanterne* (21 June 1921))*

10 *Valses nobles et sentimentales* (pf 1911; orch. 1912)

Performer	Auspices/venue	Date
Louis Aubert (pf)	SMI/Salle Gaveau, Paris	9 May 1911

The title *Valses nobles et sentimentales* sufficiently indicates my intention of composing a series of waltzes in imitation of Schubert. The virtuosity which forms the basis of *Gaspard de la nuit* gives way to a markedly clearer kind of writing, which crystallizes the harmony and sharpens the profile of the music. The *Valses nobles et sentimentales* were first performed amid protestations and boos at a concert of the Société Musicale Indépendante, in which the names of the composers were not revealed. The audience voted on the probable authorship of each piece. The authorship of my piece was recognized – by a slight majority. The seventh waltz seems to me the most characteristic.

> ([Ravel] 'An autobiographical sketch', 31; the results of the audience voting were published in *Le Courrier musical* (15 May 1911), 365. For more detail, see Orenstein, *Ravel*, 64–5.)

Ballet premiere (retitled *Adélaïde ou Le Langage des fleurs*)

Troupe of Natasha Trouhanova	Théâtre du Châtelet, Paris	22 April 1912

Maurice Ravel (scenario/cond.)
Orchestre Lamoureux
Jacques Dresa (décor/costumes)
Ivan Clustine (choreog.)

11 *Trois poèmes de Stéphane Mallarmé* (voice, ensemble/pf 1913)

Performers	Auspices/venue	Date
Jane Bathori (voice) D.-E. Inghelbrecht (cond.)	SMI/Paris	14 January 1914

UK premiere

Jane Bathori (voice) Thomas Beecham (cond.)	London	(mid-) March 1915

[The *Trois poèmes*] are among the most recent and interesting examples of modern song. The tiny orchestra is handled with utmost delicacy and intimacy of expression ... Mr Thomas Beecham conducted and Mme. Jane Bathori sang the very difficult vocal part with great insight and expressiveness.

> (Critic for the *Daily Mail* (18 March 1915), in Orenstein, *Ravel*, 68)

An attentive audience listened in absolute bewilderment to some of the strangest exercises in ultramodern cacophony which it would be possible to imagine ... Now and then the divergence between the voice part and the accompaniment seemed so pronounced as almost to suggest that Mdme. Bathori-Engel was singing one number while the instrumentalists were playing another.

> (Critic for the *Westminster Gazette* (18 March 1915), ibid.)

12 *Le Tombeau de Couperin* (pf 1914–17; orch. 1919)

Performer	Auspices/venue	Date
Marguerite Long (pf)	SMI/Salle Gaveau, Paris	11 April 1919

Ballet transcription

Ballets Suédois/	Théâtre des Champs-	8 November 1920
Rolf de Maré (dir.)	Elysées, Paris	
D.E. Inghelbrecht (cond.)		
Jean Börlin (choreog.)		
Pierre Laprade (décor, costumes)		

In bygone times they called the collecting of homages in prose, verse or music as tribute to a person deceased or still living a 'tombeau'. Louis Couperin, father [*sic;* actually uncle] of François Couperin *le grand*, had thus composed 'Le Tombeau de Blanc-Rocher' for his lute teacher ... And this evocation of the past has been most attractively staged by the choreographer M. Borlin, danced also by himself, Mlle Hasselquist, and the *corps de ballet.*   (Louis Schneider, *Le Gaulois* (15 November 1920))*

Le Tombeau de Couperin is a delicious musical entertainment composed of a brisk fast-moving introduction, nimbly and sharply executed, and full of charming coquetry, and of three dances, a forlana, a minuet and a rigaudon, traditional steps exquisitely dressed up in 'modern' garb.

> (Reynaldo Hahn, in Bengt Häger, *Ballets Suédois*
> (London: Thames & Hudson, 1990), 102)

13 *La Valse* (orch. 1919–20; also pf and 2 pfs)

Performers	Auspices/venue	Date
Camille Chevillard (cond.)/	Concerts Lamoureux/Paris	12 December 1920
Orchestre Lamoureux		

Your understanding of *La Valse* is perfect. I could never get that rhythmic suppleness in Paris ... Don't forget to have the programs mention that this 'choreographic poem' is written for the stage. I believe it is necessary, judging from the surprise which the concluding frenzy has evoked from some listeners, and, above all, from the fantastic comments of several music critics. Some situate this dance in Paris, on a volcano, about 1870, others, in Vienna, before a buffet, in 1919.

(Ravel, letter of 20 October 1921 to Ernest Ansermet, in *RR*, 212)

Ballet premiere

Ballets Ida Rubinstein	Opéra, Paris	23 May 1929
Maurice Ravel (scenario)		
Gustave Cloez (?) (cond.)		
Alexandre Benois (décor)		
Bronislava Nijinska (choreog.)		

We are, on the bank of the Danube, in a marble swimming pool surrounded by high, massive columns ... Mme Ida Rubinstein, in a silver corset and a cap with flaxen plumes, appears as a kind of water goddess of the Waltz ... Let's not debate the intellectual whim which determined it. Let's just savour the masterly symphonic score of M. Maurice Ravel, its meticulously thought-out plan, its delicate nuancing, its fastidious working amid his detours and scintillating effects.

(Henry Malherbe, 'Chronique musicale', *Le Temps* (29 May 1929))*

UK ballet premiere

Ballets Ida Rubinstein	Covent Garden Theatre,	8 July 1931
Maurice Ravel (scenario/décor?)	London	

La Valse is Maurice Ravel's *ballet* in a special sense, for, besides composing the music, he has developed the costumes and scenery. When the curtain rose upon its performance by Mme. Ida Rubinstein's company at Covent Garden Theatre last night, it was evident that M. Ravel is as skilled in the handling of colour and design in the literal sense as in the musical sense. From behind veils that slowly lifted there was disclosed a lovely vision of the nineteenth-century ball-room. Gradually the figures in uniform and crinoline awakened from the picture and began to move in waltz-rhythm, until, as in *Bolero*, all were whirling in the dance.

(Unsigned review for *The Times* (9 July 1931))

14 *L'Enfant et les sortilèges (fantaisie lyrique, 1920–5)*

Performers	Auspices/venue	Date
Raoul Gunsbourg (dir.)	Opéra, Monte Carlo	21 March 1925
Vittorio de Sabata (cond.)		
George Balanchine (ballet master)		
M. Visconti (décor)		

French premiere

Albert Wolff (cond.)	Opéra-Comique, Paris	1 February 1926

[the opera] is not convincing. It seems void of music! Why? Because the music never has the opportunity to expand.

> (Robert Dezarnaux, *La Liberté* (3 February 1926),
> in Orenstein, *Ravel*, 90)

The most refined of our contemporary composers and the most penetrating of our authors have united in order to create a work of incomparable enchantment . . . It is impossible, indeed, to enumerate all the carefully selected riches, all the subtle notations, the rhythmic forms, all the tours de force of this classical and spiritually sensual score, which is so ingeniously reconciled with contemporary taste.

> (Henry Malherbe, *Le Temps* (3 February 1926), ibid.)

It is difficult to give you a thorough account of the actions and reactions which *L'Enfant* has aroused. The family circle naturally applauded. The Institute cursed you until the seventh generation . . .

Your work is performed every night in a lively, scandalous atmosphere. Everyone is delighted that it is always possible to hear the music, particularly the performers. 'We're having a good time', Roger Bourdin [operatic baritone] confided to me, 'we're living through historic moments.'

Whether your work is greeted with praise or with reservations, the critics are stammering a bit more stupidly than usual . . . There was very keen praise from Raymond Douches (in *L'Avenir*); a short article in *Paris-Midi* with a picture of the film producer Ravel (Gaston); a very pleasant article by Vuillermoz [*Excelsior*, 3 February 1926]. Finally, a characteristic thrashing by Messager in *Le Figaro* [4 February 1926] . . . he claims you sacrifice everything for some orchestral effects, when it seems to me that *L'Enfant* is the least *orchestrated* but the most *orchestral* work you have written. That was the main point of my article in *Le Ménestrel* [5 February 1926].

> (Roland-Manuel, letter of 23 February 1926
> to Ravel, in *RR*, 269–71: 269–70)

15 Sonata for Violin and Piano (1923–7)

Performers	Auspices/venue	Date
Georges Enesco (vn) Maurice Ravel (pf)	Concerts Durand/ Salle Erard, Paris	30 May 1927

US performance

Joseph Szigeti (vn) Maurice Ravel (pf)	Gallo Theater, New York	15 January 1928

Ravel was somewhat nonchalant about his piano-playing; 'unconcerned' might better describe his attitude. It was the confidence of the creative artist that determined his stand with respect to our task. It was as if he said: 'What of it, whether we play it a little better, or in a less polished and brilliant fashion? The work is set down, in its definitive form, and that is all that *really* matters.'

(Joseph Szigeti, *With Strings Attached* (New York: Knopf, 2/1967), in Orenstein, *Ravel*, 96)

16 *Chansons madécasses* (voice, fl, pf, vc; voice, pf 1925–6)

Performers	Auspices/venue	Date
Jane Bathori (voice)	Elizabeth S. Coolidge	8 May 1926
Alfredo Casella (pf)	(sponsor and dedicatee)/	
Louis Fleury (fl)	American Academy,	
Hans Kindler (vc)	Rome	

French premiere

Jane Bathori (voice)	Salle Erard, Paris	13 June 1926
Alfredo Casella (pf)		
M. Baudouin (fl)		
Hans Kindler (vc)		

He renews himself periodically without ceasing to be himself . . . I do not see, in Europe, any other great contemporary musician who, as much as Ravel, succeeds in transforming himself continually in this way without apparent crisis. Across the last few years, Ravel's art has become more linear, more sparse, more contrapuntal. He condenses his thought in an ever more rigorous form.

(Henry Prunières, 'Les Concerts, trois *Chansons madécasses*', *La Revue musicale*, 7 (1 July 1926))*

17 *Boléro* (ballet 1928; 2 pf version 1929)

Performers	Auspices/venue	Date
Ballets Ida Rubinstein	Opéra, Paris	22 November 1928
Walther Straram (cond.)		
Bronislava Nijinska (choreog.)		
Alexandre Benois (décor)		

Concert premiere

Maurice Ravel (cond.)/	Concerts Lamoureux/	11 January 1930
Orchestre Lamoureux	Paris	

To be awakened, one only needed to hear the first bars of *Boléro* by Maurice Ravel. One was immediately taken captive, transported by an art which partakes of magic. Ravel has certainly written works with a greater musical richness; he has done nothing more successful...

Mme Rubinstein understood that the strength of the score was such that the dance must appear as a kind of projection on the visual plan of this radiant music. She had thus created, with the help of the great Russian painter Alexandre Benois, a tableau in the manner of Goya: Interior of a huge barn, a flamenco-dancer, where, on a platform, she performed a type of very stylised bolero, amid the encouragement and impassioned quarrels of the spectators.

(Henry Prunières, 'La Musique en France et à l'étranger',
La Revue musicale, 10 (January 1929), 242–5: 243–4)*

18 Concerto for the Left Hand (1929–30)

Performers	Auspices/venue	Date
Paul Wittgenstein (pf) Robert Heger (cond.)/ Vienna Symphony Orchestra	Grosser Musikvereinsaal, Vienna	5 January 1932

French premiere

Paul Wittgenstein (pf) Maurice Ravel (cond.)/ Orchestre Symphonique de Paris	Salle Pleyel, Paris	17 January 1933

It always takes me a while to grow into a difficult work. I suppose Ravel was disappointed, and I was sorry, but I had never learned to pretend. Only much later, after I'd studied the concerto for months, did I become fascinated by it and realize what a great work it was.

(Paul Wittgenstein (1887–1961), in Stelio Dubbiosi, 'The piano music of Maurice Ravel' (dissertation, New York University School of Education, 1967), in Orenstein, *Ravel*, 101)

Even those, who, as I, admire all of Ravel's achievements, feel a certain regret at so many Pyrrhic victories, and think still in all that the author of *Daphnis* should indeed have been able to let us observe more frequently what he was guarding in his heart, instead of accrediting the legend that his brain alone invented these admirable sonorous phantasmagorias. From the opening measures, we are plunged into a world [to] which Ravel has but rarely introduced us.

(Henry Prunières, 'Ravel: Concerto pour la main gauche', *La Revue musicale*, 14 (February 1933), in Orenstein, *Ravel*, 104)

19 Concerto in G (1929–31)

Performers	Auspices/venue	Date
Marguerite Long (pf) Maurice Ravel (cond.)/ Orchestre Lamoureux	Ravel Festival/Salle Pleyel, Paris	14 January 1932

M. Ravel is continually brought out as a pianist or as a conductor, whilst he cannot possibly shine in either of these two specialities. The Portuguese conductor much more efficaciously presented the works he conducted than did Ravel the scores confided to him. His *Pavane* was unutterably slow, his *Bolero* dry and badly timed. And the accompaniment of the concerto lacked clarity and elasticity.

But there is only praise for the composer of all these delicate, subtle works, the orchestration of which abounds in amusing and profound inventions, and which is really of inimitable originality of writing and of thought. The new concerto is worthy of the other masterpieces that we owe to Ravel . . . The work is very easy to understand and gives the impression of extreme youth.

(Emile Vuillermoz, 'Ravel's new piano concerto', *Christian Science Monitor* (13 February 1932), in Orenstein, *Ravel*, 103)

Notes

Introduction

1 'A visit with Maurice Ravel', 472.
2 Ravel, 'The Lamoureux Orchestra concerts', 341.
3 Jankélévitch, *Ravel*, 140.
4 R. A. Henson usefully documents this predisposition for 'nervous' or 'psychiatric disorder' (Henson, 'Maurice Ravel's illness', 1585), dating back to around the time of World War I: 'Important premorbid pyschological factors included remarkable dependence on his family (especially his mother) and his complusive or obsessional behaviour, evidenced by his self-critical and fastidious nature from an early age' (1586).
5 Russom, 'A theory of pitch organization', 13.
6 Urtext editions by Roger Nichols, publ. Peters Edition, London: *Album of Shorter Pieces, Gaspard de la nuit, Jeux d'eau, Miroirs, Pavane pour une Infante défunte, Sonatine* and *Le Tombeau de Couperin*; volumes republ. Dover, New York: *Maurice Ravel: Four Orchestral Works* (1989); *Maurice Ravel: Le Tombeau de Couperin and Other Works for Solo Piano* (1997).

1 History and homage

1 Ravel, '*Fervaal*', 359.
2 Downes, 'Mr. Ravel returns', 458.
3 Chalupt, *Ravel*, 106. (Willy was the pseudonym of Colette's first husband, the novelist and critic Henri Gauthier-Villars (1859–1931); Mistinguett was a music-hall singer/dancer, partnered by Maurice Chevalier. As Nichols notes, the 'Forlane' joke goes back to the Archbishop of Paris's ban on the tango; see Preface (para. 6) to Maurice Ravel, *Le Tombeau de Couperin*, ed. Roger Nichols (London: Peters Edition, 1995). [Ed.])
4 Cited in Nichols, *Ravel Remembered*, 13 and 10.
5 Orenstein, *Ravel*, 15 and 27–8.
6 Ravel, 'Contemporary music', 48.
7 X. M., 'Maurice Ravel's arrival', 440. (The chronology is in fact wrong. [Ed.])
8 Nichols, *Ravel*, 29 and 30.
9 *RR*, 57 and 60.
10 This and following quotation: letter from Romain Rolland to Paul Léon, 26 May 1905, ibid., 66–7.
11 Nectoux, 'Ravel/Fauré', 303.
12 Unpublished letter, Fonds Montpensier,

folder 2: 'Tournée en Europe', item 13(j).
13 Roland-Manuel in Nichols, *Ravel Remembered*, 143. (On models, see also Mawer, 'Neoclassicism and l'objet (re)trouvé': Chapter 3.)
14 'Ten opinions of Mr. Ravel', 493.
15 Ravel, 'Memories', 395.
16 Leroi, 'Some confessions', 485.
17 Deane, 'Renard, Ravel', 181, and Frank Kermode, 'Value at a distance', *History and Value* (Oxford: Clarendon Press, 1988), 93.
18 Cited in Nichols, *Ravel Remembered*, 107.
19 Ravel, 'Take jazz seriously!', 391. See Harold Bloom, *The Anxiety of Influence* (New York: Oxford University Press, 1973), in which he argues that a poet's reaction to his predecessors is not simply one of generosity, but of more complex anxiety. For Bloom's theory applied to twentieth-century music, see Joseph Straus, *Remaking the Past* (Cambridge, Mass.: Harvard University Press, 1990).
20 Letter from Fauré, 15 October 1922, in *RR*, 230–1.
21 Ravel, 'Les Mélodies de Gabriel Fauré', repr. in Orenstein, *Maurice Ravel: Lettres*, 325.
22 Calvocoressi in Nichols, *Ravel Remembered*, 182, and 'An autobiographical sketch', 30.
23 BN Ms.17649.
24 Ravel, 'Memories', 394.
25 Delage, 'Ravel and Chabrier', 548.
26 'Ravel and modern music', 421.
27 Roy Howat, personal communication, 21 July 1998.
28 Ravel, 'The songs of Gabriel Fauré', 384, and Révész, 'The great musician', 432.
29 *RR*, 58–9: 58.
30 Nichols, *Ravel Remembered*, 101.
31 'Ravel and modern music', 421.
32 Ravel, 'Take jazz seriously!', 391.
33 See Satie's letter to Conrad, in Robert Orledge, *Satie the Composer* (Cambridge: Cambridge University Press, 1990), 251.
34 Orledge, *Satie*, 64–5, and 'Maurice Ravel's opinion', 410.
35 Orledge, *Satie*, 250.
36 Ibid., 251, and Cocteau in Nichols, *Ravel Remembered*, 114.
37 Fondation Satie; I am grateful to Robert Orledge for this excerpt.
38 Downes, 'Maurice Ravel', 451.
39 Ravel, 'Contemporary music', 45.
40 Downes, 'Maurice Ravel', 450.

41 Edgar Allan Poe, *Edgar Allan Poe's Works*, ed. James Harrison, 17 vols. (New York: AMS Press, 1965), vol. XIV ('Essays, Miscellanies'), 195.

42 Poulenc in Nichols, *Ravel Remembered*, 118.

43 Poe, *The Poetic Principle*, in *Edgar Allan Poe's Works*, 271–3.

44 Ibid., 274.

45 Ibid., 275; see *RR*, 32, 433, 338. (See also Kaminsky, 'Musical *transposition* in *Trois poèmes de Stéphane Mallarmé*': Chapter 8.)

46 Cited in Nichols, *Ravel Remembered*, 78. See also Baudelaire, 'Correspondances', *Les Fleurs du mal*, ed. Jacques Crépet and Georges Blin (Paris: Librairie José Corti, 1968), 34 (and Mawer, Chapters 3 and 7).

47 Ravel, 'Memories', 394.

48 *RR*, 53.

49 Downes, 'Maurice Ravel', 450.

50 Révész, 'The great musician', 433.

51 'Ravel and modern music', 422.

52 C.B.L., 'An afternoon with Maurice Ravel', 488.

53 Downes, 'Maurice Ravel', 449.

54 Nectoux, 'Ravel/Fauré', 308.

55 Letter to the Committee of the National League, 7 June 1916, in *RR*, 169.

56 See letter to Cipa Godebski in Chalupt, *Ravel*, 106, and Scott Messing, *Neoclassicism in Music* (Ann Arbor: UMI Research Press, 1988), 50–1. (See also Nichols's comments on Ravel's 'Forlane' in the Preface (para. 7) to *Le Tombeau de Couperin* (Peters Edition). [Ed.])

57 *RR*, 155–6: 155. (See also n. 3 above.)

58 'An autobiographical sketch', 32. I am grateful to my colleague, Sohrab Uduman, for sharing his views.

59 Messing, *Neoclassicism*, 50.

60 C.B.L., 'An afternoon with Maurice Ravel', 488; see also Révész, 'The great musician', 433.

61 See Luigi Foscolo Benedetto, 'The legend of French classicism', in Jules Brody (ed.), *French Classicism: A Critical Miscellany* (Englewood Cliffs: Prentice Hall, 1966), 127–47, and Paul Collaer, *La Musique moderne, 1905–1955* (Paris and Brussels: Elsevier, 1955), 113.

62 BN Ms.17653.

63 Nectoux, 'Maurice Ravel et sa bibliothèque', 199.

64 Ravel, 'At the Théâtre des Arts', 363. For the main discussion of Ravel's transcriptions and orchestrations, see Russ, Chapter 6.

65 Calvocoressi, 'Maurice Ravel on Berlioz', 462, and Bruyr, 'An interview with Maurice Ravel', 481.

66 Mendelssohn, *Romances sans paroles*, ed. Maurice Ravel, 9 vols. (Paris: Editions Durand, 1915), vol. I, iv–v.

67 Ravel, 'Contemporary music', 44.

68 Joint letter to the Editor, *Le Courrier musical*, 25 (1 April 1923), in *RR*, 239–40: 240. See also letter to the SMI Board included with a letter to Mme Casella, 2 April 1913, in *RR*, 135–6.

69 Ravel, 'Contemporary music', 47.

70 *RR*, 136. (Nichols suspects that this is a joke, noting that 'the whole tone of the letter is flippant-cum-serious, with references to Messrs. Lalo and Pougin': personal communication to the editor, 12 February 1999.)

71 Boulez, 'Trajectoires', 123, 140.

72 Reprinted in 'La Musique française depuis la guerre', *Etudes* (Paris: Editions Claude Aveline, 1927), 7–26 (with additions), and in Darius Milhaud, *Notes sur la musique*, ed. Jeremy Drake (Paris: Flammarion, 1982), 193–205.

73 Jourdan-Morhange in Nichols, *Ravel Remembered*, 104.

74 Ibid., 114.

75 Downes, 'Maurice Ravel', 451.

76 'A visit with Maurice Ravel', 473.

77 Frank, 'Maurice Ravel between two trains', 497.

78 T. S. Eliot, 'The metaphysical poets', in Frank Kermode (ed.), *Selected Prose of T. S. Eliot* (Orlando, Fla.: Harcourt Brace Jovanovich, 1975), 64.

79 Ernest Ansermet, *Les Fondements de la musique dans la conscience humaine* (Neuchâtel: Editions de la Baconnière, 1961), in Eric Walter White, *Stravinsky, the Composer and his Works* (London: Faber, 1979), 556–7.

80 Boulez, 'Trajectoires', 125.

2 Evocations of exoticism

1 Révész, 'The great musician', 433.

2 C.B.L., 'An afternoon with Maurice Ravel', 488.

3 D. Kern Holoman, *Berlioz* (London: Faber, 1989), 314.

4 Berlioz, 'Twenty-first evening', *Evenings in the Orchestra*, trans. C. R. Fortescue (Harmondsworth: Penguin, 1963), 218–19, 224.

5 Cited by Stanley Sadie, 'Opera', in Sadie (ed.), *The New Grove Dictionary of Music and Musicians*, 20 vols. (London: Macmillan, 1980), vol. XIII, 545–647: 546.

6 See Anik Devriès, 'Les Musiques d'extrême-orient à l'Exposition Universelle de 1889', *Cahiers Debussy*, nouvelle série, 1 (1977), 25–36.

7 'A visit with Maurice Ravel', 473.

8 Nikolay Rimsky-Korsakov, *My Musical Life*, trans. J. A. Joffe (New York: Knopf, 1923, 3/1942), 291.

9 Révész, 'The great musician', 431.

10 Manuel de Falla, *On Music and Musicians*, trans. D. Urman and J. M. Thomson (London: Marion Boyars, 1979), 94.

11 Ibid., 42–3: from special Debussy issue of *La Revue musicale*, 1 (December 1920). (On 'La Soirée' and the 'Habanera', see also Howat, '*Sites auriculaires*': Chapter 4.)

12 Ibid., 95. Ravel maintained that 'the "Habanera" contains the germ of several elements which were to predominate in my later compositions', see 'An autobiographical sketch', 30.

13 The manuscript was sold at Sotheby's, London in May 1994: the harmonisations are not by Ravel.

14 See Orenstein, *Ravel*, 225, and Nichols, *Ravel*, 37–8. Three folksongs came from the collection made in 1898–9 by Hubert Pernot, published in Paris, 1903 (see *RR*, 76–7).

15 See Orenstein, *Ravel*, 230–1, and Nichols, *Ravel*, 69.

16 Letter, 27 July 1916, in *RR*, 175–6.

17 Gustave Samazeuilh, 'Maurice Ravel en pays basque', *La Revue musicale*, 19, special issue (December 1938), 200–3: 202.

18 'Une esquisse autobiographique', repr. in Orenstein, *Maurice Ravel: Lettres*, 46. For further details, see Nichols, *Ravel*, 93.

19 See the accounts of Marguerite Long and Madeleine Grey in Nichols, *Ravel Remembered*, 161–4.

20 Letter, 23 August 1905, in *RR*, 74–5.

21 Letter, 19 July 1911, ibid., 126.

22 Letter to Maurice Delage, 20 August 1906, ibid., 84–5: 84.

23 Letter, 7 February 1928, ibid., 291–2: 291.

24 Letter to Ida Godebska, 9 August 1905, ibid., 73–4: 73.

25 Ravel's friend Charles Koechlin set 'Le Voyage' as the second of his second collection of *Shéhérazade* songs (Op. 84) in 1922–3. See Robert Orledge, *Charles Koechlin (1867–1950): His Life and Works* (Luxembourg: Harwood, 2/1995), 130–1.

26 Danièle Pistone, 'Les Conditions historiques de l'exotisme musical français', *Revue internationale de musique française*, 2/6 (November 1981), 11–22: 22. This special issue on 'L'Exotisme musical français' is recommended to anyone interested in probing further into this area. (See also a recent addition to the literature: Jonathan Bellman (ed.), *The Exotic in Western Music* (Boston: Northeastern University Press, 1998). [Ed.])

27 Jourdan-Morhange, *Ravel et nous*, 227–8.

28 'A visit with Maurice Ravel', 473.

29 Nichols, *Ravel*, 12.

30 Orenstein, *Ravel*, 24.

31 Roland-Manuel, *Maurice Ravel*, 28.

32 Letter, 20 June 1923, in *RR*, 243.

33 A discussion of *Le Palais du silence ou No-ja-li* and the sketches Debussy made for it in 1914 can be found in Orledge, *Debussy and the Theatre* (Cambridge: Cambridge University Press, 1982), Ch. 8.

34 *RR*, 148–9: 148.

35 For a full evaluation of Ravel's library, see Nectoux, 'Maurice Ravel et sa bibliothèque', 199–206.

36 Ibid., 203.

37 Ibid.

38 Reuillard, 'M. Maurice Ravel', 500.

39 'A visit with Maurice Ravel', 472.

40 Jourdan-Morhange in Nichols, *Ravel Remembered*, 129.

41 Michel-Dimitri Calvocoressi, *Musician's Gallery* (London: Faber, 1933), 51. (On artificiality, see also Mawer, 'Ravel's objectivity and "l'objet juste"', Chapter 3.)

42 This and following two quotations: Ravel, '*Symphonic Scenes* by Monsieur Fanelli', 350. Fanelli had derived his inspiration from Théophile Gautier, *Le Roman de la momie* (Paris, 1856).

43 Ravel, '*The Witch* at the Opéra-Comique', 353–4.

44 Letter, 14 March 1909, in *RR*, 103–5: 103–4. Inghelbrecht (1880–1965) was also one of the 'Apaches' and Ravel did have some more positive things to say about his work.

45 Ravel, 'At the Opéra-Comique', 373–4.

46 Letter to Bruneau, 1 April 1911, in *RR*, 123–4: 123.

47 For a vivid description, see Jourdan-Morhange in Nichols, *Ravel Remembered*, 121.

48 See Orledge, *Debussy and the Theatre*, 146–7.

49 Ravel, 'New productions of the Russian Season', 381.

50 Nichols, *Ravel*, 154. (See also Kelly, 'National consciousness and tradition' and 'Technique, imitation and influence': Chapter 1.)

51 'An autobiographical sketch', 31.

52 Ibid., 32.

53 Nichols, *Ravel*, 128.

54 'An autobiographical sketch', 32.

55 Révész, 'The great musician', 433. Coincidentally this interview of 1 May 1924 was published only five days after the London premiere of *Tzigane*.

56 Ravel, 'Take jazz seriously!', 390–1.

57 Ravel told Marguerite Long that he composed it 'two measures at a time' with Mozart's help; see *RR*, 495 n. 6. (On 'models', see also Chapters 1 and 3 of the present book.)

58 Letter, 27 February 1919, in *RR*, 188–9: 188.

59 Definitions from A. M. Macdonald (ed.), *Chambers Twentieth Century Dictionary* (Edinburgh: Chambers, 1972, repr. 1980), 459.

60 Thomas Cooper, 'French Empire and musical exoticism in the nineteenth century' (Ph.D. dissertation, University of Liverpool, 1998), 296–7, 301.

61 C.B.L., 'An afternoon with Maurice Ravel', 488. (For a rather different view of Ravel and Frenchness, see Howat, introduction: Chapter 4.)

62 This is implicit in his letter to Nelly and Maurice Delage, 31 December 1927, in *RR*, 287.

63 See Ravel's letter to the stage decorator Georges Mouveau and the set designer Jacques Drèsa, early January 1912, ibid., 128.

64 Letter, 26 January 1912, ibid., 129.

65 Charles Tenroc, 'Les Avant-premières: *Thérèse* et *L'Heure espagnole*', *Comoedia* (11 May 1911), in *RR*, 412, n. 4.

66 This and following quotation: 'Dress rehearsal', 436.

67 See Roland-Manuel, *Maurice Ravel*, 113–14.

68 'An autobiographical sketch', 32.

69 Perlemuter, *Ravel According to Ravel*, 37. 'Scarbo' is the final movement of *Gaspard de la nuit*.

3 Musical objects and machines

1 Hopkins, 'Ravel', 609.

2 Ravel, 'Finding tunes in factories', 400.

3 José Bruyr, 'En marge ... d'un premier chapitre', *La Revue musicale*, 19, special issue (December 1938), 279–80: 279.

4 Maurice Ravel, 'Some reflections on music', in *RR*, 38–9: 38, and 'Memories', 395.

5 Louis Laloy, 'Le Mois: concerts', *Mercure musical et S.I.M.*, 3 (15 February 1907), 155–8: 155, and 'La Musique, Société Nationale: *Gaspard de la nuit*', *La Grande Revue*, 13 (25 January 1909), 395–6: 395. Translations are my own unless otherwise specified.

6 M.-D. Calvocoressi, 'Maurice Ravel', *The Musical Times*, 54 (1 December 1913), 785–7: 785.

7 Jankélévitch, *Ravel*, 84.

8 Louis Laloy, 'Maurice Ravel', in *Histoire du théâtre lyrique en France, depuis les origines jusqu'à nos jours*, 3 vols. (Paris: Poste National Radio-France, 1939), vol. III, 229–33: 230.

9 Jankélévitch, *Ravel*, 91–2 .

10 Hopkins, 'Ravel', 615.

11 Glenn Watkins, *Pyramids at the Louvre* (Cambridge, Mass.: Belknap Press, 1994), 326.

12 Igor Stravinsky and Robert Craft, *Conversations with Igor Stravinsky* (London: Faber, 1959), 17. On Ravel's fourths, see Teboul, *Ravel: Le Langage musical*, 37–56; for more on detachment, see Kelly, 'Technique, imitation and influence': Chapter 1.

13 Scott Goddard, 'Some notes on *Daphnis et Chloé*', *Music & Letters*, 7/3 (July 1926), 209–20: 216.

14 Ravel, 'Contemporary music', 46.

15 Ravel, 'The polonaises', 335; we should acknowledge Orenstein's concern that the text of this article is not wholly reliable: *RR*, 337, n. 1. On 'hidden meaning' and synaesthesia, see Zank, '"L'Arrière pensée" in music of Maurice Ravel'.

16 Jacques Attali, *Noise: The Political Economy of Music*, trans. Brian Massumi (Manchester: Manchester University Press, 1985), 25. For semiological readings of Ravel despite the problematics, see Lévi-Strauss, '*Boléro*', and Lassus, 'Ravel, l'enchanteur'. Beyond Ravel, see Mary Breatnach, *Boulez and Mallarmé, A Study in Poetic Influence* (Aldershot: Scolar Press, 1996).

17 See, for instance, unsigned interview, 'Ravel says Poe aided him in composition', *New York Times* (6 January 1928), in *RR*, 454–5.

18 *RR*, 35, n. 12.

19 Faure, *Mon maître Maurice Ravel*, 78.

20 Gronquist, 'Ravel's *Trois poèmes*', 507. (See also Kaminsky, 'Musical *transposition* in *Trois poèmes de Stéphane Mallarmé*': Chapter 8.)

21 Delahaye, 'Symbolisme et impressionnisme dans "Soupir"', 56.

22 Orenstein, *Ravel*, 174.

23 *RR*, 108. 'Le menuet est confectionné'; 'confectionné' tends to mean manufactured or mass produced, as with an 'off the peg' suit. Either way, we are reminded of Ravel's impeccable dress sense.

24 Ravel, 'Memories', 393.

25 See Roy Howat, *Debussy in Proportion* (Cambridge: Cambridge University Press, 1983), 189–92, and 'Motivic and geometric extensions': Chapter 4, n. 33; see also Chapter 7, n. 41.

26 Lawrence Morton, 'Stravinsky and Tchaikovsky: *Le Baiser de la Fée*', *Musical Quarterly*, 48 (July 1962), 313–26: 325.

27 Roy, '*Frontispice*', 141–4; Plebuch, 'Der stumme Schrecken, Ravels *Frontispice*', 162. I am also grateful to Roy Howat for our discussion of *Frontispice*.

28 Ricciotto Canudo, *S.P. 503, Le Poème du Vardar*, Les Poètes de la Renaissance du Livre (Paris: Lambert, 1923), xiii.

29 Rex Lawson, 'Maurice Ravel: *Frontispice* for pianola', *The Pianola Journal*, 2 (1989), 35–8.

30 Ravel, 'On inspiration', *The Chesterian*, 9/68 (January–February 1928), in *RR*, 389.

31 'Problems of modern music', 465.

32 Scott Messing, *Neoclassicism in Music* (Ann Arbor: UMI Research Press, 1988), xvi.

33 Pieter C. van den Toorn, *Music, Politics, and the Academy* (Berkeley: University of California Press, 1995), 143.

34 Max Paddison, *Adorno, Modernism and Mass Culture* (London: Kahn & Averill, 1996), 61.

35 Richard Wollheim, *Art and its Objects* (Cambridge: Cambridge University Press, 2/1980), 74–5; and Lydia Goehr, *The Imaginary Museum of Musical Works* (Oxford: Clarendon Press, 1992).

36 Roland-Manuel, 'Des valses à *La Valse*', in Colette et al., *Maurice Ravel*, 141–51: 145. See also Prost, '*L'Enfant et les sortilèges*: l'infidélité aux modèles', 59–63.

37 Frank Onnen, *Maurice Ravel* (London: Sidgwick & Jackson, 1947), 16.

38 'Ravel analyzes his own music', 520.

39 Boulez, 'Trajectoires', 122–42.

40 Ravel, 'Contemporary music', 46.

41 Igor Stravinsky, *An Autobiography* (London: Calder & Boyars, 1975), 78.

42 See Gut, 'Le Phénomène répétitif', 29–46. Extreme repetition invokes questions of signification, its 'meaning' connected with the tragic and grotesque (after Marnat) and the comic.

43 Robert Hughes, *The Shock of the New, Art and the Century of Change* (London: BBC, 1980), 15.

44 Larner, *Maurice Ravel*, 15. Regarding the 'Whirlwind of Death', Roy Howat has kindly alerted me to Ravel's own curious doodles – swirling and spiralling shapes – at the end of the manuscript of the solo piano reduction of *La Valse* dated 12/1919–2/1920 (Lehman Collection, Pierpont Morgan Library, New York).

45 *RR*, 268.

46 Jankélévitch, *Ravel*, 93.

47 Downes, 'Maurice Ravel', 450.

48 *RR*, 328–9.

49 Chalupt, *Ravel*, 238.

50 Ravel, 'Finding tunes in factories', 398–400. (This article was one of Ravel's last completed projects, postdating the composition (but not the orchestration) of *Don Quichotte à Dulcinée*, though predating an interview by Reuillard, 'M. Maurice Ravel', and an article by Ravel on 'The aspirations of those under twenty-five: musical youth', *Excelsior* (28 November 1933), in *RR*, 401–3.)

51 Ibid., 398.

52 Ibid., 399.

53 Ravel, 'New productions of the Russian Season', 380–3.

54 This and immediately following quotations: Ravel, 'Finding tunes in factories', 399.

55 Ibid., 399–400.

56 Caroline Tisdall and Angelo Bozzolla, *Futurism* (London: Thames & Hudson, 1977, repr. 1993), 114.

57 *RR*, 469, n. 4.

58 C.B.L., 'An afternoon with Maurice Ravel', 487.

59 Ravel, 'Finding tunes in factories', 400.

60 Tisdall and Bozzolla, *Futurism*, 114.

61 'Factory gives composer inspiration', 490.

62 Russolo, 'The art of noises', in Tisdall and Bozzolla, *Futurism*, 115.

63 George Antheil, 'Manifest de Musico-Mechanico', *De Stijl*, 6/8 (1924), 99–100.

64 'Factory gives composer inspiration', 490–1.

65 See discussion of fixed/free elements in Deborah Mawer, *Darius Milhaud: Modality and Structure in Music of the 1920s* (Aldershot: Scolar Press, 1997), 104.

66 See Henson, 'Maurice Ravel's illness', 1585–8, for an account of Ravel's distressing terminal illness: 'a restricted form of cerebral degeneration [possibly Alzheimer's or Pick's disease]' (1585). 'Neurological upset' was first evident in 1927 and worsened during 1933 when 'signs of organic brain disease appeared' (Ravel's taxi accident in October 1932 may have contributed to his deteriorating condition). His last four years were increasingly restricted, particularly by 'aphasia' (inability to communicate in speech or writing).

67 *RR*, 70–1.

68 André Ferdinand Hérold, 'Souvenirs', *La Revue musicale*, 19, special issue (December 1938), in *RR*, 71, n. 5.

69 Tisdall and Bozzolla, *Futurism*, 115–16.

70 Derrick Puffett, 'Debussy's ostinato machine', *Papers in Musicology*, 4 (Nottingham: University of Nottingham Press, 1996), 5.

71 Orenstein, *Maurice Ravel: Lettres*, 197.

72 Gustave Fréjaville, *Au music-hall* (Paris: Editions du Monde Nouveau, 1923), 246.

73 Davies, *Ravel Orchestral Music*, 31, and 38–9.

74 Hopkins, 'Ravel', 619.

75 Bruyr, 'An interview with Maurice Ravel', 480.

76 Downes, 'Maurice Ravel', 452.

4 Ravel and the piano

1 See, for example, Rosen's view of Ravel's forms as 'generally impeccable, if uninteresting', with those of *Le Tombeau de Couperin* regarded as 'traditional late-classical

or romantic ones': Charles Rosen, 'Where Ravel ends and Debussy begins', *Cahiers Debussy*, nouvelle série, 3 (1979), 32–3. (For a rather different view of Ravel and Frenchness, see Orledge, 'Exoticism versus exotic music': Chapter 2. [Ed.])

2 See Orenstein, *Maurice Ravel: Lettres*, 120. Ravel claimed to speak Basque (though his degree of fluency has been debated): see Marnat, *Ravel: Souvenirs de Manuel Rosenthal*, 144. (See also Orledge, 'Ravel's Basque heritage, Spain and folksongs': Chapter 2.)

3 See Elaine Brody, 'Viñes in Paris: new light on twentieth-century performance practice', in Edward H. Clinkscale and Claire Brook (eds.), *A Musical Offering: Essays in Honor of Martin Bernstein* (New York: Pendragon, 1977), 45–62; and Nina Gubisch, 'La Vie musicale à Paris entre 1887 et 1914 à travers le journal de R. Viñes', *Revue internationale de la musique française*, 1/2 (June 1980), 154–248. The interesting question arises as to which was Mme Ravel's first language.

4 Viñes's one fall from grace, over the tempo of 'Le Gibet', came in 1922, well after Ravel's solo piano output was complete: see Ravel's letter to Calvocoressi, 24 March 1922, in *RR*, 218–19: 219.

5 Although *Sérénade grotesque* remained unpublished, Brody lists it as premiered by Viñes at the SN on 13 April 1901: Brody, 'Viñes in Paris', 60.

6 See Ravel, 'Memories', 394 (and Kelly, 'Ravel and Chabrier': Chapter 1).

7 See Preface to the *Images* (1894) and *Pour le piano* in *Œuvres Complètes de Claude Debussy*, series 1 vol. II, ed. Roy Howat (Paris: Editions Durand, 1998).

8 See Gubisch, 'La Vie musicale à Paris', 198–9.

9 See the facsimile in Arbie Orenstein, 'Some unpublished music and letters by Maurice Ravel', *The Music Forum*, 3 (1973), 291–334 : 298.

10 Marcel Dietschy, *A Portrait of Claude Debussy* (Oxford: Oxford University Press, 1990), 99, n. 1.

11 See Nichols, *Ravel Remembered*, 140.

12 Debussy also liked some Erards: see François Lesure, *Claude Debussy* (Paris: Klincksieck, 1994), 317–18 and 322.

13 By contrast, 'Cloches à travers les feuilles', the title of the piece which precedes 'Et la lune descend', already figured on the *Images* contract which Debussy had signed with Durand in July 1903.

14 Gubisch, 'La Vie musicale à Paris', 205, 229.

15 See Roy Howat, 'Chopin's influence on the *fin-de-siècle* and beyond', in Jim Samson (ed.), *The Cambridge Companion to Chopin*

(Cambridge: Cambridge University Press, 1992), 275–8.

16 See Roy Howat, 'Modes and semitones in Debussy's Preludes and elsewhere', *Studies in Music*, 22 (1988), 81–104.

17 See Ravel, 'Memories', 394, for his comments on Manet, especially relative to Chabrier.

18 Ravel, pointing out this motivic identity, wrote in Perlemuter's score at the antepenultimate bar, 'comme si rien ne s'était passé' (verbal information from Perlemuter).

19 'Ravel analyzes his own music', 519–20.

20 This nicely illustrates Ravel's reported comments to Mme André Bloch about how he composed: 'A note at random, then a second one and, sometimes, a third. I see what results I get by contrasting, combining and separating them' (Nichols, *Ravel Remembered*, 55).

21 This is calculated by the continuity of pulse, as three successive accelerations to three times the preceding tempo ($= 3^3$). The first, across bars 17–22, is locked into the structure by the indicated tempo equivalence at bar 395; the third, across bars 452–9, is similarly locked in at bars 616–17, and the second is effectively written into bars 418–30 and the metrical transition at bar 430. This follows Roger Nichols ('Critical commentary', Peters Edition, 46) in reading the immediate equivalence across bars 429–30 as $\lrcorner$ = preceding bar (maintaining the perceived tempo), with Ravel's indication $\lrcorner$ = $\flat$ referring back to bar 395 and inferring that, by bar 429, the tempo of the bar has inexorably crept up to that of the quaver at bar 395.

22 In the last of his Op. 2 songs (1909), Alban Berg also quotes this passage, as well as the main ostinato of 'Le Gibet', the latter aptly set against the word 'Stirb'. In 'Le Gibet', bars 23–5 presumably depict the spider spinning its macabre cravat, an image that doubtless appealed to Ravel's love of fashionable cravats . . .

23 See Perlemuter, *Ravel According to Ravel*, 35.

24 The material of *España* comes from flamenco performances which Chabrier heard in Spain; his original title was *Jota*.

25 Ravel, who knew *Le Roi malgré lui* from memory, reportedly insisted that the opera's premiere had 'changed the course of French harmony'. See Francis Poulenc, *Emmanuel Chabrier* (Paris: La Palatine, 1961), 96; and Ravel's letter to Mme Bretton-Chabrier, 4 December 1929, in *RR*, 303.

26 An Iberian tint also opens the *Valses nobles*, which take as their starting point – in key, harmony and exact tempo – the opening bars of Debussy's 'Ibéria', a piece which Ravel hotly

defended against critical hostility. See Ravel, 'Regarding Claude Debussy's *Images*', 366–8. (For more on *Valses nobles*, see Woodley, 'Ravel's piano roll recording of *Valses nobles* (1913)': Chapter 10.)

27 Jeanne Thieffry (ed.), *Alfred Cortot, Cours d'interprétation* (Paris: Legouix, 1934), 85. This reference was kindly pointed out by Jean-Jacques Eigeldinger.

28 Verbal information from Perlemuter. The indications for the 'Prélude' and 'Forlane' tally with the orchestral score but still seem implausibly fast.

29 See Perlemuter, *Ravel According to Ravel*, 78–80; also the commentary prefacing *Le Tombeau* (Peters Edition) for tempos from recordings by Ravel's associates. Perlemuter's suggested tempo (to the present writer) for the 'Toccata' is ♩= 126–32. Mme Long's claims to authority are somewhat undermined by Ravel's reported reference to her in his last years as 'celle qui ne joue pas si bien du piano' (Marnat, *Ravel: Souvenirs de Manuel Rosenthal*, 184–5).

30 Newbould, 'Ravel's "Pantoum"', 228–31.

31 For more detail, see Roy Howat, 'Ravel, rhythm and form', *Musicology Australia*, 16 (1993), 57–65.

32 Burnett James, *Ravel* (London: Omnibus, 1987), 46.

33 GS (≈ 0.618/0.382) can be represented to nearest whole numbers by summation series like the Fibonacci series (2, 3, 5, 8, 13, 21 etc.) and the Lucas series (3, 4, 7, 11, 18, 29, 47 etc.).

34 Compare Orenstein's quotation of Baudelaire's line in relation to Ravel: 'That which is not slightly distorted lacks sensible appeal' (Orenstein, *Ravel*, 123, n. 12).

35 Ravel, 'Memories', 393. For GS proportions elsewhere in Ravel's music, see Roy Howat, *Debussy in Proportion* (Cambridge: Cambridge University Press, 1983), 189–91.

36 Perlemuter's recommended tempo, taking the orchestration into account, is ♩= 144–52 (*Ravel According to Ravel*, 90).

37 A similar bisection occurs in the finale of the Sonata for Violin and Piano, a binary-sonata form divided 88 : 88 bars up to the point where the first movement's opening theme returns as a coda to end the Sonata.

38 Perlemuter in conversation with the present writer.

5 Harmony in the chamber music

1 With the exception of the String Quartet (1893), a masterpiece for all time, and the three late sonatas (1915–17) that he completed out of a projected set of six, Debussy's instrumental chamber music is of relatively lesser importance. Of the half-dozen pieces of chamber music from his student years, the Piano Trio, composed probably in 1880 or 1881, is a particularly well-constructed example. From the middle years, there are only the *Petite pièce* for clarinet and piano (1910), *Syrinx* for solo flute (1913) and the two *Rapsodies* for saxophone (1908) and clarinet (1910): these last two are really solo pieces with orchestra. The short fragments of incidental music to accompany recitations of Pierre Louÿs's *Chansons de Bilitis*, for two flutes, two harps and celesta (1900–1) constitute a special case.

2 Orenstein, *Ravel*, 144.

3 Another surprising debt to Debussy's Quartet is found in Ravel's *Alcyone*, his 1902 cantata for the Prix de Rome; Ravel's melody for the trombones where 'the ship is tossed by the waves' (p. 50) is a direct borrowing from the second theme in the first movement of Debussy's Quartet. It can be seen in Orenstein, *Ravel*, plate 22.

4 See also Kelly, 'Ravel and his immediate predecessors': Chapter 1.

5 For more on voice-leading – essentially 'part-writing' – see Mawer, 'Analytical aside': Chapter 7 (and Russ, Chapter 6).

6 See Walter Piston and Mark DeVoto, *Harmony* (London: Gollancz, 1978; 5/1987), 524; see also H. H. Stuckenschmidt, 'Debussy or Berg? The mystery of a chord progression', *Musical Quarterly*, 51 (July 1965), 453–9.

7 The great harpist Carlos Salzedo stated explicitly that the key of the *Introduction et allegro* was G♭ major: personal communication to the author, 1951. See also Mark DeVoto, 'The Russian submediant in the nineteenth century', *Current Musicology*, 59 (1995), 48–76.

8 Orenstein, *Ravel*, 72.

9 The classic examples of *zortzico* are by Albéniz and Turina (in the *Danzas fantásticas*); there are also examples by Alkan, Sarasate and others.

10 For detailed consideration of the Malayan *pantun* connection, see Newbould, 'Ravel's "Pantoum"', 228–31. See also Howat, 'Sophistication in *Le Tombeau de Couperin*': Chapter 4. [Ed.]

11 This mode, which might equally be thought of as 'altered mixolydian' (i.e. with a flattened sixth), also features in *Boléro* (see Mawer, 'Machine and flamenco in *Boléro*': Chapter 7); it occurs too in the music of Ravel's younger contemporaries, especially Milhaud. For more detail, see Deborah Mawer, *Darius Milhaud: Modality and Structure in Music of the 1920s* (Aldershot: Scolar Press, 1997), 50–4, 65–6, 192. [Ed.]

12 Orenstein, *Ravel*, 184.

13 See Donald Harris, 'Ravel visits the Verein: Alban Berg's report', *Journal of the Arnold Schoenberg Institute*, 3/1 (March 1979), 75–82.

6 Ravel and the orchestra

1 The score was recovered by Orenstein and published by Salabert, 1975. See *RR*, 34, n. 9.

2 Letter to Florent Schmitt, 9 June 1899, in *RR*, 55–6: 55.

3 Pierre Lalo, *Le Temps* (13 June 1899), in Orenstein, *Ravel*, 25. (See also Mawer and Nichols, 'Ravel's main works', No. 1: Appendix.)

4 The first of Debussy's *Chansons de Bilitis* (1897–8). The connection is strengthened by the opening text: 'For the Holiday of Hyacinthia, he gave me a pipe made of well cut reeds.'

5 Nichols, *Ravel Remembered*, 7.

6 Nichols, *Ravel*, 12.

7 Roland-Manuel, *Maurice Ravel*, 28.

8 Orenstein, *Ravel*, 57.

9 'An autobiographical sketch', 30. (See above, Chapter 2, n. 12.)

10 Martin Cunningham, 'Spain, §II, 2: Folk music, characteristics', in Stanley Sadie (ed.), *The New Grove Dictionary of Music and Musicians*, 20 vols. (London: Macmillan, 1980), vol. XVII, 792–3: 792. For the unalloyed employment of the Andalusian scale, see the 'Prélude': Fig. 4.

11 Unsigned article, 'Malagueña' in Sadie (ed.), *The New Grove*, vol. XI, 549.

12 The Roman numbering of the three octatonic scales follows Pieter C. van den Toorn, *The Music of Igor Stravinsky* (New Haven: Yale University Press, 1983).

13 Nichols has written of 'the combination of C major with F♯ major . . . whose sinister, metallic sound on the keyboard was also the genesis of *Petrushka*'. Nichols, *Ravel*, 17. (See also nn. 15 and 24 below.)

14 Ravel, like Bartók, considered the position of the major/minor chord with the major third at the bottom to be the natural one, a point he debated with Stravinsky. See Nichols, *Ravel*, 155.

15 Ravel may have been the catalyst here for Stravinsky's *L'Oiseau de feu* though, as with octatonic writing, both men owe hugely to Rimsky-Korsakov. Taruskin has argued that, although Ravel's *Rapsodie espagnole* was the catalyst for Stravinsky's harmonic glissandos, Stravinsky then returned to Rimsky's *Christmas Eve* for his model: Richard Taruskin, *Stravinsky and the Russian Traditions*, 2 vols. (Berkeley: University of California Press, 1996), vol. I, 310–11. Taruskin also states that

'the orchestral glissando at the end of the "Danse infernale" . . . [was] rather brazenly cribbed from the ending of the *Rapsodie espagnole*.' Ibid., vol. I, 614–15.

16 Ravel, 'Concerto for the Left Hand', 396.

17 Long, *At the Piano with Ravel*, 59. See also *RR*, 594, and Nichols, *Ravel*, 142–3.

18 Roland-Manuel, *Maurice Ravel*, 111 and Long, *At the Piano with Ravel*, 57; Larner, *Maurice Ravel*, 208–9.

19 Calvocoressi, 'M. Ravel discusses his own work', 477.

20 Ravel, 'Concerto for the Left Hand', 396.

21 Calvocoressi, 'M. Ravel discusses his own work', 477.

22 Ravel, 'Concerto for the Left Hand', 396.

23 Long, *At the Piano with Ravel*, 60.

24 Quoted in Taruskin, *Stravinsky and the Russian Traditions*, vol. I, 664.

25 Larner, *Maurice Ravel*, 210; Long, *At the Piano with Ravel*, 60; Rollo Myers, *Ravel*, 177; Nichols, *Ravel*, 141.

26 Calvocoressi, 'M. Ravel discusses his own work', 477.

27 Ravel, 'Concerto for the Left Hand', 397.

28 'Ten opinions of Mr. Ravel', 494.

29 Paul Griffiths, 'Concerto §6: 20th Century', in Sadie (ed.), *The New Grove*, vol. IV, 637–9: 638; Davies, *Ravel Orchestral Music*, 47.

30 Richard Taruskin, *Defining Russia Musically: Historical and Hermeneutical Essays* (Princeton: Princeton University Press, 1997), 273.

31 'A visit with Maurice Ravel', 473, and Bruyr, 'An interview with Maurice Ravel', 482.

32 David Schiff, *Gershwin: Rhapsody in Blue* (Cambridge: Cambridge University Press, 1997), 20; see also 74–6.

33 Calvocoressi, 'M. Ravel discusses his own work', 477.

34 Schiff, *Gershwin*, 37–8.

35 'Ten opinions of Mr. Ravel', 494, and Long, *At the Piano with Ravel*, 41. (For more on the slow movement, see Woodley, 'Marguerite Long and the Concerto in G': Chapter 10.)

36 Orenstein, *Ravel*, 205.

37 Hopkins, 'Ravel', 617, and Davies, *Ravel Orchestral Music*, 17. (For a rather different view, see Howat, '*Miroirs*': Chapter 4. [Ed.])

38 Perlemuter, *Ravel According to Ravel*, 23–4.

39 *RR*, 191, n. 3.

40 For a full discussion, see Millan Sachania, '"Improving the Classics": some thoughts on the "ethics" and aesthetics of musical arrangement', *The Music Review*, 51 (February 1994), 58–75.

41 Taruskin, *Stravinsky and the Russian Traditions*, vol. II, 1526.

42 Nichols, *Ravel Remembered*, 16.

43 Ravel, 'Take jazz seriously!', 391, and 'The songs of Gabriel Fauré', 387.
44 Orenstein, *Ravel*, 141. (See also Kelly, 'Ravel and Chabrier': Chapter 1, and Howat, 'Viñes and the early piano music': Chapter 4.)
45 Nichols, *Ravel*, 114.
46 M.-D. Calvocoressi, 'Ravel's letters to Calvocoressi', *Musical Quarterly*, 27/1 (January 1941), 1–19: 11.
47 For more detail, see Michael Russ, *Musorgsky: Pictures at an Exhibition* (Cambridge: Cambridge University Press, 1992), 21–4 and 79–83.
48 Letter to Mme Claude Debussy, 8 June 1922, in *RR*, 226.

7 Ballet and the apotheosis of the dance
1 Judith Mackrell, *Reading Dance* (London: Michael Joseph, 1997), 15.
2 Jankélévitch, *Ravel*, 156. Translations are my own unless otherwise specified.
3 Mackrell, *Reading Dance*, 171 and 176.
4 For other ballets on Ravel's music, see Noël Goodwin, 'Ravel, Maurice', in Martha Bremser (ed.), *International Dictionary of Ballet*, 2 vols. (Detroit and London: St. James Press, 1993), vol. II, 1180–2.
5 Mackrell, *Reading Dance*, 15.
6 Jankélévitch, *Ravel*, 156; Jourdan-Morhange, *Ravel et nous*, 169–72 .
7 Jankélévitch, *Ravel*, 158.
8 Henry Prunières, 'Trois silhouettes de musiciens', *La Revue musicale*, 7 (1 October 1926), 225–40: 240.
9 Robert Harrold, *Ballet* (Poole: Blandford Press, 1980), 25. See also Lynn Garafola, *Diaghilev's Ballets Russes* (Oxford: Oxford University Press, 1989), 3–49; and Joan Lawson, 'Fokine, Mikhail (Michel)', in Bremser (ed.), *International Dictionary of Ballet*, vol. I, 501–5.
10 Bizet, '*Ma Mère l'Oye*', 414.
11 *RR*, 517; Russom, 'A theory of pitch organization'.
12 'Ravel analyzes his own music', 520–2.
13 Russom, 'A theory of pitch organization', 180.
14 'An autobiographical sketch', 31.
15 Calvocoressi in Nichols, *Ravel Remembered*, 187.
16 Serge Lifar, *Serge Diaghilev* (London: Putnam, 1940), 265, repr. in Nichols, *Ravel*, 80.
17 Emile Vuillermoz, 'Les Théâtres', *Revue musicale de la S.I.M.*, 8/6 (15 June 1912), 62–8: 66–7. (For more detail, see Mawer and Nichols, 'Ravel's main works', No. 9: Appendix.)
18 Mackrell, *Reading Dance*, 145.
19 Cohen-Lévinas, '*Daphnis et Chloé*', 88–95.
20 Russom, 'A theory of pitch organization', 98.

21 From *La Grande Saison de Paris, 13 mai–10 juin 1912, Programme officiel des Ballets Russes* (Paris, Bibliothèque de l'Arsenal). The woodland glade setting is typical of Parisian productions: *La Sylphide* (1832), *Giselle* (1841) and *Les Sylphides* (1909).
22 André Levinson, *Ballet Old and New*, trans. Susan Cook Summer (New York: Dance Horizons, 1982), 60.
23 Leo Kersley and Janet Sinclair, *A Dictionary of Ballet Terms* (London: Black, 4/1997), 29.
24 Cohen-Lévinas, '*Daphnis et Chloé*', 92.
25 Ibid., 91.
26 See Scott Goddard, 'Some notes on *Daphnis et Chloé*', *Music & Letters*, 7/3 (July 1926), 209–20: 210.
27 See Kersley and Sinclair, *A Dictionary of Ballet Terms*, 14.
28 Ibid., 81–2.
29 Larner, *Maurice Ravel*, 130.
30 Ibid., 132. For more on the 1910 version, see Jacques Chailley, 'Une première version inconnue de *Daphnis et Chloé* de Maurice Ravel', *Mélanges d'histoire littéraire offerts à Raymond Lebègue* (Paris: Nizet, 1969), 371–5.
31 Myers, *Ravel*, 199–200.
32 Bengt Häger, *Ballets Suédois* (London: Thames & Hudson, 1990), 299.
33 Paul Griffiths, *Modern Music: A Concise History from Debussy to Boulez* (New York: Thames & Hudson, 1978, repr. 1986), 82–3.
34 James Harding, liner notes for EMI recording of *Daphnis et Chloé; Valses nobles et sentimentales* (CDM 7-69566-2, 1988), 3.
35 Constant Lambert, *Music Ho!* (London: Penguin, 1948), 143.
36 'An autobiographical sketch', 32.
37 C.v.W., 'The French Music Festival', 423.
38 Poulenc in Nichols, *Ravel Remembered*, 118.
39 Henry Malherbe, 'Chronique musicale', *Le Temps* (29 May 1929). (For more detail, see Mawer and Nichols, 'Ravel's main works', No. 13: Appendix.)
40 Benjamin, 'Last dance', 433 and 434.
41 Cyril Beaumont, *The Complete Book of Ballets* (London: Putnam, 1951), 812–13. See also Jane Pritchard, '*La Valse*', in Bremser (ed.), *International Dictionary of Ballet*, vol. II, 1454–6 and Jacques Depaulis, *Ida Rubinstein* (Paris: Honoré Champion Editeur, 1995), 376–7, 388, 390–1.
42 Benjamin, 'Last dance', 432.
43 Igor Stravinsky and Robert Craft, *Expositions and Developments* (London: Faber, 1962), 148. See also Leo Treitler, *Music and the Historical Imagination* (Cambridge, Mass.: Harvard University Press, 1989), 40.
44 Calvocoressi, 'M. Ravel discusses his own work', 477.

45 Goss, *Bolero: The Life of Ravel*.

46 Lévi-Strauss, 'Boléro', 5–14; Miki Osada and Kengo Ohgushi, 'Perceptual analyses of Ravel's *Bolero*', *Music Perception*, 8/3 (Spring 1990), 241–9; Goffredo Haus and Antonio Rodriguez, 'Formal music representation; a case study: the model of Ravel's *Bolero* by Petri nets', in Haus (ed.), *Music Processing* (Oxford: Oxford University Press, 1993), 165–232.

47 Larner, *Maurice Ravel*, 203.

48 Henry Prunières, 'La Musique en France et à l'étranger', *La Revue musicale*, 10 (January 1929), 242–5: 244. (For more detail, see Mawer and Nichols, 'Ravel's main works', No. 17: Appendix.)

49 Unsigned article, 'Fandango', in Stanley Sadie (ed.), *The New Grove Dictionary of Music and Musicians*, 20 vols. (London: Macmillan, 1980), vol. VI, 378.

50 Willi Kahl, 'Bolero', in Sadie (ed.), *The New Grove*, vol. II, 870–1: 870.

51 See Israel J. Katz, 'Flamenco', in Sadie (ed.), *The New Grove*, vol. VI, 625–30, and Claus Schreiner (ed.), *Flamenco: Gypsy Dance and Music from Andalusia* (Frankfurt am Main: Fischer Taschenbuch, 1985; Eng. trans., Portland: Amadeus Press, 1990).

52 Chalupt, *Ravel*, 237.

53 Derrick Puffett, 'Debussy's ostinato machine', *Papers in Musicology*, 4 (Nottingham: University of Nottingham Press, 1996), 5.

54 See example of *palmas* 1, 2 and 3, in Schreiner, *Flamenco*, 152 and guitar illustrations: 127, 143.

55 See Schreiner, *Flamenco*, 137–8.

56 Willi Reich, 'In memoriam Maurice Ravel', *La Revue musicale*, 19, special issue (December 1938), 275.

57 Puffett, 'Debussy's ostinato machine', 24 and 14.

58 Leonard B. Meyer, *Explaining Music: Essays and Explorations* (Berkeley: University of California Press, 1973, repr. 1978); see too Eugene Narmour, *The Analysis and Cognition of Basic Melodic Structures, The Implication–Realization Model* (Chicago: University of Chicago Press, 1990).

59 Larner, *Maurice Ravel*, 203.

60 Rosenthal in Nichols, *Ravel Remembered*, 62.

61 Jacques Attali, *Noise: The Political Economy of Music*, trans. Brian Massumi (Manchester: Manchester University Press, 1985), 27.

8 Vocal music and the lures of exoticism and irony

1 See, for example, Ravel's letter to Roland-Manuel, 7 October 1913, 'When I received your last letter, I was finishing my 3 poems. Indeed, "Placet futile" was completed, but I retouched it. I fully realize the great audacity of having attempted to interpret this sonnet in music . . . Now that it's done, I'm a bit nervous about it.' *RR*, 142–3.

2 Arbie Orenstein (ed.), *Maurice Ravel: Mélodies posthumes* (Paris: Editions Salabert, 1988), 1.

3 Arbie Orenstein (ed.), *Maurice Ravel: Songs 1896–1914* (New York: Dover, 1990), xii. (This is the source for the translations of *Sainte*, 'Asie' and 'Soupir' used in the main text.)

4 See *RR*, 3–4.

5 The scale may be generated variously: for example, as an alternating semitone–minor third series, or as two augmented triads a semitone apart. For the properties of this prime resource for late nineteenth-century harmony, see Richard Cohn, 'Maximally smooth cycles, hexatonic systems, and the analysis of late-Romantic triadic progressions', *Music Analysis*, 15/1 (March 1996), 9–40: 18 and n. 18.

6 Deane, 'Renard, Ravel', 178.

7 Jules Renard, *Journal*, entry for 12 January 1907, in *RR*, 36, n. 18.

8 See Deane, 'Renard, Ravel', 184ff.

9 See Ravel, 'Memories', 394. (See also Kelly, 'Ravel and writers': Chapter 1.)

10 Edgar Allan Poe, *The Philosophy of Composition*, in Margaret Alterton and Hardin Craig (eds.), *Edgar Allan Poe: Representative Selections* (New York: American Book Company, 1935), 376.

11 Respective sources: Ravel, 'Contemporary music', 45–6; Révész, 'The great musician', 433; and 'An autobiographical sketch', 32.

12 Immediately following Ravel's settings and without prior knowledge of his choices, Debussy also decided to set 'Soupir' and 'Placet futile', though he was initially denied permission by Mallarmé's son-in-law. With characteristic good will, Ravel interceded on Debussy's behalf, with the fortunate outcome that we have both settings of these poems. See Orenstein, *Ravel*, 67. Comparative readings include Theo Hirsbrunner, 'Zu Debussys und Ravels Mallarmé-Vertonungen', *Archiv für Musikwissenschaft*, 35/2 (1978), 81–103, and Cornelia Petersen, *Die Lieder von Maurice Ravel* (Frankfurt am Main: Peter Lang, 1995), 168ff.

13 See also Delahaye, 'Symbolisme et impressionnisme dans "Soupir"', 31–58. [Ed.]

14 As a close reader of Mallarmé, Ravel would doubtless have been aware of the frequency with which 'l'Azur' occurs in his poems.

15 Philip Russom offers a quite different

reading of the structural bass progression in 'A theory of pitch organization', 96–8.

16 Anna Balakian, *The Symbolist Movement: A Critical Appraisal* (New York: Random House, 1967), 75–6. 'Mallarmé's poetic concerns were crystallized early in his life, when he sketched the forms they were to take; thereafter, he spent his life refining his attitudes and his forms. He was largely haunted by "ennui" [boredom], by the "gouffre" [abyss], its counterpart of "azur", and by the isolated status of the poet in society.'

17 Alfredo Casella cited both the sharpened eleventh and the unusual resolution of appoggiaturas as hallmarks of Ravel's style. See 'L'Harmonie', *La Revue musicale*, 6, special issue (April 1925), 31–2.

18 Orenstein, *Ravel*, 196, n. 46.

19 'An autobiographical sketch', 32.

20 See Orenstein, *Ravel*, 197, and James, 'Ravel's *Chansons madécasses*', 372.

21 James, 'Ravel's *Chansons madécasses*', investigates relations between the *Chansons madécasses* and indigenous Malagasy music.

22 Orenstein, *Ravel*, 206.

23 The *Tombeau de Ronsard* was published as a supplement to *La Revue musicale*, 5 (May 1924).

24 Orenstein observes the cantorial style of 'Kaddisch'; he also cites Rabbi Abraham Idelsohn's criticism of Ravel's setting of the text 'L'Enigme éternelle' as 'ultra-modern ... without regard for its scale and the nature of the mode'. See Orenstein, *Maurice Ravel: Songs 1896–1914*, xv. (For more on the *Chansons madécasses* and Hebraic songs, see Woodley, 'Recordings of Ravel's vocal music': Chapter 10.)

25 Orenstein, *Ravel*, 185.

26 On Ravel's stacking of fifths, note also the opening of *Daphnis et Chloé* (see Mawer, 'Reading dance in *Daphnis et Chloé*': Chapter 7). [Ed.]

27 Révész, 'The great musician', 433. (See also Chapters 1–3 of the present book.)

28 On Debussy and chromatic thirds, see Avo Somer, 'Chromatic third-relations and tonal structure in the songs of Debussy', *Music Theory Spectrum*, 17/2 (Fall 1995), 215–41.

9 Ravel's operatic spectacles: *L'Heure* and *L'Enfant*

1 Ravel did not refer to *L'Heure* or *L'Enfant* as operas. *L'Enfant* was subtitled a 'fantaisie lyrique'.

2 This 'affaire' is discussed in Leon Vallas, *Claude Debussy et son temps* (Paris: Félix Alcan, 1932), 231–2. See also François Lesure, *Claude*

Debussy (Paris: Klincksieck, 1994); Howat, '*Sites auriculaires*': Chapter 4; and Orledge, 'Ravel's Basque heritage: Spain and folksongs': Chapter 2.

3 Marnat, *Ravel: Souvenirs de Manuel Rosenthal*, 165–6. (See again Orledge, 'Ravel's Basque heritage': Chapter 2.)

4 Léo Claretie, 'Les Samedis de L'Odéon', *L'Art du théâtre*, supplement (August 1904), cvi–cx.

5 It was given twenty-eight times within the remainder of 1904, seventeen times in 1905 and thirteen in 1906. (Source: Edouard Noël and Edmond Stoullig, *Les Annales du théâtre et de la musique* (Paris: Charpentier, 1904–6).)

6 See, for example, Réné Maizeroy, *Le Matin* (16 October 1904), 4.

7 Plays and operas which articulated contemporary issues through earlier settings were nothing new: Puccini's *La Bohème* is a prime example.

8 See, for instance, articles in the Parisian *Revue hispanique*.

9 Julián Juderías, *La Leyenda negra* (Madrid: Revista de archivos, bibliotecas y museos, 1913). The chapter which details the nineteenth-century studies and summarises the view of Spain from surrounding Europe is in the second volume; its title translates as 'Research study of the psychology of the Spanish people as judged by foreigners'.

10 Pierre Léonce Imbert, *L'Espagne: Splendeurs et misères* (Paris: Plon, 1875), 114–15.

11 De Musset's poem *L'Andalouse* (celebrated in the salon *mélodie* by Hippolyte Monpou), was modelled on one of Goya's erotic images of a girl pulling on a stocking: 'Bien tirada está', the 'well-pulled' of its title barely concealing an erotic *double-entendre* of which Franc-Nohain would have been proud.

12 Théophile Gautier, *Voyage en Espagne* (Paris: Charpentier, 2/1845): section on 'Procession de la Fête-Dieu à Madrid'.

13 Charles Tenroc, 'Les Avant-premières: *Thérèse et L'Heure espagnole*', *Comœdia* (11 May 1911), in *RR*, 412–13, n. 4.

14 Alfred Fouillée, *Esquisse psychologique des peuples européens* (Paris: Félix Alcan, 1903).

15 James R. Lowell, *Impressions of Spain*, ed. Joseph P. Gilder (London & New York: Putnam, 1900).

16 *Le Monde et volonté* was first translated complete in 1886.

17 Tenroc, 'Les Avant-premières', 412. (There is of course no imprecision in Ravel's notation of the speeds of the clocks. Indeed, Roger Nichols has suggested that the repetition of the composite metronomic pattern every fifteen seconds might relate to the idea of 'L'Heure'

discussed later in the main text: personal communication to the editor, 12 February 1999. [Ed.])

18 Nectoux, 'Maurice Ravel et sa bibliothèque', 204.

19 Bizet, '*L'Heure espagnole*', 411.

20 Draft of letter to Jean Godebski, 17 May 1911, in *Maurice Ravel*, exhibition catalogue (Paris: Bibliothèque Nationale de France, 1975), 31.

21 'An autobiographical sketch', 31.

22 No score reprint includes a French or English translation, nor is there presently a recording incorporating a libretto. The one available recording (Melodiya (1982): Olympia (OCD 145)) has no supporting notes; conducted and orchestrated by Gennadi Rozhdestvensky, it is nonetheless of excellent musical quality. Since the Russian follows the Gogol play exactly, the English reader may use one of two available translations: that by Christopher English in Nikolai Vasilyeivich Gogol, *Petersburg Tales; Marriage; The Government Inspector* (Oxford: Oxford University Press, 1995), or Gogol, *Marriage*, trans. Bella Costello (Manchester: Manchester University Press, 1969).

23 Ravel wrote to M. Robert de Harcourt that 'he would willingly undertake this interesting work'. See Nichols, *Ravel*, Appendix E: 'Ravel and Mussorgsky's *Le Mariage*', 190–1. No readily available French translation of Gogol's play existed at this time; seemingly, Ravel was one of a small group of enthusiasts for this remarkable piece.

24 Translation given in the vocal score (Moscow: State Publishers, 1965).

25 See Richard Taruskin, '*Marriage*', in Stanley Sadie (ed.), *The New Grove Dictionary of Opera*, 4 vols. (London: Macmillan, 1992), vol. III, 223–4, and 'Handel, Shakespeare, and Musorgsky', in *Studies in the History of Music*, vol. I (New York: Broude Bros., 1983), 247–68.

26 Letter to César Cui, 3 July 1868, quoted in Taruskin, 'Handel, Shakespeare, and Musorgsky', 254.

27 Bizet, '*L'Heure espagnole*', 411. For a fuller synopsis, see Roger Nichols, '*L'Heure espagnole*', in Sadie (ed.), *The New Grove Dictionary of Opera*, vol. II, 710–12.

28 Claude Terrasse (1867–1923) successfully composed light opera and incidental music, collaborating with central (often humorous) literary figures. His output included music for Alfred Jarry's *Ubu Roi* (1896) and operas for which Franc-Nohain was a co-librettist.

29 Raoul Laparra, 'La Musique et la danse populaires en Espagne' [1914], in *Encyclopédie de la musique et dictionnaire du conservatoire*

(Paris: Librairie Delagrave, 1920), 2353–400.

30 Ravel had witnessed Fauré denounce Laparra after he had won the Prix de Rome in 1903. On 11 September 1903, he contacted Jane Courteault for Laparra's address. See Orenstein, *Maurice Ravel: Lettres*, 69–70: 70.

31 Melanie Klein, 'Infantile anxiety-situations as reflected in a work of art and in the creative impulse', paper read to the British Psycho-Analytical Society (23 March 1927); repr. in Klein, *Contributions to Psycho-Analysis, 1921–1945* (London: The Hogarth Press, 1948), 227–35. See also Christiane Milner, 'Mélanie Klein et les sortilèges de Colette', in *Cahiers Colette*, 5 (1981), 36–44.

32 Baroque, monistic forms were not infrequently used by later composers to represent authority. *Carmen*, for example, employs fugue for the authority of the guards.

33 Colette published two versions of these memoirs: firstly, as 'Un salon de musique en 1900' in Colette et al., *Maurice Ravel*, 115–24; secondly, in the celebrated *Journal à rebours* (Paris: Fayard, 1941).

34 See Jean-Michel Nectoux, 'Musique et beaux-arts: le salon de Marguerite de Saint-Marceaux', in *Une famille d'artistes en 1900: Les Saint-Marceaux* (Paris: Dossiers du Musée d'Orsay, 1992), 62–90.

35 Anyone who has played the early French editions will realise the importance of this: the two pianists are constantly clashing.

36 Like Colette, Debussy wrote for *Gil Blas*, and material outlining their reviews of the same concerts may be found in Richard Langham Smith (ed. and trans.), *Debussy on Music* (London and New York: Secker & Warburg, 1977). For Colette's musical articles, see Alain Galliari (ed.), *Colette au concert* (Paris: Le Castor Astral, 1992).

37 Marnat, *Ravel: Souvenirs de Manuel Rosenthal*, 166.

38 Letter to Colette, 27 February 1919, in Orenstein, *Maurice Ravel: Lettres*, 171–2: 172.

39 Marnat, *Ravel: Souvenirs de Manuel Rosenthal*, 166.

40 Marguerite Crosland, 'Colette and Ravel: the enchantress and the illusionist' in Erica M. Eisinger and Mari W. McCarty (eds.), *Colette: The Woman, the Writer* (University Park and London: Pennsylvania State University Press, 1981), 116–24: 123.

41 'Une esquisse autobiographique', repr. in Orenstein, *Maurice Ravel: Lettres*, 46. Pourvoyeur has questioned Ravel's reference to 'l'opérette américaine', pointing out that neither Kern's *Show Boat* nor Gershwin's *Porgy and Bess* had yet been written. Ravel may have been referring to American revues, popular

American dances and French revues (notably by Christiné and d'Yvain) in the American style. See Robert Pourvoyeur, 'Sortilèges de Colette et de Ravel', in *Maurice Ravel: L'Enfant et les sortilèges* [and] *L'Heure espagnole*, *L'Avant-scène opéra*, 127 (January 1990), 18–22: 21.

42 This and immediately following quotations: 'Avant-première', in Orenstein, *Maurice Ravel: Lettres*, 349.

43 'Dress rehearsal', 436.

44 The 'piano luthéal', also employed in *Tzigane*, was a type of prepared piano that could imitate a cimbalom.

10 Performing Ravel: style and practice in the early recordings

1 Bruno Sébald, 'Ravel's personal record collection', in *RR*, Appendix G, 601–11; according to Touzelet's introduction here, however, some additional recordings of Ravel's own music had probably gone missing before the transfer of the collection to the Conservatoire in 1975 (ibid., 601). Touzelet's complete listing of recordings to 1939 is printed in Orenstein, *Ravel*, Appendix B, 247–70; a complementary and invaluable listing of 'Historical interpretations (1912–1988)', indexed principally by artist, is provided by Touzelet in *RR*, Appendix F, 526–600.

2 *RR*, 532. Ravel's failure to record the last movement of the *Sonatine* was probably due to his own pianistic limitations.

3 Compare, however, Maurice Dumesnil's account of Debussy's view: '"It is not advisable to use relaxation constantly," he said. "In pianissimo chords, for instance, the fingers must have a certain firmness, so the notes will sound together. But it must be the firmness of rubber, without any stiffness whatsoever"' (Nichols, *Debussy Remembered* (London: Faber, 1992), 162–3).

4 Perlemuter, *Ravel According to Ravel*, 50–1.

5 Ibid., 57.

6 Ibid., 11–12.

7 Calvocoressi in Nichols, *Ravel Remembered*, 181.

8 Robert Philip discusses interesting cases of this phenomenon pre- and post-World War I (*Early Recordings and Musical Style: Changing Tastes in Instrumental Performance 1900–1950* (Cambridge: Cambridge University Press, 1992), especially Ch. 2 'Tempo rubato'); see also Robert Philip, '1900–1940', in Howard Mayer Brown and Stanley Sadie (eds.), *Performance Practice: Music after 1600*, The New Grove Handbooks in Music (London: Macmillan, 1989), 461–82.

9 Perlemuter, *Ravel According to Ravel*, 13.

10 Touzelet, in Orenstein, *Ravel*, 247–63.

11 See Elaine Brody, 'Viñes in Paris: new light on twentieth-century performance practice', in Edward H. Clinkscale and Claire Brook (eds.), *A Musical Offering: Essays in Honor of Martin Bernstein* (New York: Pendragon, 1977), 45–62; also *RR*, especially 62, 78, 80–1 and 127.

12 The contract is printed in full in *RR*, Appendix E, 524–5.

13 See Touzelet in *RR*, 533; also sleeve-notes by Jean-Michel Nectoux to the 1988 EMI LP set 'Ravel et ses interprètes' (see Table 10.1).

14 *RR*, 219.

15 Perlemuter, *Ravel According to Ravel*, 21.

16 This passage is one of the subjects for harmonic analysis discussed in 'Ravel analyzes his own music', 517–23.

17 Philip, *Early Recordings*, especially 70–93.

18 Perlemuter, *Ravel According to Ravel*, 5.

19 André Mangeot, 'The Ravel String Quartet', *The Gramophone*, 5 (1927–8), 138–9.

20 Ibid., 138.

21 Ibid.

22 Facsimile of Ravel's letter, ibid., 139.

23 'National Gramophonic Society Notes', *The Gramophone*, 5 (1927–8), 118.

24 See *RR*, 538 for further details of this recording session.

25 Henry Prunières, *La Revue musicale*, 16 (January 1935), 72.

26 Dominique Sordet, 'Ravel et l'édition phonographique', in Colette et al., *Maurice Ravel*, 177–86: 179.

27 The recording was reviewed with little understanding ('there is very little "meat" in the music') by 'A.R.', and without reference to Ravel's participation, in *The Gramophone*, 1 (1923–4), 183. Compton Mackenzie, the magazine's editor, described it as 'an extremely pleasant series of noises, with one snatch of melody very reminiscent of César Franck. A lot of space is wasted, which makes it expensive' (*The Gramophone*, 2 (1924–5), 411). The discs, priced at 15s 0d, were nevertheless regarded as among the best chamber music issued in early 1924, and Mackenzie went so far as to say that 'Ravel is really only possible on a Columbia surface, and I beg them earnestly to reprint the three snippets they have already given us from his ravishing quartet, which on the old surface sounded rather like a ship dropping anchor' (*The Gramophone*, 1 (1923–4), 219–21).

28 This white-tone effect, presupposing some vibrato in 'normal' playing, is clearly audible in several Quartet recordings studied here, for example, Fig. 2 in the first movement (lower three instruments). Far from being a modern

affectation, it is an expressive device, along with *flautando*, which was part of a string-player's repertoire in this period, and explicitly discussed in a chamber-music context: see George Stratton and Alan Frank, *The Playing of Chamber Music* (London: Oxford University Press, 1935), especially their valuable discussion of the Debussy Quartet, 46–65.

29 'We won't linger over the subtle *Chansons madécasses*, which Mlle. Madeleine Grey defends as best she can without making them very persuasive' (Sordet, 'Ravel et l'édition phonographique', 183).

30 Grey herself comments: 'In the interpretation of his songs, Ravel attached the highest importance to respect for prosody. Nobody has known better than he how to find rhythms and melodic contours which, on the one hand, underline with the greatest expressive truth the meaning of each nuance of a text, and, on the other hand, are so perfectly fitting to the genius of our language' (Madeleine Grey, 'Souvenirs d'une interprète', *Revue musicale*, 19, special issue (December 1938), 175–8: 178).

31 Henry Prunières, *La Revue musicale*, 10 (October 1929), 280.

32 Henry Prunières, *La Revue musicale*, 11 (April 1930), 373.

33 Henry Prunières, *La Revue musicale*, 11 (June 1930), 562. An anonymous English critic (pseudonym 'Terpander'), however, suggested as early as 1935 that 'Bathori recordings are quite likely to have an historical value one day' ('Ravel's *Histoires naturelles* (1906): Songs for mezzo-soprano and pianoforte', *The Gramophone*, 12 (1934–5), 428).

34 Further details in *RR*, 535–6. The final recordings apparently happened in the early hours, with Long exhausted: although one is hard pressed to hear this (even if some woodwind intonation is fairly sour), Compton Mackenzie described this version as sounding 'a little *après la bataille*' (*The Gramophone*, 10 (1932–3), 384).

35 For anecdotal examples of his conducting and piano playing, see Nichols, *Ravel Remembered*, 89–97; a little rare film footage is cited by Touzelet in *RR*, 530. Another English critic, the notoriously curmudgeonly W. R. Anderson, reviewed the 1932 recording thus: 'I have heard the Ravel in the concert-room, conducted (sometimes one doubts if the word is the right one) by the composer, and I am afraid it fails to convince me that Ravel is still a living force' (*The Gramophone*, 10 (1932–3), 357). The full English reception of Ravel pre-World War II is a study still waiting to be written. (Some further insights on this subject

are offered by Nichols, 'Ravel's influence in England': Chapter 11. [Ed.])

36 Henry Prunières, *La Revue musicale*, 13 (February 1932), 124. (For more on the conducting of Ravel and Freitas Branco, and the premiere of the Concerto in G, see Mawer and Nichols, 'Ravel's main works', No. 19: Appendix.)

37 Ibid., 125.

38 Letter from Ravel to Prunières, in *La Revue musicale*, 13 (April 1932), 320. This letter appears not to have been translated into English before.

39 See the exchange chronicled in *RR*, 590–1, and 305–8.

40 See *RR*, 540–1. Although the orchestras for the two recordings were different, there was probably an overlap of players for the more exotic wind, such as the oboe d'amore which has a very similar, fast and nervous vibrato in each.

41 Ravel's copy of the score corrects the printed metronome mark of 76 to 66; later editions compromise on 72: see *RR*, 541.

42 W. R. Anderson, *The Gramophone*, 7 (1929–30), 505. Anderson later described *Boléro* as 'just pure laudanum' (*The Gramophone*, 12 (1934–5), 347), and the Concerto for the Left Hand as 'A scratchy, unsatisfying work, bearing only too obvious traces of the composer's decline' (*The Gramophone*, 15 (1937–8), 471).

43 Basil Hogarth, 'Maurice Ravel: the man of the hour', *The Gramophone*, 8 (1930–1), 569–72.

44 Scott Goddard, 'Gramophone records', *Music & Letters*, 12 (1931), 103–5: 103.

45 Ibid., 105. Mackenzie had expressed a similar preference in *The Gramophone*, 8 (1930–1), 214.

46 Sordet, 'Ravel et l'édition phonographique', 182–3.

11 Ravel and the twentieth century

1 Jim Samson, *Music in Transition* (London: Dent, 1977), 50.

2 I am grateful to George Benjamin, Pierre Boulez, Henri Dutilleux and Alexander Goehr for giving me their views on Ravel in the course of interviews in November 1998; and to Julian Anderson, Michael Berkeley, John Casken and Robin Holloway for doing so by telephone, letter and e-mail during January and February 1999.

3 Letter to Laloy, 8 March 1907, in François Lesure and Roger Nichols (eds.), *Debussy Letters* (London: Faber, 1987), 178.

4 Charles Baudelaire, 'Le Dandy', *L'Art romantique* (Paris: Calmann-Lévy, 1924), 92–4.

5 Quoted by Calvocoressi, in Nichols, *Ravel Remembered*, 181.

6 Letter to an unknown woman, 16 February 1907, in Orenstein, *Maurice Ravel: Lettres*, 88.

7 Roland-Manuel, *Maurice Ravel* (London: Dobson, 1947, rev. 1972), 136.

8 Marcel Proust, *A la recherche du temps perdu*, 3 vols. (Paris: Gallimard, 1954), vol. III, 1025–6.

9 Edward Lockspeiser, *Debussy: His Life and Mind*, 2 vols. (London: Cassell, 1965), vol. II, 40.

10 Eric Walter White, *Stravinsky: The Composer and his Works* (London: Faber, 1966, 2/1979), 193 and 396.

11 Stephen Walsh, *The Music of Stravinsky* (Oxford: Clarendon Press, 1993), 19.

12 Richard Taruskin, 'Chez Pétrouchka: harmony and tonality *chez* Stravinsky', in Joseph Kerman (ed.), *Music at the Turn of Century* (Berkeley: University of California Press, 1990), 71–92: 74.

13 Darius Milhaud, 'La Musique française depuis la guerre', *Etudes* (Paris: Editions Claude Aveline, 1927), 7–39: 22.

14 Erik Satie, *Ecrits*, ed. Ornella Volta (Paris: Editions Champ Libre, 1977), 244.

15 Ornella Volta, *Satie Seen Through his Letters*, trans. Michael Bullock (London, New York: Marion Boyars, 1989), 89; the quotations referenced here and in n. 14 above are given in Robert Orledge, *Satie the Composer* (Cambridge: Cambridge University Press, 1990), 251.

16 Harry Halbreich, *Honegger*, trans. Roger Nichols (Portland: Amadeus Press, 1999), 255, 270, 321, 599.

17 Letters of 12 January 1932 and 23 January 1933 to Nora Auric, in Francis Poulenc, *Correspondance 1910–1963*, ed. Myriam Chimènes (Paris: Fayard, 1994), 361, 382.

18 Letters of 10 June 1919, 25 August 1928 and 8 November 1943 to Georges Jean-Aubry, Henri Sauguet and Roland-Manuel, respectively; ibid., 292, 547.

19 Letters of 10 June 1919 and 7 May 1921 to Jean-Aubry and Paul Collaer, respectively; ibid., 93, 125.

20 Francis Poulenc, 'Mes maîtres et mes amis', talk given on 7 March 1935, publ. *Conferencia* (15 October 1935), 524; *Correspondance*, 704.

21 Letter to Pierre Bernac, 24 June 1944, *Correspondance*, 553–4; Francis Poulenc, *Selected Correspondence*, ed. and trans. Sidney Buckland (London: Gollancz, 1991), 135.

22 Olivier Messiaen, *Music and Color: Conversations with Claude Samuel*, trans. E. Thomas Glasow (Portland: Amadeus Press, 1994), 195.

23 Olivier Messiaen, *Traité de rythme, de couleur, et d'ornithologie* (Paris: Leduc, 1994), vol. I, 129.

24 Boulez in interview with the present writer (November 1998).

25 This passage was noted by Alexander Goehr, *Finding the Key*, ed. Derrick Puffett (London: Faber, 1998), 52; the proportions are worked out by Nichols. [Ed.]

26 Pierrette Mari, *Henri Dutilleux* (Paris: Zurfluh, 1988), 91.

27 Hans Moldenhauer, *Anton von Webern* (London: Gollancz, 1978), 236.

28 Joan Peyser, *Boulez, Composer, Conductor, Enigma* (London: Cassell, 1977), 50.

29 Quoted in Fiona Clampin, 'Englishness revisited: the influence of Debussy and Ravel on English music 1900–1930' (M.A. dissertation, University of Exeter, 1997), 65.

30 Clampin, 'Englishness revisited', 65, 95.

31 Arthur Bliss, *As I Remember* (London: Faber, 1970), 21.

32 Humphrey Carpenter, *Benjamin Britten* (London: Faber, 1992), 15.

33 Ibid., 32.

34 Percy Scholes, *The Mirror of Music*, 2 vols. (London: Novello/Oxford University Press, 1947), vol. I, 451.

35 Norman Demuth, *Musical Trends in the 20th Century* (London: Rockliff, 1952), 54.

36 Baudelaire, 'Le Dandy', 94.

37 *R.E.D. Classical 1999 Catalogue* (London: Retail Entertainment Data Publishing, 1999), 831–7.

Appendix: early reception of Ravel's music (1899–1939)

1 Cited in Christian Goubault, *La Critique musicale dans la presse française de 1870 à 1914* (Geneva/Paris: Slatkine, 1984), 405. I am indebted to this excellent book for a number of the quotations used in this article.

2 Henri Gauthier-Villars [review of 29 May 1899], *Garçon, l'audition!* (Paris: Simonis Empis, 1901), trans. in Orenstein, *Ravel*, 24. (See Mawer and Nichols, 'Ravel's main works', No. 1: Appendix.)

3 Charles Koechlin, *Chronique des arts et de la curiosité* (7 May 1910), 148, and (3 June 1911), 172.

4 Ibid., 172.

5 Letter to Louis Laloy of 22 February 1907, in François Lesure (ed.), 'Correspondance de C. Debussy et de L. Laloy', *Revue de musicologie*, 48, special issue (1962), 3–40: 24.

6 Emile Vuillermoz, review of 15 June 1911, in 'Maurice Ravel et la critique contemporaine', *La Revue musicale*, 6, special issue (April 1925), 89–104: 99.

7 Henry Prunières, '*L'Enfant et les sortilèges* à l'Opéra de Monte-Carlo', *La Revue musicale*, 6, special issue (April 1925), 105–9: 108.

8 Pierre Lalo, *Le Temps* (13 June 1899), repr. in 'La Critique contemporaine', 91. (For more of this review, see 'Ravel's main works', No. 1.)

9 Pierre Lalo, review of the String Quartet, *Le Temps* (19 April 1904). (See 'Ravel's main works', No. 2.)

10 Pierre Lalo, review of *Histoires naturelles*, *Le Temps* (? January 1907). ('Ravel's main works', No. 4.)

11 Pierre Lalo, review of *Rapsodie espagnole*, *Le Temps* (24 March 1908). ('Ravel's main works', No. 5.)

12 Pierre Lalo, review of *L'Heure espagnole*, *Le Temps* (28 May 1911). ('Ravel's main works', No. 6.)

13 Roland-Manuel, 'Maurice Ravel et la jeune musique française', *Les Nouvelles Littéraires* (2 April 1927), repr. in Orenstein, *Maurice Ravel: Lettres*, 351–4: 352 and 353.

14 Gaston Carraud, *La Liberté* (5 February 1907). ('Ravel's main works', No. 3.)

15 Carraud quoted in the *Revue musicale de Lyon* (26 March 1911), 751.

16 Carraud quoted in *Le Guide du concert* (22 April 1911), 359. This notice was of the concert

performance of Suite No. 1 from *Daphnis* given on 2 April by the Colonne Orchestra, conducted by Gabriel Pierné.

17 Reynaldo Hahn quoted in *S.I.M. Revue musicale* (15 June 1911), 74.

18 Goubault, *La Critique musicale*, 119.

19 Respective sources: Jean Marnold in the *Mercure de France* of 16 January 1908, and 1 May 1912, 188.

20 Jean Marnold, 'Un Trio de Maurice Ravel' [November 1915], *Le Cas Wagner* (Paris: Legouix, 1920), 72.

21 Goubault, *La Critique musicale*, 116.

22 Ibid., 113.

23 Louis Laloy, *Mercure musical et S.I.M.*, 3 (15 March 1907), repr. in *La Musique retrouvée* (Paris: Plon, 1928), 163–5.

24 Laloy, *La Musique retrouvée*, 164. (For more of this review, see 'Ravel's main works', No. 4.)

25 Letter to Francis Poulenc of 16 October 1924, Francis Poulenc, *Correspondance, 1910–1963*, ed. Myriam Chimènes (Paris: Fayard, 1994), 241.

26 Ravel, 'Concerts Lamoureux', repr. in Orenstein, *Maurice Ravel: Lettres*, 294.

27 Ravel, 'A propos des *Images* de Claude Debussy', repr. ibid., 313.

Select bibliography

Main texts on Maurice Ravel

Benjamin, George, 'Last dance', *The Musical Times*, 135 (July 1994), 432–5.

Boulez, Pierre, 'Trajectoires: Ravel, Stravinsky, Schönberg', *Contrepoints*, 6 (1949), 122–42.

Chalupt, René, and Gerar, Marcelle, *Ravel au miroir de ses lettres* (Paris: Laffont, 1956).

Cohen-Lévinas, Danielle, '*Daphnis et Chloé* ou la danse du simulacre', *Musical*, 4 (June 1987), 88–95.

Colette et al., *Maurice Ravel par quelques-uns de ses familiers* (Paris: Editions du Tambourinaire, 1939).

Davies, Laurence, *Ravel Orchestral Music* (London: BBC Music Guides, 1970).

Deane, Basil, 'Renard, Ravel and the *Histoires naturelles*', *Australian Journal of French Studies*, 1/2 (1964), 177–87.

Delage, Roger, 'Ravel and Chabrier', *Musical Quarterly*, 61/4 (October 1975), 546–52.

Delahaye, Michel, 'Symbolisme et impressionnisme dans "Soupir", premier des *Trois poèmes de Stéphane Mallarmé* de Maurice Ravel', *Cahiers Maurice Ravel*, 4 (1988–9), 31–58.

Faure, Henriette, *Mon maître Maurice Ravel* (Paris: Les Editions ATP, 1978).

Goss, Madeleine, *Bolero: The Life of Ravel* (New York: Tudor Publishing, 1940, 2/1945).

Gronquist, Robert, 'Ravel's *Trois poèmes de Stéphane Mallarmé*', *Musical Quarterly*, 64/4 (1978), 507–23.

Gut, Serge, 'Le Phénomène répétitif chez Maurice Ravel. De l'obsession à l'annihilation incantatoire', *International Review of the Aesthetics and Sociology of Music*, 12/1 (June 1990), 29–46.

Henson, R. A., 'Maurice Ravel's illness: a tragedy of lost creativity', *British Medical Journal*, 296 (4 June 1988), 1585–8.

Hopkins, G. W., '(Joseph) Maurice Ravel', in Stanley Sadie (ed.), *The New Grove Dictionary of Music and Musicians*, 20 vols. (London: Macmillan, 1980), vol. XV, 609–21.

James, Richard S., 'Ravel's *Chansons madécasses*: ethnic fantasy or ethnic borrowing?', *Musical Quarterly*, 74/3 (1990), 360–84.

Jankélévitch, Vladimir, *Ravel* (Paris: Editions Rieder, 1939; Editions du Seuil, ed. Jean-Michel Nectoux, 3/1995).

Jourdan-Morhange, Hélène, *Ravel et nous: L'Homme, l'ami, le musicien* (Geneva: Editions du Milieu du Monde, 1945).

Larner, Gerald, *Maurice Ravel* (London: Phaidon Press, 1996).

Lassus, Marie-Pierre, 'Ravel, l'enchanteur: structure poétique et structure musicale dans *L'Enfant et les sortilèges*', *Analyse musicale*, 26 (February 1992), 40–7.

Lévi-Strauss, Claude, '*Boléro* de Maurice Ravel', *L'Homme*, 11/2 (April–June 1971), 5–14.

Long, Marguerite, *Au piano avec Maurice Ravel* (Paris: Julliard, 1971); *At the Piano with Ravel*, ed. Pierre Laumonier, Eng. trans. Olive Senior-Ellis (London: Dent, 1973).

Marnat, Marcel, *Maurice Ravel* (Paris: Fayard, 1986; 2/1995).

Marnat, Marcel (ed.) *Ravel: Souvenirs de Manuel Rosenthal* (Paris: Hazan, 1995).

Myers, Rollo, *Ravel: Life and Works* (London: Duckworth, 1960).

Nectoux, Jean-Michel, 'Ravel/Fauré et les débuts de la Société Musicale Indépendante', *Revue de musicologie*, 61/2 (1975), 295–318.
  'Maurice Ravel et sa bibliothèque musicale', *Fontes Artis Musicae*, 24 (1977), 199–206.

Newbould, Brian, 'Ravel's "Pantoum"', *The Musical Times*, 116 (March 1975), 228–31.

Nichols, Roger, *Ravel* (London: Dent, 1977).

Nichols, Roger (ed.), *Ravel Remembered* (London: Faber, 1987).

Orenstein, Arbie, *Ravel: Man and Musician* (New York: Columbia University Press, 1975; Dover, 2/1991).

Orenstein, Arbie (ed.), *Maurice Ravel: Lettres, écrits, entretiens* (Paris: Flammarion, 1989).
  A Ravel Reader (New York: Columbia University Press, 1990).

Perlemuter, Vlado, and Jourdan-Morhange, Hélène, *Ravel d'après Ravel*, repr. with Jean Roy, *Rencontres avec Vlado Perlemuter* (Aix-en Provence: Editions Alinéa, 1989); *Ravel according to Ravel*, Eng. trans. Francis Turner, ed. Harold Taylor (London: Kahn & Averill, 1988).

Plebuch, Tobias, 'Der stumme Schrecken, Ravels *Frontispice*', *Hommage à Ravel 1987* (Bremen: Hochschule für Gestaltende Kunst und Musik, 1987), 155–65.

Prost, Christine, '*L'Enfant et les sortilèges*: l'infidélité aux modèles', *Analyse musicale*, 26 (February 1992), 59–63.

Roland-Manuel, *A la gloire de Ravel* (Paris: Nouvelle Revue Critique, 1938; Paris: Gallimard, 2/1948); *Maurice Ravel*, Eng. trans. Cynthia Jolly (London: Dobson, 1947).

Rosenthal, Manuel, *Satie, Ravel, Poulenc* (Madras and New York: Hanuman Books, 1987).

Roy, Jean, '*Frontispice*', *Cahiers Maurice Ravel*, 1 (1985), 141–4.

Russom, Philip Wade, 'A theory of pitch organization for the early works of Maurice Ravel' (Ph.D. dissertation, Yale University, 1985).

Teboul, Jean-Claude, *Ravel: Le Langage musical dans l'œuvre pour piano* (Paris: Le Léopard d'Or, 1987).

Zank, Stephen, '"L'Arrière pensée" in music of Maurice Ravel: sound, style and virtuosity' (Ph.D. dissertation, Duke University, 1996).

Authored interviews with Maurice Ravel (page references are to *RR*)

Bizet, René, '*L'Heure espagnole*' [*L'Intransigeant* (17 May 1911)], 411–13.
  '*Ma Mère l'Oye*' [*L'Intransigeant* (28 January 1912)], 414–15.

Bruyr, José, 'An interview with Maurice Ravel' [*Le Guide du concert* (16 October 1931)], 479–84.

Calvocoressi, Michel-Dimitri, 'Maurice Ravel on Berlioz' [*Daily Telegraph* (12 January 1929)], 461–4.

'M. Ravel discusses his own work: the *Boléro* explained' [*Daily Telegraph* (11 July 1931)], 476–8.

Downes, Olin, 'Maurice Ravel, man and musician' [*New York Times* (7 August 1927)], 448–53.

'Mr. Ravel returns' [*New York Times* (26 February 1928)], 456–60.

Frank, Nino, 'Maurice Ravel between two trains' [*Candide* (5 May 1932)], 496–8.

Leroi, Pierre, 'Some confessions of the great composer Maurice Ravel' [*Excelsior* (30 October 1931)], 485–6.

Reuillard, Gabriel, 'M. Maurice Ravel is going to write a *Joan of Arc*' [*Excelsior* (24 September 1933)], 499–502.

Révész, André, 'The great musician Maurice Ravel talks about his art' [*A.B.C. de Madrid* (1 May 1924)], 431–5.

Initialled and unsigned interviews (page references are to *RR* unless otherwise specified)

'Maurice Ravel's opinion of modern French music' [*The Musical Leader,* 21 (16 March 1911)], 409–10.

'Ravel and modern music' [*The Morning Post* (10 July 1922)], 421–2.

C.v.W., 'The French Music Festival: an interview with Ravel' [*De Telegraaf* (30 September 1922)], 423–5.

'Avant-première', *Le Gaulois* (20 March 1925), repr. in Orenstein, *Maurice Ravel: Lettres*, 348–50; Eng. trans., 'Dress rehearsal', in *RR*, 436–8.

X.M., 'Maurice Ravel's arrival' [*Berlingske Tidende* (30 January 1926)], 439–41.

'Problems of modern music: from a conversation with Maurice Ravel' [*Der Bund* (19 April 1929)], 465–6.

'A visit with Maurice Ravel' [*De Telegraaf* (31 March 1931)], 472–5.

C.B.L., 'An afternoon with Maurice Ravel' [*Neue freie Presse* (3 February 1932)], 487–9.

'Factory gives composer inspiration' [*Evening Standard* (24 February 1932)], 490–1.

'Ten opinions of Mr. Ravel on compositions and composers' [*De Telegraaf* (6 April 1932)], 492–5.

Articles by Maurice Ravel (page references are to *RR* unless otherwise specified)

'The polonaises, nocturnes, impromptus, the barcarolle – impressions' [*Le Courrier musical,* 13 (1 January 1910)], 335–7.

'Concerts Lamoureux', *Revue musicale de la S.I.M.*, 8/2 (15 February 1912), 62–3 (orig. pag.); repr. in Orenstein, *Maurice Ravel: Lettres*, 294–7; Eng. trans., 'The Lamoureux Orchestra concerts', in *RR*, 340–3.

'*Symphonic Scenes* by Monsieur Fanelli' [*Revue musicale de la S.I.M.*, 8/4 (April 1912)], 349–52.

'*The Witch* at the Opéra-Comique' [*Comœdia illustré*, 5/7 (5 January 1913)], 353–7.

'*Fervaal*' [*Comœdia illustré*, 5/8 (20 January 1913)], 358–61.

'At the Théâtre des Arts' [*Comœdia illustré*, 5/9 (5 February 1913)], 362–5.

'A propos des *Images* de Claude Debussy', *Les Cahiers d'aujourd'hui* (February 1913), 135–8 (orig. pag.); repr. in Orenstein, *Maurice Ravel: Lettres*, 311–13; Eng. trans., 'Regarding Claude Debussy's *Images*', in *RR*, 366–8.

['Ravel analyzes his own music' (1913)], two-page manuscript fragment (Paris, Bibliothèque de l'Opéra, Rés. 1093 (2)); used in René Lenormand, *Etude sur l'harmonie moderne* (Paris, 1913); Eng. trans. in *RR*, Appendix D, 517–23 and Plate 16.

'At the Opéra-Comique: *Francesca da Rimini* and *La Vida breve*' [*Comœdia illustré*, 6/8 (20 January 1914)], 372–5.

'New productions of the Russian Season: *The Nightingale*' [*Comœdia illustré*, 6/17 (5 June 1914)], 380–3.

'Les Mélodies de Gabriel Fauré', *La Revue musicale*, 3 (October 1922), 22–7 (orig. pag.); repr. in Orenstein, *Maurice Ravel: Lettres*, 322–6; Eng. trans., 'The songs of Gabriel Fauré', in *RR*, 384–88.

'Take jazz seriously!' [*Musical Digest*, 13/3 (March 1928)], 390–2.

'Contemporary music' [*Rice Institute Pamphlet*, 15 (April 1928)], 40–9.

[Roland-Manuel] 'Une esquisse autobiographique de Ravel' [1928], *La Revue musicale*, 19, special issue (December 1938), 17–23 (orig. pag.); repr. in Orenstein, *Maurice Ravel: Lettres*, 43–7; Eng. trans., 'An autobiographical sketch by Maurice Ravel', in *RR*, 29–37.

'Memories of a lazy child' [*La Petite Gironde* (12 July 1931)], 393–5.

'Concerto for the Left Hand' [*Le Journal* (14 January 1933)], 396–7.

'Finding tunes in factories' [*New Britain* (9 August 1933)], 398–400.

Index

In this Index, 'names' includes some collective names of artistic groups (e.g. 'Les Six', or the 'Apaches'), companies and ensembles (e.g. Ballets Russes, Calvet Quartet), societies (e.g. SMI) and concert series (e.g. Concerts Colonne). In the case of alternative artistic names, the main entry is made under the familiar pseudonym, with the actual name given in parenthesis; more occasionally, following citation of an artist's real name, their 'nickname' is included in parenthesis. In addition to music, 'works' includes reference to Ravel's main writings cited in the text and to seminal literary works (and librettos) of writers such as Poe and Colette. References supported by music examples are denoted by '(& ex.)' or '(& exx.)', whereas '(ex.)' indicates citation only within the body of an example. Titled pieces within a larger work (e.g. songs within a collection, or Chabrier's *Pièces pittoresques*) are itemised under the main work for ease of access to the text. Some discretion has guided the inclusion of parenthetical material, cross-references and frequently cited composers (e.g. Debussy) mentioned only as part of a long listing.

Adorno, Theodor 55, 67
Albéniz, Isaac 202, 273
Alkan, Charles (Charles Morhange) 273
   Marcia funebre sulla morte d'un papagallo 75
Allais, Alphonse 253
Alphonso XIII, King of Spain 191
Amyot, Jacques 39, 142
Anderson, Julian 249, 250, 280
Anderson, W. R. 236, 280
Antheil, George 63
   Airplane Sonata 58
   Ballet mécanique 58
'Apaches' 14, 17, 23, 32, 165, 251, 269
Apollinaire, Guillaume 50
Aranyi, Jelly d' 40, 108, 112, 228
Attali, Jacques 49, 160
Aubert, Louis 185, 260
Aubry, Marcel
   L'Or 35
Aulnoy, Comtesse d' 17, 39
Auric, Georges 16, 18, 25

Bach, Johann Sebastian 93, 204, 249
Bailly (stage designer) 257
Bakst, Léon (Lev Samoylovich Rosenberg) 141, 143, 165, 259
Balakirev, Mily 256
   Islamey 81, 246
Balanchine, George 262
Balzac, Honoré de 190
Balla, Giacomo 58
Ballets Russes 12, 25, 38, 39, 44, 141–2, 143, 149, 151, 259
Ballets Suédois 150, 261
Bardac, Raoul 14
Barrès, Maurice 18
Bartók, Béla 107–8, 110, 112, 249, 274
   Music for Strings, Percussion and Celesta 63
Bathori (-Engel), Jane 232–3, 237, 256, 260–1, 264, 280
Baudelaire, Charles Pierre 17, 50, 51, 171, 241, 249, 250, 273
   Les Fleurs du mal 52, 89 ('Harmonie du soir')

Baudouin (flautist) 264
Baugnies, Jacques 202
Bax, Arnold
   Oboe Quartet 229
Beaumont, Cyril 152
Beaumont, Marie Leprince de 17, 39
Beecham, Thomas 260
Beethoven, Ludwig van 10, 22, 130, 202, 241, 249, 252
   Kreutzer Sonata 242
   Piano Sonata Op. 31 No. 3 56
   Symphony No. 9 154
Bellini, Vincenzo 23
Bellman, Jonathan 238
Benedictus, Mme Edouard 32
Benjamin, George 151, 152, 153, 154, 155, 240–1, 242, 244, 246, 280
Benois, Alexandre 141, 151, 155, 262, 264, 265
Bérard, Jean 233
Berg, Alban
   Songs Op. 2 272
Bergson, Henri 192
Bériot, Charles de 7, 71
Berkeley, Sir Lennox 248
Berkeley, Michael 249, 280
Berlioz, Hector 10, 27–8
Bertelin, Albert 19–20 (& ex.)
Bertrand, Aloysius 45, 82
Bizet, Georges 27, 32
   Carmen 189, 210, 278
Blanche, Jacques-Emile 137
Bliss, Arthur 248
Bloch, Mme André 272
Bloom, Harold 267
Boccaccio, Giovanni 193
Börlin, Jean 150, 261
Borodin, Alexander 23, 148
   Petite suite 119
   Prince Igor 142
   Symphony No. 2 23, 33
Boulez, Pierre 24, 26, 56, 57, 242, 246, 247, 280
   Le Marteau sans maître 246
Bourdin, Roger 263

Bourgault-Ducoudray, Louis
  Rapsodie cambodgienne 27
Brahms, Johannes 10, 107, 241
Branco, Pedro de Freitas 233, 237, 280
Braque, Georges 50
Bretagne, Pierre 38
Bretton-Chabrier, Mme 12
Britten, Benjamin 248
  Quatre chansons françaises 248
Bruneau, Alfred
  Penthésilée 38
Bruyr, José 67

Calvet Quartet 227, 229–30, 238
Calvocoressi, Michel-Dimitri 11, 36, 47, 143,
  220, 222, 251
Canudo, Ricciotto 52, 53
  S.P. 503, Le Poème du Vardar 52–3
Capet Quartet 228
Caplet, André 24, 185
Carraud, Gaston 189, 252, 254
Carré, Albert 257
Casadesus, Robert 9, 217, 222, 223, 224–5, 226,
  237, 238, 239
Casals, Pablo 202
Casella, Alfredo 12, 264, 277
Casken, John 249, 280
Cendrars, Blaise 50
Cervantes, Miguel de 257
Chabrier, Emmanuel 7, 9, 11, 12–14, 15, 25, 26,
  72, 78, 93
  Bourrée fantasque 56, 77
  Briséis 23
  Caprice 14
  España 29, 81, 87, 189, 272
  Habanera 29
  Pièces pittoresques (*Dix*)
    'Paysage' (I) 14
    'Melancolie' (II) 14
    'Tourbillon' (III) 77, 93
    'Sous-bois' (IV) 14
    'Idylle' (VI) 78 (ex.)
    'Danse villageoise' (VII) 93
    'Menuet pompeux' (IX) 12, 72 (& ex.),
    135, 137
  Le Roi malgré lui 12, 72–3 (& ex.), 87, 272
  Tes yeux bleus 96
  Trois valses romantiques 12, 56
Chalupt, René 59
Chaplin, Charlie
  Modern Times 58
Chevalier, Maurice 267
Chevillard, Camille 151, 261
Chopin, Frédéric 23, 49, 56, 81, 256
  Etude Op. 25 No. 1 82
  Nouvelle étude in Db 74
  Sonata Op. 35 81, 85 ('Marche funèbre'), 87
  Les Sylphides 275
Clampin, Fiona 248
Cloez, Gustave 151, 262
Cocteau, Jean 16, 194, 253
  Le Coq et l'arlequin 194
Cohen-Lévinas, Danielle 144, 147, 148
Coindreau, Pierre 38

Colette, Bel-Gazou 204
Colette, Sidonie-Gabrielle ('Colette Willy';
  'Colette'; 'Claudine') 7, 201–4, 209, 278
  L'Enfant et les sortilèges 43, 203–4
  La Paix chez les bêtes 204
Collaer, Paul 22
Colonne, Edouard (Judas Köhn) 257
Concerts Colonne 257
Concerts Durand 263
Concerts Lamoureux 237, 261, 264
Coolidge, Elizabeth Sprague 178, 264
Cooper, Thomas 43
Coppola, Piero 232, 236, 237, 238–9
Cortot, Alfred 7, 88, 202, 226–7, 237
Couperin, François ('Le Grand') 261
  Concert royal, No. IV: 'Forlane' 7, 19–22 (&
  exx.), 90
Couperin, Louis 261
Courteault, Jane 278
Croiza, Claire 202
Crosland, Marguerite 204
Cui, César 194

Daquin, Louis Claude
  Premier livre de pièces de clavecin: 'Le
  Coucou' 88
Dargomïzhsky, Alexander 36
David, Félicien 27
  Le Désert 27, 36
Davies, Laurence 129
Deane, Basil 10
Debussy, Claude 2, 9, 10, 11, 14–15, 18, 22, 23,
  25, 29, 25, 26, 33, 38, 45, 47, 49, 71, 72,
  76, 77, 81, 97, 99, 107, 122, 162, 166,
  171, 187, 188, 189, 190, 215, 240, 241,
  243, 244, 247, 249, 250, 251, 252, 253,
  255, 257, 272, 273, 277, 278
  Chanson espagnole 75
  Chansons de Bilitis (staged version) 273
  Chansons de Bilitis (songs) 119 ('La Flûte de
  Pan'), 232, 274
  Childrens' Corner
    'Doctor Gradus ad Parnassum' (I) 207
    'Jimbo's Lullaby' (II) 106
    'Serenade for the Doll' (III) 208
  Danse sacrée et danse profane 103
  Estampes
    'Pagodes' (I) 76
    'La Soirée dans Grenade' (II) 30, 74–5 (&
    ex.), 188
    'Jardins sous la pluie' (III) 76, 81, 89
  Images (orchestra) 254
    'Ibéria' (II) 115, 156, 158, 272
  Images (piano) Set I 78, 79
    'Reflets dans l'eau' (I) 81
    'Hommage à Rameau' (II) 79
  Images (piano) Set II
    'Cloches à travers les feuilles' (I) 272
    'Et la lune descend' (II) 79, 272
    'Poissons d'or' (III) 76
  Jeux 80
  L'Isle joyeuse 80
  Lindaraja 74
  La Mer 77, 80 ('Jeux de vagues'), 135
  Nocturnes 14

Le Palais du silence ou No-ja-li 34, 269
Pelléas et Mélisande 14, 38, 77, 165, 188, 189, 202, 210, 246, 253
Petite pièce 273
Piano Trio in G 273
Pour le piano
   'Sarabande' (II) 15, 72–3 (& ex.) (1896 version), 74 (& ex.)
   'Toccata' (III) 89
Prélude à l'après-midi d'un faune 14, 33, 74
Préludes (Book I) 87
   'Voiles' (II) 83
   'Le Vent dans la plaine' (III) 76
   'Des pas sur la neige' (VI) 81
   'Ce qu'a vu le Vent d'Ouest' (VII) 81
   'La Sérénade interrompue' (IX) 76
Rapsodie (1908) for saxophone 273
Rapsodie (1910) for clarinet 273
String Quartet Op. 10 26, 56, 98–9, 102, 228, 273, 280
Six épigraphes antiques 87, 243
Suite bergamasque: 'Clair de lune' 81–2
Syrinx 273
Tarantelle styrienne 15 (orch. Ravel as *Danse*), 139
Trois poèmes de Stéphane Mallarmé 276
Debussy, Mme Claude 138
Dekobra, Maurice 62
Delage, Maurice 32, 58, 63, 93, 185
Delahaye, Michel 51
Delaunay, Sonia 50
Delibes, Léo 27
Delius, Frederick 35
Demuth, Norman 248
Dinsey (violinst) 237
Disney, Walt 168
Doesburg, Theo van 57
Dommange, René 9
Douches, Raymond 263
Downes, Olin 67
Draper, Haydn P. 231, 237
Drésa, Jacques 142, 258, 260
Dubois, Théodore 8
Dukas, Paul 185
Dumas, Alexandre ('Dumas père') 190
Dumesnil, Maurice 279
Duncan, Isadora 202
Durand, Jacques 23, 272
Durony, Geneviève 258
Dutilleux, Henri 247, 280
   Flute Sonatina 247
Dvořák, Antonín
   Piano Quintet 229
Dyagilev, Sergey 39, 44, 123, 135, 137, 141, 142, 143, 151, 172, 259

Ecorcheville, Jules 19, 52
Edwards, Alfred 31
Edwards, Misia 31
Eigeldinger, Jean-Jacques 273
Einstein, Albert 192
Eliot, T. S. 26
Enesco, Georges 202, 228, 244, 263
Erlanger, Camille
   La Sorcière 38

Falla, Manuel de 30, 61, 71
   La Vida breve 38
Fanelli, Ernest 36, 269
   Tableaux symphoniques 36–7 (& ex.), 38, 269
Fargue, Léon-Paul 17, 162, 185, 186, 226–7
Fauré, Gabriel 7, 9, 11, 15, 26, 71, 99, 106, 202, 251, 278
   Nocturne No. 6 81
   Le Secret 11
Feure, Georges de (Georges van Sluijters) 34, 38
   Les Jardins d'Antinoüs 35
   Le Masque terrible 34
   Le Palais du silence 34
Février, Jacques 77
Flecker, James Elroy
   Hassan 35
Fleury, Louis 264
Fokin(e), Mikhail (Michel) 141, 143–4, 149, 259
   Les Sylphides 275
Fokina, Vera 259
Fouillée, Alfred 191
Franc-Nohain (Maurice-Etienne Legrand) 35, 189, 190–1, 192, 194, 195, 277, 278
   Le Chapeau chinois 35
   Chansons des trains et des gares 189
   Flûtes 189
   L'Heure espagnole 189, 258
Franck, César 80, 103, 250, 279
   String Quartet in D 99, 228
Freud, Sigmund 200
Frogley, Alain 248
Furtwängler, Wilhelm 9

Galimir, Felix 230
Galimir Quartet (re-formed) 230, 238
Galimir Quartet of Vienna 229–30, 237
Galland, Antoine 39
Garban, Lucien 8
Gaubert, Philippe 259
Gauthier-Villars, Henri ('Willy') 202, 251, 267
Gautier, Théophile 190–1
   Voyage en Espagne 190
Gaveau (attaché) 32
Gavoty, Bernard 77
Gedalge, André 9, 11, 104, 242
Gerar, Marcelle 232, 237
Gershwin, George 25, 42, 132, 250
   Concerto in F 115, 132
   Rhapsody in Blue 132
Ghil, René 51
Glass, Philip 243
Glinka, Mikhail 27, 133
Goddard, Scott 236
Godebska, Ida 31, 32
Godebski, Cipa (Xavier Cyprien) 7, 38
Goehr, Alexander 242–3, 248–9, 280
Goehr, Lydia 55
Gogol, Nikolay Vasil'yevich 194
   The Marriage 193–4, 278
Goossens, Leon 229
Goubault, Christian 253
Gounod, Charles 11, 12, 14, 25, 202
   Faust 12–13 (& ex.), 26

Goya, Francisco de 190, 257, 265, 277
Grey, Madeleine 231–2, 237, 238, 280
Grieg, Edvard 23
Griffiths, Paul 129
Gronquist, Robert 51
Grovlez, Gabriel 9, 142, 258
Gunsbourg, Raoul 262
Gut, Serge 52

Hahn, Reynaldo 202, 252
Halbreich, Harry 245
Harcourt, Robert de 278
Harding, James 150
Hartman, Victor 138
Hasselquist, Mlle (dancer) 261
Heger, Robert 125, 265
Heller, Stephen 24
Henson, R. A. 267, 271
Hérold, André Ferdinand 63
Heymann Quartet 255
Hindemith, Paul 9
Hogarth, Basil 236
Holloway, Robin 249, 280
Honegger, Arthur 185, 245
    Pacific 231 58, 61, 64
    Sonatina for Violin and Cello 245
    String Quartet No. 1 245
    Symphony No. 3 245
    Trois pièces 245
Hopkins, G. W. (Bill) 47, 48
Howat, Roy 12, 246, 271
Howard, Frank 228, 237
Howells, Herbert
    Quartet No. 3 (*In Gloucestershire*) 248
Hugard, Jeanne 142, 258
Hugo, Victor 190
Huysmans, Joris-Karl 16
    A Rebours 17

Idelsohn, Rabbi Abraham 277
Imbert, Pierre Léonce 190
Indy, Vincent d' 1, 9, 10, 18, 202, 253
Inghelbrecht, Désiré-Emile 38, 150, 260, 261, 269
    Pour le jour des premières neiges au vieux Japon 38
International Quartet 227–9, 230, 237
Ireland, John
    Sonatina 248

Jacobs, Rémi 238
James (cellist) 237
Jankélévitch, Vladimir 1, 48, 140, 141, 144
Jarry, Alfred 278
Jean-Aubry, Georges 15, 244
Jobert, Jean 15, 138
Johnson, Dr Samuel 28
Jourdan-Morhange, Hélène 112, 141, 214, 218
Juderías, Julián 190, 191
    La Leyenda negra 190
Juilliard Quartet 230, 238

Kaminsky, Peter 249
Kandinsky, Wassily 51
Karsavina, Thamara 141, 142, 143

Kermode, Frank 10
Kern, Jerome 42
    Show Boat 278
Kindler, Hans 264
Kiriac, Dumitru 8
Klein, Melanie 200–1, 205
Klingsor, Tristan (A. J. Léon Leclère) 7, 32, 165, 176
    Shéhérazade 32, 165, 178 ('Asie')
Koechlin, Charles 9, 32, 43, 251
    Shéhérazade Op. 84 (songs) 269
Koussevitzky, Sergey 137, 238
Kugel, Georges 9

La Fontaine, Jean de 169
Lalo, Edouard 252
Lalo, Pierre 76, 144, 188, 252, 254, 268
Laloy, Louis 47, 48, 144, 241, 253
Lambert, Constant 150, 236
    Rio Grande 236
Lami, Eugène 152
Lang, Fritz
    Metropolis 58
Laparra, Raoul 198–9 (& ex.), 278
Laprade, Pierre 150, 261
Larner, Gerald 125, 149, 160
Lawson, Rex 53
Le Corbusier (Charles-Edouard Jeanneret) 48, 58
    'Le Purisme' 58
Le Flem, Paul 38
Léger, Fernand 58
Leleu, Jeanne 258
Lenepveu, Charles 8
Leroux, Xavier 8
Lévi-Strauss, Claude 155
Levinson, André 145
Leyritz, Léon 59
Ligeti, György 250
Liszt, Franz 23, 36, 81
    Hungarian Rhapsodies 112
    Piano Sonata 126
    Waldesrauschen 81
Lockspeiser, Edward 243
Long, Kathleen 228
Long, Marguerite 9, 88, 125, 214, 233–5, 237, 261, 266, 269, 273, 280
Longus (Greek myth-teller) 39, 143
Louÿs, Pierre
    Chansons de Bilitis 273
Lowell, James Russell 191
Lucas, Blanche 38
Lully, Jean-Baptiste 19
Lyon, Gustave 103

Mackenzie, Compton 279, 280
Mackrell, Judith 140
Maeterlinck, Maurice 188
Mahler, Gustav
    Fourth Symphony 98
Mallarmé, Stéphane 7, 17, 24, 50, 162, 164, 171–2, 178, 185, 243, 247, 276, 277
    Sainte 164, 276
    Trois poèmes
        'Soupir' (I) 172–5 (& ex.), 276

'Placet futile' (II) 175, 176, 276
'Surgi de la croupe et du bond' (III) 175, 178
Manet, Edouard 82
Mangeot, André 227–8, 237
Maré, Rolf de 150, 261
Marès, Roland de 162
Marnat, Marcel 52, 254, 271
Marnold, Jean (Jean Morland) 16, 18, 31, 252–3
Marot, Clément 17, 162, 163, 186
Mason, Gwendolen 231, 237
Massenet, Jules 8, 202
Masslow, Boris 33
Mauclair, Camille (Camille Faust) 254
Maurras, Charles 18
Mawer, Deborah 124
Mead, Alfred C. 222
Mendelssohn, Felix 23, 24, 250
Mengelberg, Willem 238–9
Messager, André 202, 263
Messiaen, Olivier 53, 175, 244, 245, 246
    Trois petites liturgies 246
    Turangalîla Symphony 246
    Vingt regards 246
    Visions de l'Amen 246
Messing, Scott 19, 22, 55
Metzinger, Jean 50
Meyer, Leonard B. 160
Mignan, Edouard
    Rapsodie 34
Milhaud, Darius 14, 18, 25, 63, 111, 244
    Chamber Symphony No. 5 63
    La Création du monde 25, 115 (& ex.)
    'The evolution of modern music in Paris and Vienna' 25
    Machines agricoles 58, 64
    Soirées de Petrograd 232
'Mistinguett' (singer/dancer) 7, 267
Molinari, Bernardo 80
Monpou, Hippolyte 277
Monteux, Pierre 143, 259
Monteverdi, Claudio 250
Morand, Paul 185
Mosolov, Alexander
    Iron Foundry 61
Mozart, Wolfgang Amadeus 10, 22–3, 56, 87–8, 130, 162, 250, 252, 269
    Clarinet Quintet 43, 132–3
    'Jupiter' Symphony 90
Mulet, Henri 38
Multzer (costume designer) 257
Murchie, Robert 231, 237
Musorgsky, Modest Petrovich 36, 194, 196
    Boris Godunov 33, 109, 119
    Khovanshchina 23, 172
    The Marriage 193–4
    Pictures at an Exhibition 23, 46, 137–8
Musset, Alfred de 190, 277
Myers, Rollo 149

National Gramophone Society (NGS) 228–9
National League for the Defence of French Music 18, 24
Nectoux, Jean-Michel 23, 193, 233

Newbould, Brian 89
Nichols, Roger 2, 8, 33, 39, 40, 63, 137, 238, 267, 268, 274, 277, 281
Nietzsche, Friedrich Wilhelm 48, 242
    The Origins of Tragedy 252
Nijinska, Bronislava 141, 151, 152, 155, 262, 264
Nijinsky, Vaslav 34, 137, 141, 142, 143, 147
Noverre, Jean-Georges 141

Offenbach, Jacques 194, 208
Onnen, Frank 56
Orban, Marcel 38
Orledge, Robert 179
Orenstein, Arbie 19, 53, 61, 63, 98, 104, 107, 137, 142, 163, 164, 173, 178, 185, 238, 254, 270, 273, 274, 277

Paganini, Niccolò 113
Palestrina, Giovanni Pierluigi da 242
Paoli, Domenico de' 31
Parny, Evariste-Désiré de 39–40, 178, 179, 185
    Chansons madécasses, traduite en français 178
Pater, Walter 16
Pavlova, Anna 141
Pecker, Boris 228, 237
Perlemuter, Vlado 96, 135, 214, 217, 218, 219, 220, 223, 224, 225, 226–7, 237, 238, 239, 272, 273
Perloff, Nancy 58
Pernot, Hubert 269
Perrault, Charles 17, 39
Petipa, Marius 141
Peyser, Joan 247
Philip, Robert 225, 279
Picasso, Pablo 50, 67
Pierné, Gabriel 282
Pistone, Danièle 33
Plebuch, Tobias 53
Poe, Edgar Allan 7, 16–17, 35, 50, 171, 172, 186, 192
    The Mask of the Red Death 34
    The Philosophy of Composition 16, 50, 171, 186
    The Poetic Principle 16
    The Raven 16, 50, 67, 171
Pougin, Arthur 268
Poulenc, Francis 14, 18, 25, 245
    Les Mamelles de Tirésias 245
    Rapsodie nègre 208
Pourvoyeur, Robert 278–9
Pratella, Francesco 57, 62
    'Technical manifesto of Futurist music' 61
Pro Arte Quartet 230, 237
Prokofiev, Sergey 66
    Le Pas d'acier 58, 61
Proust, Marcel 50, 242
    A la recherche du temps perdu 242
Prunières, Henry 230, 232, 235, 251
Puccini, Giacomo
    La Bohème 277
    The Girl of the Golden West 35
Puffett, Derrick 64, 65, 67, 124, 156, 158
Purcell, Henry 250

Rakhmaninov, Sergey 107
Rameau, Jean-Philippe 19, 141
Ravel, Edouard (brother) 31, 58, 59, 62
Ravel, Marie Delouart (mother) 30, 59, 71,
    150, 188, 204, 267, 272
Ravel, (Joseph) Maurice
  MUSIC
  A la manière de ... Borodine 23
  A la manière de ... Chabrier 12–13 (& ex.)
  Alcyone 8, 273
  Alyssa 8
  Ballade de la Reine morte d'aimer 11, 50,
    162, 163
  Berceuse sur le nom de Gabriel Fauré 11, 52
  Boléro 29, 45, 48, 52, 57, 58, 59, 61, 63, 64,
    66, 79, 80, 116, 117, 140, 150, 155–61 (&
    exx.), 197, 235–9, 241, 242, 264–5, 266,
    273, 280
  Callirhoé 8
  Chanson du rouet 164
  Chansons madécasses 24, 39–40, 96, 97–8,
    111, 117, 162, 163, 178–9, 182, 185, 231,
    237, 264, 277, 280
    'Nahandove' (I) 40, 179–82 (& ex.)
    'Aoua!' (II) 40–1 (& ex.), 44, 179, 182–4
      (& ex.), 185
    'Il est doux' (III) 179, 182, 184–5
  Chants populaires 162, 170–1
    'Chanson hébraïque' (IV) 30, 231, 238
  Cinq mélodies populaires grecques 30, 162,
    170
  La Cloche engloutie 63
  Concerto in G (Piano) 9, 10, 25, 43, 45, 76,
    77, 96, 107, 116, 117, 125, 126, 129–34
    (& exx.), 233–5 (& exx.), 237, 266
  Concerto for the Left Hand (Piano) 45, 66,
    96, 125–9 (& exx.), 130, 132, 245, 265,
    280
  Daphnis et Chloé 1, 39, 49 (& ex.), 57, 66, 98,
    102, 104, 107, 140, 142, 143–9 (& exx.),
    152, 153, 161, 221, 246, 251, 252, 259,
    265, 277, 282
  Deux épigrammes de Clément Marot 22, 164
    'D'Anne jouant de l'espinette' (II) 45
  Deux mélodies hébraïques 185, 231–2, 238
    'Kaddisch' (I) 30, 185, 277
    'L'Enigme éternelle' (II) 185, 232, 277
  Don Quichotte à Dulcinée 30, 45, 162, 163,
    178, 185, 242, 271
  L'Enfant et les sortilèges 1, 28, 43, 44, 52, 59,
    87–8, 98, 110, 115–6 (& ex.), 125, 134,
    141, 166, 169, 179, 199–210 (& exx.),
    245, 252, 262–3, 277
  Frontispice 48, 52–4 (& ex.), 58, 64, 67
  Gaspard de la nuit 71, 80, 81–2, 88, 95, 96,
    97, 150, 221, 222, 242, 244, 246, 258, 260
    'Ondine' (I) 76, 77, 81, 82, 85, 95
    'Le Gibet' (II) 45, 48, 50, 77, 79, 80, 81,
      82–5 (& ex.), 87, 101, 222, 223, 224–5,
      237, 243, 244, 272
    'Scarbo' (III) 46, 76, 80–1 (& ex.), 84,
      85–7 (& ex.), 215, 246
  Un grand sommeil noir 164, 243
  Les Grands Vents venus d'outremer 171
  L'Heure espagnole 30, 44, 64–5 (& ex.), 77,

    124, 166, 188–99 (& exx.), 200, 204, 208,
    210, 245, 246, 251, 252, 257–8, 277
  Histoires naturelles 8, 47, 58, 75, 77, 162, 163,
    169–70, 171, 221, 232–3, 251, 253,
    256–7
    'Le Paon' (I) 170, 237, 257
    'Le Grillon' (II) 170, 237
    'Le Cygne' (III) 169, 170
    'Le Martin-pêcheur' (IV) 170, 237
    'La Pintade' (V) 170, 257
  Introduction et allegro 97, 102–4 (& ex.),
    221, 231, 237, 248, 273
  Jeux d'eau 11, 76–8, 80, 89, 95, 122, 188, 221,
    226–7 (& exx.), 237, 243, 244, 254
  Manteau de fleurs 164
  Ma Mère l'Oye 15, 29, 39, 44, 45
    ('Laideronnette'), 58, 78, 88, 98, 140,
    142, 150, 166, 169, 221, 242, 245, 246,
    258
  Menuet antique 22, 45, 72 (& ex.), 76, 90,
    135, 136, 137, 163, 221
  Menuet sur le nom d'Haydn 52, 76
  Miroirs 50, 78–80, 96, 221, 237, 242, 244,
    246, 253, 256
    'Noctuelles' (I) 76, 78 (& ex.), 80
    'Oiseaux tristes' (II) 52, 76, 78, 103, 143,
      222, 223–4 (& ex.), 237, 246
    'Une barque sur l'océan' (III) 77, 79 (&
      ex.), 80, 96, 135, 252
    'Alborada del gracioso' (IV) 44, 52, 56, 72,
      76, 79 (& ex.), 93–5 (& exx.), 103, 123,
      135–6, 140, 251
    'La Vallée des cloches' (V) 48, 50–1 (&
      ex.), 74, 79, 80, 222, 237
  Morgiane 34
  Myrrha 8
  Noël des jouets 17, 166–9 (& ex.)
  Pavane pour une Infante défunte 12, 72–3 (&
    ex.), 75–6, 77, 135, 186, 221, 222, 237,
    241, 248, 266
  Piano Trio 11, 31, 35, 45, 56, 89, 97, 98,
    104–7, 108, 109, 110, 113, 116, 242,
    253
  Rapsodie espagnole 30, 45, 56, 79, 118, 120,
    221, 243, 248, 257, 274
    'Prélude à la nuit' (I) 120–1 (& ex.), 122,
      274
    'Malagueña' (II) 120–2 (& ex.)
    'Habanera' (III) 120, 122–3
    'Feria' (IV) 57, 65–6, 120, 123–5 (& exx.),
      149
  Rêves 163, 185, 186
  Ronsard à son âme 22, 114, 185, 186
  Sainte 164, 276
  Sérénade grotesque 12, 71–2, 76, 272
  Shéhérazade, ouverture de féerie 8, 29, 33,
    118–20, 251, 252, 255
  Shéhérazade (songs) 14, 27, 162, 163, 165–6,
    168, 171, 221, 232, 237, 242
    'Asie' (I) 103, 165–6 (& ex.), 175–8 (&
      exx.), 276
  Si morne! 164
  Sites auriculaires 8, 163
    'Habanera' (I) 29, 30, 48, 56, 74–5 (& ex.),
      76, 132, 188, 243, 252, 269

'Entre cloches' (II) 50, 75
Sonata for Violin and Cello (Duo) 15, 25,
    45, 64, 98, 107–12 (& exx.)
Sonata for Violin and Piano (early work:
    1897) 56, 96, 98, 108
Sonata for Violin and Piano (1923–7) 33,
    42–3 (& ex.), 52, 55, 64, 107, 111, 112,
    113–17 (& exx.), 132, 134, 184, 228, 244,
    245, 263–4, 273
Sonatine 74, 76, 78, 80, 95, 219–21 (& exx.),
    222, 223, 228, 237, 241, 248, 279
String Quartet 8, 11, 26, 34, 97, 98–102 (&
    exx.), 103, 104, 105, 107, 227–31 (&
    exx.), 237, 248, 253, 255–6, 279
Sur l'herbe 171
Le Tombeau de Couperin 38, 52, 76, 80, 88–9,
    96, 140, 150, 221, 241, 242, 246, 261, 271
    'Prélude' (I) 89, 114, 273
    'Fugue' (II) 88, 89
    'Forlane' (III) 80, 88, 90–2 (& exx.), 273
    'Rigaudon' (IV) 77, 89, 90, 92–3, 246
    'Menuet' (V) 88, 90, 106 ('Musette'
        section), 114
    'Toccata' (VI) 56, 88–9, 222, 238
Trois chansons pour choeur mixte 17, 22, 31,
    185–6
Trois poèmes de Stéphane Mallarmé 15, 40,
    51–2, 56, 97, 111, 162, 163, 171–2, 260–1
    'Soupir' (I) 48, 164, 172–5 (& ex.), 276
    'Placet futile' (II) 175–6 (& ex.), 276
    'Surgi de la croupe et du bond' (III) 15,
        175–8 (& ex.), 183, 184
Tzigane, rapsodie de concert 40, 112–13, 135,
    253–4, 279
La Valse 1, 25, 39, 45, 48, 52, 57, 58, 63, 66,
    79, 80, 140, 146 (& ex.), 150–5 (& exx.),
    161, 243, 261–2, 271
Valses nobles et sentimentales 56, 57, 76, 83,
    87, 88, 106, 142, 215–18 (& exx.), 219,
    221, 238, 242, 243, 248, 253, 260, 272
    ballet version entitled *Adélaïde* 88, 140,
        142, 150, 260
Vocalise-étude en forme de habanera 170
Zaspiak-Bat 31
ARRANGEMENTS (orchestrations/pf
    reductions)
Antar (Rimsky-Korsakov): orch. excerpts 23
Carnaval (Schumann): orch. as ballet 23, 34,
    137
Khovanshchina (Musorgsky): orch. with
    Stravinsky 23, 172
Nocturnes (Debussy): reduction for 2 pfs
    14
Pictures at an Exhibition (Musorgsky): orch.
    23, 46, 137–8
Pièces pittoresques, 'Menuet pompeux'
    (Chabrier): orch. as ballet 12, 72, 135,
    137
Pour le piano, 'Sarabande' (Debussy): orch.
    15, 138
Prélude à l'après-midi d'un faune (Debussy):
    4-hand reduction 14
Tarantelle styrienne (Debussy): orch. as
    Danse 15, 138–9

WRITINGS CITED IN TEXT
'An autobiographical sketch' 14, 50, 80
'Contemporary music' 7, 15, 18, 56
'Finding tunes in factories' 59–62
'Take jazz seriously!' 11
Ravel, Pierre Joseph (father) 52, 58, 59, 60, 71,
    155
Régnier, Henri de 171
Renard, Jules 17, 169, 253, 257
    Journal 17, 169
Révész, André 30
Rimbaud, Arthur 51
Rimsky-Korsakov, Nikolay 10, 23, 25, 29, 36,
    56, 119, 122, 137–8, 149, 165, 244, 255,
    274
    Antar 23, 119
    Capriccio espagnol 29
    Christmas Eve 274
    Mlada 23
    Shéhérazade 119, 142, 143
    Songs Op. 4 23
    Songs Op. 7 23
Risler, Edouard 202
Rolland, Romain 8
Roland-Manuel (Alexis Manuel-Lévy) 14, 15,
    19, 24, 45, 48, 125, 185, 242, 252, 254
Ronsard, Pierre de 17, 162, 186
Roques, Léon 221
Rosen, Charles 271–2
Rosenthal, Manuel 14, 62, 160, 188, 203, 204
Rossini, Gioacchino 10
Rouché, Jacques 59, 142, 203, 258
Rousseau, Henri ('Le Douanier') 58
Rousseau, Jean-Jacques 28
Roussel, Albert 24, 32, 185
Roy, Jean 53
Rozhdestvensky, Gennadi 278
Rubinstein, Ida (Ballets) 34, 150, 151, 152, 155,
    156, 158, 262, 264, 265
Ruhlmann, François 257
Russian 'Five' 23, 29
Russ, Michael 240, 246
Russolo, Luigi 57, 60, 62
    'The art of noises' 57, 63–4
    The Awakening of a City 57
Russom, Philip 2, 142, 143, 276

Sabata, Vittorio de 262
Saint-Marceaux, Marguerite de 17, 201–2
Saint-Saëns, Camille 10, 11, 23, 25, 26, 32, 56
    Danse macabre 81
    La Jeunesse d'Hercule 11
    Six Etudes for the Left Hand 125
    Trio Op. 18 56
Salzedo, Carlos 273
Salzer, Felix 2
Samson, Jim 240
Sarasate, Pablo 273
Sardou, Victorien 38, 193
Satie, Erik 7, 10, 11, 15–16, 25, 29, 36, 59, 164,
    232, 244–5, 255
    Entretiens 15
    Gymnopédies 39, 133
    Parade 15, 62
    Socrate 15

Sauguet, Henri 253
Schenker, Heinrich 133, 142
Schmitt, Florent 14, 38
Schoenberg, Arnold 18, 24, 25, 26, 111, 247
    Die glückliche Hand 61
    Kammersymphonie (No. 1) 126
    Pierrot lunaire 24, 25, 40, 56, 111, 172
Schola Cantorum 8, 9
Scholes, Percy 248
Schopenhauer, Arthur 192
    The World as Will and Idea 192, 277 (Le
        Monde et volonté)
Schubert, Franz 187, 260
    Impromptu in G♭ 82
    Valses nobles 150
Schumann, Robert 137, 250
    Carnaval 23, 34, 137
    Kreisleriana 253
Second Viennese School 240, 247
Selva, Blanche 202
Séverac, Déodat de 202
Shakespeare, William
    Julius Caesar 50
Six, Les 25, 253
Skryabin, Alexander 51
Smollett, Tobias George
    The Present State of All Nations 189
Société Musicale Indépendante (SMI) 9, 11,
        15, 24, 258, 260, 261
Société Nationale de Musique (SN) 8, 9, 11, 18,
        38, 98, 255, 256, 258, 272
Society for Private Musical Performances
        (Schoenberg) 111
Sordet, Dominique 230, 232, 238–9
Steuermann, Eduard 247
Straram, Walther 155, 264
Strauss, Johann ('The Elder') 150
    Radetzky March Op. 228 154
Strauss, Johann ('The Younger') 23, 45, 150
    Tales from the Vienna Woods Op. 325 154
Strauss, Richard 10, 23, 56, 125
    Elektra 112, 244
    Feuersnot 252
Stravinsky, Igor 10, 23, 24, 25, 26, 47, 52, 55,
        57, 58, 66, 122, 129, 136, 153, 162, 172,
        243, 244, 245, 249, 250, 274
    Etude for Pianola 58, 64
    Fireworks 58
    Jeu de cartes 243
    Mavra 25, 245
    Octet 55
    L'Oiseau de feu 87, 142, 146, 148 ('Dance of
        the Firebird'), 243, 274
    Petrushka 38, 87, 126, 132, 142, 148, 244, 274
    Le Rossignol 38, 60, 243
    Le Sacre du printemps 110, 144, 145, 152,
        244, 246
    Trois poésies de la lyrique japonaise 24, 56,
        172
    Two Poems of Verlaine: 'Un grand sommeil
        noir' 243
Szigeti, Joseph 263–4

Tansman, Alexandre 10
Taruskin, Richard 130, 137, 244, 274
Tchaikovsky, Pyotr Il'yich 25, 130
    'Rêves d'enfant' 130
Tcherepnin, Alexander
    Le Pavillon d'Armide 142, 143
'Terpander' (English critic) 280
Terrasse, Claude 189, 194, 278
Teyte, Maggie 202
Thibaud, Jacques 202
Thomson, Virgil 249
Tomlinson, Ernest 237
Tortelier, Yan Pascal 97
Toscanini, Arturo 155, 235
Touzelet, Jean 214, 215, 221, 222, 279
Trouhanova, Natasha (Troupe of) 142, 260
Turina, Joaquín 71
    Danzas fantásticas 273

Uduman, Sohrab 268
Utrillo, Maurice 245

Valéry, Paul 50
van den Toorn, Pieter C. 55
Varèse, Edgard 48, 58
    Ionisation 64
Vaucaire, Maurice 193
Vaughan Williams, Ralph 248
Verlaine, Paul 17, 50
    Un grand sommeil noir 164, 243
    Sur l'herbe 171
Vidal, Paul 8
Vilzak, Anatole 152
Viñes, Ricardo 12, 23, 30, 45, 71, 75, 79, 202,
        221, 222, 256, 258, 272
Visconti (set designer) 262
Vuillemin, Louis (Louis Francis) 24, 144, 251
Vuillermoz, Emile 144, 251, 253, 263

Wagner, Richard 10, 18, 23, 241, 251
    Der Ring des Nibelungen 252
    Tristan und Isolde 14 ('Liebestod'), 85, 139
Walsh, Stephen 243
Weber, Carl Maria von 23
    Le Spectre de la rose 143
Webern, Anton 247, 249
Weill, Janine 233
Welte, Edwin 215
White, Eric Walter 243
Whiteman, Paul 42
Widor, Charles-Marie 10
Wiéner, Jean 24
Wilde, Oscar 16
Withers, Herbert 228, 237
Witkowski, Georges 1
Wittgenstein, Paul 125, 265
Wolff, Albert 263
Wollheim, Richard 55
Wood, Sir Henry J. 248
Woodhouse, Charles 237
Wyzewa, Theodor de 51